THE BROKEN JOURNEY

by the same author

Travels in a Small Country
Conversations in a Small Country
The Closing Headlines
Alastair Hetherington: A Man of His Word (Editor)
Both Sides of the Border
The Invisible Spirit: A Life of Post-War Scotland 1945–1975

THE
BROKEN
JOURNEY

A LIFE OF SCOTLAND
1976–99

KENNETH ROY

First published in 2016 by
Birlinn Ltd
West Newington House
10 Newington Road
Edinburgh
EH9 1QS

British Library Cataloguing in Publication Data. A catalogue record
for this book is available from the British Library.

ISBN: 978 1 78027 425 6

Set in Adobe Garamond Pro at Birlinn

Printed and bound by
Gutenberg Press Ltd, Malta

CONTENTS

PREFACE

I HAVE SUB-TITLED THIS 'A LIFE' OF SCOTLAND. THE STARTING POINT is 1976, and the book ends with the re-establishment of the Scottish Parliament a few months short of the new millennium. It is an account of how the country looked to one individual – its author – in the last quarter of the twentieth century. But it makes no claim to be a definitive history of modern Scotland. It lacks the necessary clinical detachment.

Formally this book is a sequel to *The Invisible Spirit*, which covered the period 1945 to 1975. That too was called 'A Life'. That too had the structure of a chronological narrative. When I started to write the present volume, I was picking up where I had left off. But I quickly realised that, despite these superficial similarities, I was writing a different sort of book: a more intensely personal one.

I said in the preface to *The Invisible Spirit* that it had been motivated by a curiosity about my own country: 'It was a belated attempt to give me an insight that I had always lacked – the knowledge of what was going on in Scotland in the early part of my life when I was too young to understand or care. Before I wrote the book I was more familiar with Robert Burns's Ayrshire, the main figures of the Scottish Enlightenment and the clearances from the Highlands than I was with the events and influences of a later and not much documented Scotland – the one in which I was brought up.'

While *The Invisible Spirit* was genuinely exploratory, with *The Broken Journey* I was examining more recognisable territory. By 1976

I had joined the BBC as a journalist and was presenting the nightly news programme, *Reporting Scotland*; throughout the period, on air or in print, I was a professional observer of the events that now form the subject matter for this book. Sometimes they felt so close that it was almost as if I was writing about current affairs – until I visited that last resting place of worldly ambition, the index, and noted that most of the people I knew and interviewed were already dead. I am too close to the project to know if this intimate knowledge of Scotland and its figures of influence has been a help or a hindrance. Perhaps it has been a bit of both.

II

It says a great deal about the nature of Scottish life between 1976 and 1999 that, for this assignment, unlike the last, so much of my study consisted of reading, analysing and deconstructing the reports of official inquiries into tragedies and scandals (often the two were indivisible). I have to wonder if any country, short of an actual war zone, suffered more misfortune than Scotland in so short a time. At one stage in the story, after Piper Alpha but before Lockerbie, an interval of only six months, the suffering was so intense that I felt obliged to give the reader a break.

Three of the main documents on which I drew were: *Report of the Inquiry into the Removal of Children from Orkney in February 1991* (HMSO, 1992), *Report of an Inquiry into an Allegation of a Conspiracy to Pervert the Course of Justice in Scotland* (HMSO, 1993), and *The Public Inquiry into the Shootings at Dunblane Primary School on 13 March 1996* (HMSO, 1996). For two reasons these reports – and in the case of Dunblane the transcript of evidence – deserve even closer scrutiny than I have been able to give them. The first is the detail with which devastating information is imparted, including important testimony that never achieved wide circulation; the second is the unsatisfactory conclusions reached in every case. I read also the

Report of the Inquiry into the Liaison Arrangements between the Police, the Procurator Fiscal Service and the Crown Office and the family of the deceased Surjit Singh Chhokar by Dr Raj Chandoo, presented to the Lord Advocate in 2001. This likewise was enlightening, not so much for its flawed indictment of institutional racism as for its perspective on the behind-the-scenes dynamic of the criminal justice system.

For the chapter, 'Lives of the Young', I read not only the report of the fatal accident inquiry into the deaths of young women in Cornton Vale Prison but the full transcript of evidence, which enabled me to include extracts from eyewitness accounts of the regime there; and I had been sufficiently intrigued by the fatal drug-related incidents at the nightclub known as Hanger 13 to attend the public inquiry in its entirety and subsequently talk at length to the family of one of the young men who died. The chapter on Lockerbie, 'Thunder in December', was partly informed by personal experience of the public inquiry and shameless eavesdropping on the lawyers in cabal over dinner at the Station Hotel, Dumfries. In writing the chapter on Dunblane, 'One of Us', I was constantly reminded of my many conversations with the father of one of the victims and of the furious reaction of fellow journalists when I delivered a speech at a seminar in London suggesting that the media bore some degree of culpability for the distress of the parents that day. For the chapter on the case of James Nelson, 'Forgiveness', I remembered how it felt to be in the Assembly Hall as a convicted murderer persuaded an impressionable Kirk that he was fit to be a minister.

Paradoxes, there were a few: the crushing dullness of Bruce Millan in front of camera, yet the realisation, when I came to write about him, that he was an unusually courageous Secretary of State for Scotland; the fragility of the miracle man John Fagan before the canonisation of the Blessed John Ogilvie, whose intercession the Roman Catholic Church believed had cured him – it seemed Mr Fagan would expire at any moment, yet he survived everyone in his immediate circle; the benign presence in my life of football's Ernie

Walker, yet the knowledge that I would have to write disobliging things about him; how the private warmth of such characters as MacDiarmid and McGahey was completely at odds with their public persona. But it was not possible to be amused by the central paradox of the book: the obsession of the political class with the constitutional question to the exclusion of so much else that should have received intelligent consideration.

III

The title is derived from an impression, or series of impressions, of broken journeys. The children of Dunblane who went to school one spring morning but never returned; the students on their way back to the United States for Christmas who never got further than the rooftops of a small town in Dumfriesshire; the 'ordinary men' of Piper Alpha, far from home, who never completed their shift but perished on a boiling oil rig; the vulnerable girls held on remand in an adult prison who could not bear to go on living; the Saturday night clubbers, bumping along the back road to Ayr, whose bodies would soon be wrecked by drugs – all of these were broken journeys, and all of them told us something troubling about the Scotland of the period.

Among the survivors, the boy from the care home who was picked up by a predator on a bus, the children removed at dawn and put on a plane, the prostitute yards from safety who was stopped for a light – each of their broken journeys rocked the established order and destroyed reputations, yet the national self-examination that should have followed, and might have proved cathartic, was conveniently avoided.

In that sense – and here I arrive at the theme of the book – the journey of Scotland itself was a broken one.

Prestwick
July 2016

1976

THE YEAR OF MIRACLES

I

ON 23 SEPTEMBER 1976, JEFFREY COSANS, A 15-YEAR-OLD PUPIL OF Beath High School in Cowdenbeath, took a shortcut over the school wall to his home nearby. His route through the cemetery had been ruled out of bounds after reports of vandalism. Two boys who defied the ban had already received several strokes of the belt across their outstretched palms – the traditional sanction for breaches of discipline in Scottish state schools. But when Cosans was sent to the assistant headmaster for the same, he explained that his parents objected to corporal punishment and that he would not accept it.

He was sent home at once and told not to return until he was willing to receive the belt. His parents were informed. The following month Mr and Mrs Cosans had an inconclusive meeting with a senior official in the Fife education authority at which they confirmed their opposition to corporal punishment. In the absence of any agreement, the boy continued to stay away from school.

There was little public sympathy for the Cosans and active support for the school from such champions of traditional methods as the Glasgow *Evening Times*: 'The headmaster has been backed by the education authority. Good. The case might seem like a storm in a teacup. But there's an important principle. The headmaster did the right thing – and sets a good example. It's probably symptomatic of today's attitudes that the situation ever arose: it almost certainly wouldn't have in the days when stepping out of line brought swift retribution and no one dreamed of challenging it.'

Not all of the paper's readers agreed. Mrs J. Small wrote a dissenting letter to the editor: 'Since the beginning of the new school term my seven-year-old daughter has had the belt twice. Once it was for talking in the line while waiting to go into school, the next time for holding a door open to let children in from the playground, which it seems contravened some school law. When I questioned the punishment I was told that it was necessary for discipline. I am sure that generations to come will look back in amazement to think that in 1976 this type of punishment was still being used in our schools.' Far from there being any amazement in 1976 at the belting of a seven-year-old girl for an act of kindness to her fellow pupils, there was almost universal endorsement of such summary justice.

For most boys, corporal punishment was an occupational hazard. A survey by the largest teaching union, the pro-belt Educational Institute of Scotland, found that 36% of 12 to 15-year-old boys were belted at least once every 10 school days, while a study by Edinburgh University's Centre for Educational Sociology conducted among 40,000 school-leavers showed that only one in 20 boys went through secondary school without feeling its sting – a much higher incidence of corporal punishment than in England and Wales. Official records were patchy, varying from council to council. While Glasgow kept no punishment record, Edinburgh did require a log to be maintained. In a single term, the city's primary teachers applied the belt in 3,978 cases and its secondary teachers in 5,589 cases – which, if repeated over a full school year, would have amounted to an annual total of 30,000 beltings in Edinburgh alone.

Documents released by the National Archives of Scotland many years later revealed the growing unease within the Scottish Education Department (SED) in the late 1970s about the belting of children, particularly of girls, but a reluctance to ban it for fear of 'violent opposition' from the teaching profession and concern that a partial ban might infringe the new Sex Discrimination Act. A letter from the SED in July 1977 acknowledged that, when the equalities legislation was being drafted, 'ministers did not want to have the subject of corporal punishment in schools raised in debate' and that, as a result, 'any rules which provide that boys should receive corporal punishment where girls do not would be illegal.'

In serious cases of indiscipline, the pupil could expect to be summoned to the office of the headmaster or one of his assistants, as Jeffrey Cosans was, and dealt with privately. But normally the offending pupil would be called to the front of the class and told to hold out one hand, 'palm uppermost', with the other hand supporting. The official regulations for its administration were specific. The tails of the belt should be rested on the upturned palm to allow the teacher to judge each stroke; the belt should then be drawn back over the teacher's shoulder and brought down on the palm with some force, so that the tails struck both fingers and palm; if more than one stroke was to be given – as it often was – the pupil should be ordered to swap hands, 'this to be repeated until the allotted punishment has been completed'. Only in approved schools – closed institutions for delinquent children or children otherwise in need of custodial care – was belting over the buttocks allowed.

Although these regulations would have revolted public opinion scarcely a generation later, there was no outcry at the time. When the Labour MP Dennis Canavan, a former teacher, introduced a bill in the House of Commons to outlaw corporal punishment – a measure doomed to failure – such support as it had came mainly from MPs in London and the south-east rather than from his left-wing colleagues in Scotland, who voted decisively against it. 'When I was teaching', said Canavan, 'I resorted to the strap on a few occasions and I never found it an answer to anything. It just increased my sheer repugnance of corporal punishment.'

Few journalists spoke out against it. An exception, Kate Kinloch, wrote: 'The other week I was visiting a friend whose husband is a teacher. He came home from school while I was still there, and flung his briefcase on the floor. "The teacher next door sent in teenage girls

again today to borrow my strap so that he could use it on them."
His face showed all the disgust he felt.' Kinloch inquired about the
age of the girls. 'Oh, about 14. And the teacher is young, in his early
thirties. It's kinky, I tell you, kinky. There's no other word for it.'
Kinloch testified in the same article to her own experience and the
'obvious relish with which a screaming dervish used the belt on the
small palms raised in front of her'. At her school, even the janitor had
the power to belt pupils.

In state schools, pupils were punished with an approved strap
(or 'tawse') known as the Lochgelly, named after the small town in
Fife where its manufacture by the family firm of Dick was a thriving
local industry. Not so in the private sector, where schools made their
own rules, teachers employed a variety of instruments, and pupils
were habitually ordered to bend over.

There were occasional prosecutions. Peter Spencer, headmaster of
St Ninian's preparatory school in Moffat, appeared in court charged
with 12 counts of assault involving seven boys over a period of five
years. The boys described how Spencer beat them ferociously over
the buttocks with a cane, a slipper and a riding crop; a doctor who
examined them said that, several days later, they were still suffering
pain and that the force with which they had been struck 'must have
been extremely excessive'. But the sheriff had no difficulty in dismissing the case on the grounds that assault required some measure
of criminal intent of which, in his opinion, there was none; he instructed the jury to return a verdict of not guilty. An elated Spencer,
who had never made any secret of his belief in the efficacy of corporal
punishment, stood on the courthouse steps declaring his hope that
the verdict would encourage other teachers who were 'trying to
uphold discipline and good behaviour'.

The possibility that there was a sado-masochistic dimension to
corporal punishment in schools – the 'kinkiness' alluded to by the
teacher who confided in Kate Kinloch – had either never occurred
to Scotland's policy-makers and opinion-formers or was simply too

embarrassing to confront openly. In the prevailing climate it required courage and tenacity to pursue an ethical objection to the practice. But two sets of parents were prepared to stick their heads above the parapet and challenge the right of local authorities – and ultimately of the British government – to sanction corporal punishment.

In March 1976, six months before Jeffrey Cosans took his short-cut over the wall into the cemetery, Grace Campbell launched an application to the European Court of Human Rights in Strasbourg over the refusal of her local authority (Strathclyde Regional Council) to give her a guarantee that her seven-year-old son Gordon would not be belted at his Roman Catholic primary school in Bishopbriggs. The fact that Gordon was never in fact belted there failed to satisfy Grace Campbell. The point at issue was the council's unwillingness to respect her deeply-held philosophical opposition to the corporal punishment of children, which she regarded as a sexual perversion. The family of Jeffrey Cosans joined her in an appeal to the European Court. The opposing party, obstinate to the end, was neither of the local authorities but their master, the British government, which invoked the full apparatus of the state to defend the beating of children.

As the case dragged on, the Pack committee of inquiry, which had been set up by the Scottish Office to investigate indiscipline and truancy in schools, recommended that corporal punishment should disappear by a process of 'gradual elimination' rather than by legislation. The teachers purred approval; if the belt had to go, it was best that it did so in no great hurry.

John Pollock, the media-savvy general secretary of the Educational Institute of Scotland, was rewarded with his usual favourable press when he commented acidly that taxpayers' money through legal aid was being used to support the parents' case, as if this were somehow unusual. Norman MacEwan, the solicitor representing Grace Campbell, explained that it would be impossible for the ordinary individual to proceed with such an application without legal aid, that the amount was 'very modest', and that it by no means covered all his client's expenses. Undeterred, Pollock went on to claim that the Scottish Council for Civil Liberties (SCCL), was behind the case, an allegation repeated by the Labour MP Tam Dalyell. An outraged David Godwin of the SCCL accused Dalyell of being 'bent on attacking the basic protection of individuals appealing to an international court of human rights'.

In January 1977, three months after Jeffrey Cosans was suspended, the local authority informed the family that it had decided to lift the suspension on condition that Jeffrey obeyed 'the rules and the disciplinary requirements of the school'. The Cosans stipulated in reply that, if their son were to be re-admitted, he should not receive corporal punishment under any circumstances. It was stalemate: the council responded that the parents had refused to accept the condition and warned them that they might be prosecuted for failure to ensure Jeffrey's attendance. The threat was an empty one, and on 31 May 1977, his 16th birthday, Jeffrey Cosans ceased to be of compulsory school age.

The barbaric excesses in Scottish schools were still being perpetrated even as the Cosans and Campbell families were doggedly pressing their case in Strasbourg and as their integrity was being impugned by such well-respected figures as the EIS's John Pollock. It emerged, through papers released under the 30-year rule, that pupils in Scotland's 26 approved schools were being abused, that the extent of the abuse was known to the Scottish Education Department and that nothing was done about it.

The SED acknowledged that corporal punishment was administered in Scottish approved schools 10 times more often than in their English counterparts and that there was evidence of 'curious things' going on in at least two of these schools: Guthrie's Girls School in Edinburgh and Wellington School in Penicuik; the nature of the curiosities was not divulged in the official papers. The highest number of beatings, however, was recorded in neither of these institutions, but in Geilsland, a school run by the Christian folk of the Church of Scotland, at Beith in Ayrshire.

An inspector of the SED prepared his briefing in longhand in order to spare the Scottish Office typist anguish and embarrassment. 'Corporal punishment,' he wrote, 'is still quite a savage business and boys scream when a stout Lochgelly is applied on their buttocks . . . the records show that many floggings are administered in our schools. Nor am I in any doubt about bruised buttocks which show scars long after the event; this would be particularly the case when special thin pants cover the behind.' He stated that there were examples of boys defecating as they were belted.

But there was no suggestion that sadistic teachers should be disciplined or that the worst cases should be referred to the police, and successive Secretaries of State went on advocating a consensual approach to abolition. They had no cause to fear public disapproval, for the Scots as a whole were almost as keen on the idea of corporal punishment as the teachers who actually dished it out.

In the winter of 1976, the Glasgow Citizens' Theatre produced a new play about the Marquis de Sade. Despite the subject matter, it proved to be rather tame. The theatre critic Christopher Small expressed surprise that it contained so little sadism. In Scotland, however, there was no need for sadism on the stage when there was so much of it in real life.

II

The many thrashings to which he testified as a product of the Scottish approved school system failed to deter Patrick (Paddy) Meehan from a life of crime. He graduated as a safe-blower and jail-breaker. When he escaped from prison in 1963, he managed to get himself to East Germany, where he offered his services to the security police, boasting that he could spring any spy. This showed a certain entrepreneurial spirit, but the Germans quickly tired of him. They handed Meehan over at Checkpoint Charlie in Berlin and he was sent packing – back to Wandsworth prison in London.

Five years later he was convicted of the murder of 72-year-old Rachel Ross at her home in Ayr. Meehan, who had no previous record of personal violence, was sentenced to life imprisonment, protesting his innocence as he left the dock. His counsel, Nicholas Fairbairn QC, and his solicitors, variously Len Murray and Joseph Beltrami, believed him. They were not alone. Even in some quarters of the Crown Office there were doubts about the credibility of the verdict.

The broadcaster Ludovic Kennedy, who was known for his interest in miscarriages of justice, agreed to chair a committee campaigning for Meehan's release. Kennedy went further, writing a book about the case which he sent to every Scottish MP. On three occasions Secretaries of State for Scotland had perversely refused to take a fresh look at the evidence. But in 1976, with the resignation of the long-serving Willie Ross, the new man at the Scottish Office, Bruce Millan, was convinced by Kennedy's deconstruction of the case in his book, *A Presumption of Innocence*, decided that Paddy Meehan had been wrongly imprisoned and recommended the exercise of the royal prerogative of mercy – a free pardon. After six years and 209 days in prison, of which the last four years and nine months were spent in self-imposed solitary confinement, Meehan was released from Peterhead jail. It would never have happened without the tireless efforts of Ludovic Kennedy and the Free Patrick Meehan committee, and the fortuitous appointment of a more open-minded Secretary of State.

Later in 1976 there was a sensational new development in the saga. A man called Ian Waddell was put on trial for the murder of Rachel Ross, mainly on the basis of his repeated confessions to the crime. The Lord Advocate, Ronald King Murray, conducted the prosecution. Although a conviction was widely expected, the jury acquitted Waddell. But it did so only after a scandalously partial summing-up by the trial judge, Lord Robertson, who stated that there was 'no legal justification whatsoever in saying that Meehan was wrongly convicted of the murder,' and that having heard all the evidence 'you might well have come to the clear conclusion that he was in fact rightly convicted as another jury found seven years ago.' Having damned the pardoned he went on to damn the pardoner, accusing Millan of 'paying attention to clamour'. Robertson was critical, not only of the exercise of the royal prerogative in general, but of Meehan's pardon in particular. 'I have always thought,' he said, 'that in the ordinary use of language, if you pardon someone, you pardon them for something they have done and not for something they have not done.'

Robertson was mistaken in his interpretation of the word pardon. He should have known – and as a judge of long experience almost certainly did know – that, although pardons were more normally granted in forgiveness of a crime, they were occasionally offered to people who had been wrongfully convicted. (The subsequent establishment of the Scottish Criminal Cases Review Commission created a more satisfactory mechanism for dealing with miscarriages of justice.)

It was true that there had been 'clamour', but it was clamour based on a rational re-examination of the case. It was also true that Millan had not exhausted what the judge called 'the obvious process of law'; Millan could have referred the case to the Court of Criminal Appeal. But the Secretary of State knew that there were severe limitations on the power of the court to consider a case afresh, rather than as simply an appeal against the original conviction. In the end, he decided that, if justice was to be done, he must bypass the appeal court and invoke the royal prerogative. It was an act of political courage by a Secretary of State in his first weeks in the job.

Robertson's personal attack on Millan, who was nothing if not a man of honour, provoked a furious reaction in the House of Commons. Millan himself, in an opening statement, defended the royal prerogative as 'an integral part of the constitutional system which exists to protect the citizen against possible miscarriages of justice'. Member after member leapt to his defence. David Steel, for the Liberals, said his party wholly rejected 'the underlying claim to judicial infallibility which seemed to lie behind so much of Lord Robertson's summing-up'. The Tory Nicholas Fairbairn, speaking with the authority of Meehan's QC, asked Millan to consider the 'very serious constitutional issue where a judge in a privileged position is able to defame the reputation of a man whose conviction has been expunged and gratuitously defame the holder of the office of Secretary of State'. Labour's Norman Buchan suggested that Robertson should attend a refresher course for judges if he believed that a pardon could only be given if an offence had been committed, while Dennis Canavan demanded that 'this interfering busybody of a judge' should apologise.

The SNP's Winnie Ewing, a Glasgow solicitor before her election to parliament, proposed an extreme remedy: 'In the long history of Scottish judges, we have rarely had a judge removed, but I suggest that this is a case where Lord Robertson's removal from the bench should be seriously considered by the Secretary of State.' Ewing described the Meehan case as 'a blot on the fair name of Scottish justice, the worst instance since Oscar Slater'. Even Bruce Millan refused to go that far.

Lord Robertson was not removed and nor did he resign or apologise. He continued as an ornament of the Scottish bench until his retirement 11 years later at the age of 75. When he died in 2005, his generous obituary in the *Glasgow Herald* made no mention of his part in the Meehan affair, though it did refer to his captaincy of the Honourable Company of Edinburgh Golfers. At a memorial service, his friend Lord Mackay of Clashfern described Robertson as 'a meticulous, courteous and diligent judge and a great believer in the reputation of Scots law and particularly the criminal law in providing a fair and balanced system for the trial of persons accused of offences'. Again, there was no mention of the Meehan case, which had so undermined 'the reputation of Scots law' that the state awarded Meehan compensation of £50,000 for his years of imprisonment.

But the judges of Scotland could never be accused of failing to look after their own. When an official inquiry into the case was set up, it was chaired not by some independent person unconnected to the Edinburgh judiciary but by one of Robertson's colleagues, the bluff Lord Hunter; and when Hunter reported in 1982 he found insufficient evidence to support Meehan's innocence. So Meehan, who died in 1994 at the age of 67, never completely cleared his name.

What, then, happened in a bungalow on the outskirts of Ayr that ended in a woman's violent death, years of solitary confinement for one of her alleged assailants and a judicial cause célèbre without precedent in the history of modern Scotland?

The Meehan case was built on a coincidence so extraordinary, so bizarre, that it almost defied belief. On the afternoon of Saturday 5 July 1969, two pairs of criminals, each pair unknown to the other, drove out of Glasgow heading south to the Ayrshire coast. That night two men who addressed each other as Pat and Jim broke into the house of Abraham Ross and his wife Rachel with robbery in mind, beat them up and took money from their safe. Later Mrs Ross died of her injuries. The police had no hesitation in nailing Jim Griffiths and Patrick Meehan for the crime, and for the very good reason that their first names were almost identical to those overheard by Mr Ross. It was, from the police's perspective, a reasonable deduction. But it turned out to be the wrong one.

Griffiths, aged 34, from Rochdale in Lancashire, was a violent criminal with a long record; Meehan, 42, had been in and out of prison for most of his life, usually for theft. On that summer evening they were travelling south of Ayr in a car with false number plates, Griffiths at the wheel, for the purpose of casing a joint: the motor tax office in Stranraer. The occupants of the other car, the one that would go no further than Ayr, were believed to be Ian Waddell and a fellow villain whose identity has never been conclusively established. Their mission was to raid the house of a bingo hall owner and his wife. But at the High Court trial for murder, it was Patrick Meehan, and Meehan alone, who faced Lord Grant and a jury. His accomplice Griffiths was dead and Ian Waddell was in prison for something else, confessing to the Ross murder to a cell-mate.

Whoever carried out the attack on Mr and Mrs Ross did so with exceptional cruelty. Two men entered their house some time after midnight when the couple were asleep. 'I remember something just coming at me,' Abraham Ross recalled in court. 'It was like a nightmare'. He was covered with a blanket and hit if he tried to move it, while his wife was struck on the face. They were both securely tied up, and before the attackers left they turned the couple over on their backs, bent their legs behind them, and tied their ankles together. Mr and Mrs Ross lay on the floor 'like trussed chickens' until they were discovered by their housekeeper on Monday morning, 30 hours later. Mrs Ross died in hospital in the early hours of Tuesday. Such an event was unimaginable in a middle-class Ayr suburb, and there was public revulsion when the details emerged. An angry crowd jostled Meehan after his preliminary appearance at the town's sheriff court.

Meehan had been on a list of up to 30 suspects, but not a strong one; he was among the last to be routinely interviewed by the police. When he was asked to account for his movements he made a statement about the trip to Stranraer which was inaccurate on two counts. It omitted any reference to the illegal purpose of the visit – the inspection of the motor tax office (as it happened he and Griffiths didn't fancy the look of it and abandoned any plan to break into it); and it excluded the fact that they had hung around a local hotel for several hours with the aim of stealing from cars parked there.

Meehan lied that they left Stranraer around midnight, which blew a hole in his alibi. For in the same statement, he described how, on their way back to Glasgow, they had come to the aid of 16-year-old Irene Burns, who was standing distraught on the road near Prestwick Airport, having been dumped there from a car by two youths after one of them had 'tried to get funny' with her. The youths had then driven off with her friend. Meehan and Griffiths set off in pursuit of the car, caught up with it, signalled to it to stop, pulled the other girl from the clutches of the youths and then, like good samaritans, drove both girls home to Kilmarnock before themselves returning to Glasgow, 'getting there, I think, about 5 am'.

The chronology made no sense. Even accounting for the detour with the girls, it was inconceivable that a car journey in the early hours of the morning from Stranraer to Glasgow would take five hours. (How long the journey did take became one of the many disputed questions of the case.) By concealing his true intentions in Stranraer, Meehan had unwittingly incriminated himself and Griffiths in the Ayr murder; five hours afforded ample opportunity for an earlier detour – to the house of Mr and Mrs Ross. Badly compromised by his own stupidity, Meehan was soon spilling the name of his accomplice. The police could hardly believe their luck: they had two criminals called Pat and Jim in the area on the night of the murder.

Better still, they were about to have a positive ID. When Abraham Ross attended an identity parade in Glasgow a week after his wife's murder, he requested that the men should use the actual words used by one of the assailants in response to his appeals for mercy: 'Shut up, shut up, we'll send [for] an ambulance'. A detective uttered the words and asked Meehan, first in line, to repeat them. As soon as he did Ross staggered back, visibly shaken, and exclaimed: 'That's the voice, I know it, I know it, I don't have to go any further.' Meehan replied: 'You're mistaken, laddie.' But Ross, in a state of near-collapse, insisted: 'Oh, that's him, that's him,' to which Meehan retorted: 'Sir, you have got the wrong man, honest.' The parade came to an end there and then, and Meehan was escorted to the bar of the Central police station. As the charges of robbery and murder were read out, he again declared his innocence: 'You are making a horrible mistake. I know absolutely nothing about it.'

The police promptly went after Griffiths and found him in a rented flat in the city. Nothing could have prepared them for the response: their prey started shooting. When the police raced to the relative safety of their car, he went on shooting – indiscriminately – from the front window. He somehow managed to escape in a stolen vehicle, and in a rampage lasting an hour and a half killed one person and wounded 13 – a trail of destruction remarkable even by Glasgow standards – before he was cornered in a tenement flat in Springburn to which he had randomly retreated, and a police marksman shot him through the heart. 'It was either him or me,' the marksman said.

For the police this settled matters, if they had not been settled before. The names Pat and Jim at the scene of the crime; a decisive ID; and now the death of Griffiths, a man who, the police reasoned, must have acted as he did because he was as guilty as sin. The Crown Office issued a prejudicial statement: 'With the death of Griffiths and the apprehension of Patrick Meehan, the police are no longer looking for any other person suspected of implication in the incident concerning Mr and Mrs Ross in Ayr.' If ever a case was cut and dried, surely this was it – or so the police convinced themselves.

The homicidal madness of Griffiths was always a problem for the defence; it pointed to a man who would have been more than capable of viciously beating up an elderly couple. Ludovic Kennedy, making the best of it, suggested that Griffiths knew somehow that the game was up, for a crime which for once in his life he had not committed, and that 'if he had to go down, then he would take as many with him as possible'. As a psychological insight, this was short of watertight.

The Crown had problems of its own in proving Meehan's guilt beyond reasonable doubt. The first and most obvious flaw, though the police chose to ignore it, was the implausibility of housebreakers using their real names in the course of a robbery. It simply wasn't done. And if it wasn't done in this case, it was wretched luck for Meehan that two criminals, in the same area on the same night, appropriated Pat and Jim as their professional pseudonyms.

More perplexing still, there was Abraham Ross's testimony about the voices of the men who broke into his house. At Meehan's trial, Nicholas Fairbairn questioned the victim closely:

'Were their voices both similar?'
'I would say so, yes.'
'Were they both Scottish voices?'
'Yes.'
'Were they both Glasgow voices?'
'Yes.'
'You are sure of that?'
'Yes, I think.'
'Are you sure they were both Scottish voices?'
'Yes.'
'Do you think they were both Glasgow voices?'
'They seemed to me both like Glasgow voices, yes.'

How could this be? It was agreed that Griffiths spoke with a pronounced Lancashire accent. Had he successfully adopted a Glaswegian one for the occasion? It seemed unlikely. But Lord Grant, in his summing-up, attached little significance to this important discrepancy and wasted few words on it.

Next there was the question of whether Meehan and Griffiths had time to visit the Ross household on their way back from Stranraer. According to Meehan's first statement, they did. But in his revised account of their movements, for which there was corroboration, they were outside a hotel in Cairnryan, on the Ayr side of Stranraer, until 2 am. Irene Burns recalled that it was around 3.30 am when she was picked up by Meehan and Griffiths near Prestwick Airport. So the window of opportunity was around 90 minutes.

The judge made much of the police's reconstruction of the journey: 'Going at a sort of family Sunday afternoon speed took about an hour and 15 minutes, and I think one of the officers said that if he had been in a hurry he would have done that, plus the journey from Stranraer to Cairnryan, in about an hour.' Ludovic Kennedy called this 'a total impossibility'. It wasn't quite, in the early hours of the morning, when traffic was light, in a Triumph 2000, even on a road twisty in places. But Lord Grant might have been influenced by his own speed as a driver. He was a notoriously fast one and, three years after the trial of Patrick Meehan, he was killed in a road accident.

Grant proposed to the jury that Meehan and Griffiths 'could have had half an hour or more at the Rosses' house and been at the Underwood Road layby [where they rescued Irene Burns] at 3.30 or thereby'. For the purpose of meeting this tight timetable, Grant shamelessly lopped 15 minutes off Meehan's stated time of departure, telling the jury that they set off from Cairnryan not at 2 am but at 1.45. Fifteen minutes made a difference.

If the jury accepted that Meehan and Griffiths had only half an hour or so at the Rosses, it would also have to accept – and no doubt did – that they were able within that time to park the car, survey the house, fetch a pair of step-ladders from the garage, climb on the garage roof, from there climb up a telephone pole and cut the wires, re-enter the garage and steal an iron bar for breaking in, creep round to the front of the house, force open the front bedroom window, climb in, tie up the couple, open the safe and empty it of its contents, help themselves to a relaxing whisky in the sitting room, leave the house and drive off – before doing their good deed for Irene Burns 12 minutes later and behaving normally in her company.

There was a further illogicality. Abraham Ross sensed that the men were no longer in the house when 'everything went all quiet' – by his reckoning about five or 10 minutes after they had gone. He managed to remove the blanket from his head and saw that it was daylight. If it was daylight, the men had not had half an hour or so at the Rosses: they had been in the house for a considerable time. (James McKillop, a Glasgow journalist, was told by David

Struthers, the head of Ayr CID, that the murderers spent 'several hours' in the house.) Lord Grant's way of overcoming this obstacle to conviction was to cast doubt on Abraham Ross's testimony: 'I think probably, in the condition he was in, he would have had some difficulty in assessing the length of time between any one particular event and another.'

The evidence about the state of the light on the edge of Kilmarnock, 12 miles away, when Meehan and Griffiths arrived there with Irene Burns, should have assisted the judge in his summing-up to the jury. Several witnesses had testified that it was 'dark' or 'quite dark' or 'very dark' just before 4 am. If they were to be believed, and Abraham Ross was to be believed, Meehan and Griffiths had accomplished a remarkable feat: they had left Ayr in daylight and soon afterwards arrived in the neighbouring town of Kilmarnock when it was still dark. But Lord Grant managed to resolve even this conundrum. He preferred the testimony of Irene Burns that it was 'quite light by then because I noticed the colour of the Anglia' (the car of the youths). What he omitted to say was that Irene had noticed the colour of the Anglia because the Anglia had its rear lights on.

There was a moment in the trial when Patrick Meehan realised he had been stitched up. The police claimed to have found a scrap of paper in Abraham Ross's safe matching one found in Ian Griffiths' coat pocket. It was the sort of forensic evidence that juries tended to listen to with great respect – even if, implausibly, the tell-tale production in this case had not been spotted by the officers who examined the safe immediately after the murder. Meehan was to curse that scrap of paper – the one that turned up mysteriously late in the investigation – for six years and 209 days.

III

When Patrick Meehan was finally released from prison, he did so into a changing Scotland. He might have blinked at the knowledge that, although corporal punishment in schools was still widely practised, it was now being robustly challenged. The Scotland of 1976 was indeed a country of small miracles – and one official one.

Among the small miracles, there was the prospect that a man just out of prison would soon be able to celebrate his freedom with a drink in a pub on a Sunday. It was three years since Dr Christopher Clayson had produced his report on liberalising Scotland's drinking laws, including the revolutionary idea that children should be allowed to accompany their parents into pubs. He was a realist; he didn't expect this to happen soon. But at least parliament was debating the first tentative step – Sunday opening.

Clayson was a good man. Struck with TB in his final year as a medical student at Edinburgh University, he spent his first three years after graduation as a patient. He became physician superintendent at the Lochmaben Sanatorium in Dumfries-shire, where the 142 beds for TB patients were always filled; much to his surprise he was elected president of the Royal College of Physicians of Edinburgh. Although his vision was to eliminate Scotland's male-dominated drinking culture, Clayson was no prohibitionist. His report described a daily intake of four units of alcohol as 'moderate'. Clayson himself enjoyed his four units a day – 'a sherry and a couple of glasses of claret with a meal' – which, in the opinion of public health specialists half a century later, would have qualified him as borderline alcoholic. After a useful life, in which he knocked back seven sherries and 14 glasses of claret a week, he died at the relatively advanced age of 101.

Clayson's relaxed take on alcohol consumption and his relatively sunny view of human nature – his belief that social drinking could be civilised by an improvement in the quality of the pubs – was not universally popular. The newspapers reported that the proposal for Sunday opening had 'split Scotland' and many influential voices were heard in protest. The churches were the most predictable.

The under-secretary for home affairs at the Scottish Office, Harry Ewing, found himself in charge of the parliamentary bill: an unhappy assignation for Ewing because he could not support the proposed reforms. His boss Bruce Millan told him to argue his case, but to accept the will of the Scottish Standing Committee when it came to a free vote. 'The legislation does not say that pubs cannot open on a Sunday,' Ewing emphasised. 'Any pub that cares to add a dining-room where people can have a meal can open on a Sunday. That is what I want. What I am against is the Sunday opening of drinking dens – pubs that are only pubs. Go to Glasgow, Edinburgh, Aberdeen or Dundee and you will see that they are often built on the ground floor of a tenement with something like 200 homes adjoining. I have a responsibility to the people who live in these houses to make sure they get at least one day a week of peace and quiet.'

Three Labour MPs and a Scottish nationalist backed an amendment sponsored by the Conservatives' Alick Buchanan-Smith opposing Sunday opening on principle. Robin Cook, one of the brightest of Labour's new generation, argued that 'in every country where there has been an extension of hours there has been a substantial increase in the consumption of alcohol and an increase in alcoholism'. Harry Ewing added that Scotland had 'the worst alcoholism in Europe'. It was undeniably bad. A report by doctors in Glasgow showed that 70% of all the patients reporting to the Western Infirmary with head injuries were intoxicated; that a fifth of all the beds in the Victoria Infirmary were occupied by people with injuries caused by drink; that 90% of all the people who died in fires in the city were drunk; that the death rate from cirrhosis of the liver was six times higher in Scotland than in England and Wales. 'Alcoholism is rampant in Scotland', concluded the report. 'We have more drunk-driving cases than any other part of Britain and most of our murders are committed when those involved in the crime are drunk.'

The supporters of the Clayson reforms won the day. Although six in the committee voted against Sunday opening, the majority – 10 – were in favour. Harry Ewing took the rebuff gracefully, admitting that he enjoyed 'a drink in moderation' and that sometimes he drank on a Sunday. Menzies Campbell, who had worked for the Clayson committee as a young advocate, called it 'a bloody good result, better than any of us could have predicted' and praised Christopher Clayson's chairmanship – 'He had all the acumen of a lawyer without any of the baggage. He is also an illustration of how alcohol in moderation does you good.'

IV

Later in the year there was a second small miracle: a startling recantation by Rangers Football Club, the Protestant half of Glasgow's 'Old Firm'. The club's general manager, Willie Waddell, called the press to the 'Blue Room' at Ibrox stadium and announced: 'No religious barriers will be put up by this club regarding the signing of players. Everything possible will be done to remove spectators from Ibrox who do not agree with this policy'. The press hailed it as a 'shock announcement' and a 'historic decision'.

The timing was, however, more than a little suspect. The *volte-face* came only days after a 'friendly' match with Aston Villa in Birmingham had to be abandoned because of rioting Rangers supporters. Thirty-five people attending the game required hospital treatment, while in the city centre shop windows were smashed, men and women were assaulted as they did their shopping and pubs became battlegrounds. The landlord of one pub told journalists: 'I have never been more terrified in my life. They went berserk, grabbed bottles from the shelves, wouldn't pay, and ripped down the curtains.' The misbehaviour was not sectarian in origin, but racist. 'Well, we certainly sorted out thae English the day,' one fan was heard to remark in New Street Station. But the reputation of the club, never high, was now in shreds. It had become impossible to discriminate between one form of prejudice and another. It was all bad.

Two Scottish teenagers each went to prison for six months, one for threatening behaviour after shouting 'Kill the bastards' as police moved in to break up fighting fans, the other for waving an air pistol during rioting on the terracing. Young people were trampled underfoot in the panic to get away from him, and police found that he had ammunition in his pockets and mouth.

Willie Waddell blamed such appalling scenes on alcohol and announced 'a purge on drink'. It was a long way from the dinner table of Dr Clayson with its sherry and claret. But according to the sports journalist Ian Archer, the sickness of Rangers Football Club could not be explained away so glibly; its supporters were fuelled as much by bigotry as whisky. 'This country,' said Archer, 'would be a better place if Rangers did not exist. They are a permanent embarrassment because they are the only club in the world which insists that every member of the team is one religion.' He felt obliged to add at the end of his column – 'because some people are so sick' – that he was not a Roman Catholic.

There had been only one Catholic player on Rangers' books since the Second World War, and only because of a mistake by the management. Larry Blyth was offered a trial with the club in 1950. 'It was all a bit of a dream,' he recalled. 'I was straight out of the army and suddenly a career in football was just around the corner. The Rangers scout drove me home to Dundee and while we were chatting I mentioned that I played a lot of football at my school, St Joseph. The car nearly left the road.' The deal was honoured: Blyth signed on the dotted line. But within a few days he learned the hard facts of life at Rangers. A groundsman pointed to a housing scheme and said: 'There are Catholics over there.' Blyth played a few games for the reserves and then ended up on the bench: 'There was this silent certainty that I wasn't going to make it at Ibrox.' After 18 months he received a telegram informing him that staff cuts were being made and he had lost his job. The cuts amounted to one redundancy – his. Blyth quit professional football altogether. His heart was no longer in the game.

Ian Archer reckoned that if, by 1980, Rangers still fielded an all-Protestant team, Waddell's announcement would be seen as no more than hot air. He was relatively hopeful. 'The Ibrox boardroom is not inhabited by confirmed bigots, merely by men who were stuck with an indefensible policy of discrimination and who were afraid to change it,' he wrote. There was, however, no great change by 1980. It was not until 1989 – 13 years after the 'shock announcement' in the Blue Room – that Rangers finally signed their first significant Roman Catholic player, Maurice Johnston; later the influx of footballers from the continent made Catholic signings more common.

V

The two small miracles of 1976 were dwarfed by the official recognition of a real one. John Fagan, 51, a dock worker, fell seriously ill in 1967 and was taken to Glasgow Royal Infirmary, where surgeons operated on a massive tumour in the stomach. They expected him to live for no more than six months. The family GP, Dr Archibald Macdonald, when he realised that the patient's stomach was breaking up, administered what he confidently anticipated would be the final shots of a pain-killing drug. By that terminal stage, Fagan's weight was down to five stones. He received the last rites and his wife Mary settled down for an all-night vigil, believing that John would be dead by the morning.

At 8 am he lay motionless. A few minutes later Mary Fagan was astonished to hear the strong voice of her husband: 'Mary, I'm hungry. Mary, I feel so different.' Her response was to make him an egg, and then to call Dr Macdonald. 'Good God,' said the doctor, 'I don't understand it.' When Fagan returned to hospital for a check-up, the cancer had disappeared from his body. There were only two possible explanations. The first and more rational was that he had been wrongly diagnosed; that he had not been suffering from cancer in the first place. This was a theory supported by at least one specialist, Dr Gerard Patrick Crean of the Southern General Hospital, who wondered if the growth might have been an abscess. But it was pure theory; Crean had never examined Fagan.

The second was that a miracle had occurred. This was the view of the parishioners of the Roman Catholic church in Easterhouse, Glasgow, who had prayed for a cure, imploring John Ogilvie to intercede. Ogilvie, a seventeenth-century Jesuit priest, was hanged at Glasgow Cross on 10 March 1615 for his beliefs; he was often invoked in prayer by the city's Catholic faithful, but never before with so remarkable a result.

By 1976, after years of pressure on the Vatican, there were high hopes that Ogilvie might at last be canonised. In March, several thousand Scottish Catholics took part in a walk from the Cross to the north side of Glasgow Cathedral, where it was supposed that the martyred priest was buried. Could Ogilvie, dead for 361 years but still active on John Fagan's behalf, become the first Scottish-born saint?

In October, 4,000 Scottish pilgrims filed into St Peter's in Rome to hear the announcement for which they had long prayed. Pope Paul VI, seated in front of the papal altar, said that after serious reflection and frequent prayers for divine assistance, 'we declare and define John Ogilvie of Scotland to be a saint'. It was reported that the applause within the basilica rose instantly and rapturously. John Fagan, whose mysterious recovery had clinched the deal, and his wife Mary were granted a private audience with the Pope, who presented Fagan with a pair of blessed rosary beads. 'I hear you nearly died, John,' said Paul simply.

Even after his recovery Fagan looked extremely frail. Nevertheless he survived for 26 years after the surgeons at Glasgow Royal Infirmary had given him six months. He outlived most of the others in his intimate circle: his wife Mary died three years after the ceremony in Rome; his GP, Dr Macdonald, and his parish priest, Father Thomas Reilly, who was prominent in the campaign to have Ogilvie canonised, both died young; the journalist Colm Brogan, who was close to Fagan, died in his thirties. The miracle of Easterhouse touched many in the company of John Fagan, but only Fagan himself with good fortune. Ogilvie, once he was canonised, ceased to intercede in the district.

VI

But it was safer to rely on John Ogilvie than to worship Bung Ho, the resident idol in an establishment known to the tabloid press as the House of Corruption. Bung Ho was a lifesize clay figure before which salesman employed by Rotary Tools were obliged to kneel. Maurice Cochrane, the Glasgow company's founder and managing director, who preferred to be known as Jimmy, started work at two or three in the afternoon and expected key staff to stay on until he left, typically in the early hours of the morning. On one occasion in this challenging environment, a salesman who had failed to hit target was ordered to stand in front of Cochrane's desk for a mock trial and a harsh spotlight was thrown on the under-performer. After the evidence was heard, the young man was found guilty and sacked, his only consolation being that he would never again have to grovel at the feet of Bung Ho.

Cochrane had a style that the popular press, in their indulgent stereotypes of chancers and bullies, called 'ebullient' or 'larger than life'. When he walked into a hotel, he would automatically slip the doorman a fiver, the head waiter a little more, and the band, if there was one, £20 – all before he sat down. Born in London, he had worked as an actor with repertory companies in England, but could never master vowel sounds. As a result his theatrical career bombed, though it did revive during his spells in prison for a variety of offences including fraud and house-breaking. Among his roles was Malvolio in *Twelfth Night*, which enjoyed a short run at an open prison in Gloucestershire.

In 1965 the resourceful Cochrane landed a job in Scotland. He then established Rotary Tools with some success, securing contracts with the National Coal Board, Scotts shipyard in Greenock, and the Chrysler car plant at Linwood, all of which involved the greasing of palms. He denied that his technique of offering 'inducements' to such clients was unconventional. 'I did not corrupt anyone who was not already corrupt,' he protested. 'This is a bent society. We started dishing out gifts and money because it was clear that was the only way we would be able to do business with some companies.'

Into the House of Corruption stepped a 25-year-old Polish model whose name might have been a gift from the gods to sub-editors. She was called Anna Grunt. Cochrane was renowned for his wild parties, and Grunt attended them as a hostess, receiving a flat fee of £35 each time she slept with a client.

John Sim, 51, 'small and balding', a production manager with the National Coal Board in the Lothians, disliked for his autocratic style, was having a meal with one of the Bung Ho worshippers in the Excelsior Hotel at Glasgow Airport when Grunt joined them. A great deal of drink was consumed – far beyond Christopher Clayson's four units, it is safe to assume – and it was soon obvious to Sim that he would be going upstairs with Grunt. He described what followed as a momentary lapse. Maretta Barnsley, a croupier in Manchester when she was not horizontally employed by Rotary Tools, followed Grunt to the bedroom floors with a second client, but when challenged to describe him said she wasn't looking that closely.

There were other visitors to the home of Bung Ho who, unlike Anna and Maretta and their clients, were persons of unimpeachable reputation. In August 1973, at his Glasgow warehouse, Cochrane hosted his most spectacular event to date, billing it the 'party of the century'. Four thousand people turned up; at 2 am guests were still queuing to get in. The jazz trumpeter Dizzy Gillespie was one of the star turns along with Miss United Kingdom, making her first public appearance since winning the title, and presiding over the evening was none other than the rector of Glasgow University, Arthur Montford, whose job as a presenter of sports programmes with Scottish Television involved the wearing of a loud check jacket on soporific Sunday afternoons of football highlights.

Montford, in addition to his duties as compere, was expected to co-adjudicate the aesthetic highlight of the night, a beauty contest in which Cochrane's girlfriend Carolyn Schulz had been installed as short-odds favourite. Schulz, the daughter of a Midlands business-man, was a secretary at Rotary Tools, where she quickly fell under the spell of its eccentric proprietor. She was sufficiently attractive to be a genuine contender for the competition, but Cochrane made sure that she was the only one. Another of the judges, Kitti Lamonte, wife of a Scottish comedian, alleged that Cochrane informed her that Schulz 'had to win' – although Lamonte had privately decided to pick her anyway. The approach to Montford was more direct: 'The only comment Mr Cochrane made to me was that Carolyn will win.'

When Maurice Cochrane entered the dock of Glasgow Sheriff Court, he faced several charges of providing sex and cash to small, balding officials of nationalised industries and other people prone to momentary lapses, and a further charge of rigging the beauty contest. The Crown dropped that one; perhaps it was beneath even the Crown's dignity to pursue it. But he was found guilty of providing both the sex and the cash and was sent for 12 months to Scotland's largest repertory theatre, Barlinnie Prison.

As he was led to the cells, he blew kisses to his young wife Carolyn, whom he had married in a registry office shortly before his trial. They were living in a council house, though not quite penniless: after the fall of Bung Ho, the entrepreneur had earned a little money selling knickers in an open-air market. 'I'll be standing by Jimmy,' said the new Mrs Cochrane. 'I believe he has done nothing wrong.' He was certainly a man of his word. Mrs Cochrane had duly won the beauty contest – even if the result was not exactly one of the year's miracles.

1977

LILYBANK TO LERWICK

I

A YEAR AFTER THE DISAPPEARANCE OF RENEE MACRAE, A YEAR IN which the police had sifted through thousands of reports, witness statements, maps and photographs in their futile search for the wife and three-year-old son of an Inverness businessman, a promising discovery was made in a water-filled quarry on the south side of Culloden Moor. An underwater TV camera designed to operate in pitch darkness produced, from 40 feet down, a five-second shot of a bundle wrapped in sacking, apparently standing upright in the water. Some who examined the grainy image claimed to detect the outline of a human face – the remains of eyebrows, eye sockets, a nose and a gaping mouth. 'Could this be Renee or Andrew?' asked the newspapers. Bemused readers were invited to judge for themselves.

At its height, the search for the MacRaes involved a hundred officers of the small Northern Constabulary, frogmen, an RAF jet, police dogs from Lancashire which had been trained to find buried bodies, as well as many civilian volunteers. It yielded nothing; not a trace of the mother and child was found. Officially it remained a case of two missing persons – but that formality deluded no-one in Inverness, least of all the police. The MacRaes were dead and buried. The question was where.

Renee MacRae – 36 years old, blonde, petite, always smartly dressed – was last seen alive leaving the office of her husband's building firm at 5 pm on Friday 12 November 1976. The couple had been living apart for a year, though on amicable terms. Gordon MacRae had given her a car – a BMW – and a house.

Little was known of her movements later that evening. Between 7 pm and 8 pm, her car was seen parked near a hotel about seven miles south of Inverness; around 10 pm, a driver stopped in a layby on the A9 to investigate a flicker of flames. He was horrified to discover a burnt-out BMW and a large bloodstain in the boot. Andrew's push-chair was missing from the boot, and there was no sign of mother or son.

Renee MacRae had told friends that she was planning to drive to Kilmarnock to visit her sister, returning on Monday to pick up her older child from school. Only her best friend, Valerie Stevenson, knew the truth: that she intended to spend the weekend in Perth with her married lover Bill McDowall, company secretary of her husband's company, so that he and Andrew could get to know each other better.

Six days after the discovery of the burnt-out car, McDowall admitted that he and Renee had been having an affair. He promptly left Gordon MacRae's employment and surprised the police by turning up at their Inverness headquarters to volunteer a statement. Before he could do so, his wife marched into the interview room and dragged him away, telling the police to leave him alone.

McDowall, who had an alibi provided by his wife, maintained that he had made an arrangement to meet Renee but had a change of heart and had not kept the appointment. Valerie Stevenson told the police that Renee had been besotted with McDowall for the four years of their relationship, but Valerie was not sure he felt as committed as Renee did. Valerie doubted the sincerity of McDowall's promise to Renee that they would run away together and start a new life in Shetland, where he said he had found a job in the oil industry.

A year later, Bill McDowall had indeed found a job in the oil industry, but not in Shetland. He had become a globe-trotting executive and was living in London with his wife and two children, far from the accusing fingers and chattering tongues of Inverness. The 'Where are they now?' posters in the shops had turned yellow, Renee's luxury bungalow had been sold, and the police inquiry had run into the sand. In the absence of any fresh leads, there was only speculation – and plenty of it.

Despite the appearance of intense activity, not everyone was convinced that the police had pursued their initial inquiries with the thoroughness that might have been expected. It emerged much later that a few weeks after the MacRaes' disappearance, a police sergeant, John Cathcart, had smelled decomposing flesh in a quarry at Dalnagarry, close to where the car was found. He reported it to his superiors, yet was subsequently told to stop digging. No reason was ever given. 'The machine we were hiring had to go back', he said, 'so I assumed the motive was financial'. Such was the scale of the investigation and the intense public interest, this seemed unlikely.

The various theories contradicted each other. Witnesses said they had seen a man dragging what looked like a body into woods surrounding the quarry. Contrary to the impression given by John Cathcart, senior officers suspected that both bodies were buried in the quarry but moved before the police arrived at the scene. An elderly farmer took his divining rods to Dalnagarry and declared the bodies to be under a track. Later the farmer decided they were not under a track but buried under the A9, which was being upgraded at the time. The police dismissed this theory, although it continued to be a popular one locally.

For a few days in November 1977, the image in the water held out the best hope of solving the case. Gordon MacRae told journalists that he hoped his wife's body would be found: 'I am sure she is dead. I don't think there is any question of that. If she had been alive she would have contacted someone within days of her disappearance.' But the police were cautious. 'There's a great danger of seeing what one wants to see,' warned the head of Northern CID, John Cameron. He was right: when a team of Royal Navy divers located the sack they found nothing sinister. 'We must presume,' said Cameron, 'that the bundles, one with what appeared to be the outline of a human face, are sacks of garden rubbish. The search for Mrs MacRae will go on. This inquiry will not be closed until we find this woman and child.'

Three years later, in October 1980, Gordon MacRae let it be known that he had divorced his missing wife and that he intended to re-marry a former receptionist in his company. The other principal character, Bill McDowall, kept a low profile. The inquiry, though still notionally open, was dormant. Years passed.

By the summer of 2004, when it was re-activated, Renee MacRae would have been 64. The police announced out of the blue that their bodies might have been dumped in the quarry at Dalnagarry. This was scarcely news: Dalnagarry had been the primary focus of the investigation at the outset. But the search abandoned in 1976 when the digger had to be returned was now resumed with a vengeance. Two thousand trees were cleared, 20,000 tons of earth moved, in preparation for a search of the quarry bottom. A forensic scientist at Dundee University, Professor Sue Black, undertook a comprehensive trawl of the case papers in preparation for what might be turned up at the quarry. Nothing was. The excavation produced two crisp packets, some men's clothing and rabbit bones. Six months later, in January 2005, the police made a further announcement: they were on the point of naming a suspect and sending a report to the procurator fiscal. Nothing came of that either.

II

The heady scent of illicit sexual intrigue, the setting of the scandal in the middle-class business community of the Highlands, the enigma of the woman at the centre of it, the enduring mystery of her last hours, the odd twists and turns of the investigation, and most of all the growing realisation that a perfect murder had been committed

– these ingredients combined to make the MacRae case endlessly fascinating. Fascinating – but otherwise of no great significance. In contrast, two premature deaths in 1977 were concerned with brave innovations in Scottish life – and the difficulty of sustaining them.

On a November evening, a Glasgow actress, Katy Gardner, former wife of a playwright, Edward Boyd, received a telephone call from Sir William Murray, the baronet of Ochtertyre in Perthshire. 'Katy, I am going to shoot myself' were his only words before Gardner heard gunfire. She contacted the police and two constables from Crieff arrived at the sixteenth-century mansion around 2.40 am. They found Murray's body with the gun at his side. He had died instantly of head wounds.

He had seemed cheerful enough the night before his death as he dished out tickets for a BBC quiz programme which was due to take place in the little theatre he had created in part of the house. But his air of unconcern was deceptive. Deep in debt, Murray was being harried by the Inland Revenue for £25,000 – unpaid capital gains tax incurred over a number of years on the sale of land. And there had been a lot of it to sell. When he came of age in the 1960s 'Sir Willie' inherited a family estate of 14,500 acres as well as the historic house of Ochtertyre, where Robert Burns once stayed and which inspired him to write one or two poems about Murray's ancestors.

Sir Willie himself would have been worthy of an elegy. The young man's inheritance had included a bank overdraft and death duties; in order to pay them off he was forced to sell two farms almost immediately. But his subsequent problems were all his own making. Restless and flamboyant, he lacked the temperament for the life of a Perthshire landowner. Instead he poured money into a succession of disastrous business enterprises. Over the years he kept herds of pedigree Herefords, shipped lobsters to France, ran a film company and invested in motor racing. The year before he died, he helped to organise a Scottish expedition to explore caves in South America.

He was no more successful in love than he was in business. His first marriage ended in divorce and his second wife, a pop singer rejoicing in the name Dee-Dee Woods, left him after only a year. His greatest love, however, was the theatre he opened in the house in 1972. A girls' school had been evacuated to Ochtertyre during the Second World War, and Murray converted the former gym into a well-equipped little theatre with 100 seats. Later he added a restaurant. His first season, opening with a performance by Scottish Theatre Ballet, was fairly modest and attracted little attention. But within two years he was mounting an ambitious season lasting nine months, with plays by authors as various as Ibsen and Alan Ayckbourn, professionally produced and earning praise from the Scottish critics.

The actors who came to Ochtertyre Theatre were not expected to stay in hotels. The laird gave them rooms in the big house and breakfast in bed, often served by Murray himself. But the venture was eating money, and the 1975 season – which included a new play by the Scottish writer William McIlvanney – had to be truncated. The Scottish Arts Council and the local authorities, original backers of the scheme, withdrew their support, and despite the last-ditch patronage of two unlikely benefactors, Bing Crosby and Bob Hope, Murray was forced to close the theatre. He had been disposing of the estate at the steady rate of 1,000 acres a year and had no more land to sell. The remnants – 220 acres out of the original 14,500 plus the family home – were bought by a Dutch businessman, Dick Groot, who allowed Sir Willie to rent a small apartment in the basement.

'Everything he touched turned to failure' was the unkind verdict of one of his obituaries. But the critic Christopher Small took a more generous view of Murray's legacy. 'It would be a pity,' he wrote, 'if the founder's tragic death should prove the fatal blow to a daring, over-rash, but at its best accomplished and imaginative addition to Scotland's theatrical life.' Despite this endorsement from a respected source, the cold heart of the Scottish Arts Council was untouched. Ochtertyre Theatre never re-opened.

III

Sir William Murray, 39, and Larry Winters, 34, died young in the same year, but there the obvious resemblances ended. Murray came from a Scotland of wealth and privilege, Winters from a Scotland of neither. The only violence in Murray's life was the self-inflicted shot to the head that ended it. Winters' whole life had been violent; he had once murdered a taxi driver for £5, a fact often recalled by the tabloid press as proof of his nature. Murray died in the grand house that had once been his, while Winters 'drowned in his own vomit' (it would have been an oddity had he drowned in anyone else's) while he sat naked on a chamber pot in Barlinnie Prison. Apart from their shocking deaths within a few weeks of each other, the lives of these men could not have been more different. But they had this in common: they were both associated with noble experiments, Murray as a creator, Winters as a participant, in a country where timidity was more familiar.

In setting up a theatrical enterprise of serious ambition away from the traditional centres of artistic excellence, Murray had in-vested – or squandered – what was left of the family fortune; though the funding agencies had briefly supported him, he was essentially a lone wolf. Another Murray – Ken Murray – was that unusual combination, a prison officer and a penal reformer. He would have admired his kinsman's willingness to challenge established systems. In that most entrenched of all, the Scottish prison system, Ken Murray too was trying to challenge orthodox thinking.

In the early 1970s, with the help of a Scottish Office minister, Alick Buchanan-Smith, Murray had persuaded the authorities that there might be a better way of dealing with society's most violent offenders than by incarcerating them in punishment cells and treat-ing them like wild animals – a policy that had provoked a number of well-publicised riots. So came into being the Barlinnie special unit, a therapeutic community separate from the main prison in which inmates and officers shared responsibility for decision-making and the prisoners were encouraged to explore their innate gifts as human beings.

Its most celebrated success, Jimmy Boyle, had been brutalised in a succession of mainstream prisons. The governor of Porterfield Prison in Inverness once said of Boyle that he was 'likely at any time to attack and kill anybody with whom he is liable to come into contact'. Long before the end of his 15-year sentence, he had – in the words of the journalist and Labour MP Brian Wilson – 'metamorphosed through the special unit into a high-profile paragon of creativity and liberal humanity'.

The special unit never appealed to the atavistic tendencies of the popular press and the political class, though hardline socialists from the backwoods, rather than humane Tories such as Alick Buchanan-Smith, were among its harshest critics. With the death of Larry Winters, who was serving a life sentence plus 26 years for the attempted murder of four prison officers, the relentless drip of hostility became a flood.

At mid-day on 11 September 1977, an inmate of the special unit called John Neeson fetched Winters' lunch from the kitchen and took it up to his cell. When he walked in, he found Winters sitting on the chamber pot. 'I tapped him on the back of the head but got no response and realised something was the matter. When I touched him he fell off the pot on to the floor. His body was cold.'

A week or so before his death, Winters had approached Neeson with a request. He wanted him to collect 'some stuff' from a lavatory in the Douglas Inch psychiatric clinic that Neeson was attending as an out-patient. On his next visit to the clinic, Neeson found a matchbox behind a lavatory seat. He didn't open it. When he got back to the special unit that night he was not searched; he had never been searched on his return from an outside escort and, so far as Neeson knew, it was policy not to search. The matchbox contained a drug on which Winters then overdosed. He fell into a coma.

Jimmy Boyle, who had known Winters for 18 years, gave evidence at a fatal accident inquiry. Asked about Winters' physical and mental state the night before he died, Boyle replied: 'To be quite honest I have never seen Larry looking better. I would absolutely discount any suggestion of him taking his own life.' Sheriff Principal Robert Reid QC agreed, ruling that there was no suicidal intention and that Winters' death could have been avoided by the strict searching of prisoners.

The case was a disaster for the special unit and Ken Murray. It was immediately followed by a succession of damaging stories in the press about drink, drugs and sex in the cells, including an allegation that prostitutes were admitted to the unit. 'The possibility that certain of the allegations may be true cannot be completely eliminated,' acknowledged the Secretary of State, Bruce Millan, in a strained official euphemism barely concealing the extent of official frustration.

Bowing to the inevitable pressure, Millan announced that visitors would be more closely vetted, supervision during visits stepped up, while telephone contact with the outside world had already been restricted. Prisoners would still be allowed to wear their own clothes and to possess such personal items as wristwatches, radios, TV sets and tape recorders; and the weekly shopping expedition, in which an inmate under supervision went out to buy food which the prisoners then cooked themselves, continued as before. But mail was now being opened by staff and former inmates were no longer permitted to visit the unit. By the end of the year, the emphasis seemed to be shifting from therapy back to old-fashioned discipline, albeit in a relatively mild form. It was a change regretted by such friends of the unit as the Labour MP Norman Buchan, who called on the Secretary of State to resist 'the many voices calling for its destruction' and suggested that conjugal visits should be introduced.

Such enlightened reforms were not introduced. Instead the death of Larry Winters foreshadowed the unit's slow decline and eventual extinction. In what he interpreted as a deliberate insult, Ken

Murray was moved to another prison, a low-security establishment for young offenders, and returned to Barlinnie only in his last year before retirement in a role unconnected to the special unit. Without him it withered into insignificance, although it was not officially closed until 1994.

The writer Tom McGrath, who collaborated with Jimmy Boyle in a stage work called *The Hard Man*, gave a dark context to the fall of the special unit. He claimed that there were people in key positions in the Scottish prison system who had a Calvinistic belief in the devil, that governors regarded violent men as intrinsically evil, and that this consciousness, which he felt was 'very alive in Scotland', was directly linked to sexual oppression. It was a point of view endorsed by the social worker and broadcaster Kay Carmichael, a frequent visitor to the unit and an admirer of Ken Murray's pioneering spirit. But by the end of 1977, Carmichael was distracted by problems of her own.

IV

Unlike many of Scotland's housing ghettos, Lilybank in the east end of Glasgow had not had much of a press, good or bad. Ignored and neglected in the shadow of Parkhead (the home of Celtic Football Club), the people listened to the distant roar of the crowd every second Saturday, but for the rest of the time the outside world seldom intruded; and from the city council, owners of most of the 534 houses, there was silence in the face of muted protest. The scheme had never had a public telephone, there was only one shop, and there was no hall, playground or community centre.

The front door of the two-bedroom home of Marion Oakes, secretary of the tenants' association, had never fitted properly and consequently a draught blew through the hall; the windows, with their rotting frames, rattled; the doors of the built-in cupboards in the kitchen opened directly over the naked flame of the gas cooker;

there were radiators in the hall, where they weren't needed, but none in the bedrooms, where they were. 'The rooms are so narrow that you can't rearrange the furniture,' said Marion Oakes. 'The people are trying to bring this place up after years of neglect, but I think it might have been better to knock the whole lot down.'

Kay Carmichael, born in 1925, was herself a product of the east end (Shettleston), the child of a mixed marriage, which in the Glasgow of her childhood meant a match between a Catholic and a Protestant. She contracted polio, spent a long time in hospital, and at the age of four was sent to a convent school in Girvan, where she was mistreated by a sadistic mother superior and punished for refusing to eat the disgusting porridge. These were the roots of her social activism, which found expression not only in her work as deputy chair of the Supplementary Benefits Commission and on other public bodies, including the BBC's Broadcasting Council for Scotland, but less formally with such groups as the Gareloch Horticulturalists. Armed only with flowers and vegetables, its women members staged peaceful raids on the nuclear base at Faslane. During one of these raids, she managed to break through the perimeter fence of the base and received a prison sentence of 14 days. She was sent to Cornton Vale, Scotland's women's prison, where she instantly rebelled against being addressed as Catherine, preferring to be known as Mrs Carmichael. The governor was not amused.

While employed by Glasgow University as a senior lecturer in social work, she applied to Glasgow City Council for the tenancy of a house in Parkhead, close to Lilybank, took leave from her job – she was believed to be abroad – and stayed there for three months, living on the social security level of £10.50 a week. Adopting the identity of an impoverished widow called Cathy Price, she soon began to question how any civilised society could tolerate such living conditions. She wrote later that, from the age of three, children in the area bore 'the stigmata of deprivation' and that their aggression frightened her.

Long after she had completed this unusual experiment in social research, Alastair Hetherington, controller of BBC Scotland, got to hear about it and decided that it would make a valuable television documentary. He asked the head of current affairs, Matt Spicer, to supervise the project. The result was a three-part series, *Lilybank*, produced by David Martin and presented by Magnus Magnusson. Carmichael was unapologetic about the deception at the heart of the series; she insisted that the nature of poverty in such places as Lilybank could not be understood from behind a desk and that exposure of it excused her 'little white lie'. Hetherington stoutly defended the series, saying that it had been made with care and thought – 'it was not just a hit and run affair'.

In his obituary of Kay Carmichael, who died in 2009, Brian Wilson wrote that when the truth emerged about Cathy Price, 'the community expressed outrage at being used in this way' and that 'a project that had intended to demonstrate empathy with the poor had turned into an indictment of how little better-off people know about the lives of others in the same city'. The ethics were certainly complex, but the outrage of the community was by no means unanimous. One tenant, Charlie McCrindle, alleged that the BBC had tried to bribe young people: 'This guy came up and offered us a plastic bag filled with cans of beer. He wanted us to stand in the street and drink while they filmed.' But the treasurer of the tenants' association, Elizabeth Kane, disagreed with a city councillor, Susan Baird, that the series had 'degraded' the people of Lilybank: 'Conditions were depressing long before Mrs Carmichael came along.' A teacher in the east end wrote that the tenants' fears that the series would demean them had proved to be groundless.

Most contributors to the letters pages of the newspapers supported Kay Carmichael. 'She is to be commended for her physical and mental courage in living among the people of this unfortunate area, so that she might come to terms with the feelings, the atmosphere and the attitudes of the people,' wrote Alex Bremner. 'Her action to my mind is much more commendable than many of the whistlestop visits by local authority officials.' Robert Millar reminded detractors of the series that the east end was once a hive of manufacturing: 'Now we have an industrial desert, sprinkled with samples of industrial archaeology. Additionally we see the prospect – which terrified Mrs Carmichael – of a younger generation growing up and never working from the cradle to the grave.'

The professional critics were less impressed. One said that, although she had identified the scheme as 'hostile and ugly', she had failed to pinpoint the causes. Another lambasted Magnusson for his 'sentimentality' in observing that we were 'all' responsible for the mess. 'So once again,' wrote Robert Myddleton in the Catholic paper, *The Tablet*, 'we had a programme which appeared to be boldly facing up to radical social issues, only to duck away at the vital moment. The viewer could let his social conscience out for a trot, without actually being required to do anything.'

Alastair Hetherington was justified in claiming that the series broke new ground in television documentary. More than 30 years later, when a similar series – *The Scheme*, filmed in Kilmarnock – was shown on the BBC, the repertoire of outrage, from those in power with most to lose from such exposure, had scarcely changed. For Hetherington, however, *Lilybank* was the beginning of the end of his troubled association with the BBC (which he had joined after 20 years as editor of the *Guardian*). His fellow Scot, the director-general Alasdair Milne, when he saw a preview, made it clear that he did not care for *Lilybank* and declined to include it in the network schedule. At first it was shown only in Scotland. Under some pressure from the Broadcasting Council for Scotland, of which Kay Carmichael was still a member, an hour-long version of the series eventually went out on BBC2, but Hetherington felt that Milne never forgave him for it. His dealings with senior management in London continued to deteriorate, particularly when he persisted in demanding more autonomy for BBC Scotland, and his tenure came to an abrupt end.

V

In his classic *Scottish Journey*, a meditation on the state of Scotland loosely constructed as a travel book, Edwin Muir observed as long ago as the early 1930s that many of the places in his native country had never met. He might have been thinking of the east end of Glasgow in relation to Shetland, a group of islands 500 miles north of Scotland's most populous city, and much closer to Norway than to Scotland. They shared the same small space on a map of the world and were constitutionally part of the same country, yet they were as disconnected from each other socially and culturally as it was possible to imagine. When a Shetland farmer sent a bull to the mainland he talked of sending it 'to Scotland', as if Scotland were a foreign country, which in many ways it was.

By the end of 1977, however, a migration was taking place that would bring the world closer to Shetland and change the character of these islands for the indefinite future. It was no longer inconceivable that someone living in Lilybank, someone who wanted a job and saw no hope of getting one in the east end, would speculatively take a train to the far north and then a ferry to the distant capital of Shetland, exchanging Lilybank for Lerwick, one kind of loneliness for another. The Sullom Voe terminal was scheduled to receive its first piped oil from the North Sea in May 1978, and construction workers were struggling to have the 1,000-acre site ready in time. So there were jobs, many jobs, but demand far exceeded supply, placing an intolerable strain on the fragile infrastructure of the islands.

From all over Britain they came, camping in tents in the hope of securing work at Sullom Voe. By the summer the labour force was expected to grow from 3,000 to 4,500. But the lucky ones were outnumbered by the rejects. Some went hungry and were in danger of freezing to death. Lieutenant John Howie and his wife were doing their best to accommodate the most vulnerable in the Salvation Army's Lerwick citadel; every night, 15 or 16 slept in camp beds or sleeping bags on the floor. 'Even in winter it still goes on,' said Howie despairingly. But he objected to the term 'hobos' to describe them: 'They are not tramps, vagrants or ne'er do weels. They are men, and we've also had women, who are determined to find work. I've known them to walk 50 miles from Sumburgh airport to Sullom Voe. Even if they manage to get a job they find it hard to get accommodation.'

At the terminal, men were being turned away from the camps at the rate of a hundred a week. The director of environmental health for Shetland, Douglas Smith, admitted that he had had to 'clear out' men who were staying in disused lorries and even in wartime gun emplacements in the wilds. 'We may have to think about turning them back at the gangways of the ferries,' he said. But the message from the oil company BP, 'Stay away,' went largely unheeded in the scramble for work.

From Shetland's perspective, the trouble was that the oil industry paid too well. Unskilled men got £100 a week – good money in 1977 – with overtime on top; a skilled worker could expect at least £170 a week. These high wages for all levels of skill had contributed to a flow of labour reminiscent of the great gold rushes of the nineteenth century; then, too, the opportunities had been exaggerated. 'It is ironic,' said an editorial in the *Glasgow Herald*, 'that after a very long time of neglect, the Shetland Islands are now a magnet for a population which they cannot and do not want to absorb.'

In anticipation of the oil bonanza, the local authority had sought to minimise the impact on a long-settled way of life and to ensure that 'certain distinctive characteristics of Shetland survive and advance', identifying as two of those characteristics the sense of belonging felt by individuals within small communities and the absence of serious crime. It aimed in particular to protect fishing and farming, through loans and investments, in the belief that, once the oil had run out, the islands would again be dependent on traditional industries 'tried and tested over generations'.

Its practical vision went further. Through an act of parliament, Zetland County Council was able to take 'any action it considered necessary or desirable' for the controlled development of coastal and harbour areas; it was able to acquire land compulsorily; and it was given jurisdiction over the amount of financial compensation it could claim from the developers. These exceptional powers should have ensured that the disruptive effects of large-scale industrialisation were mitigated and that, as one of the historians of modern Shetland, J.R. Nicolson, put it, 'the Shetlanders would enjoy the advantages of an economic boom without compromising their cultural identity'.

To a limited degree the strategy worked. The local authority showed an admirable sensitivity to local needs and was resolute in protecting the interests of Shetland. What it did not foresee – and perhaps could never have foreseen – was the massive scale of oil extraction, well beyond the estimates in its initial plans. It was forced to extemporise, not always with happy results.

Many more temporary workers needed to be housed at Sullom Voe than originally expected, and the council decided that they should be accommodated in work camps away from permanent settlements. This policy was intended to discourage crime, but had the inevitable effect of isolating the oil workers and creating a sense of dislocation from the wider community. Nor did it discourage crime. The number of offences increased dramatically during the construction phase of the terminal, when the population of the islands rose from 19,000 to 23,000. In his Lerwick courtroom, Sheriff Alastair Macdonald had once been able to count on his fingers the number of criminal cases which came before him every week. Now there was a ceaseless procession of offenders in the dock, mostly immature young oil workers whose wads of ready cash were often their undoing.

The council's next decision did nothing to instill harmony in an already divided community. It decided to discourage the locals from applying for jobs at Sullom Voe by barring them from staying in the work camps and excluding them from the dislocation pay received by outsiders. Not surprisingly, the policy proved unpopular with many Shetlanders and had to be watered down; the natives wanted their share of the action and made sure they got it. But the big money came at a price: local businesses were suddenly unable to compete. Only one baker in Lerwick now made bread; the rest had to be shipped in from Aberdeen. The biggest dairy on the islands no longer delivered milk.

The scrawled verse on the lavatory wall of a shabby Lerwick pub told its own cynical story of progress:

> *Hey, Jimmy, this Shetland's a wonderful site*
> *Where the people are working by day and by night*
> *They 'don't like this oil' but it's right up their street*
> *And there's gangs of them digging for gold in the peat*

Of the people who 'don't like this oil' but nonetheless were taking full advantage of it, J.R. Nicolson wrote more philosophically: 'Had oil been discovered 10 years earlier it would have been hailed as the economic salvation of Shetland. But instead it came at a time of optimism and full employment, in marked contrast to the situation elsewhere in Britain at that time.' He detected that many Shetlanders saw the oil boom as a threat to their renewed prosperity and their way of life 'even as they realised that their islands would perform a meaningful role in securing the national interest'.

The population statistics show that these fears were partly justified. In agriculture, employment dropped from 1,245 to 476 between 1976 and 1979, the period which coincided with the building of the Sullom Voe terminal. It did, however, rise again fairly sharply afterwards. The number of jobs in fishing fell more slowly over a 20-year period (1971 to 1991) from 1,774 to 1,353. A team of American academics who conducted an impact assessment of the oil industry on Shetland concluded that the council had done well to sustain employment in the traditional industries and hailed it as a remarkable example of managed growth. The lord lieutenant of Shetland, R.H.W. Bruce, agreed: 'We have moved from a state of comparative poverty to a state of plenty' – a claim in marked contrast to Nicolson's more measured judgement of the local economy before the boom. Bruce, the Queen's man, was scornful of 'all sorts of influential people in the south who tell us it [oil] is a complete disaster'.

Physically as well as economically and culturally, the industry was transforming Shetland. The abandoned croft houses with their tarred or corrugated iron roofs stood ever more forlornly in a landscape dotted with expensive new properties. The little airport at Sumburgh was bursting at the seams, handling more passengers in a week than it used to do in a year, and the local hotels could afford to pick and choose. When a journalist attempted to book a hotel room in Lerwick, the first question he was asked was: 'Are you a workman?'; it was only when he assured them that he wasn't that they allowed him to enter the premises. A second journalist was told that there was no room at the inn, that all the rooms were booked. They were: but most of them were empty night after night, reserved by oil companies for executives who might or might not turn up and usually didn't.

It was to this changing Shetland that Renee MacRae, if she had lived, might have come to live with her lover, who had boasted of having found a job there: two more migrants to the faraway islands where the milk float didn't stop any more.

1978

ENDSVILLE

I

On a spring evening in 1978, a bizarre event took place at Hampden Park, home of Scottish football. In what the newspapers agreed was a 'gala atmosphere', 22,000 fans celebrated a rare sporting triumph, wildly cheering when the heroes made their entrance. The choice of a comedian (Andy Cameron) to introduce them should have been a clue. They paraded round the ground on an open-topped bus – twice, in case anyone missed them the first time – to the accompaniment of *Flower of Scotland*, an unofficial national anthem dripping with anti-English sentiment. Two hundred musicians from 10 of the country's finest pipe bands serviced the proceedings, along with the twirling patriots of the Barmulloch Majorettes.

One banner among many characterised the feeling in the stadium and in the country as a whole: 'Argentina. We came, we saw, we conquered'. The confident use of the past tense underlined the historic inevitability of the occasion. It was assumed that Scotland's footballers would win the World Cup; it was regarded as a foregone conclusion. Only the formality of the competition itself stood between Scotland and its destiny.

After their ecstatic reception in Glasgow, the team drove 30 miles to Prestwick Airport, where 4,000 supporters saw them off. They boarded a British Caledonian Airways' jet for the 24-hour flight to Argentina and were not long in their seats when the party began with a drink specially concocted for the flight. 'Ally's Tartan Cannonball' had been named in honour of the team manager, Ally MacLeod, an otherwise rational individual who had so conjured up a national mood of ludicrous certainty that the travelling fans were known as 'Ally's Tartan Army'. The Scottish press loved it. 'Scotland will be given the VIP treatment when they fly into Cordoba,' enthused one fan with a typewriter. 'They are staying at a ranch-type hotel with a heated pool.'

Back home, where heated pools were in relatively short supply, the news from Scotland seemed particularly colourless by comparison. The go-ahead for a nuclear power station at Torness in East Lothian, the usual rumblings of civic corruption in Dundee, a financial crisis at the Royal Lyceum Theatre in Edinburgh, all passed without much comment. There was, however, mild interest in an outrageous suggestion by the broadcaster Tom Weir, a kenspeckle character in hiking boots, that fewer mountain rescue teams would bring irresponsible climbers to their senses. Weir spoke with some authority on the subject. Having broken most of the bones in his body in a succession of climbing accidents, he was often described as Scotland's greatest survivor.

At the Free Kirk Assembly in Edinburgh, a figure of Presbyterian rectitude, Willie Ross, urged the faithful not to despair in the face of 'present-day moral laxity'. Across the road, at the General Assembly of the Church of Scotland, the Reverend Erik Cramb of St Thomas's, Gallowgate, insisted during a debate on ministerial stipends that he had enough to live on while admitting: 'I have a wife and two weans and Partick Thistle to support, and this is a big enough burden for any man.' In Hamilton, a parliamentary by-election was entering its final stages with the photogenic Margo MacDonald, the so-called 'Boadicea of the Nats', commanding most of the media attention. One commentator found it necessary to point out that 'she lives apart from her husband' but that 'people are less sniffy about such sad situations these days.'

For entertaining diversions in the run-up to Argentina, there was a choice between the Kelvin Hall in Glasgow and the bill-topping

Sydney Devine, a country and western singer adored by women of a certain age, and the sheriff court in Edinburgh where two go-go dancers went on trial. Georgina McKechnie, 29, and Maureen Lawrence, 30, denied 'exposing their persons in a shameless and indecent manner and performing dances of a lewd and libidinous nature' in the Steamboat Inn, Commercial Street, Leith. The prosecution alleged that they performed obscene acts with 30 men at a stag night – further proof of moral laxity in the very week of the General Assembly.

It fell to a plain-clothes police constable, Dugald Cameron, to expose the salacious goings-on in the Steamboat Inn, a role he performed with an impressive dedication to duty. Having 'received certain information', he and a colleague bought tickets for the stag night and spent two hours in the pub before they decided that enough was enough and called for reinforcements. A solicitor for the accused said that none of the customers had complained – an assurance that should have come as no surprise to the court – and that stripping was accepted all over the world. The sheriff fined each woman £50 and the landlord £100 for breach of the peace. McKechnie said afterwards: 'I don't regard what I did as indecent – it's all in the mind. I draw the line at overt sex. I think the judgement was wrong, but I'm not really bothered about the fine – £50 is nothing. I'll be carrying on and I get plenty of work. A couple of gigs will cover it.' She added that a male sheriff might have arrived at a different verdict.

Far from the Steamboat Inn, the young athletes on whom Scottish hopes rested were ensconced in the ranch-style Sierras Hotel in Cordoba. The tournament had still not started, but out on the streets of the city the foot soldiers of Ally's Tartan Army were being proclaimed by the doting press corps as the stars of the World Cup. 'We have taken Argentina by storm,' wrote another of the fans with typewriters. 'We are being treated like royalty. The Argentinians have just one complaint – there are not enough Scotsmen around.' Some had stayed behind in Scotland, where the last frantic preparations were being made for a war that would be fought in front of the television set. The women had their orders. 'I must not vacuum while the match is on,' said Heather McDougall of Jordanhill, Glasgow. 'I must warn friends not to phone or call at the house. I must buy in plenty of beer and crisps. I've also been told by my son that anyone who doesn't know the names of the Scottish squad is a dummy.' These were among the last reported words of happy expectation.

Scotland lost the first of their three qualifying games 3-1 to the unfancied Peru. 'Is there something about the press in Scotland that is reticent about preparing us for unwelcome truths?' inquired the Labour MP Tam Dalyell, who had once managed the football team at Bo'ness Academy. 'In spite of the fact that any inquiry among friends from the Latin American community in Britain would have revealed that Peru had developed a formidable side, Scottish journalists have persisted in suggesting a walkover for Ally MacLeod's Tartan Army.' Dalyell might have added that the journalists took their cue from MacLeod himself, who had described the Peruvians as 'old men' (and another of their opponents, Iran, as 'minnows'). But these same journalists were less impressed by the unexpected skill of the Peruvians than by the ineptness of the Scots. 'I watched in disbelief,' wrote Jim Reynolds of the *Glasgow Herald*, 'a nightmare of sheer inefficiency, a third-rate performance which must rank as one of the worst ever by a side in the dark blue of Scotland.'

The team hotel was instantly rebranded Chateau Despair. The morning after the terrible night before, Ally MacLeod 'sat in the sun in a glum mood, still trying to figure out the answers'. The manager's deadpan quip before leaving Scotland, 'You are either looking at a millionaire or a condemned man,' was quoted back at him in ironic rebuke. MacLeod replied that 'the way we played, we couldn't have beaten Muirend Amateurs' and, when a stray dog sidled up to him, added: 'Look – my only friend.' But the self-pitying manager had nothing to say about the disgrace engulfing his squad.

Even before the Scots had arrived to face the ordeal of a post-match drinks reception organised by the British Embassy, rumours were circulating in the media centre that one of the players, Willie Johnston of West Bromwich Albion, had failed a drugs test. When Johnston was confronted at the reception by a crew from ITN, MacLeod angrily intervened. 'There is a time and a place to interview players, and that place is not here,' he bawled at the interviewer, Trevor McDonald. 'You are here as a guest of the embassy, not to interview players. I am going to ask you to leave.' McDonald did leave, and the reception broke up in disarray. Until then Johnston had been unaware of the result of the test. His immediate response was to protest surprise; he said he had been suffering from a heavy cold but refused to divulge if he had taken anything for it.

The initial evasiveness failed to survive much scrutiny. It was soon disclosed that, in a routine check before the match, the Scottish team's medical adviser, Dr John Fitzsimmons, had given each of the players an opportunity to state that they had taken drugs and no-one did. The hapless Johnston finally admitted popping Fencamfamine – a stimulant on the tournament's list of banned substances – because he was feeling low with hay fever: 'I have taken them at West Bromwich. I just didn't realise it would cause all this trouble.' The disciplinarian secretary of the Scottish Football Association, Ernie Walker, promptly announced that Johnston was to be sent home and would never play for Scotland again. The players, who were said to be 'numbed' by the affair and 'walking about the camp like robots', were instructed to stay in their rooms while Walker solemnly read out a prepared statement.

Suddenly, Ally MacLeod was nowhere to be seen. He had earlier said that if he was asked to attend Ernie Walker's press conference he would be there – 'if not, then I will be absent'. He was absent. Soon the post-mortem was in full swing; and it was MacLeod's reputation on the slab. 'Did we ask too much of him?' wondered Miller Reid, chairman of Partick Thistle. 'He was public relations officer, financial consultant, salesman and a host of other things as well as team manager.' Others were less tolerant. The Argentinian media denounced him as 'Mr Big Mouth', alleged that he rarely spoke to his players, gave them no advice about drugs and tolerated a culture of heavy drinking.

Whatever the truth about MacLeod, the immediate problem was how to get rid of Johnston. Ernie Walker wasted no time. The morning after the press conference, 'the man who disgraced Scotland' was covered in a blanket, smuggled out of the hotel at the crack of dawn, driven a punishing 440 miles to Buenos Aires and put on the first plane home. This was unnecessarily cruel; the Scottish Football Association could have booked him on a local flight to Buenos Aires and allowed him to leave with a little dignity.

Ally's Army, stunned by the triple blows of defeat at the hands of Peru, a farcical draw with Iran a few days later, and the Johnston scandal, retreated in ignominy from the streets of Cordoba. Among the celebrity supporters, the rock singer Rod Stewart did not conceal his despair: 'This is goodbye. It's Endsville. We are out. I just can't believe it.'

The supporters of the national team revealed themselves as fair-weather friends. During the Iran game, 14 who were displaying obscene banners critical of the Scottish Football Association were escorted out of the stadium at gunpoint and detained in the local police station for several hours. 'They said they would shoot us unless we came with them,' explained one tartan-clad youth, the son of a High Court judge. At half-time, the players were jeered off the park; at full-time they were 'lucky not to be lynched' according to one erstwhile fan with a typewriter. 'Scotland's on the pill, ee-eye-addio, Scotland's on the pill,' they yelled at the team bus.

Seven thousand miles away, in the pubs around Ibrox stadium, Willie Johnston was remembered as a former Rangers star, a player given to throwing tantrums but a dazzling talent at his best. The punters resorted to the dark humour they reserved for situations of dire emergency. 'Stimulants?' mused one. 'I thought they were all on tranquillisers.' 'A Scottish player takes drugs and we still get beat,' reflected another. In one of the city's record shops, Andy Cameron's excruciating ditty, 'Ally's Tartan Army', could be obtained at the knockdown price of 1p. The manager said that some customers handed over the money and then smashed the record across the counter.

For their last game, with the mighty Dutch, the Scottish team were required to travel several hundred miles to the city of Mendoza. Only 300 mutinous fans made the journey with them. Before the game, one of them lunged at a Scottish Television producer, Clarke Tait, who was ill-advisedly wearing the official badge of the Scottish Football Association. The drunken Scot made a clumsy attempt to smash a bottle over his head, narrowly missing, and when Tait fell to the ground, kicked him and ran off. A victory against Holland by three goals to two – an empty result, for Scotland had already been eliminated from the tournament – restored the good humour of the home support. 'O Scotland, O Scotland, we'll walk a million miles for one of your goals,' chanted the same fans who had taunted the players, throwing scarves at them in disgust, only a few nights earlier. 'Scotland died gloriously in the World Cup last night,' reported the fans with typewriters. 'We are on our way home with honour restored.' It didn't take much.

Such was the temporary national amnesia, the nationalist MP Douglas Crawford was not laughed off the park when he tried to make political capital out of the 'triumph' over Holland. Pointing out that Scotland was the only World Cup finalist that was not a sovereign nation, he said it was 'not certain' that FIFA, the governing body of international football, would allow such a situation to continue. How, he asked, would the Scots feel if there was to be no Scottish team at future World Cup finals? The possibility that, after the events in Argentina, many Scots would feel only relief might not have occurred to him.

With the return of the team to Scotland, a sense of reality returned. The home-based players, 'tired and drawn', touched down at Glasgow Airport to a lukewarm reception. A bus was waiting for them on the tarmac to allow them to avoid a crowd of young female admirers which the press, never good with figures, estimated at around 200. Ally's Tartan Army had been granted premature demobilisation. There was no more talk of death with glory or honour restored. It was time for recriminations. To allegations from the Scottish squad that the press corps had filed exaggerated stories about excessive drinking, and that such reporting had upset the players' wives at home in Britain, the journalists replied indignantly that they would not have filed the stories if they had not been true.

The manager, so recently a national hero, was now a fallen idol and fair game for the unforgiving media. One allegation followed another: the players had gone drinking in the bars of Cordoba because they were bored and had nothing to do; there had been a row about bonuses; even the ranch-style hotel with its heated pool was not all it had been cracked up to be – there had been no water in the pool. MacLeod dealt stoically with his bad press and stayed on as Scotland manager for several months until he found an alternative berth for his modest talents – the vacancy at Ayr United. Later, in a self-justifying memoir, he wrote: 'I am a very good manager who just happened to have a few disastrous days, once upon a time, in Argentina.' He died in 2004 at the age of 72, from Alzheimer's Disease, and his obituaries were kind: he was recognised as an essentially decent and well-meaning man.

The Scots, a rather canny lot most of the time, had a periodic weakness for messianic figures offering them a tantalising vision of the promised land. Half the population had attended the rallies of the American evangelist Billy Graham in 1956 and many stepped forward as converts; in the opening years of the twenty-first century, a silver-tongued nationalist with the common touch, Alex Salmond, would do for the Scots politically what Graham had done for them spiritually. But of the three great persuaders, MacLeod was the least plausible. Beyond a native wit – had he not pursued a career in sport he might have been a passable comic – there seemed to be nothing remarkable about him, and even his admirers struggled to identify the source of his alchemy. Willie Miller, captain of Aberdeen during MacLeod's tenure there, said after his death that his old boss had lifted Scotland's spirits: 'His power was getting people to listen. No matter how outrageous his statements, Ally had you believing what he said could happen.' And Scotland lived the dream – if briefly.

The career of Willie Johnston never recovered. He was in his early thirties when he was selected for Argentina: the best of his career was behind him. But had he returned to England after a successful World Cup, he could have looked forward to a few more good years with West Bromwich Albion. Instead he had to endure the insults of opposing fans at away games, the cries of 'Junky! Junky!' from the terracing. The club dropped him and Johnston emigrated to Canada. Years later, in an interview with the sports journalist Graham Spiers, he recalled the worst day of his footballing life: 'After the match they're wanting a urine test, aren't they, and I think Archie Gemmill was meant to do it. For some reason Archie wasn't up to it, so I said "I'll go". The next thing I knew we're at that reception for Scotland players and officials and Trevor McDonald and the ITV crew are suddenly on me and switching on their lights. I genuinely didn't know what was going on. Then Asa Hartford yanked me and said: "Hey, wee man, you've failed the test!". Well, that was it. Ernie Walker ordered me to my room and the next day I was being driven away under a blanket, like a criminal.'

In his crude handling of Johnston, an innocent abroad in many ways, and as prime mover of the Hampden send-off, the secretary of the Scottish Football Association had much to answer for. After his death in 2011, one of his obituarists, Archie Macpherson, said that in organising such a *folie de grandeur* Ernie Walker had 'succumbed to the populist terracing tendency which did indeed inform much of his thinking'. He was nevertheless a figure of immense stature in Scottish sport and, despite his outwardly stern demeanour, a man of considerable charm. As Macpherson wrote: '[He] could portray authority simply by flicking his cigar ash nonchalantly into a tray, while sipping a good malt.' He was also a uniquely successful administrator, taking Scotland to five successive World Cup finals. In Macpherson's deft phrase, he had the heart of a punter. But the punter was never the same after Argentina. The Tartan Army continued without Ally, often as boisterously as before, but with a welcome dash of self-parody in the ranks. The irony had entered their souls.

II

So overwhelming was the obsession with the World Cup and its quarrelsome aftermath, another story about football came and went almost unnoticed, yet its washing of grubby socks in public was equally revealing of the dysfunctional nature of the 'national sport'. A young manager, Alex Ferguson, formerly of East Stirlingshire, was dismissed by the Paisley side, St Mirren, and took his employer to an industrial tribunal. This course of action was almost unheard-of. Football managers were as resigned to the likelihood of the sack as schoolboys were to the belt. In the game of managerial musical chairs, an alternative club swiftly beckoned for the talented ones. Sure enough, two days after he was fired by St Mirren, Ferguson was installed as manager of a bigger club, Aberdeen, with his growing reputation more or less unimpaired. He persisted, however, with his case against the board of St Mirren, claiming that he had been unfairly dismissed.

Ferguson had half a year in which to reconsider his position, before the case came to a public hearing. He then faced a well-prepared opponent in a fixture with all the makings of a grudge match. The club chairman, William Todd, went on the attack with 13 allegations against Ferguson, including rows over expenses and a feud between the manager and his secretary so bad that the pair were barely on speaking terms. Todd told the tribunal that his own relationship with Ferguson had been amicable until near the end, when Ferguson complained that he was not being paid enough. 'He seemed particularly perturbed,' said Todd, 'and we knew he was in certain financial difficulties.' According to the chairman, the manager was helping himself to an extra £25 a week and writing off the money as expenses. Ferguson claimed he was entitled to the money; the directors disagreed. 'At the end,' said Todd, 'he was virtually forcing us to dismiss him.'

The company secretary, James Aitken, and the vice-chairman, John Corson, were implacable in defence. Aitken described a 'stormy meeting' at which Ferguson's salary was discussed, which ended with the manager storming out shouting 'Just sack me and I'll sue you.' Corson claimed that Ferguson was 'impossible to live with' and that the decision to dismiss him had been taken at a board meeting in the Excelsior Hotel at Glasgow Airport, a hotel last in the news in the interesting case of Bung Ho and Anna Grunt.

Alex Ferguson, giving evidence on his own behalf, explained the main source of his disillusionment: the fact that, in an average season, three of the players earned more than he did. Todd had been unsympathetic to his request for an increase in salary, pointing out to Ferguson that Johan Cruyff – a European star of the time – earned more than his manager at Barcelona. Ferguson's riposte was that the three players at St Mirren who earned more than he did were not in the same class as Johan Cruyff.

Ferguson lost the case. The tribunal dismissed him as petty and immature, a fair enough judgement in the circumstances, but could not resist the gratuitous observation that Ferguson 'possessed neither by experience, nor talent, any managerial ability at all' – the equivalent of one of those school reports that return to haunt the teacher. After the reputational damage of the St Mirren case, Ferguson never made such a silly mistake again. He retired in his early seventies as manager of one of the greatest clubs in the world, Manchester United, garlanded with honours, a knight of the realm, a national treasure.

Although nationalist fervour inspired the World Cup misadventure, it failed to translate into electoral advantage for the SNP. In the first of the year's three by-elections, Donald Dewar was returned to Westminster after eight years in the wilderness, holding Glasgow Garscadden for Labour by a majority of 4,552. It had been a bitter, nasty campaign and in its final hours, outside the count, Labour chants were drowned out by the lusty refrain of *Flower of Scotland* from the SNP contingent. The song may have been a bad omen that night, as it was a few weeks later at Hampden Park: the result, in a seat the SNP were so confident about winning that they had booked a hall in Partick for the victory party, stunned the nationalists into silence.

A beer can narrowly missed the new MP's head as he emerged from the count to address the crowd. 'This changes the whole psychological mood of Scottish politics,' declared the victor. The 27-year-old secretary of the Labour Party in Scotland, Helen Liddell, said that the Scots had taken 'a massive step away from separation' and the *Glasgow Herald* called it 'the most serious blow suffered by the Scottish National Party since its breakthrough 11 years ago at Hamilton' (when Winifred Ewing took what had been a safe Labour seat and ignited her party's revival). But the commentators also noted that, in Donald Dewar, Labour had fielded an exceptionally able candidate, and that the SNP's Keith Bovey, a Glasgow lawyer known for his work with the Campaign for Nuclear Disarmament, looked less than sure-footed in comparison.

The Garscadden by-election had the incidental result of killing off the breakaway Scottish Labour Party, founded two years earlier by the disillusioned Labour MP Jim Sillars. From the derisory 583 votes of its candidate, Shiona Farrell, there was no way back. The *Glasgow Herald* dashed off an obituary, claiming that it was 'always hard to launch a new party', that there was 'less ideology in British political culture than committed ideologues like Mr Sillars like to imagine' and that there had been 'simply no room for the SLP'.

It had not seemed at all like that in the early weeks of 1976, when the new party enjoyed the ringing endorsement – and in some cases active support – of several prominent figures in the Scottish media. James Callaghan's government had recently published a White Paper recommending a Scottish Assembly with a wide range of devolved powers, but retaining UK responsibility for the economy. One of Labour's rising stars, George Robertson, Scottish organiser of the General and Municipal Workers Union, infuriated the more ardent devolutionists such as Sillars by asserting that there was no such thing as a distinctive Scottish economy and that close links with the rest of the British economy could not be 'artificially ruptured' without doing serious harm to job prospects north of the border.

The electorate gave the devolution package a lukewarm reception; in the first opinion poll of 1976, only 37% said they were satisfied with the proposals and the SNP continued to lead Labour by 6%. Sensing a gap in the market for a non-nationalist party more genuinely committed to devolution than his own, a frustrated Sillars decided to risk political suicide and form one. He was joined by a second dissident, the Labour MP for Paisley, John Robertson.

The party's birth in a Glasgow hotel was delayed by the issue of membership cards to the unexpectedly large number of supporters who turned up: 396 instead of the anticipated 100 or so. At 5.20 pm – it was the sort of momentous occasion that required journalists to check their watches – the Scottish Labour Party formally came into being. Sillars delivered one of his trademark speeches, rich in fiery imagery, in which he denounced 'the once magnificent institution of the Labour Party . . . debauched by careerism, its idealism quenched by wave after wave of Wilsonian pragmatism'. He prophesied that his party's demands for a powerful Scottish parliament would 'make the Cabinet quiver with anxiety, the mandarins of Whitehall choke on their pheasant, and half the Parliamentary Labour Party faint at the prospect'. The 396 card-carriers listened with every impression of seriousness. They consisted, noted one observer, of 'old men in cloth bunnets who talked of the ILP, smart young women, business types, Marxists, the plain curious, and even an official observer from the Italian Embassy in London'. The secretary of the new party, Alex Neil, a former Labour Party researcher, assured them that they were attending 'the most historic political event in Scotland since the Scottish Trades Union Congress was formed at the turn of the century'.

On the same day, the Secretary of State for Scotland, still Willie Ross at that stage, pulled an audience of 250 – 146 fewer than Sillars elsewhere in the city – for the launch of Labour's 'Devolution not Separation' campaign. Ross avoided any direct reference to the SLP, who were launching while he spoke, but said pointedly that the separation of the economy was 'a very dangerous and difficult' concept. James Milne, the influential general secretary of the Scottish Trades Union Congress, dissented, arguing for 'substantial' devolution of economic powers.

Later in January 1976, the depth of the split in the Labour Party over devolution was exposed at the end of a four-day debate in the House of Commons by the refusal of 19 of its backbenchers to support the proposals. When it came to a vote on 'noting the White Paper', the government won easily: so feeble was the motion that it would have been a spectacular disaster had they not. Three Scottish Tories – Tam Galbraith, Michael Clark Hutchison and Iain Sproat – opposed even taking note. 'I do not want such an assembly', Sproat wrote a few days later in a newspaper article, 'because it would lead inevitably to the disintegration of the United Kingdom. This is because everything good would be credited to the assembly and everything bad would be debited to London.' From the opposite perspective, the Liberal leader David Steel was just as unhappy. He feared 'a low-grade talking shop' and emphasised the importance of getting the terminology right: it should be a 'Parliament' rather than an 'Assembly'. The White Paper was not a crowd-pleaser, yet when the Leader of the House, Edward Short, appealed to the Scottish people to tell him what they thought about it, he received only 29 replies in two months. Were the politicians who got so excited about it in danger of overestimating public interest in devolution? Only a referendum would settle the question and the smart money was now on just that.

By March 1976, an opinion poll showed that the breakaway SLP had converted a quarter of the Labour vote. Alex Neil said he was 'staggered and delighted by this wonderful result', which had taken the seven-week-old party from nowhere to fourth place, above the Liberals. But a week was indeed 'a long time in politics', and a week later the author of the aphorism, Harold Wilson, mysteriously resigned as Prime Minister. The 'Hammer of the Nats', Willie Ross, promptly bowed out and Wilson's successor, James Callaghan, appointed the more emollient Bruce Millan to the Scottish Office portfolio. In a second smart move, Callaghan fired Edward Short and put Michael Foot in charge of the devolution bill with an able young Scot, John Smith, assisting him. With these deft strokes, the new Prime Minister revived the devolution project and made it more likely that Scotland would soon have a meaningful assembly.

For Jim Sillars, it was wretched luck: the gap in the market had abruptly closed. Labour's fortunes improved at once, and by April they had recaptured all of their lost support and were leading the SNP by 5%. Alex Neil insisted that he was not downhearted by the SLP's poor showing and that the true test would be the party's performance in a council by-election in Darnley, Glasgow, which he regarded as potentially fertile territory. But the SLP took only 15% of the vote in Darnley, and the party was effectively over before it had begun. Long before the Garscadden by-election two years later, the Whitehall mandarins had ceased to worry about choking on their pheasant.

In the long-running comedy of Scottish constitutional politics, the careers of performers who fell carelessly through the trapdoor were not always doomed by derisive laughter from the auditorium. Some dusted themselves down in time to make a further appearance later in the play. Jim Sillars gave up being a devolutionist and, by the end of Act II, was the SNP member for Govan. Alex Neil did even better for himself, as a cabinet member in the Scottish government of Alex Salmond (and later of Nicola Sturgeon).

The two other 1978 by-elections also went to Labour. George Robertson, the trade union official who doubted the existence of a separate Scottish economy, 'roared with delight' when the result in Hamilton – scene of Winnie Ewing's great victory – gave him a majority of 6,492. 'The greatest psychological victory for the Labour Party in modern political history,' Helen Liddell called it – a hyperbole almost as fanciful as Alex Neil's likening of the breakaway SLP to the founding of the STUC. Outside, while the SNP supporters did their usual rendering of the ill-fated *Flower of Scotland*, the Labour crowd chanted 'If you hate devolution, clap your hands'. Worryingly for the party, many did.

In July 1978, the Labour intellectual John P. Mackintosh died suddenly at the age of 48. Only weeks before his death he announced that although he had been appointed professor of politics at Edinburgh University, he intended to remain an MP and would try to retain his marginal seat of Berwick and East Lothian at the General Election. The news caused consternation in the academic community, particularly as Mackintosh had a dodgy heart. His obituaries lauded him as an inspired House of Commons debater, whose maiden speech had convinced even his enemies that he was destined for great things. But he spread his talents too thinly, dissipating them in writing, journalism and public speaking; the Renaissance Man worked himself to death but never achieved the success in politics for which his natural talents should have equipped him. 'He was a man of parts,' said one admirer. 'Possibly too many for his own good.' His early death was reminiscent of the fate of another of the party's thinkers, Hector McNeil, but while

McNeil did briefly achieve high office (as Secretary of State for Scotland 1950–51), Mackintosh never did.

In the by-election campaign caused by his death, there was a fatuous distraction. The SNP unceremoniously dumped the candidate who had been selected to fight the seat in the General Election and installed 34-year-old Isobel Lindsay, the party's vice-chair. When the newspapers discovered that Lindsay was pregnant, a fact she had omitted to disclose when she handed in her nomination papers, it became an issue. 'Even in a normal situation,' pontificated the *Glasgow Herald's* political editor, Geoffrey Parkhouse, 'this would raise interesting questions as to whether or not it is valid that this information should be available about a person who is putting herself up for public office.' Lindsay polled only 9% of the vote, a long way behind Labour, and the fuss kicked up by such dinosaurs as Geoffrey Parkhouse was quickly forgotten. But the incident showed how far the Scotland of the late 1970s still had to travel to the ultimate destination of an enlightened society.

IV

In the summer of the World Cup misadventure, when the Scotland of modern times had never felt more male, Heather McDougall of Jordanhill spoke for the majority of women when she cheerfully acknowledged her allotted place. She had received her orders: to fetch sufficient quantities of beer and crisps for the big match and to ensure by her smooth organisation of the household that the men were undisturbed by extraneous irritations.

Although the Scottish husband was unreconstructed in his habits, a new phenomenon had begun to transform the lot of the urban wife. She was no longer popping out to the corner shop for the pre-match beer and crisps; she tended to do most of her shopping in the new 'superstores' – supermarkets as they came to be known. A female journalist marvelled at the attractions of the recently opened branches of

Tesco in Ayr, Greenock and Irvine: 'All sell fresh fish brought daily from Arbroath. The food is cheap, the aisles are wide, and the different sections easily found. At Greenock's meat counter there is a telephone and customers are invited to ring for butchers' advice. The atmosphere of these stores is deceptively casual – they are highly organised and work efficiently.'

The newspapers were intrigued by the growth of the superstores and their impact on the lives of women. But there was less discussion in the press about the intellectual lives of women and why so few of them contributed to the public life of the country. The pregnant Isobel Lindsay, and her nationalist colleague Margo MacDonald, whose separation from her husband had been written down as a 'sad situation', were exceptions. Both were objects of media curiosity – mostly for the wrong reasons.

The *Sunday Post*, a bugle of the respectable working class, ran an improving column, arranged in the form of a diary, called Francis Gay. There was no-one of that name in the office, and the word gay had not yet been appropriated by emancipated homosexuals; when Francis Gay arrived in Scottish journalism it was as the pseudonym for a fictional columnist of orthodox conservative views, a Kirk-attending sort of chap, much given to sentimental homilies on the human condition, whose wife was known as the Lady of the House. A figure of immense dignity, the Lady of the House rarely ventured out alone except to attend Sunday worship and the monthly meeting of the Scottish Women's Rural Institute. Mrs Gay, though a stereotype, was an instantly recognisable one. Eighteen years after the end of the supposedly liberating Sixties, she represented something real. There was a lot of her about.

Safe in its eternal verities, the Gay household felt blessed to have been untouched by the sexual revolution. But in the insecure world outside it, the real one, even as late as 1978 there were residual areas of confusion about relationships and their boundaries. Lise Miles, an 18-year-old aspiring model from Ayrshire, articulated them in a newspaper series about the lives of young Scots.

Lise, who was described as 'very pretty', had a boyfriend called Callum, a disc jockey. 'We are thinking of moving into a flat together in Troon or Ayr,' she said, 'but I'd discuss it first with my parents, although I don't think they would object. They are quite open-minded people. I feel sorry for my friends who are sleeping with their boyfriends and having great rows with their parents about it.' Lise thought she and Callum would 'travel around Europe for a while' before they pursued careers. There was no suggestion that either would go to university: degrees and diplomas were not yet regarded by most young people as the designated route to the holy grail. 'I want to do something with my life, make a name for myself. I've never wanted ordinary, conventional things,' said Lise. If she ever did make a name for herself, it was not by using her own. But in her yearning to break free from the stifling limitations of a small society, she too represented something real – the Scotland of youthful if often frustrated ambition.

In the spring of 1978, the ambition of 26-year-old Anne Hannah was severely limited. Not for her the luxury of travelling around Europe for a while. The hapless victim of a bureaucratic tangle, she spent much of April travelling around the new town of Livingston with her two sons aged seven and five, shuttling between the social work offices of Lothian Regional Council and the housing offices of West Lothian District Council.

A new piece of legislation which came into force that month gave district councils – the second-tier local authorities – responsibility for homeless people. A dispute arose within days when West Lothian refused Anne Hannah emergency accommodation though it had 20 vacant houses set aside for the purpose. The SNP chairman of the council's housing committee, James McGinley, personally vetoed the application on the grounds that the Hannahs were not genuinely homeless and that the family had been 'a social work case of some long standing' – a claim denied by Lothian social work department. The Scottish Office was helpless to intervene, admitting that under the new law the Secretary of State had no powers to resolve a dispute between region and district.

The facts were simple enough: Anne Hannah had given up the tenancy of her house and gone to live with a man; the relationship had ended badly; the man had thrown her out, leaving her and her children on the street. It was a familiar situation for which there was a practical solution: there was no dispute about that. Only the intransigence of an obstinate minor politician prevented her from being re-housed at once. Instead she and her children had to be put up in a hotel. On eight successive mornings, officials of the social work department presented her at the housing office; on eight successive mornings she was turned away. Finally, a third authority – Livingston Development Corporation – stepped in and offered Mrs Hannah one of its own houses. The ludicrous affair ended with an admission from McGinley that the council had been in breach of the legislation and an undertaking that the council would honour its obligations in future.

The dispute was widely cited as an example of the many anomalies of the two-tier system of local government introduced by Lord Wheatley's reorganisation. But there was a deeper dimension to the story. The needless humiliation visited on Anne Hannah and her children by a male councillor was expressed in a language drained of warmth or personality. In the quoted utterances of McGinley, there was no reference to Mrs Hannah and her two sons as people; rather they were reduced to the status of a file, 'a social work case of some long standing'. Used consciously or unconsciously, this dehumanised official-speak, which George Orwell had been among the first to expose, was a powerful weapon against the weakest, most vulnerable people in society, including and especially women and children who had been left without a roof over their heads.

The Hannah children and their mother were safely re-housed; that much could be said for the outcome in West Lothian. The same week, the body of a 10-year-old girl, who had been missing for three days, was found in Glasgow; in this tragedy there was a lack of humanity at every level. Lord Wheatley, who was seldom far from the centre of Scottish public life, was discreditably involved in it – as the judge who presided over its denouement.

V

Andrea Hedger went missing on 5 April 1978 on her way to Willowbank Primary School, 300 yards from her home in the Woodlands district of the city. She was a shy girl, described by one of her teachers as a well-behaved child who caused no trouble. On the morning of her disappearance she carried a note from her mother, Margaret, apologising for Andrea's late arrival and explaining that the family had slept in.

As she approached the school, Andrea stopped to speak to a young man, someone she had never met before, whose demeanour startled her. 'Why is a big man like you crying?' she asked him. Robert Tervet, the weeping stranger, had just quarrelled with his 15-year-old girlfriend, who was heavily pregnant with their child but had abandoned him for someone else. Tervet forced Andrea to accompany him to a derelict basement, where he pushed her on top of a mattress, put a hand over her mouth, raped her, strangled her with a scarf, and left her body hidden under a pile of rubble and wood, covering it with a 6ft-high plywood cutout of a red-painted dragon. When the case came to court, his counsel suggested that the rape had been a form of displacement activity: Tervet had 'imagined' Andrea to be the girlfriend who betrayed him.

On the night of the murder, Tervet turned up at a police station in Glasgow to speak to a detective who had had previous dealings with him. He was told that the officer was not available. He then went to see his father, who was staying in a lodging house. His father would not see him either. Next he took a bus from Glasgow to Manchester, where he stayed with relatives in Stockport until the police tracked him down. His alibi was checked and found to be false. He was escorted back to Glasgow and appeared at the sheriff court, where screaming women besieged the van taking him to Barlinnie Prison. There he was detained in solitary confinement, afraid to take the half-hour exercise he was allowed each day.

The child murderer was not long out of childhood himself. He was 19, one of a family of 11, with a string of previous convictions. When Tervet needed money he stole lead and sold it. He was of low intelligence (though judged sane and fit to plead) and had slept rough for much of his life in a succession of derelict tenements in a twilight area of the city's west end. In their search for Andrea, detectives visited every house and basement in the neighbourhood and unearthed dozens of other crimes, including rapes and serious drug offences, admitted by people who would rather volunteer information against themselves than be suspected of so terrible a murder.

Woodlands had once been a solid middle-class preserve. By the late 1970s the core of it was a ghetto of slum housing, a local byword for social dysfunction, blighted by prostitution, drugs and vagrancy. Many of the tenements were owned by a London-based landlord, Grenadier Properties. The chairman of Charing Cross and Kelvingrove Housing Association, Gordon Rennie, wrote to the company three times asking if the association could buy their properties in Woodside. He got no reply. Eventually, prompted by the Hedger case, he rang Grenadier's contact man, one Peter Colenutt, and was told that Colenutt was too busy to speak to him. Later Grenadier made it clear they were not selling.

Many houses owned by another of the Woodside landlords, Mustafa Khan, were empty and rotting. The playwright Edward Boyd, who lived in St Vincent Crescent, started a campaign to have the vacant houses acquired and sold for the general good of the area. Khan referred him to his solicitor – who turned out to be the chairman of the Scottish Development Agency, Sir William Gray, a former Lord Provost of Glasgow and a well-known champion of poorly housed people. Gray, when he was confronted, replied that his law firm could not be expected to know what all its clients were doing with their properties. It was not a great answer: Khan was no ordinary client; he was a notorious slum landlord. But the urbane Gray was a popular figure among Glasgow journalists and, during his term of office as Lord Provost, would relax with them in the city chambers on a Friday afternoon. Of the apparent conflict of interest, no more was heard.

Among the large immigrant community, many of whom attended Andrea's funeral, there was dismay and bewilderment at the decline of a district in which they had once been happy. The press published the testimony of Mrs Manorma Sood, who was raising five daughters in a two-room and kitchen flat in Woodlands with a toilet but no bath. After an arranged marriage in the Punjab, she and her husband emigrated to Scotland, where he worked on the buses; in 1971 they moved to Woodlands and sank £800 into the flat. At first life there was good – until, for reasons she found impossible to comprehend, the locality deteriorated rapidly. There were three brothels in her close now, and almost nightly men hammered on her door assuming that her flat, too, was a brothel. Her husband died in 1977 at the age of 40; without him she was frightened, never leaving home after 4 pm, when her children returned from school. Her 12-year-old daughter Anita had been Andrea Hedger's best friend. They played records together the night before Andrea met the big man crying in the street.

Robert Tervet admitted murdering Andrea, but the prosecution alleged that he showed no remorse – only self-pity. Lord Wheatley, sentencing him to a minimum of 15 years, said that he could feel 'no sorrow' for any treatment Tervet might receive in prison. The Howard League for Penal Reform was appalled: 'It is no part of his duty to give expression to those feelings in open court in a way which could be held to condone, if not incite, the maltreatment of one prisoner at the hands of another.' The League called on Wheatley to set the record straight, while the Scottish Council for Civil Liberties demanded a reprimand for the judge. But there was no reprimand, no setting of the record straight; Wheatley, who had mishandled the case of the last man to hang in Scotland (Harry Burnett), sailed on regardless. For his own safety, Tervet was transferred to the high-security prison at Peterhead, where he was kept in protective custody in a special unit.

VI

Two years earlier, in a talk for the BBC about Scotland and its future, the historian Christopher Smout had delivered a withering anatomy of the national character. He asked: 'What do Norway and Sweden have that Scotland does not, apart from separation from England?' His answer was that history had made the Scandinavians more co-operative, innovative and flexible, that they had a more honest and democratic voting system, that they used less autocratic methods in schools 'and therefore do not grow up to become industrial paranoics alienated from the State'. Smout concluded that nothing less than a crusade would be required to change Scottish attitudes. But where was such a crusade to start? Not with the politicians, preoccupied as they were by the constitutional question; and certainly not with the bench of judges who gave every impression of being above imperfect democracy. The Solicitor-General for Scotland, Lord McCluskey, used the platform of the Glasgow Bar Association to condemn the interference of 'remote international institutions' – a reference to the European Court of Human Rights – in such domestic matters as the use of the tawse in Scottish schools and the treatment of prisoners. He contended that Scotland should be left to take its own decisions 'in the light of what it saw to be the prevailing circumstances and the worthwhile traditions of Scotland'. It seemed that McCluskey was prepared to defend as 'worthwhile traditions' the retention of corporal punishment in schools and the degrading conditions in

Scottish prisons, where men shared tiny cells and defecated into chamber pots.

Radio Scotland, which had commissioned Smout's talk and had once been a civilised home of enlightened discussion if never exactly a rallying point for a crusade, was reborn in the autumn of 1978 with a more populist agenda. The critic Kathleen Rantell, after a marathon listen-in from 6 am till midnight, mourned the loss of Alastair Hetherington's blueprint for the station and its substitution by 'endless hours of needle time and mush'. The flagship *Good Morning Scotland* was 'as dreich as the weather', its amiable host Neville Garden 'trapped in an impossible format'. She had nothing good to say about Tom Ferrie, presenter of Scotland's first radio bingo game, or the 'awful' afternoon show, or Joanna Hickson's *Rhythm and News* at teatime; and by the evening 'very few' would be listening to Kenneth Roy's 'interesting but not brilliant' investigative series. It was this enfeebled station – 'drivel all day long' – which was expected to serve Scotland in the historic year ahead, the year of the referendum granted by the Callaghan government in the hope of sorting out the constitutional issue, the year in which the race of alienated paranoics would be invited to determine the future of their country.

The same critic was not always so harsh in her judgements. She wrote warmly of the playwright Joan Ure, who died in February 1978. 'She was exceptionally beautiful,' said Kathleen Rantell. 'Her smile was sometimes too dazzling for comfort. So was her perception. It is easier for less highly tuned people – which means nearly everybody – to be in the company of others of their own kind who are without the talent to sense life as acutely as Joan.' Her real name was Elizabeth (Betty) Clark; she took a pseudonym, she hinted, because of family sensitivities about her chosen vocation of writer. In her own words she felt starved by the neglect of her country. Her work was produced less often than it deserved to be, partly because she was resolutely non-commercial. She confined herself to one-act plays, which managements were reluctant to promote.

She was a feminist whose creed was expressed in such titles as *Something in it for Ophelia* and *Something in it for Cordelia*. She would have believed that there had to be something in it for Anne Hannah, the young woman abandoned on the streets of Livingston, for Heather McDougall, the compliant supplier of beer and crisps, and for Manorma Sood, the Indian widow in a close of brothels. She would have been profoundly affected by the death of Andrea Hedger, for whom, dead at 10, there was nothing in it. She believed that, if you could make it through till Easter, you would be all right; and one year she didn't. In a play called *The Hard Case* inspired by the Ibrox disaster, she wrote that football was carrying a burden too great for a game to bear – the curse of sectarianism. She thought there should be a wailing wall in Glasgow and that the wall of Barlinnie Prison would suit well enough. She died, at the age of 59, early enough in the year to miss the World Cup.

1979

WEE WILLIE MCTAGGART

I

SCOTLAND'S 'YEAR OF DESTINY' – THE FIRST IN A SERIES – BEGAN WITH an unexplained panic. Early one morning in January, long queues formed outside bakers' shops and customers walked away with armfuls of loaves. There had been no shortage of bread until the panic created one. Jim Connor, manager of Oliver's Hot Bread Shop in Sauchiehall Street, Glasgow, pointed in disbelief to a queue of 150 customers: 'We have trebled production, but we still can't meet this demand. I don't understand it.' Nor could anyone else.

Many roads in the north and west of the country were blocked by snow, and a British Rail survival kit went on show in Inverness. It was a food hamper, with its own gas stove for heating, for use on northbound trains in the all too likely event of passengers and crew being stranded by severe weather.

The case of the headmaster of Kiltearn Primary School in Evanton, Ross and Cromarty, who had been demoted for his opposition to Christmas, rumbled on into the new year. Iain Macdonald had refused requests from parents to have a Christmas tree in the school, blocked a proposed trip to a pantomime and refused to obey an order from the director of education to allow carol practice during school hours, all because the Free Presbyterian Church, of which the headmaster was a member, regarded Christmas as a papist feast.

The body of Richard Ewart, 92, was recovered from his house in Edinburgh after a fire on New Year's Day. He too had opposed Christmas, though for different reasons. He left strict instructions for his funeral in the Cloister Chapel of Warriston Crematorium: *La Marseillaise*, the hymn of the French Republic, was to be played 'at full blast with all the stops out'. It duly was. In a note to his solicitor, he referred to himself in the third person: 'He did not believe in the grotesque theological history of the world that had dominated – and crippled – human thought for many centuries.' During his long and useful life, Ewart invented many contraptions, including one of the earliest golf club trolleys and a self-starting device for cars. He devised the first butter-ball maker and sold it to the Lyons organisation, which was still using his original design to produce butter pats for hotels and restaurants. He loved France and visited it regularly. According to a neighbour, 'He was just as likely to say, "I'm off up the Amazon", and actually go.' He was unmarried.

The comedian Billy Connolly was not off up the Amazon, but his expedition to England – 68 one-man shows, including a week at the Theatre Royal, Drury Lane – was ambitious enough; the promoters rated it 'one of the biggest concert tours ever undertaken by an entertainer in Britain'. Every date was a sell-out. Derby, which had been the last stop in a tour by an earlier Scotch comic, Bonnie Prince Charlie, received Connolly more warmly; an advance party the length of a Glasgow bread queue started to form outside the theatre at 6.30 am and all the tickets were gone within half an hour of the box office opening. 'People in his own patch don't realise how huge Billy is in England,' explained Connolly's manager, Frank Lynch. 'He is in bigger demand than any of the English comedians.'

The Equal Opportunities Commission established an office in Scotland headed by Ron Miller, a native of Dundee, a city so matriarchal by reputation that it was known as She-Town. The truth was that women in Dundee, like women everywhere else in Scotland, were less emancipated than their sisters south of the border. Progress in advancing their rights had been painfully slow, prompting the Scottish Law Commission to recommend a number of measures for bringing Scots family law closer to the contemporary ideas on marriage and sexual equality enshrined in English legislation. The commission proposed that women should have a right to the matrimonial home even if the house was not in their name, and that they should be given civil protection from violent husbands.

Miller – 'Scotland's first custodian of fair deals' – had his work cut out. Although 44% of the working population were married women, a couple applying for a joint mortgage found that some building societies took only the husband's income into account – disregarding the higher income of many wives; and although it was no longer legally necessary for women in Scotland to have a male guarantor before they could sign a hire-purchase agreement, most stores omitted to pass on this little-known fact to their customers. 'The patriarchal system remains dominant here,' said Miller, 'and an awful lot of Scottish women are still guilty of conditioning their children. They buy a little girl a nurse's uniform and a little boy a hammer.'

Some bought their little boy a putter. If he was a posh little boy he might one day join one of the exclusive male golf clubs, among them Prestwick, Royal Troon, Western Gailes and the Royal and Ancient, the governing body of the sport. When Bob Muir, the secretary of Glasgow Golf Club, another of the male enclaves, was challenged to defend his club's discriminatory policies, he replied that he doubted if women would be prepared to pay the hefty membership fees. Warming to his theme, he asked: 'What are we going to say to the men who've been waiting for six years to join?' Even in clubs open to both sexes, women were poorly catered for; Belle Robertson, Scotland's best-known woman golfer, said she knew of no mixed club with full facilities for women. (As this chapter was being written 36 years later, she had just been admitted to membership of the R & A – as one of the first beneficiaries of the club's decision to lift the ban on women.)

If Christopher Smout was correct in his diagnosis, it was conceivable that a race of paranoics would continue to discriminate against half its population. But leaden meanness of spirit, one of the unhappier Scottish traits, was non-discriminatory: it applied to both sexes and was particularly rampant in council chambers, as the antics of Councillor McGinley in West Lothian had so recently demonstrated. The first recorded case of 1979 concerned an application by Cranhill Community Council to name a new adventure playground in memory of their late councillor, Geoff Shaw, who had devoted himself unstintingly to the poor as a minister of the Church of Scotland and proved an inspired choice as first convener of Strathclyde Regional Council.

Claude Thomson, a journalist who followed his career, doubted that he had the streak of toughness necessary to have fulfilled his ultimate ambition – to be a leading figure in a reborn Scottish Parliament. 'He was, I think, too nice, considerate and compassionate . . . He was too influenced by the Christian ethic not to feel bound to look at every side of a question before making up his mind.' For these reasons, said Thomson, he was a poor delegator whose indecisiveness put great strains on his relationship with colleagues. After this grudging tribute, a fine biography by Ron Ferguson, a ministerial colleague, provided a more balanced view of his accomplishments.

Whatever Geoff Shaw's weaknesses as a politician, no-one should have doubted his qualities as a human being, yet when Cranhill Community Council put up the idea of commemorating him in a simple, affectionate way, the proposal was resisted by his political opponents. One of them, the SNP's Stewart Ewing, husband of the celebrated Winnie, dismissed Shaw as a 'do-gooder'. The chairman of the Scottish Council of the Labour Party, Janey Buchan, wondered why 'do-gooder', if it denoted someone who had done good, as Shaw certainly had, should be a term of abuse and contempt.

II

There had been no shortage of bread, only a rumour of one, which psychologists might have diagnosed as hysterical in origin. After the bread came the circus: the referendum on devolution. An opinion poll published on the birthday of Robert Burns gave the Yes side a 64% to 36% lead. Donald Gorrie, a lanky Liberal who was often to be seen riding his bike purposefully along Queen Street in Edinburgh, spoke for the Yes campaign: 'It is essential for the Yes voters actually to turn out and vote. If they don't, then we could well fail to get the 40%.'

The 40% referred to the percentage of the Scottish electorate – not just of those voting – who were required to say Yes to devolution in order to satisfy the proviso adopted by the House of Commons on the recommendation of the Labour MP for Islington South and Finsbury, George Cunningham. 'If Cunningham is remembered in history,' said the leader of the SNP's parliamentary group, Donald Stewart, 'it will be as a footnote to a squalid and undemocratic piece of sabotage of a straightforward ballot. The vagaries of the weather, the old and the infirm, the number of dead persons, the holiday home owners, the sheer number of wrong entries in the register make the 40% clause the serious obstacle it was intended to be.' Some were not as diplomatic in their language about Cunningham, a former pupil of Dunfermline High School. Margo MacDonald said she despised him.

With only six weeks to go, Yes's huge lead would have seemed unassailable had it not been for the 40% threshold. The research officer of the Labour Party in Scotland, Alf Young, worried that there had been a slight drop in support for Yes since the last poll, while Brian Wilson, an equally articulate voice of No, was a long way from conceding defeat: 'A lot of people still feel obliged to say Yes because they feel it's the patriotic response. As the debate goes on, this illusion can be overcome.'

For the illusion to be overcome, it was necessary to have a working knowledge of the Scotland Act. Few did. W.M. Henderson of Oban complained in a letter to a newspaper that he had set out to buy a copy and failed; even his local public library had declined to stock it. In Dumfries, Tam Farries of the Blacklock Farries bookshop described it as 'the world's worst seller . . . we've got stacks of them – I could paper the walls with them'. He claimed that people were bored with the devolution saga: 'It was the same when the bill came out. We had two or three hundred copies and sold about twenty.' HM Stationery Office admitted that they had several thousand unsold copies of the legislation in their shop in Edinburgh.

Those who did trouble themselves to read it might have been struck by its resemblance to a dog's breakfast. The Assembly would be responsible for the operation of the NHS in Scotland – but not for abortion. Education was to be delegated to Edinburgh – but not the universities. Criminal law – that too was going to the Assembly – but not motoring offences. Freshwater fisheries were being devolved – but not sea-fishing. The Secretary of State for Scotland would continue to oversee industrial development – yet, illogically, the Scottish Development Agency and the Highlands and Islands Development Board, the principal drivers for achieving it, would be devolved. Westminster would retain control of the economy in general and the Assembly would be financed through a block grant, with no independent revenue-raising powers – at least that much was clear.

The former Royal High School was being converted into a a 150-seat debating chamber, with offices, public and members' lobbies, a press centre and a tearoom; it was announced that the work would be finished on target by the end of April. Preparing for the result before the match had been fought made the Assembly the political equivalent of Ally's Tartan Army, a project based on an unproven assumption. And even if the electors compliantly gave the go-ahead, and the former Royal High School was actually required, the Scotland Act had precious little to say about the day-to-day working of what was to go on inside the building. How many departments would be needed? How many ministers? What hours would the Assembly keep? On so many counts, it was anybody's guess.

John Smith, who had piloted the legislation line by line through the Commons, adopted his usual pragmatic approach in newspaper interviews, but his answer to a question about the powers of the Assembly was leaden: 'We have always been very clear about what the Act does and does not do. The main functions in the social field, like housing, education and health, already have distinctively Scottish policies, administered by the Scottish Office, but where the Act makes a big difference is that it gives legislative control. We have been at pains to point out that control of economic, industrial and energy policies, of employment and taxation matters, remains at Westminster because these are British matters. We will be able to decide on education policies because these are distinctively Scottish matters.'

It was a clumsy piece of legislation, riddled with inconsistencies, and Smith's laborious defence of it did the cause no favours. Jim Sillars and Tam Dalyell attempted to inject some spirit into a lacklustre campaign with a travelling Yes/No road show, for which there was seldom a queue. They did play to an overflow house of 230 in Helensburgh and 160 in Livingston, but only 30 turned up in Fort William during a blizzard, and hardly anyone in Dundee on a night when the buses were off. On the penultimate night of their tour, at Jordanhill College of Education in Glasgow, 'they looked a little tired' according to one report, 'and were friendly and polite almost to the point of tedium.' The tedium was widely felt throughout the land.

In the Borders, where anti-devolution sentiment was especially strong, a Church of Scotland minister, the Reverend John Cairns, objected to his church's edict that the official Kirk statement in favour of the Assembly should be read from every pulpit. He told his congregation that he had been ordered by the Church and Nation Committee to read it and he would – before repudiating it. 'I don't think the church should involve itself in politics,' he said. In Langholm, birthplace of Hugh MacDiarmid, one of the poet's relatives, Jean White, though a Yes voter herself, detected widespread apathy. Bowman Little, who owned, wrote, printed, sold and distributed the town's newspaper, the *Eskdale and Liddesdale Advertiser*, said that many people saw the Assembly as expensive and unnecessary.

In a front-page editorial, the *Scottish Daily Express*, in one of its rhetorical flourishes, demanded to know why Scotland should put the Union at risk. 'And for what?' it thundered. 'To allow wee Willie McTaggart, who might have been a passable councillor in Cumbernauld in a bad year, to prance and preen as a Scottish Assemblyman.' The paper had discounted any possibility that the Assembly would attract candidates of the quality of the late and keenly missed Geoff Shaw; it was confronting its readers with what it saw as an inevitability – a legislature of wee Willie McTaggarts, the personification of national incompetence. 'Not to put too fine a point on it,' wrote the novelist William McIlvanney, 'I think a lot of us are feart. It's a feeling I share . . . "Better the devil ye ken" – that great Scottish cliché that has so often been fitted like manacles round the prospect of change.' McIlvanney thought that the *Express*'s leader said a lot about the state of the Scottish psyche. 'If we're that bad, it's time we weren't. The only way we're going to improve is by the practice of government.'

Among the UK political weeklies, there was some support for McIlvanney's point of view. Tom Nairn wrote in the *New Statesman* that, although the 'national nihilism of our *chiens de garde* may cause a temporary setback', opponents of devolution were crying against wind and tide. A leader in the *Economist*, while acknowledging the defects of the legislation, went on: 'A bad scheme does not destroy a good principle, which is that a nation – such as Scotland undoubtedly is, with its own legal, educational, and other systems, not to speak of a strong sense of national identity – has the right to govern its own affairs.' Only the right-leaning *Spectator* sounded sceptical: 'The Union was a political work of genius which for more than 250 years has conferred incalculable benefits on both Scotland and England. Scotland especially benefited. She retained her distinctive institutions, above all her law and her Kirk, while enjoying all the economic ad-vantages of a united island. Those Scots who wish for an end to those advantages, for a complete separation of their country from England, should certainly vote Yes. All other Scots should weigh the consequences of their vote carefully.'

In weighing them, open-minded Scots did not lack advice: there were no fewer than six main groups involved in the propaganda war. Scotland Says No, dominated by the business community, headed by the industrialist Lord Weir of Cathcart and assisted by the Scottish Conservatives, had big money at its disposal and was able to hire professional staff. Labour Vote No, a group of rebels, including Brian Wilson, Tam Dalyell and Robin Cook, claimed to speak for many ordinary members of the party but operated on a shoestring. The Alliance Group was an eclectic coalition of Jimmy Milne (STUC general secretary), Alick Buchanan-Smith, who had lost his Conservative shadow portfolio because of his devolutionist stance, and Donald Dewar. Lord Kilbrandon, whose report on the constitution had anticipated a devolved assembly but had done so with greater clarity, chaired Yes for Scotland, an umbrella organisation whose star turns were Margo MacDonald and Jim Sillars. Labour Movement Yes, the official party campaign headed by Helen Liddell with support from the trade unions, struggled to overcome grassroots scepticism over the project. Finally, Stephen Maxwell directed the SNP Yes Campaign, for what that was worth: not much, as the party languished at 18% in the polls.

The proliferation of lobbyists, particularly on the Yes side, was counter-productive. Helen Liddell, so recently the heroine of the party for pulling off three successive by-election victories in 1978, had to concede that electors seemed to have 'other things on their plate'. She said nothing of the damaging split in her own party. So inept was the diffuse Yes campaign, and so effective the opposition by such populists as Teddy Taylor, that a poll on the eve of the referendum showed that the gap had narrowed from 28% to 4% in six weeks: it was now obvious, if it had not been obvious before, that the 40% rule would not be satisfied. The SNP's deputy leader, Gordon Wilson, prophesied that if the country voted No, Scotland would become 'a demoralised province ignored by Westminster and scorned by the world'.

On polling day – 1 March – the *Glasgow Herald*, sensing a low turnout, was likewise concerned about international opinion: 'Above all we must send a clear message to the world today . . . The Scottish question has dominated British politics for the last five years and it would reflect badly on the Scots if they failed to respond to the challenge.' But the paper's own message lacked consistency. The promise of an assembly had 'diminished the potency of the nationalist appeal and its eventual establishment is unlikely to reverse that process'. At the same time, the present scheme would create 'a near-permanent conflict between the Assembly and Westminster by failing to equip the new chamber with even the most modest tax-raising powers'.

The Scots declined to send a clear message to the world, or even to each other. Yes won by 51.6% to 48.4%, which translated into a popular vote of 1,230,937 for the Assembly, 1,153,502 against – a margin of 77,435. It was a majority that fell some distance short of the 40% threshold: on a turnout of 64%, only 32.8% of the electorate voted Yes. Not one of the 13 regions mustered 40%, though six registered simple majorities for Yes, including incomparably the largest – Strathclyde. This narrow victory for devolution was perversely interpreted as a crushing defeat. 'Scots Assembly RIP' screamed the headline across the front page of the *Glasgow Herald*. 'The Assembly is dead – killed by the Scots themselves, who wrote it off yesterday as irrelevant to their immediate needs', concluded political correspondents Geoffrey Parkhouse and Stuart Trotter. A simple majority of those voting had nonetheless voted for an assembly. Thirty-five years later, in the independence referendum, that simple majority would have been sufficient to kill off, not an assembly, but the United Kingdom itself.

George Cunningham, the assassin of the hour, declared at once: 'Devolution cannot go ahead – there's no chance of that.' It was a reminder that the referendum had been purely advisory and that the

UK parliament had the last word. Another of the anti-devolutionists, Ted Garrett, a Labour MP on Tyneside, gloated that the Scots had been 'saved from themselves' and that James Callaghan's government could no longer make devolution a vote of confidence, which it might have done had the Yes vote been higher. When two of the leading No campaigners, Dalyell and Taylor, entered the House of Commons a few days later they were cheered. Dalyell got the bigger ovation – followed by a suggestion from one of his own side, Dennis Canavan, that he should join the Tories. He didn't – but remained a thorn in the flesh of his own party and of the body politic in general.

From the nationalists, any hope of a well-judged response to the predictable outcome vanished within days when the party chairman, the normally level-headed William Wolfe, called a press conference in Edinburgh and blundered into a fatal ultimatum. He gave notice that, if Callaghan did not immediately introduce legislation to introduce a Scottish Assembly, the SNP would bring down his government. Such was Labour's fragile hold on power, this was no empty threat. It was repeated by Donald Stewart at a private meeting with Callaghan at Westminster. The SNP's parliamentary leader bluntly informed the Prime Minister that unless there was a firm commitment to setting up an assembly he would deliver the votes of 14 Scottish and Welsh nationalists into the grateful hands of the Conservative leader, Margaret Thatcher, by the end of the month. He was as good as his word. On 28 March 1979 the government lost a confidence motion by a single vote out of 621 cast – the first time in 55 years that any administration had suffered such a humiliation. It triggered a general election.

In devising its high-risk strategy, the nationalist high command had calculated that the Scots would be so incensed by the denial of their wishes on devolution, and the realisation that the Scotland Act could no longer be delivered, that they would turn in protest to the SNP. But the pre-supposed mood of national indignation, on which the strategy depended for success, failed to materialise. Instead the indignation was directed at the SNP itself – for giving Thatcher the opportunity she had been waiting for to finish off the Labour government and put herself in Downing Street. The party was to pay dearly for its fundamental error of political judgement and its misreading of the Scottish electorate.

III

The Thatcher era began incongruously with a Franciscan pledge. The new Prime Minister stood on the steps of 10 Downing Street and offered harmony for discord, truth for error, faith for doubt, hope for despair. These were her first conciliatory words and they may have been her last. When James Milne of the STUC said that her attitude to the trade unions would be 'a potential area of conflict', he little knew at that early stage the implications of his own understatement.

On the same morning, a well-wisher left a spray of blue irises and white carnations at the door of the vanquished Teddy Taylor at his home in Glasgow. At election after election he had hung grimly on to his marginal constituency of Cathcart, defying the odds by taking many votes in the working-class estate of Castlemilk. The irony of his defeat was bitter indeed. It came on the night of a famous Conservative victory, and if only he had retained his seat he would have been Secretary of State for Scotland and a senior member of Thatcher's cabinet. Instead the job went to George Younger of the Alloa brewing dynasty, a more emollient character, or so it seemed at the time. One journalist claimed that Taylor 'refused to cry over the loss of such glittering prizes', but journalists themselves mourned his departure, if only because he had always been a rich source of easy copy.

True to form, in one of his last acts as an MP he had voted in the Scottish Standing Committee for the restoration of corporal punishment for crimes of violence. 'We are being asked,' said Donald Dewar, 'to go back to some tartan equivalent of Islamic law by the member for Cathcart, who is a sort of latter-day Ayatollah demanding an eye for an eye and a tooth for a tooth.' Thatcher herself had first come to prominence as a defiant backbencher advocating the return of the birch, though neither she or Taylor ever went as far as Helen Hodgkins, a Glasgow teacher and Tory councillor, who recommended the public flogging of hooligans at the start of football matches and offered to administer it herself.

On a night of many scalps, none was more prized by the Labour Party than the volatile head of Jim Sillars, who lost South Ayrshire to George Foulkes, the candidate of his old party. Echoing William McIlvanney, the great defector had dismissed No voters in the referendum as 'fearties' and accused opponents of the Assembly of being unable to grasp that the Yes side had won. (In 2014, after the independence referendum, it was Sillars who seemed unable to grasp that the No side had won. Otherwise not much had changed in the lexicon of Scottish politics; Sillars was still accusing No voters of being fearties.) But the main losers in 1979 were the nationalists. They had prepared themselves for a bad night, but not for the disaster that engulfed them. Seat after seat slipped from their grasp: Winnie Ewing by 420 votes in Moray and Nairn; Douglas Henderson by 558 in East Aberdeenshire; Hamish Watt by 799 in Banff; Andrew Welsh by 963 (to a future Lord Advocate, Peter Fraser) in South Angus; George Reid by 984 in Clackmannan and East Stirlingshire. As well as these narrow defeats there were undisguised calamities: a heavy slump in the SNP vote in Hamilton, Dalyell's thumping 20,000 majority over William Wolfe in West Lothian, Margaret Bain pushed into third place in East Dunbartonshire, big wins for the Tories in Perth and East Perthshire and in Argyll. By the end of the night, the party had lost all but two of its 11 seats; the only survivors were Donald Stewart in the Western Isles and Gordon Wilson in Dundee East.

'The party could hardly have bargained for such a devastating series of defeats,' wrote the *Glasgow Herald*'s Anthony Finlay, whose early death robbed Scottish journalism of one of its outstanding young talents. Finlay's judgement that the SNP had largely brought it on themselves was the generally prevailing one. The party had been instrumental in facilitating Margaret Thatcher's triumph, after all; and now it would have to live with the consequences of its folly. Against the national tide, Scotland had gone its own way and voted decisively Labour, but this affirmation of a separate political culture north of the border counted for nothing. Devolution was dead, and the last person who would be disposed to try to revive the corpse was the new Prime Minister.

IV

The reality of industrial life in the dissident north quickly impressed itself on the incoming government. In the first nine months of 1979 the Department of Employment recorded 21,400 redundancies in Scotland, 80% of them in manufacturing. Four thousand jobs went in shipbuilding, 900 with the closure of the Monsanto plant in Irvine, 500 when Goodyear pulled out of Glasgow, 180 with the contraction of the British Aluminium plant in Fort William. There was continuing uncertainty over the future of the Massey Ferguson tractor plant in Kilmarnock and the familiar threat to steel jobs in Lanarkshire. But the year's biggest blow was the announcement that the Singer sewing machine factory in Clydebank was closing with the loss of 3,000 jobs.

Although Singer had long ceased to be the mass employer in the town that it was at its peak, when 14,000 people worked there, it possessed an immense historical and symbolic significance. Along with the ship, the sewing machine had been proudly incorporated in the burgh's coat of arms. The ship was becoming lost to history. Soon the sewing machine would be an anachronism too. The company's head of corporate relations, Larry Mihlon, blamed the low productivity of the workers, the worst of Singer's 28 factories worldwide. 'It is the inflexibility of their attitudes more than laziness,' he added. Under questioning, however, a second, more plausible reason for the closure emerged: Mihlon admitted that the plant had been running at less than 50% of capacity.

David Livingstone discovered a Singer in a primitive African village: the machine had somehow got there before him. Mahatma Gandhi, who learned to sew on one, lauded it as one of the few useful things ever invented. 'They were marvellous machines,' agreed the journalist William Hunter. 'Buyers could have one in any colour they liked – provided it was black.' But changing fashions and the availability of cheap, ready-to-wear clothes, particularly from the Far East, were steadily reducing the consumer demand for the product.

Back in 1882, Clydebank was not the company's first choice. The American owners wanted to locate their plant in the village of Bonnybridge, near Falkirk, but a stubborn landowner refused to sell and Singer went instead to a place which did not exist in any real sense; it was Singer – and the shipyard – that created the town. It was so central to Clydebank's identity that the local railway station was named after it. Only the station survived the closure of the plant – still manned, almost the only thing left in Clydebank that was.

The news from Scotland embarrassed a deputation from the Scottish Development Agency who were touring the United States in search of investment. The Scottish industry minister, Alex Fletcher, had damned the Agency with faint praise in a speech in the Waldorf Hotel, New York. It was a shabby way of undermining the chairman, Sir William Gray. His replacement, the cricket-loving Robin Duthie, announced himself as 'not a Scottish nationalist but a nationalist Scot', a statement so meaningless that it attracted derision. Gray's replacement by Duthie solved nothing: jobs continued to haemorrhage and in Clydebank, once they had made their last sewing machine, unemployment rose to 20%.

Far out in the North Sea, there was still work aplenty for men who were prepared to tolerate the environment and the working conditions. Seven thousand construction workers from 14 oil platforms went on strike over health and safety issues. One of them, a Clydebank man, said the public had the wrong impression: 'All they ever hear about is the big money. The conditions on some platforms are hair-raising and that's why men have died. I've been in boats taking us out to the platforms which should only carry 40 but have 100 on board.' They had other grievances, particularly over sleeping accommodation. 'We are put up in camp beds and paid an allowance of £17.50 a night,' said the Clydebank man. 'We are then expected to go back on a 12-hour shift. It is physical suicide. We are not interested in their £17.50. We need a decent sleep before we can carry on with that kind of work.' The strikers pointed to a recent report on the high incidence of broken marriages and nervous illness among North Sea workers.

Elsewhere, the much-heralded oil bonanza had been a severe disappointment to several depressed communities. Off the Clyde island of Bute, the Ardyne oil platform yard, which had promised 25 years' work, lay empty, starved of orders, and one month Bute recorded the highest unemployment rate in Britain – 23.2%. Among the islands of the Outer Hebrides, Lewis was badly hit by the closure of the offshore fabrication yard at Arnish, which had provided work for 300 people in an area of low population and high unemployment. The chairman of the Highlands and Islands Development Board, Kenneth Alexander, spoke with feeling of the 'enormous fragility' of many of the islands, uniquely burdened as they were by high transport charges and the arrogance of the ferry operator, Caledonian MacBrayne, a monopoly which often behaved like one.

A socio-economic profile of the Western Isles made sobering reading. A third of the housing stock was below what was officially classed as a tolerable standard. Some of the schools still had outside toilets. Many children were obliged to live away from home during term-time, in hostel accommodation in Stornoway, but calls for a six-year secondary school at the southern end of Lewis, which would have allowed many children to be with their parents, went unheeded.

The Western Isles had the highest proportion of elderly people in Scotland – nearly a quarter of the population – and yet the poorest provision for residential care. The crofts provided only two days' wages a week. Other work was scarce.

In a remote valley on the rocky island of Harris, south of Lewis, lay the tiny village of Rhenigadale, which was sometimes described as the most materially deprived community in the kingdom. There was no road to it; the 10 inhabitants walked a four-mile-long rough path, hewn out of the mountainside, little more than a sheeptrack in places. Their supplies came by boat from Tarbert, but only when they could justify the expense of hiring one and when the wind was blowing in the right direction for landing. The post came three times a week. For heat and light there was electricity, fitfully from a generator, and when that failed Calor gas. There were no shops. There was no church. But they did have a school, with one pupil – eight-year-old Lorna MacInnes, the only child in Rhenigadale. Half a century earlier, there had been 23 pupils. 'It is our home,' said one of the women of the village, 'and we have no intention of leaving it.' Nor did they leave it; 36 years later, the population had risen by 20% – from 10 to 12.

Such island stories were faithfully chronicled in the weekly *Stornoway Gazette*, founded by William Grant in 1917, mainly to bring news of home to the 6,200 Lewis men – an exceptional number – who were serving in the First World War. Only yards from home, 181 local servicemen drowned when the troopship *Iolaire* sank on New Year's morning 1919; it was a colossal tragedy from which the Western Isles took many years to recover, if they ever did. The *Gazette* then had to report the departure of the emigrant ships carrying thousands of islanders to a new life in Canada in the 1920s. This too was an island tragedy, without the high drama of the *Iolaire* but just as profound in its sense of deprivation and loss. The diaspora did, however, create a new market for the *Gazette*: 800 of its 12,000 copies went overseas, including a dozen to some Lewis cowboys in

Argentina – though the order was reduced when the ranch manager discovered that it was easier to read the paper to them over the telephone than to deliver the copies on horseback.

James Shaw Grant inherited the paper from his father and edited it for 30 years until he embarked on a second career in public life, latterly as chairman of the Crofters' Commission. 'It was very much a community paper,' he recalled. 'Much of it was written by our district correspondents – crofters, fishermen, housewives, schoolmasters, ministers – and their copy was edited as little as possible. My father felt that we were there not to impose a style on the community but to let it express itself.' In the *Stornoway Gazette*, no-one ever died. Rather they were 'carried off to the great bourne'. One obituary read: 'It was evident that she spent much of her time in secret sanctuary with her Lord in prayer and meditation, which showed itself outwardly both in her conversation and in her walk of life.'

The *Gazette* was not so much a newspaper as an institution, but the institution became set in its ways, a little smug and complacent, and by the 1970s was superseded as the principal paper of the islands by the livelier, more radical *West Highland Free Press*, founded on Skye by Brian Wilson – the same Brian Wilson who went on to play a prominent part in the referendum campaign. In 1979 James Shaw Grant decided to sell the *Stornoway Gazette* and the paper passed from local ownership into less sympathetic hands.

V

Elizabeth the Second (or First of Scotland) was not carried off to the great bourne in 1979. But one night in Queen Margaret Drive, Glasgow, at the studios of BBC Scotland, a young, inexperienced radio announcer, Robert Sproul-Cran, received an urgent message on an internal telephone line from Broadcasting House in Edinburgh. Someone later described as a 'senior official' of the corporation informed him tersely: 'The Queen has just died'.

A week before this aberration, the controller of BBC Scotland had introduced a radical departure for the troubled Radio Scotland. Patrick Ramsay announced that news and current affairs would henceforth be 'the spice' of the station and that wallpaper music would be dropped. Guidelines approved by the Broadcasting Council for Scotland, the BBC's watchdog, set out that 'no very English or very Glaswegian voices' would normally present a long daily programme – an implicit rejection of several of the station's star names as well as a startling endorsement of racial and cultural discrimination. The commentator Murray Ritchie welcomed the changes: 'At long last it seems that the BBC has finally capitulated in the face of sustained and vociferous criticism from its middle-class audience which felt betrayed when Radio Scotland arrived to the accompaniment of pop music and vacuous chat.'

The abrupt move upmarket came in the wake of a damning review of the station commissioned by BBC management. Its author, Bob Atkins, a producer with the World Service in London, was dismayed by what he found. He described *Good Morning Scotland* as 'the station's flagship, and frankly a pretty leaky one at times' and the *Tom Ferrie Show*, which followed it, as 'slick, professional and totally characterless'; he noted how Gerry Davis, host of the afternoon programme, 'blethered his way through an odd assortment of records and sometimes embarrassing callers'. Atkins acknowledged a fellow feeling for the predicament of the amiable Davis. It was strange, he said, that a man who had been filling two hours of airtime every weekday for nine months had had so little contact with anyone from the management: 'He claims that I am the first person ever to discuss with him the problems and doubts about his own show.'

Despite this indictment and the subsequent shake-up, the head of Radio Scotland, John Pickles, kept his job – though not for long. Around 8 pm the following Friday, during Gerry Mackenzie's *Tartan Terror Show*, the duty announcer was faced with a terror of his own: how to deal with a call from one of his managers about the monarch's unexpected death. Sproul-Cran, who had been in the job for only four months, had to decide on the spot whether to accept the word from on high and broadcast the sensational news. He decided that he should not. When the details of his smart thinking leaked out, he was hailed as the silent hero of the corporation. But the identity of the culprit – the 'senior official' – was never revealed.

The suave head of information at Queen Margaret Drive, William Carrocher, a former courtier to the non-deceased Queen, attempted to deal with the media storm by claiming fatuously that the call had been part of 'an emergency fire drill, perhaps a little too realistic'. A few days later, Radio Scotland's senior executives, Pickles and Leslie Robinson, left their posts, Pickles returning to the obscurity of English local radio. Perhaps only the BBC could have come to the conclusion, after the usual internal inquiry, that although the call had been 'mishandled' the procedure itself had been 'quite proper'. Scotland had spent much of the final year of the decade pondering its constitutional future. Even the land of Wee Willie McTaggart deserved rather better of its public broadcaster than such a seasonal pantomime at the end of it.

AN AWFULLY GOOD BOY

I

ON THE EVENING OF HALLOWEEN 1980, A YOUTH CALLED STEPHEN Cameron went to the house of another youth, Joseph Sweeney, in the east end of Glasgow. They were sitting there drinking when 14-year-old Gordon Sweeney, brother of Joseph, arrived with news. He told them that he 'had a bird' in a scrapyard in Davaar Street nearby and that the 'bird' was available. The three of them went to the yard, where a fourth youth, John Thomson, was having sex with the woman in a cabin or container of some kind. The brothers then had sex or attempted to have sex with her; only Cameron abstained, giving as the reason that he had had sex with his girlfriend earlier in the evening. Cameron and Gordon Sweeney left the yard, leaving Joseph Sweeney with the woman. When he re-appeared, he was covered in blood and carrying a razor. 'I have ripped the lassie,' he said.

The victim, a prostitute in her late twenties known only as Carol X, had been walking down London Road after leaving a pub. She was 300 yards from home when 'two young boys', as she called them, approached her. One asked for a light. As she went into her shoulder bag to fetch a lighter, she felt 'something from behind'. She was dragged backwards by the arms. When she recovered consciousness, it was dark. She was naked from the waist down and someone was brandishing a razor over her. 'You don't have to use that,' she said. A voice replied, 'You are getting it, you cow,' although it could have been 'you bitch' – Carol wasn't sure. Joseph Sweeney, who explained that he was too illiterate to write his own statement and instead dictated it to the police, gave as his excuse that 'she started screaming and I had a razor so I gave it to her'. John Thomson told the police that he was standing at the door of the cabin when Joseph Sweeney launched his attack on Carol. 'I went in and pulled him by the back of the collar and pulled him out.' When Carol arrived at Glasgow Royal Infirmary, she was seen by a casualty surgeon, Robert Simpson. She had several cuts, each of about five inches long, across her face, forehead, eyebrows, cheeks and the tip of her nose, as well as deep cuts in her thighs. Simpson was in no doubt that the injuries could have killed her. She required 152 stitches and was permanently disfigured.

The public was subsequently asked to believe, and there seemed no reason to doubt it, that when the case papers arrived at the Crown Office neither of the law officers – the Lord Advocate, Lord Mackay, and the Solicitor-General, Nicholas Fairbairn – dealt with them at any stage. The ordeal of Carol X provoked an outpouring of revulsion, as well as genuine sympathy for the victim, when the details were finally exposed in the press. But in the autumn of 1980, the case was not deemed important enough to trouble Mackay or Fairbairn; it was referred further down the chain of Scotland's prosecuting authority, to a Crown counsel whose identity was not disclosed.

The alleged perpetrators should have gone to trial at the High Court in Glasgow in June 1981, seven months later. But, though the case was scheduled, it was not called. When a psychiatrist examined Carol for the first and only time, he concluded that a court appearance would be detrimental to her health and carried the risk that she would attempt suicide before or after the trial. The case could have been postponed – 'left on the table' as the lawyers put it; that would have been a normal expedient in the circumstances. Instead, the unidentified Crown counsel decided – again without reference to the two law officers, and without a further psychiatric assessment – that Carol's health would 'never' improve sufficiently to allow her to give evidence, that the whole indictment should be dropped, and that the accused should be informed accordingly. Under Scots law no further prosecution by the Crown would then be possible. The only party who was not informed of this unsatisfactory result was the victim herself.

The handling of the case raised important questions. Why was Carol not granted the courtesy of a letter setting out the reasons for the Crown's decision and instead allowed to find out for herself that her assailants were not being brought to justice? Why did the Crown not seek a second opinion on her fitness to give evidence? Why were the two law officers never consulted about the case and the decision to drop it? How could any civilised society permit a crime of such brutality to be left untried without the knowledge and authority of its two senior prosecutors? And there was a disturbing sub-text: what did the conduct of the case say about the attitude of Scotland's legal establishment to violence against women? Did the fact that Carol was a prostitute play any part in the Crown Office's decision not to proceed? Fifteen months elapsed before any of these questions were raised on the floor of the House of Commons, in an atmosphere of intense anger, after a ministerial statement of woeful inadequacy which finished the political career of Nicholas Fairbairn. But they were 15 months in which the Solicitor-General was rarely out of the newspapers for other reasons.

II

When Margaret Thatcher came to power in 1979, her instinct was to make Fairbairn Lord Advocate. As an experienced member of the Scottish Bar, he was the only Tory MP qualified to do the job; and he expected to be offered it. Sensing an impending disaster, the Lord Justice General, Lord Emslie, let it be known to the Prime Minister that the bench of judges was implacably opposed to the appointment of such a man to the office of Lord Advocate. As a result of this high-level pressure, Thatcher gave the job to James Mackay – ennobled as Lord Mackay of Clashfern – who was not a Member of Parliament and at that stage not even a member of the Conservative Party; while an embittered Fairbairn was left to curse his luck, and his enemies, in the lesser role.

Who was this man who so offended his elders that the Lord Justice General took the extreme step of counselling against his advancement? The son of a Freudian psychoanalyst in Edinburgh, he made his first political impression at the age of 12, responding to the Labour landslide in 1945 by smashing the shop windows of the Musselburgh Co-op. In *Who's Who* he described himself as a 'dress designer, bon viveur and wit' and listed his recreations as 'making love, ends meet, and people laugh', in this way advertising himself as one of life's glorious characters. He looked rather the dandy in his tartan trews and exotic cravats, a presentation risible or endearing according to taste, but his thin lips curled easily into an expression of disdain, even cruelty. Socially and intellectually he was an old-fashioned snob.

For one reason or another, many in the Scottish literary and artistic sets, who knew him as 'Nicky', adored his company, and for a while he was chairman of the Traverse Theatre, a den more frequented for its fashionable bar than as an experimental playhouse. His marriage to the daughter of Lord Reay produced three girls before he and Elizabeth were divorced in 1979, and the self-portrait of eighteenth-century panache was finished off with his acquisition of a small castle in Fife, where he styled himself Baron of Fordell. In his professional life he was a clever if erratic defender of the criminal classes, a key figure in the campaign to free Patrick Meehan, an able cross-examiner; but he alienated the judges by his various eccentricities in and out of the courtroom. He was known as a heavy drinker and a sexual adventurer, and it should not have come as a surprise to anyone who knew him that the peacock had a dark side.

None of the many press profiles hinted at the less attractive features of Fairbairn's personality. In October 1981, just before his life began to unravel, he gave an interview to the *Glasgow Herald*'s Jack Webster in which he lamented 'the lack of colour and romance in our world', assured Webster that he loved to see 'beautifully dressed women', and confessed that he wished to be remembered as a great painter. (He did paint, though no more than competently.) It was the usual obliging piece, topped off by Webster's tribute to the 'ancient mould' of the Solicitor-General's face and a reference to the 'sculptress' waiting in the wings to resume her work on his bust. Around the same time, in one of his periodic outbursts from nowhere, Fairbairn demanded to know why the sportsman John McEnroe had been elevated to the front pages of newspapers. 'Because,' he replied to his own question, 'he behaves outrageously, because he shows appalling bad manners, because he demonstrates complete lack of control.' It was a broadly accurate character assessment, not only of the tennis 'superbrat', but of Fairbairn himself.

In the interview with Jack Webster, the Solicitor-General had described himself as a lonely man: 'There is no woman in my life at present, but I would hope to change that at some point in the future.' He had recently broken it off with his mistress Pamela Milne, a 35-year-old former House of Commons secretary. Milne's reaction to being ditched was to reach for pills and whisky and go round to Fairbairn's London flat. He was not at home; he was in Scotland conducting the Crown case in a High Court trial. Milne, having remonstrated with his 17-year-old daughter, tried to hang herself with a pair of tights from a lamp-post outside the house. The daughter was reported to have cut her down.

Although this occurred in October, it was not until Christmas Eve that the story broke; Fairbairn alleged that it was maliciously leaked to the press by one of his enemies in the Conservative Party. 'Suicide Bid Girl Breaks Her Silence – My Love for Nicky' splashed the *Evening Times*. Milne, 'a highly attractive brunette', told the paper that she and Fairbairn had been together for 'a number of years' and that she felt 'a strong love' for him. 'I want to make it clear that he was not to blame for what I did,' she said. 'There are two kinds of depression, one where you know what's wrong with you, and one where you don't. With me it was the latter. I'd been staying at his home for about five days and I was really down – acutely depressed. He had gone away to Scotland and I got drunk and took an overdose. I discharged myself from the hospital that day because I was terrified they were going to put me in a loony bin. He phoned me at the hospital when he found out what had happened, but I was unable to talk.' It was then that Fairbairn decided to end their affair. 'I haven't seen him since. He has not tried to visit me to see if I am all right.' She added that she did not expect to see him again. Had she been besotted with him? 'No,' she said. 'I always thought he was besotted with me.'

While the jilted mistress was confessing all to the press, the other half of the partnership was skulking in his castle refusing to come out. Reporters, who had begun their vigil before dawn, were encouraged by the brief opening of the door at 8 am, only for it to be slammed in their faces. Rumours circulated that Fairbairn had hosted one of his late-night parties the night before and was too hungover to talk. But not too hungover to call the police; the only visitor who was admitted during the morning, a chief superintendent, emerged to say that the Solicitor-General had no comment to make. 'He says that your presence here is an annoyance to himself, his family and his workers. This is private property and so is the whole driveway down to the main road. If you remain here you will be committing a breach of the peace.' After five hours, the vigil came to an end.

There was an assumption at Westminster that his days as a member of the Thatcher government were numbered. As one report stated: 'MPs believe that the traditionally ruthless Conservative hierarchy will see to it that Mr Fairbairn is removed as painlessly as possible'. But this view of his prospects discounted Thatcher's weakness for a certain type of louche male and her tolerance of bad behaviour in the private lives of her ministers. Fairbairn survived the scandal, and years later brazenly denied that Pamela Milne had tried to hang herself. 'Totally bogus – a complete fabrication,' he insisted.

III

Having survived one scandal, he was overwhelmed within weeks by another. On 11 January 1982, he was tipped off in the High Court that the *Daily Record* was preparing to run a story about the case of Carol X. Fairbairn was genuinely baffled. 'What's it all about?' he asked his informant. He was to find out soon enough. Carol had gone to the paper with her story, Carol had been taken seriously, and Arnot McWhinnie, its crime reporter, had done a superb job, extracting a confession to the rape. The impact was explosive: a public outcry made more indignant by the stated opinion of Ross Harper, a prominent solicitor and Scottish Tory grandee, that the Crown had forfeited its right to prosecute and that the only remaining hope was a private prosecution, which he offered to try to facilitate.

For the Crown Office, which had dealt ineptly with the case, and the two men in charge of it, who had presided over a regime so lax that allegations of rape did not require to be considered by the law officers, the only dish left on the menu was humble pie. Thatcher's aides decreed that it should be served while still hot. Mackay would make a statement to the House of Lords explaining that the decision not to prosecute had been taken in good faith on the basis of psychiatric advice, but that in future such matters would be determined by the Lord Advocate; the statement was to include an undertaking that the Lord Advocate would not stand in the way of a private prosecution. Had the brief been Mackay's alone, this strategy of damage limitation might have reduced the severity of the media fallout. But there was no way of avoiding a similar statement in the Commons from the accident-prone Solicitor-General. Therein lay risk.

Nicholas Fairbairn was roused at his London flat by an early morning telephone call from the *Evening Times*. He must have wished he had never answered it. Later that day the paper published a quote in his name: 'By presenting the true facts, which I have established from a thorough personal inquiry, I sincerely hope that I will allay public anxiety. The excellence of the Scottish legal system has been impugned by misunderstanding. The over-riding factor which finally decided the matter was the simple, inescapable fact that the prosecution did not have sufficient competent or available evidence to stand a chance of gaining a conviction.' At 6 am, from a man who had only just woken up, this was a fluent composition; it had the quality of a prepared response. But though there may have been a degree of paraphrasing in the editing of his words, there was no mistaking the arch tone of the Scottish Bar and the unmistakable sound of Nicholas Fairbairn putting his foot in it.

The quote damned him on two counts. First, it was a breach of protocol for any minister who was due to make an important state-ment to Parliament to divulge its contents to the press in advance. Second, it flatly contradicted the statement that the Lord Advocate was about to make: that the case had been dropped because Carol X was medically unfit to give evidence. Now the outraged public, whose anxiety Fairbairn wished to 'allay', was being offered a con-flicting explanation: that, despite the confession in the *Daily Record*, there was insufficient evidence to bring a successful prosecution. On both counts it was folly, the political equivalent of a suicide note.

Thatcher's inner circle decided enough was enough. One of them prevailed on the Labour opposition to demand an apology for Fairbairn's discourtesy; Michael Foot obliged, clearing the way for the Leader of the House, Francis Pym, to tender the apology, saying he was 'mindful of the need for the House to be informed at the first opportunity of matters of public importance'. Fairbairn was told nothing of Pym's intention; the first he knew of it was when Pym delivered the statement. It was a calculated insult, a piece of treachery, and when he rose later to make his own statement, he was a drowning man. But his humiliation was not quite complete. His last hour as Solicitor-General for Scotland was described by one political correspondent as 'a cross between a political gang-bang and the closing stages of a stag hunt'.

He began by apologising for the disrespect he had shown to the House and then fumbled his way through the approved script – the one he had so recently rejected in his interview with the *Evening Times*. He denied ever saying that the case had been dropped because of lack of evidence, but the denial convinced no-one. Bruce Millan condemned him for 'a wholly unsatisfactory statement about an absolutely horrifying case' and said that had it not been for the persistence of the Scottish press, 'we would not have had a statement to this House at all'. Was Fairbairn aware that the victim had said she was perfectly willing to give evidence? Was he aware that it looked as if there was a considerable body of evidence justifying a prosecution? Fairbairn answered feebly: 'I am astonished that it may be that this unfortunate woman who underwent these terrible events wishes now to give evidence.' It was an abject performance.

The Labour MP for Shettleston, David Marshall, called for the Solicitor-General's resignation 'as he has no credibility left', and demanded to know the name of the person in the Crown Office who had decided to drop the charges. 'I shall not name any person who took the responsibility in the Crown Office,' countered Fairbairn – to cries of 'Why not?' from his fellow MPs. He also resisted the clamour for an inquiry. By the end of the ordeal, the face from an ancient mould was flushed with embarrassment. Apart from the kindly James Douglas-Hamilton, who uttered a few consoling words, his own party deserted him – the Prime Minister sending a clear message about her feelings by leaving the chamber before the crucifixion scene was over. Later that afternoon, the Prime Minister's parliamentary private secretary, Ian Gow, had a meeting with Fairbairn and delivered the *coup de grace*. He told him that he should 'consider resignation': code for 'go at once'. According to one account of their conversation, Fairbairn admitted: 'The department for which I am responsible has made a very serious mistake. It was an appalling blunder, quite contrary to anything I would have sanctioned. I will resign.'

The issue thus became one of personal ministerial responsibility, yet in his resignation letter, he made no attempt to repeat, even in a milder diplomatic form, what he had said privately to Gow. He said that although he had made errors of judgement in his dealings with the press he was entirely satisfied that the case had been handled 'with total propriety'. How could Fairbairn accept the responsibility for 'an appalling blunder' if he was publicly unwilling to concede that a blunder had taken place? In any case, even if he had made such a concession, why should he take the blame for serious failings in the Crown Office when it was not the Solicitor-General but the Lord Advocate who bore the ultimate responsibility? If anyone had to resign, should it not have been Lord Mackay of Clashfern?

Looking back at the events of that day, the political analyst Grant Jordan concluded that Fairbairn was not driven from office by the massed concern of the House, which in Jordan's opinion was mainly concerned with the affront to its dignity, but by a classic 'squeeze' engineered by Francis Pym, whose pre-emptive apology put Fairbairn in a very bad light. The ministers closest to Thatcher – including the Home Secretary William Whitelaw – had already decided that Fairbairn was expendable, and Thatcher, for all her forgiving nature in matters of personal indiscretion, had little option but to accept their recommendation. In retrospect, Jordan saw Fairbairn as a classic scapegoat who performed his function well, diverting attention from blame in other quarters and disposing of the need for a potentially awkward investigation. Jordan was disappointed that the press, 'cause of so much fuss', should be content with a transparent gambit. And the gambit, if that is what it was, worked a treat: there was no inquiry and Lord Mackay of Clashfern, who was fortunate to escape with his job, went on to still greater eminence as Lord Chancellor of England.

On the night of his downfall, Nicholas Fairbairn fled from the clutches of the rampant media. Malcolm Rifkind, then a junior minister at the Scottish Office, arrived in an official car at his flat in

Waterloo, the one notorious for its lamp-post, and spent a fruitless
10 minutes knocking on the door without reply, while back in his
Perthshire constituency the local Tory chairman, Charles Crichton,
made no attempt to conceal the extent of the personal misfortune:
'Three youths in Glasgow have destroyed the life and happiness
of a woman and the career of a man.' Fairbairn spent the night
at the house of a friend in Kensington, hoping that he would not
be tracked down to his 'secret address', which, in the way of secret
addresses, was not a secret for long. First thing in the morning, there
was a journalist at the door. Fairbairn received him in an 'impeccable, double-breasted, grey pinstripe suit' and stood throughout the
interview, sipping from a glass of whisky. Courteous and choosing
his words carefully, he was contemptuous of the media's role in the
affair: 'Each man must answer for himself, and this is a case of physician heal thyself.' Of the disloyalty of his own colleagues, including
the Leader of the House, he had nothing to say.

A few days later, in a BBC television interview, when James
Cox asked him what he intended to do with the rest of his life, he
replied that he would write, paint, and serve his constituents. How
difficult had it been for him? 'Immensely difficult. Very difficult
for one's children, family, friends and for oneself, very difficult. A
public humiliation, assault, everybody trying to get you, photograph
the body, ask it whether it enjoyed the sacrifice.' He was close to
breaking down on air. Cox then invited him to express an opinion
about Lord Mackay. Should he have resigned? There was no difficulty
in reading between the lines of his reply – 'It is for people to make
their own decisions where their consciences are' – and then came a
revealing metaphor: 'The dullards got me with the second barrel of
the shotgun.' The first barrel, fired after the incident involving the
mistress's tights, may indeed have been the work of an enemy, but
only a man sunk in self-delusion could have failed to acknowledge
that it was Fairbairn himself who pulled the trigger for the second
and fatal shot.

IV

A tragedy which began in the east end of Glasgow on an autumn evening in 1980 had claimed two victims who were permanently disfigured, but the only victim whose scars were physical was Carol X and not the self-pitying Nicholas Fairbairn. On the day of the 6 am telephone call, Carol had also been talking to the press. She told journalists that every time she undressed she shuddered. 'A woman is naturally proud of her body. But look at me. I needed all those stitches to put me together again. A razor played noughts and crosses on my skin. My flesh was gouged apart'. She thought the blade must have been so sharp that she had not felt the slashes. In a full-page interview for the *Evening Times*, she expanded on her views about her treatment by the judicial system: 'I think the psychiatrist said I couldn't give evidence for my sake, and he can't be blamed. He knew my state of health better than I do. I was bad with nerves, but I wanted to see those boys put away. I want to see them put away for a long, long time. I'd like to see them castrated so they couldn't do it again.'

Lord Emslie, who had single-handedly destroyed Fairbairn's loftier ambitions three years earlier, would now decide, with the assistance of Lords Cameron and Avonside, whether to grant a private prosecution. Such prosecutions were extremely rare; the last successful one in Scotland had been in 1909. When the application to serve a bill of criminal letters on the accused – the device enabling a private prosecution – came before the High Court, Mackay informed the Lord Justice General that he would not oppose it; rather he would adopt a neutral stance, so indicating that he did not intend to influence the court's decision. But it was clear from his opening statement that the Crown Office's narrative had been radically revised. The woman who would 'never' recover sufficiently to testify was fit to do so. She was no longer afraid to face her alleged attackers in court; she was prepared to relive her experience; the deep psychological wounds which had prevented an earlier appearance had 'healed'. Furthermore, she was willing to give immunity from prosecution to a fourth youth, who might have been regarded as an associate of the others – a reference to Stephen Cameron, the fastidious member of the party, who claimed to have abstained from molesting Carol because he had had sex with his girlfriend earlier in the evening.

Mackay faced searching questions from the bench. Lord Avonside wished to know why the Crown Office had not sent the woman a letter when the charges against the youths were dropped. Had she known of the decision at the time, speculated Avonside, she might well have tried for a private prosecution at an earlier stage. Mackay 'regretted' this had not been done. It was an answer that fell short of an apology; indeed an expression of regret was a well-known substitute for an apology; but in this case, as in others, apologies from the Scottish legal establishment were a rarity.

Towards the end of the first day of legal submissions, the first of three, Emslie wondered aloud whether the accused would receive a fair trial after the 'saturation coverage' in the media. When the court reconvened the following morning, Donald Macaulay QC, counsel for one of the youths, was happy to enlarge on this convenient possibility. He laid it on thick: to allow the prosecution to go ahead 'would be doing an injustice to the very concept of justice itself'; if people were to be allowed to challenge every decision of the Crown Office it would 'open the floodgates'; if private individuals could intervene in such cases, the post of Lord Advocate would become 'rather useless'. Macaulay reminded the court that the press had brought to light the decision not to prosecute; he was not criticising them for it, but the case had achieved a notoriety which could never be displaced in the public mind and the tone of the publicity had assumed or implied the guilt of the youths, who maintained their innocence. 'Even after statements were made in Parliament warning that publicity might be damaging,' said Macaulay, 'the publicity did not let up.' He was right. It had not. But there was one aspect of the case that he failed to mention: its exceptional character.

The Dean of the Faculty of Advocates, Charles Kemp Davidson QC, spoke for Carol X. He contended that, despite the publicity, a jury should be allowed to consider the case so that the matter could be 'defused': a reference to the hinterland of public anger. Emslie observed that, if it did go to trial, jurors would need 'courage and a sense of duty' beyond what was normally expected of them. Kemp Davidson did not demur. But he suggested that in recent years the courts had become more confident in the ability of juries to deal with pre-trial publicity and that, in any case, their memory would be blurred by the passage of time.

The arguments were finally balanced. Donald Macaulay had made a spirited plea for throwing out the application on the grounds that a fair trial for his client had been hopelessly compromised. But there was a sense of inevitability about the judgement: Emslie decided, 'after considerable hesitation', that the interests of the accused had not been prejudiced and that the prosecution should go ahead. The bill of criminal letters was served, the youths were taken into custody, and an early trial date was fixed.

Stephen Cameron, having been granted immunity, was the Crown's main witness, incriminating his fellow visitors to the scrap-yard with his detailed account of the night's events. Carol could add little, repeating that she had no memory of what happened between the moment she was dragged backwards by the youths along London Road and the moment she regained consciousness in the cabin. Why, then, asked Joseph Sweeney's counsel, Donald Findlay QC, did she think she had been raped? 'Because,' she replied, 'I was naked from the waist down.' She agreed with Donald Macaulay, representing the other Sweeney, that it was the police who suggested to her she had been raped, but denied that the case had only come into the public eye because of her horrible injuries.

Gordon Sweeney admitted in evidence that he had had sex with her, but maintained that she was conscious and made no protest. Joseph Sweeney would only admit to having tried to have sex with her, claiming he was put off by her drunken condition. The third youth in the dock, John Thomson, said that when he first saw her she had been 'a bit drunk', that he put his arm round her, that she had gone willingly to the yard, that she had consented to intercourse. Lord Ross told the jury there was no evidence that Gordon Sweeney or Thomson had attacked Carol with the razor, or that they had been complicit in the attack, and the charge of rape against them was reduced to indecent assault, for which they received deferred sentences and walked free. Only Joseph Sweeney went to prison – for 12 years – after Ross had described him as a dangerous young man. When the verdicts were given to her, Carol broke down in tears: 'I don't think I will ever really get over it. I am still afraid when I see groups of young boys.' She said she would probably move to England because the memories of her ordeal in Glasgow were so painful.

Bruce McKain, the *Glasgow Herald*'s law reporter, dismissed the possibility that the jurors had been influenced by the pre-trial publicity: 'To say originally that it was trial by newspaper has turned out to be an insult to the jury, who so obviously devoted great care and attention to the evidence.' The *Daily Record* called it 'a victory for public opinion, a victory for women, a moral victory for prostitutes'. But its post-trial commentary cast fresh doubt on the contradictory motives at the heart of the affair. The paper implicitly rejected the Crown Office's repeated assurance that it had dropped the prosecution only because Carol had been judged unfit to give evidence. 'It wasn't the cops but the Crown who decided the woman made an unreliable witness because she was a prostitute,' said the *Record*. Had it been as simple as that all along? If it was, Fairbairn's unguarded early morning quote showed more regard for the facts than his subsequent retraction to parliament. Ultimately it may have been a case of truth by newspaper rather than trial by newspaper.

It was not over; in the east end there was always the chance of a sequel. Stephen Cameron was never forgiven for testifying against the Sweeney brothers and was subjected to a campaign of hatred and harassment. He was labelled a 'grass', chased and attacked in the street and shunned in local pubs. Even when he moved away from the neighbourhood and went to live in another part of Glasgow with his girlfriend and two young children, his reputation preceded him and he was forced to move a second time. He became a fugitive in his own city. One night he made a misguided decision to return to see his mother. Gordon Sweeney, determined to pursue the vendetta, promptly arranged for some armed friends to attack him and one of his brothers as they walked home after a night's drinking. The Camerons managed to escape to the shelter of their mother's house, leaving another brother talking to a neighbour in the street. Fearing for his safety, the Camerons grabbed a long, ornamental sword from the wall of the house – it was the sort of house in which long, or-namental swords went with the decor – and left to go looking for him. Instead they came face to face with Gordon Sweeney, who had a weapon of his own, a baseball bat that he swung at the brothers before he lost his balance and slipped to the ground. The Camerons fell on him with their sword, inflicting terrible wounds. Sweeney was carried to his home but bled to death before an ambulance arrived. Stephen Cameron, meanwhile, hid his bloodstained clothes in a dustbin – a futile gesture since most of the neighbourhood had watched the showdown from their windows. A jury at the High Court found the brothers not guilty of murder but convicted them of culpable homicide; Stephen got 12 years – the same sentence as his enemy Joseph Sweeney three years earlier – while his brother went down for 14.

Six lives had now been ruined as a direct or indirect result of a single alcohol-fuelled incident in a Glasgow scrapyard. Gordon Sweeney was dead at the age of 17. Joseph Sweeney and the Cameron brothers faced many years in prison. Carol X was physically wrecked and mentally fragile. Only the sixth of these lives continued to be the subject of occasional public scrutiny: the degenerate Nicholas Fairbairn.

V

With his dismissal as Solicitor-General, the best was over for Fairbairn. He remained an MP and in 1988 received the consolation prize of a knighthood. When the journalist Hunter Davies went to interview him one afternoon in 1992, Fairbairn was drinking vodka from a two-litre bottle and asked Davies if he would care to join him in a snifter. His wife Suzanne – he had remarried in 1983 – came into the room from time to time – 'an attractive-looking woman in tweed knickerbockers and bright red socks'. (She died an alcoholic in 2002 at the age of 59.)

Had he been faithful to her? 'Good Lord, no,' said Fairbairn. 'It's the sanctimony of fidelity which destroys marriage.' Davies asked Lady Fairbairn if she agreed with her husband's views on marriage. 'I think monogamy does matter,' she replied. Had she been unfaithful? 'Good gracious, no.' What about Sir Nicholas? 'I know about him,' she said solemnly. Davies wondered what people would make of him when he had gone. 'I don't care,' said Fairbairn, 'but I think there's a chance I will be thought of as an awfully good boy.'

Dead three years later at the age of 62, he received grudging notices in the obituary pages. The verdict of the political journalist Patrick Cosgrave that he was 'bizarre' scarcely flattered his memory, while the publisher John Calder wrote that he was someone with a high opinion of his own accomplishments and the principal victim of his own vanity: 'Everything he did seemed to be aimed at a single goal – to attract attention.' Calder noted how he began as a human rights libertarian but moved sharply to the right in the years of Thatcher's supremacy, even supporting the reintroduction of capital punishment.

Privately, his behaviour was beyond eccentric. When he was Solicitor-General, he boasted in the bars of the House of Commons that he possessed a bound volume of crime scene photographs; his listeners got the impression that he derived a perverted pleasure from images of butchered women. Ian Hernon, the *Evening Times* journalist who had made the fateful 6 am telephone call, claimed that, long afterwards, when he brought up the case of Carol X in his company, Fairbairn replied that it was 'normal' for women to be treated that way during a night out in Glasgow. He was unimpressed by Hernon's reminder of the grotesque nature of Carol's injuries.

At the time of his death there was no suggestion that he had been other than 'a notorious ladies' man' (as John Calder quaintly referred to him). But gradually a more ambiguous view of Fairbairn's sexuality emerged. He had once risen unsteadily to his feet during a late-night Commons debate on the age of homosexual consent, attempting to describe the mechanics of sodomy before being called to order by the Speaker. Although he spoke of the practice as if it disgusted him, it may well have been part of his sexual repertoire. One political editor remembered him crudely as 'an equal opportunities shagger – either sex, any age, creed or colour, it didn't matter to him'.

In 1983 a Tory MP, Geoffrey Dickens, handed a dossier to the Home Secretary, Leon Brittan, containing allegations about the abuse of boys at a gay brothel in Barnes, south-west London, known as Elm Green House. Nothing more was heard of the dossier. Years later, when the Home Office organised a search for it, no trace could be found. But in 2014 there was a startling development in a scandal kept under wraps for three decades: the police acquired documents handwritten in Elm Green House, which showed that on 7 June 1982 a number of public figures, including 'N Fairburn' and 'C Smith', visited the property and that 'N Fairburn' had 'used boys in sauna'. 'C Smith' may have been the late Cyril Smith, a Liberal Democrat MP. Despite the spelling discrepancy, there was speculation – though only speculation – that 'N Fairburn' was N Fairbairn, who had been dismissed as Solicitor-General five months earlier.

How did this man achieve high office in Scotland? Why was he the darling of artistic Edinburgh? Is it credible that his personal excesses were never known or suspected by people of influence? It is tempting to conclude that Fairbairn was essentially the product of a society in which awkward questions were seldom asked and where a little talent, even a talent as corrupted as Fairbairn's, went a long way. Had it not been for a blood-soaked night in a Glasgow scrapyard in October 1980 – the night that marked the beginning of the end, after which there was only drink and dissolution – the awfully good boy might even have got away with it.

THE NEW DOORS

I

A GUIDEBOOK SPONSORED BY THE BRITISH TOURIST AUTHORITY, published with the aim of attracting visitors to Scotland from the continent, and written by a German journalist, Peter Sager, pulled no punches in its chapter on Glasgow. Thousands of copies were distributed before the book came to the notice of the Lord Provost, Michael Kelly, who worried about the damage it might do, particularly as it included a reference to a tour of Glasgow known as the Horror Trip. In the east end, where the big fights involved ornamental swords and baseball bats, Sager discovered that the child mortality rate was twice that of any English city and that one in five of the working population was out of a job.

'By the Clyde the unemployed sit and drink,' he wrote. 'Weeks ago, whole rows of houses still stood here. Now piles of rubbish burn in the city centre. In Glasgow, this is called the blitz of the bulldozers – a town breaking up. I have seen districts, in Calton and Anderston, which resemble a battlefield rather than a redevelopment area. I went through streets and empty houses as if there had been an epidemic of the plague . . . Is this the city which in the nineteenth century called itself, after London, the Second City of the British Empire? Today Glasgow is first: its social and economic problems are worse than those of England's worst city, Liverpool.'

History has failed to record how many readers were sufficiently enticed by Glasgow's allure as a tourist destination to witness the scenes of devastation for themselves. But there was a larger-scale horror trip which, as yet unnoticed by visiting journalists, would never feel quite the same again. The bleak rows of Scotland's council estates – the 'schemes' into which most of the people had been re-housed – both defined and disfigured the urban landscape. Change was in the air – or, at any rate, on the statute book.

Margaret Thatcher's right-to-buy legislation, introduced in the summer of 1980, was the second great reforming act of twentieth-century housing. In the first, 61 years earlier, the Addison Act, named after the then minister of housing, Christopher Addison, provided for state-subsidised local authority housing for the first time. Until then, the Scottish people endured living conditions of a wretchedness without parallel south of the border. The 1911 census showed that more than half the population lived in houses of one or two rooms compared with 7% in England, and that 45% of Scots shared a room with more than one other person compared with 9% in England. The deprivation of space was intense in such towns as Kilsyth and Coatbridge, where 71% of the population inhabited houses in which more than two people co-existed in the same small room. Even in relatively prosperous Edinburgh, there were 7,106 one-room houses, almost all of which shared a common toilet and almost half a common sink.

The Royal Commission on Housing in Scotland (1917) confirmed that the death rate was much higher in one-room houses than in houses with two or more rooms. In Edinburgh, infant mortality in 1910 was 110 per 1,000 deaths for the city as a whole, but this figure concealed wide variations. In the three- or four-room houses of middle-class Merchiston, it was 46 per 1,000, while in squalid inner-city Cowgate, it was 277. The commission reported that the risks to health of such dense living were compounded by the custom of keeping dead bodies in the home for three days before burial. The corpse occupied the family bed during the day and was then moved for the night to the one table in the house. A witness to the commission described living in one room as 'a constant succession of lifting, folding and hanging up, and if this regime is relaxed for even a short time the confusion is overwhelming'. Many children who survived such conditions suffered long-term damage to their health; in Dundee, 44% of school children were diagnosed with impaired hearing and 48% with poor eyesight.

The Addison Act sought to bring about a radical improvement in the living conditions of the British people by placing an obligation on local authorities to build houses for let by working-class families. The results in Scotland were striking: between 1919, when the legislation was passed, and the start of the Second World War 20 years later, 67% of all the houses built in Scotland were in the public sector compared with 26% in England. Rents were, however, generally higher and wages lower; in Dundee, the rent of a council house in the period between the wars accounted for around half of a textile worker's wage.

The post-war Labour government, answering the battlecry of 'Homes for heroes', dedicated itself to an ambitious programme of house-building. In Scotland, although the enormous demand far outstripped supply, most local authorities made an effort to meet the challenge and fixed rents at a more affordable level. But the explosion in public-sector housing created an undesirable imbalance in the stock; by the end of the 1960s, 63% of the houses in Glasgow, 57% in Dundee, were publicly owned. This gave councils and councillors, mostly Labour councillors, enormous power in the allocation of houses, and there were many complaints of favouritism. In a culture of dependence, few of them were actively pursued.

Margaret Thatcher's plan was to liberate tenants from the shackles of state control. Her mission, though it applied also to England and Wales, had a more potent significance in Scotland because of the much higher proportion of council-house dwellers. Iain Sproat, among her most ardent disciples, wrote in the week of its introduction: 'Nothing that has been achieved in Scotland for a generation is likely to change the political landscape of our country more dramatically than this Act. Instead of being the country with the worst record for owner-occupancy in Western Europe – almost incredibly, worse even than some Communist countries in Eastern Europe such as Hungary and Czechoslovakia – men and women in Scotland will now have the chance to fulfil our old traditions of individual independence, and to enjoy the freedom which ownership brings.'

By the time Thatcher was ejected from office by her party 12 years later, almost a quarter of a million council tenants in Scotland had exercised the right to buy. Unexpectedly, the first gesture of the liberated, one which sent a clear message to the neighbours, was to tear down the standard front door erected by the council and replace it with a door of their choice, often of incongruous suburban design. The doors thus became the physical symbols of a distinctive and increasingly visible form of social division. Behind the new doors, the 'hard-working families' championed by Thatcher suddenly had access to equity. Behind the old doors, rent continued to be paid and material aspiration counted for less; in popular mythology – it was by no means invariably true – the gardens of these houses tended to be messier, the cars shabbier. Uneasily juxtaposed, new doors and old symbolised diverging branches of the same class; the rough democracy of the council scheme disappeared in less than a generation. But the revolution anticipated by Iain Sproat turned out to be social rather than political. There were limits to the gratitude of the Scots who seized the opportunity to buy their own homes: most of the new capitalists continued to reject the Conservative Party at successive general elections.

II

There was no danger of Margaret Thatcher's revolution touching Possilpark, which lay at the socio-economic extremity of the Glasgow horror trip, an unreconstructed ghetto of old doors. The children of Possilpark loathed Thatcher with a passion. We know this because in the spring of 1981 an enterprising young teacher at the local secondary school set an essay for his pupils aged 12 to 14 entitled 'The virtues and shortcomings of the Prime Minister' and splashed the results across the pages of a far-left periodical, *Socialist Worker*.

The virtues were non-existent. Among the many shortcomings, some were personal: the Prime Minister was variously 'an ugly old hag' and 'an evil bitch'. Opinions of her policies, real or imagined, were no more flattering: 'Anyone unemployed in the future might be made to sign up with the Army'; 'She is putting bus fares up in April for old folk and not putting their pensions up'; 'She is also stopping school meals altogether and trying to get us to go to school on a Saturday'; 'I hate her because she puts up the prices and wants to start a war'; 'She makes the police search anyone they suspect carries stolen goods'.

All this was too much for the Conservative MP Allan Stewart, the tribune of Newton Mearns, who wrote at once to the Secretary of State, George Younger: 'No doubt you will be as appalled as I am to learn that this has been going on in a Scottish school.' Stewart demanded 'a special investigation' (as distinct from the 'top-level probe' invariably favoured by the tabloid press) into what was 'actually being taught' in classes of modern studies. The Labour chairman of Strathclyde education committee, Councillor William Harley, agreed that the teacher had acted 'in a totally unprofessional manner in this most unfortunate matter' and, in a rare show of cross-party unity, the leader of the Tory opposition, Councillor Len Turpie, believed that 'these extracts are unique in my experience and must remain unique because they are fostering hatred and violence in the minds of the young'.

The *Evening Times*, never slow to censure, condemned the children's work as 'filthy and obscene', but counselled the people of Glasgow not to panic: 'The best protection of all against this kind of abuse is the sensible and vigilant parent who takes the time and trouble to ask: What did you do at school today?' The *Glasgow Herald*, though it was prepared to acknowledge that the children's comments might have been expressed 'spontaneously and unprompted', trusted that the episode would 'serve as a warning to any teacher tempted to bring their political preconceptions into the classroom'.

When the guilty party was unmasked as Harry 'Jock' Morris, the newspapers were soon billeted outside his tenement flat in Maryhill, hoping for a glimpse of the Possilpark revolutionary. Emerging only briefly, though long enough for the photographers to snap him looking suitably furtive, he refused to talk to journalists, maintaining what one paper called a 'stony silence'. Unlike Nicholas Fairbairn in a tight spot, he left the telephone unanswered. His 'pretty' wife, on her way back from the shops, also declined to respond to repeated inquiries, leaving the journalists free to speculate that Morris had phoned his headmaster – a term still in use in 1981 – to report sick for a second day in succession. This ludicrous witch-hunt was encouraged by the pennyworth of the Scottish education minister, an accountant by the name of Alex Fletcher, who instructed headmasters to ensure that 'teaching does not degenerate into indoctrination'.

In their rush to judgement, the politicians and the leader writers had not paused to consider how an assignment entitled 'The virtues and shortcomings of the Prime Minister' amounted to indoctrination; or to ask themselves whether it was not fairly remarkable that children in one of Scotland's most disadvantaged communities had managed to write so passionately about politics. Morris's only error – the unauthorised publication in *Socialist Worker* – seemed to be the least of his sins; the issue for his critics was not that the essays had seen the light of day in a Trotskyist magazine but that they had been written in the first place.

In the face of official hysteria, a more humane view began to surface in the correspondence columns of the newspapers. Wilson Jamieson, a lecturer at Jordanhill, the teachers' training college in Glasgow, noted that, although it was not surprising that the pupils of Possilpark had found it difficult to write with conviction about the virtues of Margaret Thatcher, not much had been said about the virtues of the pupils themselves; the essay title seemed to him 'perfectly reasonable and balanced' and the subject matter worthier of study than many he had seen. Five teachers at St Augustine's, a Roman Catholic secondary in the city, co-signed a letter reminding the education minister that there was a difference between political education, which all parties supported, and indoctrination. Another of Morris's supporters, Jack Collins, detected in the over-reaction a symptom of more general attitudes: 'By and large the school tends to be a rather conservative institution. The general effect is to reinforce the current values in society, and not to undermine, let alone question them. We have only to look at the present batch of students in our colleges and universities to note that a clear drift to acquiescence in the system has occurred since the heady days of 1968.'

When the storm passed, the schools' inspectorate in the Scottish Education Department quietly made it clear that there would be no 'special investigation'. Instead it offered a token concession to the Stewarts and Fletchers: a 'review' of how the modern studies curriculum was being managed. Of the Possilpark essayists, who had exhibited a raw instinct for polemic, and their beleaguered teacher, nothing more was ever heard; from the saddles of the high horses, there was no suggestion that there might have been writing ability in Possilpark worth nurturing – however inconvenient the message to the interests of the established order. The episode had a certain value in confirming several unattractive national characteristics: the mistrust of independent thinking, the determination of those in power to quash any hint of subversive individuality, the insecurity behind the desire for order and submission, as well as the prescriptive nature of education.

With unintended irony, the Possilpark rumpus coincided with the unveiling of the latest of many reforms – a plan to replace the O-grade (junior) exam with a superstructure of 'Credit', 'General' and 'Foundation' exams guaranteeing that no-one left school uncertificated. A system unwilling to tolerate an innocuous challenge to its authority now hoped to tranquillise the consumers with the offer of awards for all: as the mantra had it, 'None shall fail'. The official justification was that the Foundation certificate, though essentially meaningless and with the potential to be regarded in adult life as a stigma, provided the bottom 30% of third- and fourth-year pupils with 'a record of achievement'. What of those who had made a conscious decision not to 'achieve' or who were incapable of doing so in the required manner? For this perverse minority, there was no longer a choice. Scotland was destined to become a land of compulsory achievement, in which failure was not only unthinkable but formally expunged.

In a pilot study for the Foundation exam, teachers and pupils met in an 'informal setting' for mathematics. 'On occasion,' said the authors of the study, 'teachers have taken pupils on a picnic or to the fairground. Although the mathematical content of this outing was minimal, the exercise proved beneficial. The pupils were more willing to work and were able to communicate with the teacher in a better way after seeing him in a different light.' Another example of an 'enrichment exercise' was headed 'Decorating a Room'. The report described how pupils should measure areas for painting or papering, calculate the costs and work out the time for the job. Teachers were advised to assess the listening powers of Foundation pupils by asking them to repeat what they could remember from a television programme and to test their ability to talk by getting them to use the telephone. 'Pupils responded very well when authentic samples of language were brought into the classroom: a vehicle registration form; a diary or a log; a questionnaire; a newspaper, a sign or a notice. All of those carried a conviction that no work book can imitate.'

The more unorthodox teachers – among whom R.F. Mackenzie was renowned – would have supported the idea of informal settings as an aid to teaching. Mackenzie himself was fond of taking disaffected pupils from his school in a pit town in Fife on a climbing expedition to the top of a nearby hill, where he introduced them to the natural life of the habitat, including the insects. But this was education for its own sake – an expression of joy in simple curiosity and discovery – rather than an approved route to the holy grail of 'achievement'.

The chairman of the Scottish Certificate of Education Examination Board, Farquhar Macintosh, whose West Highland lilt had a hypnotic effect on many an educational conference, opposed the Foundation in principle; he said he would be happier with no examinations at all apart from the Highers. 'An examination system for pupils up to the age of 16 is a very expensive exercise which is perhaps not justified. It is not the bit of paper which is important, but the motivation and improvement in morale which it provides.' Days later, however, Macintosh was forced on the defensive by a report from the Scottish Universities Council on Entrance which claimed to have found evidence of serious gaps in freshers' knowledge of maths, physics and chemistry and a decline in the quality of their French and German. Macintosh 'refuted' – more accurately, he denied – that standards were declining in the Highers, complaining lamely that the Council had conducted its tests when students were not at their best, soon after the summer break.

In Strasbourg, the excuses for the defects of Scottish education were more feeble still. Lord Mackay of Clashfern – of the Carol X case – was reduced to pleading before 11 judges of the European Court of Human Rights for the retention of the belt in Scottish schools. The hearing in 'L'affaire Campbell Cosans' followed five years of legal wrangling, during which thousands of pages of documented evidence had accumulated, as well as several examples of the instrument itself, imported from the manufacturer, Dick of Lochgelly. The two mothers, Grace Campbell and Jane Cosans, who maintained that the presence or threat of corporal punishment in schools breached the Convention on Human Rights by failing to respect the philosophical convictions of parents who opposed it, had pursued their case with extraordinary persistence, despite many obstacles. Grace Campbell, who observed the proceedings from the public gallery, was refused the opportunity to give oral evidence in support of a report she had prepared on the use of the belt in infant classes – a practice the education authority insisted was forbidden. The judges decided she should not be heard, sparing Scotland the embarrassment of a discussion in Europe about the belting of children as young as five.

She was, however, eloquently represented *pro-bono* by Cedric Thornberry, an international lawyer based at the United Nations in New York, who told the court: 'Corporal punishment poisons the soil for the growth of respect for human rights. It is time for our society to abandon it or to grant an alternative to the many parents who believe as Mrs Campbell does, and to give legitimacy and respect to their views.' The Lord Advocate's response was to accuse the two mothers of making 'highly emotive' and 'misconceived' attempts to discredit corporal punishment and of trying to mislead the judges into believing that 'informed opinion' was in favour of abolishing it.

Mackay confessed that he found it difficult to understand how corporal punishment differed from other forms of disciplinary sanctions. 'Why are the considerations so different between extra homework or detention and a stroke of the belt on the hand? Why is the punishment of the mind trivial when punishment of the body is regarded as of supreme importance? . . . The implications of the child having to do extra homework on a beautiful summer's evening, when other children are out playing, is at least as serious for most children as receiving a stroke on the hand.' Evidently it had not entered the Lord Advocate's head that some teachers derived sexual pleasure from the physical punishment of children or that, factually, it often consisted of more than 'a stroke on the hand'. A teacher who submitted written testimony to the court referred to 'these savage, barbarous beatings which collectively comprise the daily round of legal assaults in Scottish schools'. Who was misleading the court? Was it the teacher on the front-line of Scottish education's disciplinarian regime? Or was it the Lord Advocate? The unrelenting pressure of the mothers changed 'informed opinion' to the extent that the Secretary of State for Scotland, in the long interval between the case being raised and its determination, gave a commitment to abolish corporal punishment by 1983–84. (The target was missed: the belt did not finally disappear from the classroom until 1987.)

The mothers won. The court ruled that the British government had failed to protect the philosophical convictions of the parents and that Fife education authority had been wrong to suspend Jeffrey Cosans over his refusal to accept corporal punishment at Beath High School. But the landmark victory was achieved at heavy personal cost. Suspended from the school in September 1976 when he was preparing for his O-grades, Jeffrey never sat the examination, was refused a place at a further education college and learned that his school suspension had been vindictively entered on his records at the local employment exchange. By the age of 20 he had gone six years without schooling or work of any kind. The other child in the case – Gordon Campbell, whose parents could afford to transfer him from a state primary school in Bishopbriggs to a fee-paying school in Glasgow – flourished academically and became a doctor in general practice.

The reaction of the general secretary of the Educational Institute of Scotland, John Pollock, to the European judgement was mean-spirited. He called it 'irrelevant' for no better reason than that two local authorities, Lothian and Strathclyde, were already 'making moves' to phase out the belt. Pollock was never minded to acknowledge that Scotland had been shamed into reluctant abolition.

The reluctance was well illustrated by the case in 1981 of Margaret McGuire, a mother in Dunbartonshire, who was prosecuted for failing to send her son Daniel to St Columba High School in Clydebank after he refused to take the belt for playing a game called

'Tig' in a school corridor. The magistrate at Clydebank District Court, Julia Handley, acquitted her on a technicality which exposed a loophole in equalities legislation: the parent who was liable under the Education Scotland Act was not the wife and mother but the husband and father, in this case Daniel McGuire, a taxi driver; yet it was Margaret, not Daniel, McGuire who was harried all the way to the dock by Strathclyde Regional Council, whose policies on corporal punishment made the European judgement 'irrelevant' in Pollock's opinion. Having been exposed as incompetent, the council refused to let it drop, lodging an appeal in the name of the depute director of education, Walter Lunn. The Lord Justice General, Lord Emslie, had no difficulty throwing it out – but it was an example of how far education authorities were prepared to go to uphold their injured dignity and defend the punishment culture in Scottish schools.

But there was hope. The retiring president of the Ayrshire branch of the EIS, William Deans, made a valedictory speech accusing long-haired, sloppily dressed young teachers of sitting with a foot on their desks and inviting pupils to address them by their first names. Deans, 'a Kirk elder', feared that these newcomers to the profession were giving pupils the impression 'that moral development and academic training are undesirable'. The old order was changing, even in Scotland, and soon the politicians and the petty officials of the strap-happy teachers' union would be helpless before the advance of the new. In due course many thousands of redundant school belts would be traded on the internet for high prices – if the teachers could no longer use them, there was still profit to be made from their disposal. Grace Campbell, a Scottish prophet without honour, died young, before 'informed opinion' came to regard corporal punishment in schools as a form of institutional child abuse. As for Lord Mackay of Clashfern, who was baffled that anyone would object to a stroke of the belt on the hand – why, he simply carried on up the greasy pole of Margaret Thatcher's Britain.

III

Though there was much to do before Scotland could lay any claim to enlightenment, in the treatment of its children or in much else, the circular sideshows of party politics were a familiar substitute for practical accomplishment. By the early 1980s the music hall was more or less dead, though the Glasgow Pavilion battled on twice nightly; but there was no need for music hall when the Scottish National Party was around. In draughty seaside halls out of season, the kilted troupers of the nationalist movement, some of whom had been treading the boards since before the 1945 election, struggled for top billing with younger entertainers subversively attired in trousers. The internal convulsions in such conference resorts as Rothesay and Ayr were talked up as a battle for the soul of the party, with regular intervals for fortifying refreshments.

In 1980, it was Rothesay's turn for the horror trip known as the SNP's annual conference. In a gesture of contrived harmony, the party's new chairman, Gordon Wilson, a Dundee accountant, had a conciliatory stroll along the prom with the troublesome recruit Jim Sillars, formerly of the defunct Scottish Labour Party, who had been persuaded by his friend Alex Neil that the only way to salvage his career was to join the Nats, as Neil himself proposed to do. It was commonly assumed that the 79 Group, a cabal within the party, had been formed to give Sillars a power base. Not so, according to Sillars's wife, Margo MacDonald; it seems the formation of the group preceded his arrival. No matter: it gave him a power base anyway.

One political journalist wrote that the 'almost theatrical move' – the pre-arranged walk along the prom – was typical of the lengths the party was determined to go to disguise the hostility felt by the old guard towards what it saw as the left-wing entryists of the 79 Group. Robert McIntyre had been ousted as president after 22 years – a personal humiliation for the party's first MP (though only briefly an MP: having been elected in a by-election at Motherwell in the spring of 1945 he lost the seat in the Labour landslide a few months later). His temper at Rothesay was not improved by the spectacle of Wilson and Sillars taking the air together. 'In my view this [the 79] is a party within a party', he told the press, 'and as such I consider it to be politically immoral. I see this group's existence as nothing less than a conspiracy to subvert the party. It will take some time before we realise what these people, with their slick, tricky type of practices, are up to.' His successor, William Wolfe, who had himself recently been ousted as the party chairman, professed some sympathy for the 79 Group and disagreed with McIntyre that it undermined the party's constitution. But now it got complicated. For Wolfe was also marginally involved in a second and more combustible splinter group, though he claimed it was 'only to keep an eye on it'.

Siol nan Gaidheal – Seed of the Gael – had a murky pedigree: two of its members had been among the accused in one of the trials of the so-called 'Tartan Army' (which bore no relation to Scottish football's relatively law-abiding alternative). Gordon Wilson branded the group 'proto fascist' – a description dismissed as 'ludicrous' by another of the party's office-bearers, Isobel Lindsay. The editor of the *Glasgow Herald*, Arnold Kemp, believed that it 'fed off the boredom and disillusionment of the housing schemes' and that, while it had been infiltrated by extremists, its importance was 'unduly enlarged'. The historian Murray Pittock, impressed by its followers' 'quasi-para-military appearance based round elements of Celtic design' and its 'aggressive combination of militant activism and Jacobite romanti-cism', drew a loose parallel with the Irish Volunteers before conclud-ing sardonically that, unlike the Volunteers, Siol nan Gaidheal was 'mainly sartorial' in its threat to the stability of the state.

The daft lads from the schemes, as Arnold Kemp preferred to think of the majority, burned the Union Jack, wore black shirts and the obligatory kilts, marched in public with broadswords and accord-ing to reports reaching the party headquarters were not above singing Nazi songs, yet Siol nan Gaidheal was tolerated within the SNP even after an internal investigation into its activities. Seven months after Rothesay, the party moved east to Arbroath for a pre-Christmas debate on whether the two awkward squads – Siol and 79 – should be proscribed. Neither was. Gordon Wilson, in a startling departure from his earlier damning judgement, said after the meeting: 'We did not feel the case against Siol was made out. You could say the verdict was not proven.' The *Glasgow Herald* was unimpressed: 'It seems there is a place in the Scottish National Party for militant nationalists bearing dirks and threatening to bring down the Government by direct action.'

By the summer of 1981, the left-wing had tightened their grip on the party. In a speech to the annual conference Sillars too was talking about direct action: 'We have a very serious strategy . . . Individuals in the party must be prepared to go all the way to jail. We have got to be prepared to accept that the cell doors will clang on some of us.'

The backdrop to these self-sacrificial undertakings was a hatred of Margaret Thatcher's economic policies, which extended well beyond Possilpark Secondary School. She was personally blamed for soaring unemployment – more than 200,000 out of work, the highest total since the Second World War – and for a demoralising series of shutdowns, of which the most spectacular was the closure of the Linwood car plant with the loss of 4,800 jobs. In declining to intervene, the government was accused by the local Labour MP, Allen Adams, of 'behaving like Pontius Pilate', while his colleague Norman Buchan predicted 'the death of a town as surely as happened to Jarrow in the 1930s'. There was a reluctance to face two unpalatable facts: the record of the workforce in contributing to the dismal industrial relations at the plant; and the folly of establishing a car factory too far from the principal suppliers and major markets ever to be commercially viable. Linwood was doomed long before Thatcher came to power. It was doomed from the start.

No government could have saved Linwood. Nor could the Secretary of State, George Younger, reasonably have offered false promises. But the Thatcher administration gave the impression that it cared nothing for the people thrown out of work: it was seen as heartless, even cruel, in its indifference to an ailing Scotland. Alan Devereux, a prominent business leader of moderate views, delivered an alarmist warning; he could see a future in which the 'have nots' raided the homes of the better-off. He was mistaken: affluent Strathblane, where Devereux lived, was unaffected by raiding parties of the starving proletariat.

Nevertheless, there was public anger and frustration that the 79 Group felt entitled to exploit. 'Scotland will be a crippled nation in five years unless we grab independence', claimed one of its publications. 'The unionist parties aren't going to give us an inch – we must take it'. Many in the right-of-centre mainstream of the SNP were aghast at the major influence being exercised by Sillars and his supporters, yet powerless to halt their advance. In June 1981, the left-wing scooped half of the 10 seats vacant on the national executive, with the 79 Group's leading thinker, Stephen Maxwell, topping the poll with 131 votes. One unnamed 'mainstream activist' protested to the newspapers: 'It was one thing when they were a group within the party out to promote discussion and theories. But they have caballed so successfully that a group with a paid-up membership of less than 100 now controls more than half the 23 seats on the national executive of our party.' Maxwell was joined on the executive by four other members or sympathisers of the 79 Group: Ron Wylie with 97 votes, Rob Gibson with 85, Jeff Lockhart with 84 and – squeezing in with 79 votes – a promising newcomer called Alex Salmond. Never in the history of British politics did so few votes come to count for so much as those 79.

But if 1981 was the year of take-off for a future first minister and catalyst of the independence movement, the outlook for Kermit, a patriotic iguana, was less certain. From the bedroom of his house in a Kilmarnock suburb, Kermit's owner, the self-proclaimed founder of Siol nan Gaidheal, Gordon Walker, 24, founded a new party named the Scottish Movement. Kermit, a native of Brazil, was three-foot-long and growing rapidly on a diet of dog food and courgettes; informed opinion, the kind trusted by the Lord Advocate, had it that Kermit would soon reach six feet.

Walker was described in the press as an unemployed employment officer, a member of the Church of Scientology and a former office-bearer in the SNP. He informed journalists that he gave up work in order to concentrate on politics full-time and that he set up Siol nan Gaidheal believing it meant Sons of Scotland. It was only when one of the group's office-bearers (the treasurer) began teaching himself Gaelic that the founder was disabused of this notion. Walker decided that the chairmanship should be for life – a unilateral declaration which had the other members twitching on their broadswords. He was toppled during a night of the long dirks in 1979 and had since languished on the sidelines while his creation took off, forming its own drum corps. Would the Scottish Movement, even with Kermit rooting for it, fare any better than other breakaway parties? The auguries were discouraging. Only five people attended the inaugural meeting, of whom two failed to re-appear, and there was an issue with the motif when someone pointed out that that it could be misconstrued as a swastika. Walker was nonetheless hopeful that by the time Kermit reached his full length he – Walker, not Kermit – would be prime minister of an independent Scotland. Young Salmond with his 79 votes seemed a likelier bet, all things considered.

IV

In the pretty village of Drymen, close to the bonny banks of Loch Lomond, lived two famous Scotsmen with opposing opinions on nationalism: the entertainer Billy Connolly who could see nothing of value in the SNP's ultimate aspiration and the department store tycoon Sir Hugh Fraser, who helped to bankroll the party in the 1970s and made no secret of his belief that the English were constantly putting Scotland down. In 1981 there were so many horror trips to Drymen that the men from the tabloids might as well have been billeted permanently in the Buchanan Arms Hotel. Not that the conflicting politics of the resident celebrities interested them. What brought them to the village was the usual thing: the whiff, at times more than a whiff, of scandal.

Connolly and his wife Iris, an interior designer, had gone to live in Drymen with their children Jamie and Cara in 1974, soon after Cara was born. His second wife, the actress Pamela Stephenson, thought of Drymen as 'a peaceful town'. Peaceful it might have been before the press arrived; town it never was. 'Billy was happy that his children were having the kind of life he had only dreamed about,' wrote Stephenson, 'and, on the surface, his life was quite jolly; but inside he was lost.' Billy was getting drunk 'very regularly', having blackouts and what Stephenson called 'psychotic rages'; he decided that the trick was never to let the hangover catch up with him – just to stay drunk. By the end of the 1970s, both Billy and Iris had a problem with alcohol without either acknowledging it, and the marriage was collapsing. Then Billy met Pamela.

When rumours of the relationship reached Hugh Farmer, Scottish news editor of a scandal sheet, the *Sunday People*, he hot-footed it to a pub in Drymen where there was every chance that Connolly would be found. Sure enough there he was, in the company of his drinking friends. Farmer decided not to approach him; according to a private detective who was assisting him, and who gave evidence in the news editor's civil action against Connolly at Stirling Sheriff Court, Farmer regarded the nature of his inquiries as too 'private and delicate' to be raised in public. He left the pub and headed for the Connolly household, where Iris invited him inside. Farmer's version of what happened next – which he related in court – was that Iris told him what she knew of the story, was open about it, seemed relieved to get it off her chest. Farmer then asked her to telephone her husband at the pub. Minutes later, Connolly came storming up the driveway and into the house, ordered Farmer to leave and on his way out rabbit-punched him in the neck and kicked him 'up the backside' so severely that he was off work for a fortnight.

When the private detective, William Blyth, was asked in court why he had been hired, he replied that it was partly to confirm that Farmer had 'conducted his business in a proper and ethical manner'. But there was an alternative view of how journalism operated in Drymen: Pamela Stephenson claimed that the Connolly children were seriously harassed by reporters as they walked about the village. The events of the summer of 1981 soured Connolly's relationship with the Scottish press and many years later he was still talking bitterly about named journalists who had crossed him. Farmer, who was so jealous of his reputation that he required a private detective to vouch for it, underwent a strange metamorphosis, exchanging the ethical world of Sunday tabloid journalism for the editorship of the *Scottish Catholic Observer*, from which he was fired in 1999. Still in litigious mood, he threatened to sue for unfair dismissal. Meanwhile Iris Connolly was living out her days in the Spanish resort of Benidorm, where the *Sunday Mail* tracked her down, 'haggard and drawn, shuffling across the sun-scorched yard of her secret hideaway'.

A second private detective – name unknown – may have been sniffing around Drymen in 1981; the village was small enough to have made it possible for the two of them to have bumped into each other. The story was that the ruthless Tiny Rowland, chief executive of Lonrho, the conglomerate bidding to take over the House of Fraser, had hired a detective to tail Sir Hugh Fraser, dissolute son of the chain's founder. Although Lonrho denied it, Fraser himself was in no doubt: 'I admit I was gambling again. I was losing heavily. I've got to hand it to that private eye. As an ex-CID man he did his job marvellously.' Having discovered that his friend Rowland, who he was backing in the takeover bid, so mistrusted him that he had a private detective on the case, he was promptly fired from the board of the House of Fraser for his disloyalty, an outcome that had been on the cards since the family lost their controlling interest in the company. He rejected an offer to become president, 'because I associate that title with an elder statesman and I don't think I am old enough yet'.

Unlike his distant neighbour in Drymen, Fraser had an easy relationship with journalists, seemed not to mind their prying, and confided in them. 'I have given up gambling for ever,' he declared, not for the first time. He disclosed that he had a new woman in his life and that they hoped to marry when their respective divorces went through; he had three daughters from his two previous marriages but longed to have a son to carry on the family name. He had promised her that he would stop visiting casinos: 'If I let her down I would be the biggest damn fool in the world.'

There had been an earlier new woman in his life, Lynda Taylor, a former air stewardess, and she too had briefly been 'the girl who stopped me gambling'. In March 1979 her body was found in her car in the garage of Fraser's house, Cattermuir Lodge; she had drawn a hose connected to the exhaust pipe into the car and sat there waiting to die. No convincing reason was ever given for her suicide. There was a suggestion that she had intended to end the relationship; her father believed that the couple had had a rift of some sort. But Fraser professed to be baffled; to him she had seemed fine. Cattermuir Lodge – renamed 'Heartbreak House' by the newspapers – was put up for sale and Sir Hugh moved to a spacious whitewashed cottage on the outskirts of the village, where he lived with his 18-year-old daughter Patricia, a 'strikingly pretty' horsewoman. She too was charming to the journalists who pestered her. 'I'm sure he will win at the end of the day and be chairman of the House of Fraser,' she predicted at the height of the takeover battle. She said she had never worked in any of her dad's stores; only in his shop in Drymen selling riding equipment.

The latest new woman in Fraser's life was revealed as Annabell Finlay, who was only six years older than Patricia, a teacher in the infant department of Glasgow High School and the only daughter of the late Andrew Murray, a House of Fraser executive. The newspapers reported that, although they had known each other since Annabell was a child, 'romance blossomed following a Variety Club ball in the Albany Hotel'. Fraser's memory of the night was that 'the two of us just hit it off as soon as we met'. When the news broke, the rector of the High School, confronted by a phalanx of reporters and photographers clamouring at the gates, was not best pleased. The media's day was saved by the quick thinking of pupils who held up a notice in a classroom window: 'She's up here'.

The affair was shortlived. Fraser would say only that he had made enough mistakes. He continued in business in a small way, buying an old-fashioned Glasgow department store (Paisley's), but the venture flopped. He never did become chairman of the House of Fraser again, and nor did he acquire a son and heir. In the spring of 1987 he felt unwell, went to hospital, and was diagnosed with lung cancer. When he was told that he did not have long to live, he returned to his elderly mother's house in Milngavie, where he stayed until the end. After his death at the age of 50, the Fraser trustees bought the island of Iona for the nation; Fraser himself had donated unobtrusively to many benevolent institutions. He was a weak man but a kind one. 'His plain Glasgow accent somehow made this vulnerable millionaire one of the people,' wrote the journalist Murray Ritchie. 'I cannot think of one person who disliked him.'

The conventional theory was that the bloated inheritance from his father, old Hugh, was not so much a blessing as a poisoned chalice. Old Hugh – Fraser of Allander – was hailed as 'the last great Scottish entrepreneur' and it would have been difficult for any son to follow him, far less a playboy who squandered millions on roulette and women. 'In the words of the old cliché,' said one obituary, 'we shall never see his like again'. In the words of the old cliché, we never did. Young Hugh never had it in him and the few who came later – entrepreneurs such as the steel man David Murray and the bus magnate Brian Souter – were lesser fry. Fraser was the sad remnant of an extinct breed: an anachronism in the impersonal world of the branch factory. The time was ripe for a new cliché.

PILGRIM'S FOOT

I

IN THE WEEK OF THE POPE'S VISIT TO SCOTLAND, THE BBC DISC jockey Jimmy Savile attracted the doting press to which he was accustomed when he 'dropped in on some old friends at the State Hospital, Carstairs' (the *Glasgow Herald*'s chummy description of the occasion) and the criminally insane inmates presented him with a garden gnome. 'It would do some politicians good to come and talk to the patients here,' preached the serial child abuser, though it was not until after his death 26 years later that 'Sir Jimmy' was exposed as one of the more prolific sexual offenders of modern times.

In the same week, a strike of workers at the Royal Edinburgh Hospital, a psychiatric institution, caused a shortage of linen for the patients – 600 of whom were over the age of 70 – and many were confined to bed naked. They risked cross-infection and food poisoning because of the walk-out by kitchen and laundry staff; refuse was not being collected, pigswill was said to be 'lying around'. Many other workers were idle that week, though not through choice. The jobless figure in Scotland fell slightly to 14.5%, a figure massaged by the Conservative government's youth opportunities programme, which employed 50,000 school-leavers on short-term work placements. The few permanent vacancies were keenly contested: in Kirkcaldy in the last week of May 1982, 401 teenagers applied for 13 building and horticultural apprenticeships with the council.

Seven weeks earlier, Margaret Thatcher, a friend of Jimmy Savile, had consigned a naval fleet to the Falkland Islands in order to repel an

Argentinian invasion. Nicholas Fairbairn claimed in a debate in the Scottish Grand Committee that there had been a reduction in crime in these seven weeks because 'people in Britain believe once again that we live in a great society and not an effete one'.

From behind a tenement block in north Glasgow, the police recovered the body of Ian Waddell, a prominent figure in the local underworld, whose main claim to notoriety was that, having been impeached by one of Fairbairn's clients, Patrick Meehan, for the murder of Rachel Ross, he was unexpectedly acquitted when he stood trial for the same crime after Meehan's release from prison. As the case has been extensively dealt with in an earlier chapter, there is no need to elaborate; it is enough to note that in the week of the Pope's visit, Waddell ended up in a shallow grave in Springburn.

None of these events, interesting enough in retrospect, particularly for the audacity of the two debauchers, detained the Scottish public unduly in a week when there was only one show in town. 'Until recently,' wrote the journalist Tom Shields, 'a visit by the Pope would have seemed too dangerous a proposition. These 40 hours will be a stern test of how far the Scottish community has overcome the pitfalls of its history.'

II

Two centuries earlier, in 1782, there were only 20 Roman Catholic communicants in the west of Scotland. By 1882 there were 200,000. By 1982 there were 600,000 – as well as a further 200,000 elsewhere in Scotland. These were the bare statistics underlying Tom Shields's timely reminder of the pitfalls of history.

The explosive growth in the Roman Catholic population as a result of Irish immigration created a potentially incendiary situation, especially in overcrowded Glasgow. A contributor to one of the city's newspapers protested in 1847 that the poverty-stricken Irish who were flooding into Glasgow in their tens of thousands were 'the most improvident, intemperate and unreasonable beings that exist on the face of the Earth'. The following year, the City Chamberlain urged that 'the strongest barriers be erected against immigrants'. In 1851 *The Bulwark* magazine, one of many anti-Catholic propaganda sheets, reported under the heading 'More nuns at Glasgow': 'We observe that eight young ladies in the full bloom of womanhood have been consigned to a living sepulchre at Glasgow. There are now 18 priests and two nunneries in that city and Popery seems determined, if possible, to erect one of her strongholds there.' But the immigrants and their Scots-born descendants hit back with propaganda sheets of their own. A paper called *The Exile* commented in 1884: 'It is amazing that in a city like Glasgow with such a large population there is not a single Catholic member on the council. This is sufficient to show the bigotry that exists in Glasgow and that Catholics require to depend entirely on themselves.'

The hostility intensified with the 1918 Education Act, which gave Catholics their own schools within the state system. At the height of the debate over separate education, the demagogues coalesced under an umbrella organisation known as Protestant Action, successfully contesting seats on the city councils of Glasgow and Edinburgh and putting thousands of supporters on the streets, sometimes with stones in hand. The Catholic thinker Father Anthony Ross, reflecting on these events many years later, believed it was the influence of the bishops and clergy that dissuaded the flock from retaliation and eventually earned the respect of less extreme elements in the Protestant community. Evidence in support of this generous evaluation of moderate Protestantism is hard to find. In 1923 the official voice of the Church of Scotland – its General Assembly – approved a report entitled 'The Menace of the Irish Race to Our Scottish Nationality'. It was the same word – 'menace' – that the popular newspapers, taking their cue from the Presbyterian Kirk, habitually used to characterise the social and economic problems supposedly posed by the newcomers.

In 1927 the Dundee journalist and controversialist George Malcolm Thomson unleashed a polemic exceeding even the Church of Scotland's vitriol. 'The first fact about the Scot,' he wrote, 'is that he is a man eclipsed. The Scots are a dying people. They are being replaced in their own country by a people alien in race, temperament and religion at a speed which is without parallel in history outside the era of the barbarian invasions.' He prophesied that by the 1980s the Scots would be reduced to the status of aborigines in their own land, in a Scotland which had become 'merely part of Greater Ireland'. In this apocalyptic vision, the cities and towns would have separate Irish and Scottish quarters and by 1981 – he was specific about the date – 'the slowly deepening irritation between the races' would erupt into open war and the English army would require to keep the peace.

Thomson's sentiments did him no harm professionally; well aware of his opinions, Leslie Mitchell (Lewis Grassic Gibbon) nevertheless dedicated the novel *Cloud Howe* to Thomson. Tom Gallagher, a Catholic historian, who met Thomson in the 1980s, said that the old man had recanted his anti-Irish opinions. He had also been shown up as a poor prophet. There were no ghettos of Irish and Scots, there was no open war, no need for military intervention. The mutual antagonism was of a relatively peaceful nature, finding its main expression in the sour encounters between the two footballing rivals, Protestant Rangers and Catholic Celtic. This state of 'relative harmony', as Tom Gallagher charitably described it, impressed such scholars of Scottish history as John McCaffrey of Glasgow University, who said that, given the latent possibilities for violent friction, it was surprising there had not been more of it. Tom Gallagher offered several explanations: that the political parties had not invoked the sectarian issue for electoral ends; that industry and commerce had not used religious affiliations to split and dominate their workforce; and that, though the Irish tended at first to live together in their own areas, Scotland had managed to avoid the spectre of Protestant and Catholic ghettos on the disastrous scale of Northern Ireland.

The editor of *The Exile*, who complained of the absence of Catholics in civic life, would have been delighted to know that a century later the Catholic community was playing a vigorous part in Scottish Labour politics. By 1982, 10 of Scotland's 71 MPs were believed to be Catholics, even if a few were lapsed; more than half the ruling Labour group on Glasgow Corporation were Catholics; the last three Lord Provosts of the city were Catholics. 'It is easy to see why people might assume there is some kind of Catholic mafia,' said Bailie John McQueenie, 'but it does not work that way.' Even the chairman of the Scottish Tories was a Catholic, an aristocratic one at that: Michael Ancram, son of the Marquis of Lothian. 'I am the first and only Scottish Conservative Catholic MP,' he confirmed, 'but that will soon change when Gerry Malone wins Hillhead.' (Malone, a *Sunday Times* journalist, did not win Hillhead. In the 1982 by-election in that constituency, the victor was Roy Jenkins, co-founder of the new and short-lived Social Democratic Party.)

There was another reason, less often discussed, for the assimilation of the Irish into modern Scotland. By 1976 a remarkable 49% of all Roman Catholic marriages in Scotland were 'mixed' – not between people of different ethnic origins as the word 'mixed' implied in some societies, but between partners of different faiths. Such unions of Catholics and Protestants often disclosed more about ingrained prejudice than any Old Firm football match. The archbishop of Glasgow, Tom Winning, testified that 'there are still many non-Catholics in Scotland who would rather see their kids dead than see them become a Catholic', adding that he knew of young people in mixed marriages who had been driven close to insanity by the attitudes of their families. But the old divisions were slowly breaking down: the ground that Pope John Paul II was expected to kiss on his arrival in Scotland was more malleable than it had ever been before.

III

But there was no embrace with the actual ground. When the papal flight touched down on 31 May 1982 at Turnhouse Airport, Edinburgh, one minute late at 5.25 pm, John Paul went straight to a grass verge for the traditional kissing ceremony.

The leader of the Scottish Catholic hierarchy, Cardinal Gordon Gray, a plain-spoken native of Leith, introduced him to the Lord Provost of Edinburgh, Tom Morgan, and then it was off by car through west Edinburgh to Murrayfield Stadium, headquarters of Scottish rugby, where 44,000 'ecstatic young Scots' received him as an idol. 'Young people of Scotland, I love you' were the Pope's first words. 'Enormous shouts of joy' constantly interrupted his address and there were repeated cries of 'John Paul, John Paul', rising to a level of hysteria which reminded a few jaundiced commentators of a Nuremberg rally. The Pope was reported to be so astonished by his reception that he departed from his script to extemporise, repeating his name in Italian, Polish and Spanish.

Among the 'Catholic youth of Scotland' – the term used by Cardinal Gray in his introduction – a 17-year-old harpist from Barra, Anne MacNeil, recited in Gaelic a song she had composed for the occasion. John Paul attempted a little Gaelic himself. But mostly the singing was spontaneous. 'He's got the whole world in his hands'. 'You'll never walk alone'. And, unavoidably, the unofficial national anthem, *Flower of Scotland*, last heard this lustily on the playing fields of Argentina, several years before the junta's misadventure in the Falkland Islands.

Just before 7 pm, he was driven from Murrayfield to the centre of Edinburgh. His destination was St Mary's Cathedral, where he would address 1,000 priests, monks and nuns. But halfway along Princes Street there was a controversial detour: the papal procession took a turn up the Mound to the home of the General Assembly of the Church of Scotland. Two hundred placard-carrying zealots led by the Reverend Ian Paisley demonstrated in front of the Assembly Hall and had to be prevented by police from breaking through the barriers. They threw eggs at the Pope's car and chanted anti-Catholic slogans. When three of the troublemakers appeared in court, Sheriff Neil Macvicar imposed fines and told them that they had brought the name of religion into disrepute.

Popes were for life; Moderators of the General Assembly (or 'Moderators of the Church of Scotland' as the media sometimes mistakenly referred to them) for only a year, signifying that the head of the church was not the Moderator, who was a mere chairman and ambassador, but Jesus Christ in perpetuity. Moderators being 10 a penny, exactly that number greeted the Pope in the quadrangle of New College, where the current holder of the office, the Right Reverend John McIntyre, did his teaching as professor of divinity at Edinburgh University; nine others, former Mods still in the land of the living, though a few only just, were present for what one observer described as 'the historic first meeting of a Pope and Moderator on Scottish soil, a reconciliation of 450 years of antipathy and sectarian warring'. The Reverend Henry Munroe, a bilious visitor to the correspondence columns of the newspapers, objected that the Moderators' wives curtsied before the Pope and that McIntyre addressed him as 'Your Holiness'. Munroe, an unreconstructed Calvinist from Dunipace, dismissed the concept of papal infallibility: 'The Pope is just a man.'

If the etiquette offended the vigilantes on the theological right of the Kirk, the Moderator's public words of welcome could hardly be faulted as a lesson in how to negotiate a minefield: 'From the spirit of reconciliation which informs our meeting today we, for our part, look forward to further dialogue with your Church not only on subjects of disagreement, but also on the joint themes on which we agree in the face of a hostile world.' At a press conference later, McIntyre praised John Paul as a man of peace who had redrawn the character of the papacy, but was careful to add that he understood why people were unhappy about the meeting. 'They are understandably afraid that the things for which the martyrs died should be lost. Nobody has ceded an inch on these basic points so far.'

The symbolic nature of the reconciliation was underlined by the Pope's defence of separate schooling on the grounds that education must support 'the spirit as well as the intellect', an implied rebuke for all those schools – the majority – which operated in the apparently heathen non-denominational sector. John Paul, a hardliner on doctrinal issues, offered the fathers and brethren of Scottish Presbyterianism no more than the hand of friendship. The media agreed that between Pope and Moderator the hand of friendship had been a firm one. But that was as far as it was ever likely to go.

The Pope slept that night in sedate Morningside, at the residence of Cardinal Gray and his Cairngorms terrier Rusty, whom the cardinal had considered boarding for the week until he thought better of it, in the end allowing Rusty to be photographed with the visitor. In the morning the Pope prepared to set off for Glasgow by helicopter for a vast gathering of the Catholic faithful in Bellahouston Park. It was the first day of June 1982, a day 'bathed in sublime sunlight' as one of the 300,000 worshippers recalled it. Michael Turnbull, a biographer of the Catholic Church, was a member of the papal choir. 'We were bussed through from Edinburgh early in the morning and the groups which had rehearsed separately in every Scottish diocese met together for the first time at Bellahouston, where we were assembled on a hastily-erected raked stand, all 850 of us.' Turnbull cherished the experience as 'a little glimpse of Heaven'.

If this was Heaven, it bore at least one uncomfortable resemblance to the other place. The attendees had been warned not to bring their cars, not to bring their dogs (Rusty stayed at home), not to bring alcohol, not to bring their sleeping bags. There was only one unofficial visitor overnight – a teenager with petrol and matches who failed in his ambition to set fire to the papal dais and was remanded in custody for the whole of the momentous day. But in preparing their list of do's and don'ts, the organisers had failed to plan for the most unlikely contingency: that, in Glasgow of all places, the weather would be as hot as Hell.

The crowd sweltered for up to 12 hours in soaring temperatures before the arrival of the helicopter; by the time it landed many of the men in the congregation were stripped to the waist, many of the women in bikini tops, many of the children in swimsuits. Hundreds needed medical treatment for sunstroke, nose-bleeds and faints. 'People are utterly exhausted by the heat,' said Dr Desmond Reilly, co-ordinator of medical services. 'So many people have blisters that we have dubbed it pilgrim's foot.' One four-week-old baby became ill from dehydration. An Edinburgh woman, Ellen McDermott, went into labour and later in the day gave birth to a daughter in the Southern General Hospital. Three heart-attacks were recorded. Other facts of the day were almost as impressive: the number of police on papal duty – 6,000, including 3,000 in the park itself; the number of volunteers – 7,000; the number of unofficial extras taking part in anti-papal demonstrations in George Square – 1,800.

Among the mementos, the 'Popescope', a small cardboard telescope, enjoyed a brisk trade as a visual accessory. In an act of civic vandalism which alienated many local inhabitants, 59 majestic trees in Bellahouston Park had been demolished in advance, again to enhance the viewing of the spectacle. For those viewing remotely, the BBC mounted, according to the producer David Martin, 'the biggest and most complex TV event ever organised in Scotland', requiring the services in the commentary box of Tom Fleming and David Dimbleby, two masters of gravitas, assisted by the more avuncular Donny B. MacLeod. One way and another it was a day of the big cast; a Hollywood biblical epic, Glasgow-style.

Viewed with the clarity of detachment, however, it was hard to see what the Pope's visit achieved. There was an uneasy parallel with the Billy Graham revivalist meetings of 1957, which seemed at the time to re-energise Protestant devotion in Scotland until it became painfully obvious that the influence of the Kirk was continuing to wither and that the pews were emptying fast. Similarly, in the Roman Catholic Church, there was a limit to the power of short-term charisma. A succession of sex scandals led to a debilitating loss of reputation, particularly with the long-delayed realisation that some were occurring beneath the noses of the Scottish hierarchy at the time of the papal visit.

The sun shone on John Paul. Outside the usual circle of fanatics, most of those who opposed his visit were icily polite about it. Scotland coped well enough with the 'pitfalls of history'. But the Popescope was never designed to give more than a partial and misleading view of Catholic life in Scotland, its circumscribed range failing to detect the private torments and cruelties not far from the surface. Its lens was essentially a distorting one.

IV

Perhaps the most remarkable thing about the visit was that it happened at all. The outbreak of war with Argentina made the timing unfortunate, to say the least, inevitably raising questions about the wisdom of going ahead with a papal tour of Britain while UK troops risked their lives in the Falkland Islands. On the day of the Mass in Bellahouston Park, the Argentinians were close to surrender in Port Stanley after grievous losses on both sides. John Paul dealt with the issue in an even-handed fashion, mourning the victims but drawing no distinction between the protagonists, awarding moral legitimacy to neither.

The president of the Scottish National Party, William Wolfe, was less even-handed. In two successive letters to the Church of Scotland's magazine, *Life and Work*, he criticised the appointment of a papal ambassador to Britain and referred to Argentina as a 'Catholic Fascist state' which had moved against a mainly Protestant group of islanders in the South Atlantic. By a piquant coincidence, the party's annual conference in Ayr had been scheduled for the weekend of pilgrim's foot, so there was no way of dodging the huge embarrassment of the president's intervention.

Wolfe, a rather decent man, had somehow survived with his standing in the party more or less intact despite a series of general election defeats at the hands of Labour's eccentric Old Etonian, Tam Dalyell, in a seat, West Lothian, which should have been winnable for the SNP. But there was seldom any hope of political recovery from a full-frontal attack on the Roman Catholic Church. A furious Gordon Wilson, the party chairman, opposed an attempt to allow Wolfe to chair a session at the conference and he was duly de-invited by a crushing 245 votes to 14. The national executive had already disowned his comments, in effect a vote of no confidence compelling him to withdraw from the annual presidential contest and allowing the MP for the Western Isles, Donald Stewart, to take his place unopposed. The party's imperious grand dame, Winifred Ewing, known as Madame Ecosse on account of her membership of the European Parliament, completed his humiliation with a speech blaming him for the loss of two council seats in South Uist 'because the Catholic population have got it into their heads that we are against Catholicism'. It was a sad end to Wolfe's many years of devoted service to the nationalist cause, as well as sobering proof that a politician who meddled in religion did so at risk to his reputation, if not necessarily to his immortal soul.

But the president's unaccountable rush of blood to the head was the least of the SNP's problems in Ayr. Metaphors about 'open warfare' – the trite currency of so much political reporting – sounded more insensitive than ever that weekend, but such was the fractious state of the party, the newspapers found them impossible to resist. Gordon Wilson, who had initially been fairly tolerant of the two troublesome fringe groups, the left-wing 79 Group in which Jim Sillars and Margo MacDonald were the prime movers, and the near-deranged Siol nan Gaidheal, decided that he had had enough of both of them – and of the more recent, anti-left, Campaign for Nationalism in Scotland. He staked his future in the party by putting to the vote a proposal to proscribe all fringe groups. Although the conference supported him by 308 votes to 188, the majority was too narrow to disguise the deep splits between right and left, moderate and radical, old guard and new.

Two of the party's elders were in especially venomous mood. Winifred Ewing, who had spoken little of her socialist (Independent Labour Party) roots since her reincarnation in Brussels as voice of the Highlands, was loudly cheered at a fringe meeting – at a point in the weekend when it was still constitutionally possible to attend such a meeting – for alleging that the 'leftward shift in the SNP' had caused a significant decline in membership. 'I am glad that it has all come out in public like this', she said, 'so that people can see what this group [the 79] is like. They were a boil that had to be lanced'. The venerable Robert McIntyre added that he mistrusted the 'conspiratorial element' in the 79 Group and suspected that they would continue to operate underground.

Jim Sillars, who could often be relied on for the neat phrase, claimed that 'the heather and haggis brigade' had won, while another 79 activist, Ron Wylie, the party's candidate in Coatbridge and Airdrie where a by-election was pending, likened the atmosphere at the conference to a Nuremberg rally. (That made two Nuremberg rallies in a week: the first inspired by His Holiness the Pope, the second presided over by Gordon Wilson, a chartered accountant from Dundee.)

The political journalist William Russell, witnessing the party's agonies from the relative safety of the press benches, wrote sympathetically of the 79 Group's 'inescapable political logic'. If, he argued, Labour was in its death throes in Scotland, the Labour voter had to look for a palatable alternative: 'Scotland is a socialist country and therefore a nationalist party offering a socialist alternative ought to stand a chance of real success.' His reflections were prophetic, viewed through the Popescope of the party's route to electoral success a quarter of a century later. But, as Russell was quick to acknowledge, such thoughts were anathema to Ewing, standard-bearer of the traditionalists, 'a European MP for an area of Scotland which does not have a socialist tradition'. The barbed innuendo was that Madame Ecosse had been motivated largely by self-interest.

For Sillars, the personal implications of the 1982 conference were dire. Not only was the 79 Group banned along with the others. The delegates had also voted, on their opening day at the seaside, to reject his crusade of civil disobedience, which they had embraced only a year before. He had prepared himself and his supporters for martyrdom; he had alerted them to the glad prospect of cell doors clanging behind them. But in the tangled prose of chairman Wilson, 'the great sweep towards that policy has evaporated'.

The crusade in its early stages had not been the spectacular success that Sillars, as convener of the demonstrations committee, was fond of boasting. He boldly took the credit for the decision of the UK Atomic Energy Authority to abandon a Galloway hill, Mullwharchar, as a possible site for the dumping of nuclear waste. 'No one could have doubted our intentions about Mullwharchar,' he said, 'and that is what led to an important victory.' The committee had threatened to occupy the site. But it was factually incorrect to claim that the SNP was wholly or even mainly responsible for the outcome; the local community, irrespective of party allegiance, as well as many environmental groups, had agitated long and tenaciously to save Mullwharchar, while the scientists from Harwell had done themselves no favours by sending to Scotland for exploratory tests a vehicle unsuited to the rough terrain, which got nowhere near the site, and retreated in defeat to the police compound in Ayr. It would have been just as accurate to claim that the UK Atomic Energy Authority was laughed out of town than that the SNP's threat of occupation convinced it of the error of its ways.

Jim Sillars further maintained that the committee had shown 'ability and discipline' in its occupation of the building on Calton Hill earmarked for the ill-fated Scottish Assembly. This triumph, too, was not all it was cracked up to be. The evidence in Edinburgh Sheriff Court, where Sillars and others went on trial on a charge of vandalising a property of the Department of the Environment, amused Sheriff Neil Macvicar – the same Macvicar who had dealt leniently with the more rabid opponents of the papal visit – into various irreverent interjections from the bench.

A security guard at the building, the former Royal High School, described how he found Sillars sitting on a chair in the debating chamber. He was nursing a cut in his hand, accidentally inflicted when members of the demonstrations committee smashed a window to gain access to the premises. Two other men were inside the building. All three had rucksacks containing sleeping bags, hammers, nails and putty, chocolate and packets of crisps. 'I asked him [Sillars] to leave and he complied immediately,' said the guard. 'I handed him over to the police.' The guard admitted he had read of SNP plans to break into the building and hoped the SNP was responsible and not the Tartan Army, which had made two armed raids on the premises. 'As far as I know, the SNP is non-violent,' he added. When he told the court that the chair on which the accused Sillars had been sitting was the Speaker's, Macvicar intervened: 'He wasn't wearing a full-bottomed wig or a crown, was he?'

The next witness, Detective Sergeant James Cowan, said it appeared that the men were 'preparing for a siege'. On chocolate and packets of crisps? Derek Bateman, reporting the case, noted that it was being conducted in 'an informal and sometimes light-hearted atmosphere' – unlike the Nuremberg rallies for which Scotland was now famed. When Sillars informed the sheriff that he, the sheriff, had to make a decision of the greatest constitutional importance, Macvicar responded: 'I have the feeling you should stop calling me My Lord and start calling me Your Majesty.' The constitutional issue in question, a rather arcane one, was whether the Criminal Justice (Scotland) Act under which Sillars and his co-accused were charged had been passed unlawfully. Macvicar said that a humble sheriff court was hardly the place to test such a question: 'It is not what we are designed for. There should be nine old men doing it. You are putting a very heavy burden on me.'

Once, when two young men came before him for causing a disturbance at a Hearts-Hibs football game, Macvicar had reminded them that football was only a game. 'Football only a game, claims sheriff' was the incredulous headline in the Edinburgh *Evening News* that night. Macvicar, a lover of poetry and all things Greek, adored giving parties and every February hosted one in fancy dress, with himself as the mad hatter. He died at the age of 90. Richard Holloway, giving the eulogy at his funeral, called him 'kindly', an assessment borne out by his handling of the Sillars trial in which he used gentle wit rather than a heavy hand to puncture the pretensions of the celebrity in the dock. He found Sillars and three of the others guilty of 'recklessly and without reasonable excuse breaking a window with an axe or similar instrument' and fined Sillars £100 and the others £50: about par for the course if they had been anti-papal demonstrators rather than crusaders for an independent Scotland. The case against a fourth accused, the party's research officer, was found not proven.

Funnier than a papal visit or an SNP conference, the trial was an unexpected delight. It deserved a longer run. But it left unresolved not only the constitutional question of the greatest importance, whatever it was, but the question of how smashing a window, and then sitting briefly in a deserted building with a cut hand until security appeared, involved 'ability and discipline'. Any of Nicholas Fairbairn's clients could have done it in their sleep – had they not been inspired by the Falklands war to give up their life of crime in the interests of a better, less effete Britain.

V

On the day of the great gathering in Bellahouston Park, the mother of a young man accused of murder was giving evidence at the High

Court in the same city. She told the jury that, while in custody awaiting trial, her son had written letter after letter disclaiming responsibility: 'He prays to God that the legal process will establish his innocence.' His prayer was answered – a quarter of a century later.

The case of Raymond Gilmour was a miscarriage of justice which reflected badly on the police, the Crown Office and the profession of forensic pathology. It was the thinnest of prosecutions – as the prosecution itself privately acknowledged – and the barest of majorities – eight-six in favour of conviction. But it was enough to send Gilmour to prison for 21 years for a crime he did not commit.

There is no transcript of the trial. When the Lord Justice Clerk, Lord Gill, exonerated Gilmour in 2007 he did so without the benefit of a verbatim account of the proceedings; in its absence, he had to rely on the summing-up of the trial judge (who was dead by then), statements from some of the principal parties, and intelligent supposition. He could also have referred, if he wished, to newspaper reports of the case, a poor substitute as we shall see.

The facts were these. On the afternoon of 4 November 1981, a 16-year-old girl, Pamela Hastie, was returning from school along a narrow path through Rannoch Wood in Johnstone, Renfrewshire. It was not unusual for Pamela to make her way home by this route and she had a particular reason for doing so; she was carrying out a nature study project for her school. St Cuthbert's High was one of those Roman Catholic secondaries that the Pope defended for their emphasis on the spirit as well as the intellect; and Pamela was a credit to it. She had earlier that day been made a prefect and was hurrying home to sew yellow braid on her blazer, denoting her new status. A classmate happened to look out of the window of his house and spotted her walking towards the wood alone, with no sign of anyone following her. A few minutes later, a short distance from her front door, she was set upon, raped, and strangled.

At first her parents Jimmy and Christine were unconcerned by her late arrival. She had a part-time job in a local cafe and they assumed she had gone there – until her absence could no longer be explained and they contacted the police. Early next morning, Sergeant John Ross discovered scuff marks along the path through the wood and a trail of clues, including one of Pamela's shoes and a scattering of school books from her satchel. About 40 yards from the path, he found her body covered with ferns.

The report of two forensic pathologists, Dr Walter Weir and Dr W.D.S. McLay, who conducted the post-mortem, filled scarcely more than one side of an A4 page. It concluded that Pamela was strangled with a rough piece of string, wound three times round her neck with extreme pressure, something that Weir testified in court he had never seen before. He described it as 'particularly ferocious'.

The police suspected Raymond Gilmour, 20, a local flasher well known to them, 'shy, inadequate and sexually disturbed' as Lord Gill came to refer to him. He lived with his mother near Rannoch Wood and regularly went there to masturbate and expose himself, sometimes to schoolgirls. He admitted that he had been in the wood the day before the murder, but he had an alibi for 4 November: he insisted he was at home all afternoon. The police raided the house and found pornographic magazines in his bedroom – magazines similar to ones found at the scene of the crime. In the wood they also found pornographic letters in his handwriting. Incriminating? The police thought so. But the discoveries proved nothing – except that a sexual exhibitionist was a frequent visitor to the wood and may have been in the habit of leaving stuff there.

A few days later, one of the pathologists – McLay – carefully examined Gilmour's hands for any sign of the frictional burning which would almost certainly have resulted from pulling tightly on rough string. There was none. In fact there was no forensic evidence of any kind: no blood, no hairs, no fibres on Gilmour linking him with the dead girl. McLay acknowledged that the absence of such evidence was 'surprising'; he would have expected it had Gilmour been the murderer.

Nevertheless the police convinced themselves that they had got their man. On 9 November, Gilmour was taken to Paisley police station and made the first of his confessions: 'I was masturbating as I didn't expect anyone to appear there or arrive. I think the next thing I realised was a girl whom I recognised but didn't know her name. I jumped on her because I thought she knew me. I knocked her down and fell on top of her. She was screaming and shouting. I tried to quieten her. I put my hands over her mouth. She kept shouting. I picked up a piece of branch lying on the ground and I hit her with it. I tried to have sex with her but I couldn't manage properly. I remember pulling on her tie or the strap of her bag or something slim, a belt or something. She calmed down quite a lot. I held the thing on her neck for a length of time, but I couldn't be specific.' The confession also included a statement that, after the murder, Gilmour got up and walked away.

All this was nonsensical. The police knew that Pamela had not been strangled with a tie or a strap from her bag. They knew that she had not been attacked with the branch of a tree. They knew that the attempt at sex had been all too successful; there were horrible injuries to prove it. They knew, too, that the murderer did not immediately leave the scene but that he dragged the body some distance.

The detective superintendent in charge of the case, James Brown, had left the interrogation in the hands of two of his officers. Later in the afternoon he looked at the confession and saw it for what it was worth – not much. He then questioned Gilmour himself. Could he describe her underwear? No. What was on her legs? White socks. What kind of shoes? Black. Pamela had been wearing tights, not white socks, and her shoes were grey, not black. Brown asked him if he was telling the truth in his confession. He replied: 'I didn't kill the girl. I only made it up to please the other police'. Brown asked him what he meant. 'I couldn't take any more questioning', he said. In evidence at his trial Gilmour alleged that it was violence – kicking, punching and jostling – and threats of violence that made him give a false confession. He provided a detailed account of an incident in a lift, just before the confession, in which Detective Sergeant Dennis Mair punched him in the stomach and then produced a cigar. 'They said they wanted to give me time to think about it and that he needed a cigar to keep calm'. Gilmour also alleged that Mair advised him to seek special protection in prison as it was likely that other prisoners would want to beat him up.

After the confession, Gilmour drew a sketch of the scene, marking with crosses the spot where he attacked Pamela. The prosecution made much of the sketch, claiming that it was proof of special knowledge. In successive attempts over the years to have the case reopened, it was suggested that Gilmour was able to draw it having seen a map of the crime scene which appeared in the *Evening Times* on 6 November 1981. This would have been a plausible explanation had anyone bothered to check the map in the newspaper, which gave only a general impression of Pamela's intended journey home from school. The more likely scenario was that Gilmour had more than enough time between the afternoon of the murder and his confession five days later to visit the scene and observe for himself where the police activity was concentrated.

Superintendent Brown decided that the confession was so riddled with inconsistencies and plain lies that he had no evidence to justify a charge and released Gilmour. In a statement when the case was being reviewed, he explained his reasoning – that in his experience criminals in their confessions were always able to describe accurately 'some intimate detail' pointing conclusively to their guilt; there was no such detail in Gilmour's case. Brown admitted not only that he was 'never happy' about the conviction but that he suspected that officers under his command had assaulted Gilmour.

Towards the end of January 1982, Gilmour was the only suspect who had not been eliminated from the inquiry. Brown, having failed to deliver, was taken off the case and replaced with another of the same rank, Charles Craig, assisted by a team of officers who were new to the case, though with one exception – the cigar-smoking Mair. Craig was acutely aware that in the absence of any forensic evidence a second confession was his best if not only hope, and after a fortnight he obtained one. Brown was dubious: 'It is not my place to comment on the conduct of other officers', he wrote later, 'but it seemed too convenient that Gilmour confessed so soon after a new team took over the case'. Gilmour claimed that, before the second confession, a detective inspector named Corrie threatened him with violence.

This time the police did charge him, and a tragedy of false accusation and wrongful imprisonment began to unfold. The second confession was no more credible than the first. Relying on titbits of misinformation he had picked up from press reports – including the erroneous claim that Pamela had been 'battered to death with a blunt instrument' – Gilmour returned to the theme that he had attacked her two or three times with the branch of a tree. There was still no mention of the rough string actually used to kill her and, equally significantly, no suggestion that he had cut her fingers and may have used a knife to do so. The injuries to Pamela's fingers were noted by Weir and McLay in their post-mortem report, but neither attached any special significance to them and the trial judge, Dunpark, failed to mention them in his summing-up. Were they discussed at all during the trial? Lord Gill, in his appeal judgement in 2007, 'assumed' the jury was told of the cuts – the law of Scotland was now reduced to assumption – but in the absence of a transcript there could be no certainty about this matter or several others of relevance.

After an interval of more than 20 years, when the Scottish Criminal Cases Review Commission started to take an interest in the case, two distinguished forensic scientists – Professor Anthony Busuttil of Edinburgh University and Professor Peter Vanezis of Glasgow University – re-examined the post-mortem report at the request of the defence. Their conclusions were damning. They described the work of Weir and McLay as 'perfunctory and lacking in the detail to be expected from such a report'; Lord Gill agreed, accusing both doctors of a lack of professionalism. Busuttil and Vanezis were particularly critical of their dismissal of the cuts to the fingers, which they regarded as 'consistent with the deceased having attempted to ward off blows with a sharp pointed instrument such as a knife'. The jury, had it known that a knife was involved, would have been entitled to wonder why Gilmour made no mention of it in either of his so-called confessions. He made no mention of it because he knew nothing about it – just as the jury knew nothing about it.

Likewise, the jury was not told of Brown's suspicion – which he confided to the procurator fiscal before the trial – that Gilmour had been beaten up in Paisley police station. Brown should have been asked in court what grounds he had for this allegation, a material fact strongly to the advantage of the accused. It seems he was not asked; and nor did he volunteer the information. The Crown Office was also aware of the allegation that Mair, before the first confession, had attempted to frighten Gilmour by warning him that he would require protection in prison; the same procurator fiscal had flagged it up in a report to his superiors six months before the trial. Again the jury was kept in ignorance.

In 1993 and again the following year, Gilmour petitioned the Secretary of State for Scotland, Malcolm Rifkind, to have the case referred back to the appeal court (which had originally refused an appeal 18 months after the trial). Although the disgraceful conduct of the police was known to the Crown Office, and had been since the start, Rifkind – an advocate by profession; a Queen's Counsel – refused both applications. Gilmour was finally released in 2002, reverted immediately to form, and was sent back to prison for indecently exposing himself. Whether this vulnerable individual ever received psychiatric help – in prison or out of it – is unknown. Five years later, on the instigation of the Scottish Criminal Cases Review Commission, he was finally cleared of Pamela Hastie's murder. In the same year, St Cuthbert's Roman Catholic High School closed because of falling numbers. Had she lived, one of its former pupils would have been 42 years old.

A few months after he gave his post-mortem findings to a High Court jury, Dr Walter Weir received a pleasant surprise: the Queen rewarded him with an OBE for 'services to forensic pathology'. He died unexpectedly in 1986, while Gilmour was still in the early years of his long sentence. The *British Medical Journal* paid Weir a handsome tribute, remarking that his wise advice as an expert witness was eagerly solicited throughout Scotland. His colleague, the much-initialled McLay, in his brief biography for a scientific textbook to which he contributed, gave his address as Strathclyde Police Headquarters, Pitt Street, Glasgow, where he was employed as chief medical officer of the constabulary which investigated Pamela Hastie's murder. Before he was done he too received a gong (OBE again).

Christine, mother of the dead girl, found over the years that her religious faith helped her a great deal and that she was able to forgive 'whoever did this thing to my daughter'. She added that her husband Jimmy 'doesn't like to talk about it'. Before Christine Hastie's death in 2011, there were rumours in the press that Pamela may have been murdered by a serial killer of women, Peter Tobin, who was born in Johnstone and knew the area well. Was he, perhaps, the hooded figure who was seen running from the wood on the afternoon of the murder but never sought by the police?

1983

FORGIVENESS

I

WHEN JAMES NELSON WENT AS A MATURE STUDENT TO ST ANDREWS University to study divinity, it was with the intention of becoming a minister of the Church of Scotland, a vocation to which he believed God was calling him. He was a dedicated scholar and preached from several local pulpits, so it came as no surprise to those who knew him that he applied to be a candidate for the ministry as soon as he graduated.

In the Presbyterian system of church government, candidates required the blessing of their home presbytery – St Andrews in this case – and the presbytery was then responsible for supervising their progress through trials. The outcome of Nelson's application was a foregone conclusion. He enjoyed the patronage of several powerful figures in the Kirk, including the theologian Professor James Whyte, who had been one of his university teachers. He was welcomed into the fold without a single dissenting voice.

Two years on, in the autumn of 1983, he was well on his way to being licensed as a minister when a sensational story broke in the press: James Nelson was exposed as a murderer. Fourteen years earlier, he had been found guilty at the High Court in Glasgow of battering his mother to death and sentenced to life imprisonment. After 10 years in prison, he was not long released when, answering the call from above, he offered his services to the church. These salient facts were unknown to members of St Andrews Presbytery when they endorsed his candidature – unknown because his patrons had decided that Nelson's past should be kept a tightly guarded secret. The small circle of conspirators included presbytery office-bearers, one or two officials at Kirk headquarters in Edinburgh and a few senior academics at the university. Nelson himself claimed later that he had been uneasy about the lack of transparency: 'My instinct was to breach the confidence from the word go. I was persuaded it would not be in the best interests of the church, the university or myself.'

The deception strained Christian charity to its limits. Many of those who had in good faith endorsed him felt betrayed. Some expressed their displeasure openly, demanding that the question of his candidature should be re-visited. Malcolm Black, an elder (lay officer) of the church in St Andrews where Nelson was to be assigned as assistant minister on the completion of his trials, led the opposition. He wrote letters of protest to the press and got in touch with Nelson's estranged father. 'There have been occasions,' said Nelson, 'when I have been a little disappointed and hurt as a result of the positions taken by some people.' But he remained hopeful that the presbytery would reaffirm its earlier decision and that he would be allowed to continue his preparations for the ministry.

When the issue came to be debated, Nelson and his supporters were shocked by the outcome. The presbytery narrowly approved a motion by Norman Warnock, an elder of conservative opinions, to reject his candidature. 'I feel particularly bitter about the meetings in October 1981 when we should have been given the basic facts,' said Warnock. 'Mr Nelson was accepted unanimously as a student, but I, for one, would not have voted for him had I known the facts. If the Yorkshire Ripper repents, is he eligible on theological grounds to be a minister of the Church of Scotland?' He was supported by the presbytery clerk, the Reverend John Patterson, who regretted with hindsight that he had agreed to the secrecy over the candidate's background. Patterson's change of heart may have been influenced by his position at the sharp end of the many objections, not only from Nelson's father and individual members of the Kirk but from other presbyteries. It was unusual for presbyteries to meddle in each other's business; in this case no fewer than 14 had done so – all of them opposed to Nelson's ministry.

It was left to his minister, the Reverend Lawson Brown, to make a plea for compassion: 'We are talking about the man for whom we have pastoral care. Is there nothing we can do to show to this man whose name is being bandied about all over Scotland that his own presbytery has not reneged on its decision?' By a single vote – 43 to 42 after the initial vote produced a tie – the Presbytery did renege – if renege was an appropriate word to use against a body so badly deceived. A wounded James Whyte, who had stood resolutely behind his former student, announced that he intended to lodge a formal complaint with the General Assembly about 'this matter of great controversy and bitterness within the Kirk'.

The bitterness was not without justification: Whyte, a man much respected, even revered, had been a party to the deception. The presbytery had in effect been lied to about Nelson. But the disingenuousness of the procedure to admit him as a candidate, and the graceless reluctance of his supporters to apologise for their folly, were not the only issues in the case. There was the question, theologically contentious and endlessly debated, of a murderer's fitness to be a minister. And there was the related question of repentance – the degree and quality of the repentance – which proved to be the most perplexing of all and, ultimately, the most damning.

Had James Nelson genuinely repented? And if he had not, what was he doing as a candidate for the ministry?

His trial for murder in 1969 yielded disturbing clues to his character. The jury heard of his unhappy, frustrated childhood in Garrowhill, Lanarkshire, as the only son of a strict church-going couple, of rows with his domineering mother and authoritarian father, whom he regarded as a classic Calvinist. He left school at the age of 15 and for a while worked in his father's joinery firm, continuing to live with his parents while longing to escape from their disapproving shadow. He got a clerical job with a trade organisation, the Scottish Road Haulage Association, which paid better – though not well enough to finance his hedonistic lifestyle. His father viewed him with contempt: 'He always wanted to be a big person, big Jim, who was a big show-off with his flashy cars, doing things I didn't like.' He wondered how Jim could afford to finance his latest purchase, a Jaguar, or repay overdue income tax amounting to hundreds of pounds. His mother nagged him ceaselessly about his laziness in the home and about his new girlfriend. But by the age of 24 Jim was still not living independently. Instead he went on enduring the taunts.

On the night of his mother's death, he shared an early dinner with the family before going out around 6.30 for a date with his girlfriend. His father and sister also had an appointment – at a local church where Nelson's father, Robert, was the organist. Elizabeth Nelson was left alone in the house. When her husband and daughter arrived back from choir practice several hours later, they found a trail of blood leading from the house to the garage, and in the garage they found the body of Mrs Nelson.

Nelson's story was that, when he returned home from the date, his mother mounted a tirade about the girlfriend, denouncing her as 'a dirty whore to keep you out till these hours', although it was only 10 o'clock. (Later he was to make a claim that he did not make at the trial: that he had told his mother of his intention to marry the girlfriend and that this had provoked Mrs Nelson's fury.) Nelson sat on a chair reserved for his mother and was told to 'get the hell out of it'. He retreated with a cup of coffee to the kitchen for a respite from the vicious monologue. 'Some outside force' – he was never more specific – motivated him to go into the hall and pick up a police baton which had belonged to his grandfather. He took it with him back to the living room, hit his mother over the head with it, and went on hitting her until the baton broke in his hands and she fell dead to the floor. He denied dragging her body to the garage in an attempt to deceive the police into thinking that someone else had assaulted her; he claimed that he had moved it in order to 'reduce the shock' awaiting his father and sister. Nelson washed, changed his clothes, packed a holdall and put £25 of his father's money in his wallet: these were the actions of a man with self-preservation, rather than consideration for others, as his primary concern. He fled only as far as Glasgow before deciding to drive home and confess his crime.

According to Stewart Lamont, the broadcaster and journalist who revealed Nelson's past to an astonished Kirk, Nelson cultivated a reputation as something of a hard man in prison. Lamont – a Church of Scotland minister himself, though not a practising one at the time – had encountered Nelson during the making of a programme in Saughton Prison in Edinburgh. But by 1983, the hard man had developed a softer public image and was resorting to cod psychology to explain the brutal murder of his mother: 'It is not just enough to say I am sorry. There is something more powerful than that. I am still surprised at what happened. I ask myself, "Did this really happen?" Rationally, I look back to see it was almost inevitable, because one does not suffer total subjugation for 20 years without some climax. All our lives are intertwined in some way. Our errors, mistakes and successes are intertwined in one huge canvas and the only person who has a proper perspective is the artist.' Whatever else this was, it was not an expression of repentance, yet some were impressed, even moved, by the self-justification of a man who regarded the murder of his mother as 'almost inevitable' and who pleaded diminished responsibility on the grounds that some mysterious 'outside force' had been to blame.

The next stage in James Nelson's spiritual journey was the General Assembly, the highest court in the Church of Scotland, which had the power to overturn the decision of St Andrews Presbytery and sanction his continued candidature. On the eve of the debate, Stewart Lamont made his own preference clear: he wrote that it would 'take a cool head not to react bitterly if he is rejected by the Kirk'. Rejection was, however, a distinct possibility. After months of intense disagreements and personal antagonisms publicly ventilated, the result was difficult to predict. Whatever the outcome, this much could be said about the Nelson affair: it had engaged the wider public of Scotland as no other business of the Christian church had done in years; it had stimulated discussion on such fundamental issues as sin, forgiveness and the nature of repentance. Having moaned repeatedly to the BBC about its limited television coverage of the General Assembly, the Kirk took the perverse decision to ban the broadcasters from bringing a compelling debate into Scottish homes.

Members and spectators blocked the entrances of the Assembly Hall and packed the aisles when Nelson stepped forward to argue his case for the first time in public. The Moderator, the Right Reverend John Paterson (not the John Patterson of St Andrews Presbytery), had warned at the start of the three-hour session that there should be no applause or interruptions. Nelson, speaking in a firm voice, was heard in complete silence as he read from a prepared speech: 'I stand before you utterly convinced that God is calling me to preach the Gospel in the ministry of the church to which I have belonged all my life.' Responding to the repeated claims of his father, he said only that he had 'repented of my crime and repent of it still', which was the least that might have been expected of him. He added that he was still willing to be reconciled to 'a member of my family' – the nearest he came to identifying his father – but that he would not be drawn into 'a battle of words which would surely injure him more than it would me'.

There was another telling passage in which Nelson dealt with a suggestion from opponents that accepting him into the church would, as he put it, 'open the floodgates so that people such as homosexuals, rapists and lesbians would flock into the ministry'. He went on to argue that these attitudes encouraged the Presbytery to treat him as an object rather than as an individual with 'a unique set of circumstances'. He might have been challenged to say whether he believed that gay people also had a right not to be objectified, a right not to be stereotyped in the same breath as rapists – but Scotland's Christian representatives heard the offensive comment without protest.

They were less minded to tolerate the speech of a former presbytery clerk in Paisley, the Reverend William Bell, when he got hot under the dog-collar about the 'ruthless and reprehensible' manipulation of St Andrews Presbytery. 'In their heart of hearts,' said Bell, 'they [those who shared Nelson's secret] knew this candidate was totally unsuitable for . . .'. The rest of the sentence was drowned out by a communal hiss, which the Assembly always did rather well. It was the only moment of spontaneous dissent.

The turning point in the debate came with the speech of a former Moderator, the Very Reverend James Matheson, a gently persuasive Hebridean who had been aligned to as many denominations as Jim Sillars had had political parties (three apiece). 'When we put our trust in God,' said Matheson, 'God regenerates us anew – new birth, new creation, a new man. The other part of us is written off and we are set at liberty with the future God has for us.' The New Testament message of forgiveness and unqualified redemption preached by Matheson won the day: the Assembly voted by 622 votes to 425 to accept James Nelson into the ministry. In the same session it decided that a former bank manager who had served two and a half years in prison for embezzling the funds was also fit to be a minister, but that a minister near Falkirk who employed 'a Roman Catholic style of worship' was not; by the end of the busy afternoon the murderer and the embezzler were in, the heretic was out.

Nelson and his wife Georgina, a fellow divinity student at St Andrews, were swamped by a media scrum as they struggled to leave the hall, and the business of the Assembly was briefly suspended to allow order to be restored. Nelson said he was delighted that the Church of Scotland had 'confirmed that it believes the Gospel it preaches'; his wife added that the Assembly had come to 'the Christian decision'. The *Glasgow Herald*, which had brought the case to the public notice, applauded the decision, claiming that it was a fine example of 'the forgiving nature of the Kirk'. The paper pointed out that Nelson's opponents had argued that the case had nothing to do with forgiveness, but was about his suitability as a ministerial candidate. 'Yet it is hard to sustain that argument when there seems to be so little doubt about either the reality of his repentance or the suitability of his personal qualities.'

So little doubt? Robert Nelson predicted in a television interview immediately after the vote that the church would come to regret its decision: 'I am in no doubt that he has not repented, no doubt at all. I am not bitter. I am sad. I am sad for the church, because they will find out one day.' Despite his entrenched position, within 24 hours there was an ill-advised move to bring father and son together at 'a secret rendezvous' (a Glasgow hotel). The meeting was a mistake. 'It is correct to forgive,' said the father. 'I know that. But I cannot say anything simply to please the press or anyone else.' Nelson said: 'I saw that my father was approaching our disagreements in a certain way. I realised there was no possibility of effecting a reconciliation at this meeting.' Or ever, as it happened.

But it was possible to arrive at a reasonable view of James Nelson without relying on the testimony of the two surviving victims: his father and his sister, Anne, who 'started to see him for what he really was'. There was the incriminating testimony of Nelson himself. His friends in the church and the press chose to turn a blind eye to his capacity for self-delusion. He criticised the conduct of his trial, claiming that 'the profundity of some areas' had not been explored, that the jury had not been aware of 'the complete situation' and that the murder had been 'explicable, always explicable'. He believed that, in an exercise of leniency which would have been unique in the annals of Scottish justice, the judge should have sent him home and instructed him to sin no more. On another occasion he said he had forgiven himself – 'because I came to realise the universality of forgiveness'. And then, in an interview for the BBC in 1993, the guard dropped completely. He admitted that he felt 'no great remorse or anything like that' for his crime and added that he could just as easily have killed his father instead.

By then the Reverend James Nelson was in the seventh year of his one and only ministry, in the parish of Chapelhall and Calderbank in his native Lanarkshire, not far from the scene of his mother's murder. His marriage ended in divorce in 1997 and the following year he re-married a divorcee in his congregation. When he died in 2005 at the age of 60, the obituaries were subdued. Later, outside the timescale of this book, the Church of Scotland showed less willingness to allow gay people into the ministry than it did for admitting its first and, to date, only convicted murderer.

II

Despite its preoccupation with personal morality, the 1983 General Assembly found time to clarify its policy on a larger question: the future of the nuclear arsenal in the Clyde. For many years it had listened to an annual speech from the pacifist voice of the Kirk, the Very Reverend George MacLeod, advocating unilateral nuclear dis-armament. Even when his oratorical power deserted him in old age and he began to ramble, MacLeod had many admirers – though few converted into supporters. Year after year the Church of Scotland rejected the unilateral case which he espoused so tenaciously.

In the early 1980s, a familiar argument was re-energised by the proposal of the British government to replace the Polaris submarines off Faslane with the more powerful Trident missile system. The 1981 Assembly called on Margaret Thatcher's administration not to proceed with Trident – an entreaty doomed to fall on the deafest of prime ministerial ears. In 1983 the church announced as its official view that 'nuclear arms, including the readiness to use them, are by their nature morally and theologically wrong'. This declaration, which came to represent its 'consistent position', fell short of unilateralism and its political influence was negligible, perhaps even counter-productive. In the same month the Labour Party included a commitment to cancel Trident in its manifesto for the general election, a document described by one commentator as the longest suicide note in political history. The party under Michael Foot's left-wing leadership went down to a heavy defeat.

Post-Falklands jingoism, on the back of which Margaret Thatcher swept to her second successive victory, was noticeably less pronounced north of the border, particularly in the west of Scotland where the population lived with weapons of mass destruction on their doorstep. Their votes counted for little in the year of an English Conservative landslide, and the anti-nuclear campaigners who maintained a 'peace camp' close to the naval base seemed to be whistling in an icier wind than ever.

But then they found an unlikely ally – on the Scottish bench of all places. Two of the protesters left the dock of Dumbarton Sheriff Court, one after the other, having heard expressions of judicial sympathy. When a young man called James Rae pleaded guilty to causing a breach of the peace by obstructing the highway outside the Faslane base, Sheriff David Kelbie admonished him with the words: 'I appreciate and accept the sincerity of the views you hold. I can't deny a certain admiration of people prepared to behave in this way and who are prepared to accept the consequences of putting their views forward.'

Next came Leo Robertson, also of the peace camp. He told the court: 'War is a crime against humanity. I cannot in all sincerity accept your unjust laws. The people who use Trident and Cruise are the real criminals.' The loud applause which greeted these remarks would normally have incurred the wrath of the bench. Instead Kelbie nodded approval: 'There is very little you say with which I would disagree.' He admonished Robertson for breaching the peace, fined him £15 for breaching his bail conditions and asked if he wanted time to pay. 'I don't intend to pay the fine at all,' Robertson replied. Kelbie had no choice but to impose the alternative sanction of seven days' imprisonment, whereupon the accused's supporters began singing anti-war songs from the public benches. That night, 11 of them held a vigil outside the gates of Low Moss Prison, near Bishopbriggs.

By the following morning the obscure sheriff was in need of a vigil himself. Overnight he had become a target of the Conservative Party, whose Scottish chairman, Michael Ancram, was demanding an 'investigation' into Kelbie's conduct. It was the default position of politicians with a few cheap headlines in their sights. But what Ancram had in mind for a fellow member of the Scottish Bar was more threatening than the usual publicity-seeking ploy. He wrote to the Secretary of State for Scotland, George Younger, calling for a joint inquiry by the Lord President of the Court of Session and the Lord Justice Clerk to decide if Kelbie was a suitable person 'to continue to hold the office of sheriff'.

Only one sheriff had been removed from office during the twentieth century. Was Ancram seriously proposing that Kelbie's minor offence, if it was an offence, qualified him to be the second? 'I believe that the reported statements of Sheriff Kelbie warrant such action on your part,' he informed Younger, 'if only for the assurance of the public. While he may legitimately hold these views, to express such a political view while in court in what was undoubtedly a difficult and delicate case is in my view contrary to his judicial and therefore unbiased status. Moreover it can and may well be taken as encouraging a course of behaviour which is criminal, a motive which is wholly inappropriate to someone holding judicial office.' Ancram urged the Secretary of State to invoke his powers under the Sheriff Courts (Scotland) Act to establish whether the sheriff's remarks amounted to 'misbehaviour' – a sufficient cause for dismissal. The public took a more lenient view, giving Ancram's posturing the reception it deserved in the letters pages. Francis Middleton, a retired sheriff in Glasgow, accused him of coming 'very close to murmuring a judge' – a legal term meaning slander, which, if pursued, might have landed

Ancram in Low Moss Prison, and without benefit of a vigil in his honour.

Bill Heaney, editor of the *Lennox Herald*, the local paper covering Dumbarton Sheriff Court, weighed into the debate with a letter which destroyed Ancram's credibility as an arbiter of judicial misbehaviour. Unlike the others who had given so freely of their opinions, Heaney had been in court and observed Kelbie's performance at first hand. He said that, although the sheriff had expressed sympathy, even admiration, for the peace people, he had also made it clear that he could in no way condone what they had done and that it was his job to uphold the law. Before shooting from the hip, Ancram could have spoken to Heaney or Kelbie. Instead he chose to rely on perfunctory press reports which disregarded the sheriff's essential qualification.

There was no investigation. Younger said he would ask Kelbie's immediate boss, the sheriff principal, to 'look into the matter internally'. Nothing more was heard. Precious little was heard of Ancram either – he advanced no further than a middle-ranking job at that well-known graveyard of political ambition, the Northern Ireland Office – but David Kelbie, then 38 years old, a native of Aberdeenshire, one of the few beards on the Scottish bench, went on to greater prominence.

Later in 1983 an unusual public inquiry began into the development of Coulport, in the Rosneath peninsula, as the loading and storage base for the Trident missiles. It was called by Strathclyde Regional Council and chaired by Professor John Reid, an academic at Glasgow University. The main interested party, the Ministry of Defence, declined to be represented or examined and was obstructive at every turn. Of the 112 submissions, almost all were opposed to the scheme, making it possibly the most one-sided public inquiry in history. And despite an angry consensus of opposition to Trident – from the Scottish Trades Union Congress, the Labour Party and the SNP, as well as the Church of Scotland – the number in the public gallery never exceeded 20. Even the peace-campers who had filled the public benches of Kelbie's court found it too boring to tolerate for more than a few hours.

One of the first witnesses, Ivy Sutherland, a local resident, spoke emotionally of the environmental and human impact of siting nuclear weapons on the Clyde. She described how the freedom of local people had been eroded since the arrival of the Polaris submarines in 1968: 'We have seen acre after acre of land disappearing behind chain-link fences, we have seen favourite picnic sites, beaches, even a glacial relic – the biggest free-standing stone on the peninsula – become part of an area declared out of bounds'. Recently, she said, sailing had become another victim. A few days earlier, a police boat had approached the Cove Sailing Club's regatta and ordered it to clear off because naval exercises were taking place. Mrs Sutherland claimed that anonymous notetakers attended public meetings and took a record of those who voiced objections. 'The very idea of this coming here scares me,' she admitted. 'We have contributed enough to the national defence.'

On the second day, the convener of planning at Dumbarton District Council, Councillor Ian Leitch, challenged the official secrecy over the type and quantity of missile fuel to be stored at Coulport, arguing that such information should be made public to allay fears over safety. 'A blanket security is used to cover incompetence and inefficiency and is designed to keep the British public in a state of ignorance,' said Leitch. Chairman Reid disagreed: 'We have to tolerate a good deal of secrecy in the national interest on the grounds that intelligence of this sort can be used in an obstructive way by people of evil intent. That is a price I am willing to pay.' Leitch: 'Maybe I am absolutely naive, but I believe in giving freedom a chance.' Reid: 'I am not so optimistic.'

Next the inquiry heard from a firm of consultants who had been commissioned by the council to assess potential hazards. 'In view of the Ministry of Defence's refusal to subject their safety procedures to independent scrutiny,' they reported, 'we can only deduce that they have no particular policy or awareness.'

On the third day, the inquiry continued with a visit to the peninsula. A bus full of Strathclyde personnel parked in Coulport's naval car park and was promptly instructed by the ministry's police to move on. 'Are you with them?' a policeman asked one of the delegation, pointing to members of the Faslane peace camp who had come to welcome the bus. 'No,' said a man from the council. The assurance made no difference: the delegation was told to rejoin the bus: all but Reid, who never left it. The driver then made two attempts to negotiate the steep incline to Garelochhead, before he finally took a successful run at it.

On the fourth day, a local minister, the Reverend Ralph Smith, referred to the moral dilemma facing workers at the base. Likening those who took jobs at Coulport to the gas man at Belsen concentration camp who protested that he was only doing his job and was then hanged as a war criminal, he acknowledged that, although nuclear deterrence was offensive to the Christian conscience, it might be the only employment available. 'Society should not place so many people in this predicament,' said the minister. 'It should find ways of investing money for peaceful purposes.' A 19-year-old student of politics, Jane Vassie, testified on behalf of Helensburgh CND. She claimed that areas built specially for the incoming population had become ghettos: 'They make up a large section of the community, but contribute very little to it. They appear to have neither commitment nor responsibility to our town.'

On the fifth and final day, two scientists disagreed on whether the absence of missile bases would make the Strathclyde area any safer in the event of nuclear war. Granville Blackburn, an independent consultant, said the result would be catastrophic either way and forecast an immediate death toll of one million and a doubling of that figure through the effects of radioactive fallout. Alan Longman, representing a group called Scientists against Nuclear Arms, maintained that the presence of Trident missiles at Coulport would make the site a 'Time Urgent Target', one that an enemy would attack at once. He said that a missile exploded at the mouth of Loch Long would create a five-megaton water burst, sending a tidal surge up the loch and sweeping away everything in its path. Its rumble would be heard many miles away, presaging death on a colossal scale.

When Reid's report came to no firm conclusions, it was dismissed by Conservative members of Strathclyde Regional Council as a waste of time and money. With no classified information to work with, it yielded nothing not already in the public domain; faced with the intransigence of the Ministry of Defence, it was hobbled from the start. But as a public relations exercise it had its uses. The people of Scotland now knew what they might not have known before: that in a nuclear bunker uncomfortably close to home, many warheads would be stored, each with a power eight and a half times the force of the bomb dropped on Hiroshima.

The opposition of the trade unions, the main Christian denomination and two major political parties, together representing a decisive majority of the Scottish population, counted for nothing. The once-peaceful Rosneath peninsula had yet more to contribute to the national defence: eight years later Trident became operational on the Clyde.

III

In the absence of an ominous rumble from the other side of the country, Edinburgh relied on the daily ritual of the One O'Clock Gun to keep it approximately alert. Alastair Dunnett, the former editor of the *Scotsman*, despaired of its complacency. 'The greatest single handicap to Scotland in her present predicament,' he wrote, 'is that Edinburgh has quite forgotten how to act like a capital.' He admitted that, in the 30 years he had lived there, he could not recall a single practical stroke of civic imagination. He feared that

Edinburgh was in terminal decline, citing the 'blasphemy in Princes Street, with some gallant old businesses struggling to survive in a cheapjack thoroughfare of shoddy goods' and the indifference of its leaders to the responsibility of hosting the annual festival. 'We don't need the Festival,' Dunnett was repeatedly told. 'August is our busy time anyway.'

Dunnett recalled how he used to pay a courtesy call on the new Lord Provost, whoever he – it was always a he – might be. 'How would you like your lord provostship to be remembered?' he would ask. 'One of these new incumbents treated this question gravely. He rose silently from his chair and walked over to the window which has that marvellous prospect to the north across the gardens and Princes Street, and after pondering long, he answered: "I should like to be remembered as the Lord Provost who solved the parking problem". This seemed to me a fair summing up of the current state of thinking.'

Glasgow, in contrast, was fortunate to have as its Lord Provost the energetic Michael Kelly, who sensed an urgent need to improve the desperate perception of his city. In partnership with an advertising executive, John Struthers, who had been inspired by New York's successful rebranding, Kelly spearheaded an advertising campaign with the slogan 'Glasgow's Miles Better'. The campaign featured Mr Happy, a cartoon character from a children's book, who was improbably adopted as an honorary Glaswegian with the blessing of his creator, Roger Hargreaves. Kelly had to work hard to persuade his colleagues to stump up cash for the campaign; it was only when he managed to secure initial funding from the city's private sector that the council agreed to match it.

Miles better than what, though? It was an example of what the advertising industry called a 'null comparative', in which the starting point for comparison was left unstated; it was in the same vague category as, say, 'Our burgers have more flavour'. Kelly, when pressed to state in what way Glasgow was miles better, would reply that it was miles better than it used to be. 'There was a time when the description of a tourist here was someone who was lost,' he would add wittily.

But the breezy assurance that it was miles better than it used to be owed more to Michael Kelly's optimism than to the reality of life for the majority. While Kelly and Struthers were preparing to reveal Mr Happy as Glasgow's smiley new mascot, a BBC documentary unit from Manchester was filming a series of 'impressionistic portraits' of the inner city. The journalist Julie Davidson applauded the programmes as sensitive, even affectionate, and rounded eloquently on detractors of the series, who protested that it was being done by a crew from Manchester. As she pointed out, after the *Lilybank* fiasco BBC Scotland no longer made probing documentaries and Scottish Television had axed its own documentary unit. Davidson wrote that, if those who attacked the series failed to realise they were living in 'the sinkhole of post-industrial Europe . . . with vast areas of post-apocalyptic desolation', they had been living in Glasgow too long. She had visited Toxteth, not long after the summer riots of 1981, and thought: 'Yes, it's bad, but nothing like as bad as Springburn.'

Or, she might have added, the Gorbals, where the pre-war slums had been bulldozed, only to be replaced by a grim new set. A local resident, Bill Sharkey, showed the film-makers round the Hutchinson 'E' block, built to house 700 people. He remembered the day the damp began to creep in, how the fungus flourished and the smell penetrated everything – and everyone. The tenants wrote to the Queen, who had opened the block 10 years earlier, and were pleased by her sympathetic reply. But for their landlord, the local authority backing Mr Happy, they had only contempt. 'They said we should open the windows and turn the heating up, that we took too many hot baths, even breathed too much, and when they did send an official round, he always had a cold, so he couldn't smell,' said Sharkey. One of his neighbours, Connie Cullen, a widow in her seventies, recalled how 'awfy cheery' it had been in the beginning before the start of the early morning knocking on her door. 'There's no peace from the glue-sniffers now,' she said.

A fatal accident inquiry into the death of a 13-year-old girl, Patricia Morrison, gave an insight into the city's glue-sniffing epidemic. The inquiry was told that solvents and lighter fuel were 'easily available' in shops on the south side. Patricia's friend, 15-year-old Anne McGarvey, admitted that she and Patricia had experimented with inhaling lighter fuel. They bought it from a shop called the Wee Embassy Regal and another called the Space Invaders. On the night of Pamela's death, they went into a close to inhale: 'Pamela started to breathe the gas. Then we heard someone coming down the stairs. We ran out into the back court and I heard Patricia falling and turned back. Her face was white and pale. She was breathing heavily, and her eyes were closing. Then her face started to turn blue.' Anne rushed into the street and asked some boys to help her. They tried without success to revive Patricia with heart massage. Sixteen-year-old John Roberts said he had seen teenagers sniffing glue in the back shop of the Space Invaders and that local people were so angry they were threatening to attack the shop (which was forced to close down). He admitted he had been addicted to lighter fuel himself, and had spent three months in hospital trying to break the habit.

The city's hard drugs scene, once concentrated on a few pubs in and around Byres Road, had moved into the housing schemes. Dr Jason Ditton, a sociologist at Glasgow University, said that speed and acid were 'a commonplace, no longer exclusively west end, but capable of pulling down young people of every class'. The murder of Rab Kane, a drugs pusher, testified to the severity of the crisis.

Kane had deserted his wife and five children to become the latest boyfriend of Avril Rado, a rebellious young woman from a dysfunctional background. Avril had lived among dropouts near Oban, taking amphetamine and LSD ('a good experience, it clears a lot of the nonsense out of your head') before moving to Glasgow. She described her introduction to hard drugs as 'frighteningly casual'. Two young men approached her at a bus stop in the west end and offered her a drug called Diconal. 'They crushed the pills by rolling them with a lemonade bottle, mixed it with water, and then we injected it. It was like an orgasm, except it lasted all night.' Later she gravitated to heroin when it was offered free at a party. Her life was itinerant, restless, involving frequent changes of flats and boyfriends, until she met Rab Kane. 'I was quite shy of him because he was nice, very quiet, very good-looking.' He had a criminal record – for robbery – but Avril 'never regarded him as in any way an evil man'. If Avril and Rab got word that a chemist's had been broken into, they would head to the shop, usually in the west end, and join the stampede for drugs.

Rab lost his job with a drugs rehabilitation unit – he found he could help others, but never himself – and so he and Avril would relax in the west end with books, music and heroin. But then Rab started leaving the flat without explanation for long periods. 'I was getting telephone calls,' said Avril. 'A man who wouldn't say who he was demanded to know where Rab was and said Rab owed them money.' One night, a Glasgow hard man called 'Toe' Elliot came to the flat and there was an argument about money. Another night, she returned to find Rab with his arm in plaster. 'He said he'd been in the Gorbals when a car pulled up beside him. He was told to get in and pushed down on the floor and struck on the head. They took him to Cathkin Braes and beat him up. He was then thrown over a tree trunk and his arms were held out. They smashed his arms and hands with a baseball bat and left him unconscious.' Rab's problem was that he used some of the heroin regularly supplied by Elliot, with the result that he could never sell enough of what was left to settle Elliot's demands. 'Everyone told him time and again that if you were dealing with Toe Elliot, you got out of it fast. He denied it to me, but he was dealing with them, and he was trapped.'

Shortly before Rab died, Toe Elliot said to Avril: 'If you were no use to me, you would both be dead.' Avril thought he had been watching too many bad movies. In the city of Mr Happy people did watch too many bad movies. But when Rab cheated Toe out of one heroin deal too far, he was batoned and stabbed to death in the flat he shared with Avril in Maryhill. 'Tiny of stature, perfectly dressed, half-bald and wearing exaggeratedly large, fashionable spectacles' – as one press report had it – and looking much older than his 36 years, Toe was said to have acquired his nickname when it was discovered that he had a deformity of the foot. He had many enemies. Two of them once tried to kill him by firing through a letter-box. He was jailed for life for the murder of Rab Kane and served 17 years, seven years longer than James Nelson for murdering his mother. He was one of the 'successes' of the Barlinnie special unit, writing several prison-related plays and founding his own theatre company. In 1999, four weeks after his release, he moved to Iona to work as a volunteer with the inter-denominational community founded there by the Very Reverend George MacLeod. He had already married, in the special unit, the membership secretary of the Iona Community in Glasgow. Having 'found' religion, as many addicts had before him, he might easily have become the second convicted murderer to be admitted into the ministry of the Church of Scotland. On this occasion, however, history did not repeat itself.

1984

LOSERS AND LIARS

ON 25 JUNE 1984, A MAN WHO MIGHT HAVE BEEN BORN TO participate in a major industrial dispute turned up at a pit in County Durham to volunteer as a flying picket. His name – it was his real one – was Norman Strike. The diary he kept that summer is among the most vivid contemporary accounts of a pivotal event in British post-war history – the showdown between the miners and Margaret Thatcher.

Strike's was one of 16 names picked out of the hat. They were each given a little subsistence money – £32 in cash – and told they would be heading for Scotland that night. Strike correctly assumed that this meant Bilston Glen, one of Scotland's 12 remaining pits, one of the deepest in Europe, often described as a 'showpiece' of the industry.

'We had to wait two hours for the coach to arrive,' wrote Strike, 'and because we'd been paid, a lot of the lads took the opportunity to have a pint or five, which made for a boisterous journey . . . The driver took a discreet route over the border because we didn't want to be stopped by the pigs, and we had to make quite a few piss stops so we didn't get to Dalkeith Miners' Welfare until after midnight. So here we are, lying on seats in the concert room after being fed a supper of soup and bread. The possibility of sleep is looking remote seeing as a pool competition is taking place (it's 2.24 am!). We've been told picketing starts at 5 am and I have been promised better accommodation later today. I bloody hope so because I am shattered.' After the picket he did manage to grab an hour's sleep in the TV room of the miners' welfare 'before being turfed out by the cleaning woman'.

In the *Glasgow Herald*'s report of what happened at Bilston Glen that morning, Derek Bateman wrote: 'Two miners who defied the picket line to go to work were set on by a mob of their colleagues and punched and kicked . . . One of them was butted and suffered a cut on the head before being knocked to the ground. His workmate was also punched and both men were kicked on the body as picketing miners to the rear of the group shouted "Kill, kill". Police who were blocking roads outside the pit rescued the men from the worst single incident of inter-miner violence at Bilston Glen since the stoppage began 15 weeks ago.'

In Norman Strike's recollection of the same incident, the police 'lashed out viciously with feet and fists [and] some of the lads grabbed bricks and began lobbing them at the advancing pigs'. These eye-witness accounts, one emphasising the protective role of the police, the other exposing their aggression, were typical of the dispute's two competing narratives. In one narrative, the police arrived mob-handed at pit heads not so much to defend a few dissident miners crossing picket lines as to stir up confrontation. The general secretary of the National Union of Mineworkers in Scotland, Eric Clarke, claimed that they resorted to such tactics as pulling picketers' hair knowing they would get a reaction, and that the reaction would be well publicised.

At Bilston Glen in the early morning of 26 June, the 500 pickets were far outnumbered by the police. The local Labour MP, John Home Robertson, said he believed Bilston Glen was being used for propaganda purposes – to show men turning up for work and being intimidated by mass picketing. But when he was asked if he thought the heavy police presence amounted to provocation, he avoided direct criticism, saying only that he 'wouldn't like to try to go through them'. In this other narrative, the one supported by most of the media, the actions of the police were defended, excused or overlooked and there was only one 'mob' in the dispute: the picketing miners.

As Norman Strike left Bilston Glen around 8.30 am, he spotted the vice-president of the NUM, Mick McGahey, and Eric Clarke emerging from police lines. Strike suggested to them that the pickets should be co-ordinated more effectively 'so we could concentrate our forces at the best points'. McGahey replied: 'Picketing has nothing to do with me, son.' A bemused Strike went off for his sleep in the TV room.

'The sun was burning hot,' he wrote of the afternoon picket, 'and I was dressed for it in white jacket, shirt, trousers and white shoes. The lads all took the piss and voted me best-dressed picket, but I was going to the theatre after the picket and wanted to look as smart as I could.' The play was Chekhov's *The Three Sisters*, a study of loneliness and desperation, of uncomplaining resignation, which ends with a rueful comment on the human condition: 'If only we knew, if only we knew'. Not long after it was written, there was a revolution in Russia and rueful comments on the human condition suddenly seemed self-indulgent. Norman Strike, resplendent in white jacket in the auditorium of the Royal Lyceum Theatre in Edinburgh, having earlier in the day been part of what the *Glasgow Herald* was to call a mob, was taking part in a very British revolution, a small, relatively bloodless one. Though, as the curtain fell on *The Three Sisters*, he was not to know that the Prime Minister of his country was making plans to declare a state of emergency and bring in the troops to deal with him and insurgents like him. Her true intentions in those heady days were not made public for 30 years.

Strike enjoyed the play. But after the excitements of Bilston Glen, the next day was something of an anti-climax. He spent most of it at 'an open-cast site called Bonnyrigg, and at least here we had some small success in turning back two lorries, purely by putting our case to the drivers. This proves that peaceful picketing does work if the pigs are not there to provoke confrontation.' Meanwhile, back at Bilston Glen, there was no repetition of the violence. The two men who had been kicked and punched the previous day again defied the picket line, one claiming that pickets had threatened to smash the windows of his mother's house. Mick McGahey, invited to condemn the excesses of his members' behaviour, replied: 'How can you be violent to scabs? You should be asking about the police violence.'

On 28 June, after an early morning picket at Bilston Glen which passed without incident, Strike and his mates set off for home. 'Our visit was not an entire waste of time,' he wrote, 'because at least the number of scabs hasn't gone up as the NCB were hoping for, and we've all gained some valuable experience. We need mass pickets to really make a difference to this strike and that means trying to get the majority of men who are sitting on their arses at home out onto the picket lines.'

A month later, the Secretary of State for Scotland, George Younger, appealed to pickets from south of the border to leave. 'I have heard reports that some are not Scots, and if that is so, I hope I can ask them to go back to England and leave us to sort out our problems ourselves.' This was almost in the McGahey class of eccentricity. Where had the Secretary of State been if he had only just received this intelligence? And what made him think that the 'problems' of the miners' strike were somehow specific to Scotland? He was doing what politicians did: pretending to address one audience (the pickets, who he knew would regard his invitation with contempt) while actually addressing another (the Scottish public, which was instinctively sympathetic to the miners).

Rather than risk interception at police roadblocks, some of the Durham pickets were billeted in houses in East Lothian, accepting the hospitality of fellow miners. Others came and went in raiding parties, relying on drivers to plot a devious route over the border. The Home Office knew that the strategy of 'stop and turn back' was failing and warned Thatcher that it was not the 'unmixed blessing' that she had hoped. The hidden agenda of July 1984 – kept under wraps for three decades – was that, even as the Secretary of State for

Scotland was imploring the pickets to go home, Margaret Thatcher, determined to break the strike and apparently fearful that Britain would run out of food, was devising a scheme to employ 2,800 troops in 13 specialist teams to unload 1,000 tonnes of coal a day at the docks.

Norman Strike arrived back in Scotland in late July and was immediately caught up in another violent episode at Bilston Glen – 'the most militant so far', he noted in his diary. 'News came though that a coachload of Durham miners had been arrested in Tranent allegedly harassing a scab and everyone seemed to go mental. Lads began tearing down the fence outside the pit yard which the NCB had spent thousands having strengthened. Huge tyres were rolled over from a nearby garage and then set on fire, and within minutes thick black smoke was belching out from the flames and two trees had also caught alight.'

Strike and others headed for Dalkeith police station to protest about the arrests. 'No sooner had we got there when we were scattered by pigs coming straight for us with truncheons drawn. It was a mad stampede for safety with the pigs tripping anyone who got too close to them. I managed to reach our coach and jumped on, gasping for breath.'

The target that day was Philip Inverarity, 49, who woke before dawn to find dozens of pickets outside his house in Tranent. 'I had to call the police for help because I didn't know what they might do,' he told journalists. He was given an escort to Bilston Glen. 'This is my fifth week back at work, and it won't be my last,' he said. 'They will have to make me a stretcher case to stop me from going to work.' He alleged that his 18-year-old daughter had been threatened at a club in Dalkeith after she admitted that her father was a working miner and that his car had been daubed with paint and with the word 'scab'. Inverarity said that he returned to work because his family were starving. Perhaps he exaggerated. In East Lothian, soup kitchens fed the children of the striking miners.

II

There was trouble at Bilston Glen from the start. On 9 March, when the NUM gave official backing for strikes in Scotland and Yorkshire and pledged support for any other area which took similar action, the Scottish coalfield was sharply divided. Polmaise in Stirlingshire and Bogside in Fife, both earmarked for closure, were certain to strike. At Killoch in Ayrshire, which employed 1,750 men, and at the Seafield/Frances complex in Fife, the mood was equally militant. But there were strong pockets of resistance at Polkemmet, Monktonhall and especially at Bilston Glen. The issue, ostensibly at least, was the failure of the union to organise a ballot. 'If there has to be a strike,' said one of the Bilston miners, Leslie Miller, 'there has to be a ballot. We also don't know what we're being asked to strike for. Is it over pay or is it over pit closures? It is a tragedy because it has been done without the best interests of the miners at heart. It is a battle between the NUM hierarchy and the Tory government.'

Four days later, in the first of many ugly scenes outside the colliery, flying pickets, mostly from Polmaise, tried to prevent Bilston men from working. Punches and kicks were thrown; press photographers were manhandled; a BBC film crew was attacked. But by the evening heavy picketing had brought Bilston Glen, along with the rest of the Scottish coalfield, to a standstill. Only 70 men were still working – all of them at Bilston Glen, though not enough to keep the pit operating – and the propaganda war had intensified. The NCB claimed that many men wanted to work but had been intimidated from crossing picket lines, while Mick McGahey brazenly insisted that the union was 'forging unity among the miners'. After the exhibition of 'unity' between miners at Bilston Glen a few hours earlier, only McGahey could say how disunity might look.

By early May, eight weeks into the dispute, it was no longer simply a matter of miner fighting miner. Union was now fighting union. Ravenscraig, the steel plant at Motherwell, itself threatened with closure, became a potential flashpoint when it was learned that the British Steel Corporation intended to use an overnight convoy of lorries to transport supplies of coking coal from the deep-water port of Hunterston in Ayrshire and that the shop stewards at Ravenscraig supported their employer's bold move to keep the plant open. Miners were reported to be organising a mass picket, but only a few arrived in Motherwell in time for the first convoy. A second swept unimpeded through the gates after minor scuffles. When a third convoy approached the plant, about a hundred pickets surged forward into the middle of the road and a few risked life and limb by throwing themselves at the lead lorry, clinging on to it for several yards until the police pushed them back. Tommy Brennan, convener of shop stewards at Ravenscraig, was unrepentant. 'The miners are fighting for their industry,' he said, 'but we are fighting for the survival of ours. We do not want to strike-break. We would rather have reached agreement round a table. We can't win.'

Eighty-nine truckloads of coal reached Ravenscraig over a 24-hour period and the mass picket failed to materialise. 'There were only four of us, and about five carloads of police,' said one miner on the second day of the convoys. 'There was nothing we could do.' Stones were thrown at a lorry in the streets of the town, shattering the windscreen, but apart from that futile gesture there was little resistance. Mick McGahey brushed off the setback, claiming that the picket would have been more successful had miners from Fife not been stopped by police on the Forth Road Bridge in what he condemned as an infringement of civil liberties. But the high-profile failure of the Motherwell action was expensive on two counts. It created bad blood between the miners and the steel workers; and it was a minor propaganda coup for the government.

The miners struggled to overcome three basic obstacles. First, the timing of the dispute at the end of winter, when demand for their product would soon start to decline, was strategically poor. Second, coal stocks were high at the start of the strike; in Scotland alone, the

NCB was holding 2.8 million tonnes, the South of Scotland Electricity Board a further 3 million, the equivalent of six months' supply, and the miners' leaders seemed to be unaware of a stockpile of cheap Polish coal being held in reserve. Third, without a proper mandate, the NUM leadership faced an uphill battle to assert its authority and defend the legitimacy of its actions. In August, after two working miners took the union to court, the English judges ruled that the NUM had breached its constitution by calling a strike without first holding a ballot. This decision exposed the union to the risk of sequestration.

A few weeks later in Scotland, however, when three working miners at Bilston Glen made a similar move, there was a different outcome. Harry Fettes, John Pupkis and Tom McConnell asked the High Court in Edinburgh to grant an order banning the NUM from instructing them to strike and not to cross picket lines, on the grounds that the strike was unlawful under union rules. Their counsel, Donald Macaulay QC, quoted article 43 of the constitution, which stated that, in the event of a national strike being proposed, it could be entered into only if a ballot was held and a simple majority voted in favour. Macaulay accused the NUM of hiding behind article 41, which exempted the national executive committee from organising a ballot if the strikes were in individual areas. 'Having created a national strike,' said Macaulay, 'it is their plain duty to play the game with their members and allow them to vote one way or the other.' He added that, if the NUM tried to claim that the dispute was not a national strike, it would be 'the laughing stock of the nation'.

For the union, John Horsburgh QC argued that the interdict the three men were seeking could be justified only if an 'appreciable wrong' had been done to them. 'My information', he said, 'is that all three are working and the inference to be drawn from that is that they are crossing the picket lines and ignoring instructions or encouragement being given by the union which they consider to be illegal.' Where, then, was the 'appreciable wrong'? Horsburgh went on to submit that the strike could not be described as national or nationwide so long as three areas in England were not on strike. To general astonishment, Lord Hunter refused the interdict and ruled that the Scottish leadership had acted within its rights in restricting the strike vote to a show of hands at pitheads.

The same court was less well disposed to the union in the case of David Hamilton, a miner at Monktonhall and chairman of the central strike committee, when he was charged with assault while on picket duty and refused bail. He appealed to the High Court and might have expected some consideration from Lord Wheatley, a judge with roots in the socialist movement. But Wheatley refused to release him, and the imprisoned Hamilton achieved the instant status of a martyr. Four hundred people attended a rally in Loanhead, Midlothian, in his support. When the case finally came to trial some weeks later, he was cleared of the charge and walked free, protesting that it had all been a ploy to keep him out of the way for as long as possible.

The many conspiracy theories were hard to prove one way or the other. But at least one was undoubtedly justified. Long after the strike, in a well-sourced book on the history of the security services, Christopher Andrew gave details of MI5's routine tapping of Mick McGahey's telephone. McGahey's thickly accented voice, hewn from the deeper seams of industrial Lanarkshire, defeated the English spooks, who struggled to understand what he was saying but heard enough to be impressed by his addiction to whisky. One agent reported that he had 'more or less invented heavy drinking', while another filed that he was confined to bed with alcoholic poisoning. Certainly McGahey's consumption was legendary – when he was asked what he would like to drink he would reply 'A wee Bells,' and when he was asked what he would like in it, 'another wee Bells'. One evening during the strike, a journalist in his company probed in vain for a quote. 'That's the seventeenth time you have asked that question,' said McGahey, 'and no matter how many times you ask it, you will get the same answer.' Finally, around 4 am, the journalist had to be assisted upstairs to his room. 'The trouble with journalists,' mused

McGahey, nursing his umpeenth Bells of the night, 'is that they have no staying power. Had he stayed for another drink, he might have got the quote he wanted.'

Like their leader, the Scottish miners did have staying power. Nine months on, 94% of them were still on strike, though at growing cost to themselves, their families and their communities. George Bolton, a former Scottish president of the NUM, recalled: 'It became more of an endurance test than a strike. There was a tremendous spirit in the mining communities in those days, with their miners' welfare, brass bands and football clubs. But it was a harsh time.' Michael Hogg, one of the pickets at Bilston Glen, called it 'desperate'. He praised the women, 'the wives who did everything from making sure the miners were fed before and after picket duty to keeping up morale with fun days'. But fun was a luxury in short supply. 'There were marriage break-ups, houses repossessed and no holidays or family cars. Some people who went back to work had to move away because of resentment.' Hogg, 23, became the first Scottish miner to be arrested for picket-line violence. He struggled with the police at Bilston Glen and threw a punch at an 18-year-old apprentice, John McDonald, one of his neighbours in the village of Mayfield, for crossing the line. He was fined £500, sacked for gross misconduct, and spent two months in Saughton Prison for this and other picket-line offences. Twenty years later, Hogg continued to view McDonald as a scab. 'I see all the strike-breakers as scabs. Some of these people I speak to today quite amicably. Some I don't speak to. But I don't socialise with any of them. They know why and I know why.'

In the early weeks of 1985, as the dispute entered its second year with no hope of a settlement, support ebbed. By February, the number still out in Scotland had fallen to 75%; by March to 69%. South of the border, four out of 10 were back at work. Mick McGahey's influence, if he had chosen to exert it, might have brought the ordeal to an end long before, when there was still a chance of avoiding outright humiliation, but he remained loyal to the union president, Arthur Scargill, while privately despairing of his obstinacy and refusal to compromise. The Labour leader Neil Kinnock later claimed that, over a drink in a hotel bar, McGahey admitted to him that he had been marginalised by Scargill during the strike but that he said nothing publicly because it would have made no difference to the result.

A few days before the first anniversary, at the London head-quarters of the TUC, a special delegate conference of the NUM ordered the men back to work. There were emotional scenes outside Congress House as the news leaked out, including cries of 'Sell out' and 'We're not going back'. Some of the Bilston Glen men who had been sacked for their over-zealous picketing wept on the steps. McGahey and Scargill left the building to the jeers of a crowd re-sentful of their leaders' capitulation and aware with painful clarity that the fight had been for nothing.

At Polmaise colliery in the village of Fallin, the journalist Margaret Vaughan found the workers 'united in anger and defiance'. John Hotchkiss, a member of the local strike committee, told her: 'The strike started here and can go on indefinitely. You won't find a man in this village prepared to go back to work until the pit's future is assured. Don't forget our 11 sacked mates. They won't get their jobs back.' Vaughan reported: 'In Fallin, the reasons for this strength of feeling are clear. If the pit goes, so does the community. There is no other work.' She quoted an elderly miner: 'What about the future of the youngsters around here? If we give in, there will be no hope for them.'

The heartfelt words from Polmaise were swiftly overtaken by the farcical rout of their union's leadership. Having gone along with the national executive's decision to call off the strike, the Scottish office-bearers then promptly voted to stay out. McGahey blamed the change of mind on the intransigence of the NCB's Scottish area director, Albert Wheeler, in refusing to offer an amnesty to any of the dismissed miners – 180 according to Wheeler, 250 according to the union's own figures. Wheeler was hardline and abrasive, an unappealing character, but McGahey's last stand was quixotic. His members were voting with their feet and coal was on the move to power stations in Scotland for the first time in a year. Twenty-four hours later, pressure from local branches compelled the Scottish executive to think again. The strike was finally over.

Among the many post-mortems, McGahey tried to make the best of it, predicting unconvincingly that the NCB's programme of pit closures would be dropped and that no damage would be done to the Scottish miners. Arthur Scargill castigated the trade unions, with a few exceptions, for leaving the NUM isolated – 'to their eternal shame' – and blamed the judiciary and the media for aiding and abetting the Thatcher government. The press laid into Scargill for his maladroit handling of the dispute – the *Glasgow Herald* accused him of grotesquely misusing his energy, commitment and rhetorical flair – and there was general condemnation of the violence on the picket lines. 'So what do we find as the saddest strike of the last 60 years comes to a tragic end?' asked the *Daily Record*. 'We find losers. And that's all we find.'

The paper had forgotten one obvious winner. 'We had to stand out against intimidation,' said Margaret Thatcher. 'We could never give in to blackmail or to impossible demands. This is a victory for common sense and for those who stayed at work. I hope we will never see again in Britain some of the terrible scenes we witnessed. I did not think we would ever see such things in Britain.' George Younger, in a television interview, adopted a more emollient posture: there could be no rejoicing at the end of a 'sad, sad strike'. But the Secretary of State for Scotland could not resist adding that 'ministers make a distinction between the NUM leadership and the striking miners, most of whom were misled by Mr Scargill'. It would be a long time before the disingenuousness of these statements was exposed. By then, George Younger was dead and Margaret Thatcher had lost her memory.

The strike was triggered by the National Coal Board's announcement that, for the purposes of 'rationalising' the industry, it intended to close 20 pits with the loss of 20,000 jobs. Scargill alleged at the time that the government had a long-term strategy of shutting more than 70 pits. Few believed him. The government issued a categorical denial and the board chairman, Ian MacGregor, wrote to every member of the NUM informing them that Scargill was deceiving them by making such an allegation and that the board had no plans for further closures beyond those already announced.

Mick McGahey once described MacGregor as an alien ('whose clan does not even have its own tartan'), but the chairman, despite his American twang, was a Scot by birth and upbringing, the product of a strict Christian family which was virulently anti-union. His elder brother contributed to the breaking of the General Strike by driving trams in Glasgow in 1926, while young Ian got involved in a strike of crane drivers at Parkhead Forge, impressing his employer, Sir James Lithgow, by driving the cranes himself. He emigrated to the United States, where he prospered as a hard-nosed entrepreneur.

When Margaret Thatcher gave him the job of sorting out the coal industry he was almost 71 and long past his best, whatever his best had amounted to. He had none of the diplomatic skills necessary for the handling of a long strike, particularly of a group of workers held in general affection, and his media relations were poor. At the height of the strike he turned up in a car for a meeting in an Edinburgh hotel observed by a handful of journalists, picked up a green plastic bag from the passenger seat, stepped out, placed the bag in front of his face and walked into the hotel, peering out through the handles. 'He seemed to be trying to deny the photographers a picture,' recalled the BBC reporter Colin Blane. 'Instead he gave them an unforgettable one.' Even Thatcher lost confidence in MacGregor, though she rewarded him afterwards with the inevitable knighthood.

Despite his attachment to the Ten Commandants, he was a proficient bare-faced liar. The wholesale deception only came to light in 2014 with the release of cabinet papers into the national archives. Among the many documents relating to the miners' strike, one dated September 1983 was particularly significant. It was marked 'Not to be photographed or circulated outside the private office' and recorded a meeting attended by seven people, including the Prime Minister, at 10 Downing Street. The meeting heard that the NCB's pit closure programme had 'gone better this year than planned' and that there had been 'one pit closed every three weeks'. The new chairman, Ian MacGregor, now intended to go further. 'Mr MacGregor had it in mind over the next three years [to 1985] that a further 75 pits would be closed: first, 64 which would reduce the workforce by some 55,000 and reduce capacity by some 20 million tonnes; then a further 11, with manpower reductions of 9,000 and capacity reduction of a further 5 million tonnes.' The total workforce would be reduced from 202,000 to 138,000. A third of the Scottish miners would lose their jobs. The final paragraph read: 'It was agreed that no record of this meeting should be circulated.' A week later, another document by a senior civil servant suggested that the same small group of ministers should meet regularly but that there should be 'nothing in writing which clarifies the understandings about strategy which exist between Mr MacGregor and the Secretary of State for Energy'.

The conclusions were inescapable: there was a cover-up in which the Prime Minister and the chairman of the NCB colluded; MacGregor told a blatant lie in his letter to the miners assuring them that there were no plans for further closures beyond the 20 he had just announced; and the much-reviled Arthur Scargill was accurate in his assessment that the government had a long-term strategy to close 'more than 70 pits'. The Government and the board success-fully maintained the deception for the duration of the strike and, at the end of it, had the audacity to accuse the picketing miners of bad behaviour and Scargill of misleading his members.

David Hamilton, the union leader who had gone to prison because Lord Wheatley would not release him on bail on a charge of which he was innocent, became the Labour MP for Midlothian. When the shocking truth emerged, he wrote in the *Morning Star*: 'If we'd known just how many pits she planned to close, would the communities involved have fought back even harder and stopped her? . . . Were the lies the only thing that kept Thatcher from defeat?' The industrial correspondent Nick Jones, who covered the dispute for the BBC, wrote that if the incriminating document of September 1983 had emerged during the strike it would have been 'devastating for the credibility of Margaret Thatcher'. Instead she came out of the dispute with her reputation as the Iron Lady of British politics enhanced. The *Economist* summed up her achievement in an editorial: 'Mrs Thatcher had decided that Britain no longer needed a large coal-mining industry . . . Each night for a year television showed the shirt-sleeved miners confronting the state in the form of well-trained police. They looked like amateurs against professionals. The miners eventually gave in and returned to an already depleted industry. For Mrs Thatcher it was a major victory in her campaign to curb trade union power in Britain.'

When Mick McGahey joined the industry as a 14-year-old in 1939, there were 426 pits in Scotland employing 92,000 miners. By the time of his death in 1999, there was nothing left. An industry gone in its entirety, communities laid to waste, a culture destroyed: it had all come to pass. On the site of Bilston Glen pit, which once produced 1 million tonnes of coal a year and employed 2,300 men, and where Norman Strike once picketed in the heat after being turned out of the miners' welfare by the cleaning woman, they built a police communications centre, of all things. Half a century earlier, on the island of Jura, a dying George Orwell had managed to finish a novel about a dystopian state in which human beings were controlled and cowed by misinformation. That too was called 1984.

FOR CLUB AND COUNTRY

I

THREE DAYS AFTER THE EVENT, IT MERITED A DOWN-THE-PAGE STORY in the Scottish newspapers. 'Death of SNP vice-chairman' was the restrained but not strictly accurate headline over the *Glasgow Herald*'s brief account of a fatal crash involving 61-year-old William MacRae, 'a prominent Glasgow solicitor', north of Invergarry, Inverness-shire. He was not the vice-chairman of the SNP. He had given up the post or the post had given up him. In the strange case of William MacRae the disentangling of fact from fiction was to prove almost impossible.

The paper reported that MacRae's car had been found on the morning of Saturday 6 April, that he had been taken to Raigmore Hospital in Inverness and transferred to Aberdeen Royal Infirmary (where he died), and that on Sunday a post-mortem had been carried out. There was no hint of anything untoward. Anyone reading the piece would have assumed that he had been killed as the result of a straightforward accident on a lonely stretch of road in the Highlands.

A short tribute to the deceased accompanied the news item. The former chairman of the SNP, William Wolfe, wrote: 'Willie MacRae was like a brother to countless folk of all ages, of different creeds, and many nationalities. To those who knew him, his loving kindness was his outstanding quality.' He had been a member of the party since the 1930s and was a popular conference speaker on land use, particularly in his beloved Highlands. As convener of a policy committee on the subject in the late 1970s he had steered the party into adopting 'the most radical and practical set of detailed proposals for land use of any party today'. Wolfe wrote that he believed MacRae had been of help to the leaders of the young state of Israel, drafting their mercantile law, and had also known some of the leaders of the Congress Party in India following his active service in the Indian Navy during the Second World War. A few months before his death he had arranged for Indira Gandhi to have a holiday in Scotland and was 'as distressed as I had ever known him' by her murder.

It was a colourful obituary, especially of a man who, despite his close connections with the young state of Israel and the late Mrs Gandhi, had not enjoyed a high public profile in his native country or even in his beloved Highlands; in his own party, where he was rather better known, he once stood for the leadership and attracted only 52 votes. But such were the respectful standards of the Scottish obituary, William Wolfe knew more than he would have considered it decent to commit to print. He made no attempt to sketch the darker features of MacRae's complex personality.

The morning after the initial reports, a more intriguing story began to emerge. 'Mystery surrounds the last few hours of William MacRae, who was found dying in his car', reported the *Herald* in a single-column piece on page 7. He was believed to have been driving to his holiday home in Wester Ross when his car left the road near Loch Loyne. It was found 'standing upright, straddling a stream, but was not badly damaged'. The paper said that two Australian tourists (later identified as Alan Crowe, an airline pilot, and his wife) spotted the car on moorland some 30 yards from the road and flagged down the next car to pass. In an extraordinary coincidence a passenger in that car happened to be someone who knew MacRae: a Scottish National Party councillor from Dundee, David Coutts, who was travelling with friends to Skye on holiday. Coutts immediately recognised MacRae, who was sitting in his car with his hands folded on his lap, his head slumped on his right shoulder, covered in blood.

The driver of the car was a doctor, Dorothy Messer, who examined MacRae and concluded that, although he was still breathing, he was brain-dead and had been in that condition for around 10 hours. Coutts summoned the police. 'The only thing that I thought peculiar,' he was quoted as saying, 'was that his watch, cheque cards and personal effects were some way from the car. A lot of the things were ripped up.' Coutts said that he had been asked about bullet wounds but had not seen any. 'I went through the car myself and picked up all the things that might be relevant to the accident and gave them to a policeman, but there was no sign of a gun.' The paper had got hold of another curious titbit: early on Friday morning, the day before his death, firemen were called to MacRae's home in Glasgow, where some bedclothes had caught fire. MacRae, though suffering from the effects of smoke inhalation, refused medical attention.

Already his death had the makings of a ripping yarn, though one still confined to the inside pages; the editor of the *Glasgow Herald*, Arnold Kemp, must have been unimpressed by its potential as a whodunnit. For the authorities, it was an open and shut case: 'The death has been fully investigated,' announced the procurator-fiscal at Inverness, Thomas Aitchison, 'and there are no suspicious circumstances'. MacRae's body was discovered on Saturday morning. By Monday afternoon Aitchison was already preparing to close the file (though it was not formally consigned to the shelves until July that year with a statement from the Crown Office that 'no further information on the circumstances of this death will be made public'). If it was a 'full' investigation, it was completed with remarkable speed.

Although its results were unpublished, 'no suspicious circumstances' was a well-known euphemism for suicide. The official verdict, though acknowledged only implicitly, was that MacRae killed himself. The basis for this finding was the discovery by a nurse at Aberdeen Royal Infirmary, when she was washing the dying man's head, of the entry wound of a gunshot, the subsequent confirmation that he had been shot above his right ear, and the detection of a bullet in his head. Somehow the wound had not been spotted on his earlier admission to Raigmore Hospital, where a certain casualness of approach extended to a failure to conduct routine tests for traces of alcohol or drugs.

On Sunday there were two decisive developments: after consultation with next-of-kin MacRae's life support machine was switched off; and at noon that day, although no weapon had been found, a chief superintendent of Northern CID gave the order to move the car without taking a careful note of its location. This ineptness, if ineptness it was, led to confusion and a fundamental disagreement about the car's original position. According to David Coutts, the police were a mile out in their estimate.

On Monday, the day the procurator fiscal announced the completion of his 'full' investigation, a weapon was recovered from the burn where the car finished up. It was said to be a Smith and Wesson .45 revolver allegedly belonging to MacRae – though this was later disputed by some of the cases's many self-appointed experts – and it had been fired twice. If it was true that MacRae had not been wearing gloves, the conspiracy theorists were now able to enjoy a field day: how come there were no fingerprints on the gun? But there was no consensus about the fingerprints, or lack of them. The authors of a book, *Britain's Secret War*, counter-claimed years later that there were indeed fingerprints: those of MacRae's alone.

The critical and unresolved question was how far from the car the weapon was found. Since the car had been so quickly moved, this too was fraught with difficulty. Sixty feet, according to some original reports. In an off-the-record conversation with a journalist in 1987, the Solicitor-General for Scotland, Peter Fraser, gave and dismissed an alternative estimate: 'I don't think the gun was found 40 to 50 feet away, though it was certainly further away than it would have been if it had just fallen from his grasp, and it is unlikely, given his head injury, that he could have thrown it.' True to form, Fraser denied ever having made this statement. How far, then? One guess was as good as another's. But in a sensational article in the *Glasgow Herald* in 1995, the columnist John MacLeod articulated what many believed: Willie

'McRae' (he got the spelling of the surname wrong) was murdered. 'A man who has just shot himself cannot then fling the weapon of self-murder a distance of 60 feet,' he reasoned. We were back to 60 feet rather than 40 or 50 – or some lesser distance that the Solicitor-General would not define but was anyway inconsistent with suicide.

MacLeod drew an informative pen-portrait of MacRae: born near Falkirk, excelled at school, left Glasgow University with a first in history; a penchant for three-piece suits; pugnacious in appearance; a heavy smoker; a lover of whisky; unmarried. In 1980, said MacLeod, he was prominent in the public inquiry into the proposal to dump nuclear waste in the Galloway hills and may have 'single-handedly' thwarted the intentions of the United Kingdom Atomic Energy Authority. (As already noted, the same claim was made by Jim Sillars.)

The many versions of the solicitor's last movements, before he set off for the far north, were extensively rehearsed and, unlike so much else in the cloudy narrative, did coalesce at one or two key points. MacLeod's version was that, on the night of 4 April, MacRae returned to his flat after attending a ceilidh with his godson. Early next morning, two passers-by saw flames from the window and the householder was found unconscious on the hall floor. He explained that he had fallen asleep while smoking in bed and awoke to find the bedclothes smouldering. Embarrassed by the incident, he decided to have a quiet weekend at his cottage in the Highlands and drove off on Friday evening in his maroon Volvo. This was a possible motive for MacRae's decision to embark on the journey, although he must have known that he would be driving in the dark for the last and most hazardous part of it.

What was his state of mind as he disappeared into the night? The testimony of his business partner Ronnie Welsh, who had trained with MacRae and later joined him in his new practice in Buchanan Street, Glasgow, should be treated with caution: Welsh kept the business going after his death but was struck off the solicitors' roll in 1987 for alleged financial irregularities. Still, perhaps his recollection of the Friday of MacRae's departure was as credible as any. According to Welsh, when MacRae left the office at mid-day he was in cheerful spirits and had made appointments for the following week; he gave 'no indication that he was suicidal'. The fact that he had made plans impressed Winifred Ewing, queen of the nationalist movement, who wrote to Gordon Wilson, Wolfe's successor as party chairman, in 1988: 'While he [Wolfe] thought Willie had a lot of worries and was often disturbed, he also thought that at that time he had many forward plans. It has come to my attention that Willie had engagements in Plockton the morning after he left for the north and that he had a full diary for the following week.' As suicide is so often an impulsive act, particularly where alcohol is involved, these appointments proved nothing.

Another witness, a former Strathclyde police officer, Donald Morrison, who was routinely described in the press as a friend of MacRae, agreed that MacRae was 'in fine fettle' when he bumped into him outside a shop in Glasgow shortly before he started the drive to Wester Ross. The solicitor was carrying two bottles of whisky and a bag of paperwork. He told Morrison that he was 'going to go through all this' – pointing to the bag – and that 'I've definitely got them this time.' In 2007 the *Daily Record*, in one of the many media retrospectives, said that MacRae left his office 'laden with his usual bulging briefcase and armfuls of legal documents, a big grin splitting his face'. He turned to his office staff and declared, 'I've got them,' leaving without further explanation. Had he told both Morrison and his office staff that he had 'got them'? Or had he told only Morrison? In the MacRae case anything was possible. But there may have been something of a mission about his ultimate journey.

He left Glasgow around 6.30 pm and was next seen, barely alive, at 10 am the following morning. If Dorothy Messer was correct in her assessment of the patient's condition, the crash occurred around midnight.

Morrison claimed in 2010 that he had been told by (unnamed) senior officers that MacRae was under surveillance by Special Branch and MI5. According to another press story, MacRae was said to have been suspicious of a car – a Triumph – that he believed was following him. When he raised the matter with a friendly policeman – Morrison, perhaps – the officer checked the police computer and it came up with 'Blocked vehicle – Special Branch'. A private investigator named Iain Fraser informed the media in 2006 that he was paid to 'watch' MacRae one Saturday in 1985 and did so from mid-afternoon until 6.00 pm and again from 8 pm till 11 pm. Fraser was vague about the commission: 'The cheque came from Newcastle. I can't remember the individual who signed it. I wished I had kept a copy.'

The question of what MacRae knew which so interested Special Branch and MI5 that someone in Newcastle put a tail on him, though only for six fruitless hours, and later went to the bother of shooting him, was the subject of several conflicting theories. It was speculated that it may have been because of his links with the loopy fringe movement Siol nan Gaidheal or with the more violent Scottish National Liberation Army. Hamish Watt, a Scottish National Party MP, claimed that MacRae was assassinated because of his 'extensive study of NATO activities in Scotland'. Another theory – supported by John MacLeod – was that he had got hold of classified papers related to the nuclear industry and was preparing to blow them. There were rumours, presumably inspired by MacRae himself, that his house was burgled on several occasions and that he had taken to carrying copies of sensitive documents about with him. These documents were said to be concerned with the proposal to dump nuclear waste from Dounreay into the sea – but, if they were, they were never found. The items recovered from the car by David Coutts included a couple of books, a Bible, a half-consumed half-bottle of whisky (there was no sign of the two full bottles he was reported to have had with him prior to departure), while a local policeman despatched to the scene found 'a small pyramid of the dead man's personal papers all carefully torn up, topped with his smashed wrist watch'. The famous bag, stuffed with secrets, was missing.

The notion that MacRae may have been bumped off by MI5 was not entirely implausible. When Hilda Murrell was found murdered in her cottage in rural Shropshire a year before MacRae's death, it was revealed that papers about her anti-nuclear campaigning had been stolen from her house by the perpetrator or perpetrators. If the spooks found it expedient to dispose of an elderly rose-grower, they would have had a more pressing interest in Willie MacRae, who did not smell of roses and who was rumoured to have links, not only with fringe nationalist organisations in Scotland, but with Mossad and Asian extremists. And if it was not an agent of the British state who fired the fatal shot one spring evening in 1985, might it have been some sinister figure from a drug cartel in the Highlands? That too was proposed at one stage. More recently, long after the dumping of nuclear waste ceased to be a fashionable issue, a new theory surfaced: that the bag of stash contained evidence of a paedophile ring in the Scottish judiciary, sufficiently incriminating to have the guilty parties searching their contacts book for a hit man. Ultimately there seemed to be few public scandals of the late twentieth century with which the former vice-chairman of the Scottish National Party was not intimately familiar.

There was a further ever-present possibility: that MacRae was simply a fantasist who enjoyed dropping dark hints about inside knowledge that he did not possess. He was accused variously of mental instability, alcoholism and advanced megalomania, all of which would have supported the theory that the bag contained nothing of interest. But the failure of the authorities to account for the oddities at the crash scene meant that the whiff of a conspiracy persisted.

'There do appear to be unanswered questions,' wrote Winifred Ewing to Gordon Wilson in 1988. 'At present I cannot get over the fact that no gun was found in, under or near the car.' Wilson replied that the authorities were 'blameless' for not carrying out a site inspection as they believed MacRae had been involved in a simple car accident. 'The whole question of whether there should be an inquiry,' he told Ewing, 'was taken up with the family through Billy Wolfe, who explained the position to them. The family decided they wished Willie to remain at rest and they did not request the procurator fiscal to carry out an inquiry.' When Ewing pressed her case, Wilson responded curtly: 'The clear view from both Billy Wolfe and Dr MacRae [Willie's brother] is that it would be in no-one's interest to have an inquiry. Billy was under the impression from Willie's actions that his mental balance at the time was questionable.' There may, however, have been another reason for the family's reluctance to have the case examined: the fear that he would be exposed as gay at a time when his elderly mother was still alive.

Arnold Kemp, whose paper's reporting of the incident had been so uninquiring, wrote in 1993 that the truth about MacRae's death was 'much less glamorous' than the conspiracy theories put about by his friends. MacRae had one conviction for drunk driving with another pending; had he survived the crash he would 'almost certainly' have been sent to prison. In Kemp's mental revisiting of the scene, the solicitor sat trapped and injured in his crashed car and decided that he preferred death to slopping out. 'The probability that he shot himself with his own .22 pistol, a memento of his India days, is overwhelming,' wrote Kemp. According to this theory he discharged his pistol once to see if it was working and then committed suicide. The Kemp version added yet another minor inconsistency to a story riddled with them. Now it was a .22 pistol, not a .45 revolver. It also contributed fresh but unsubstantiated detail. He claimed that MacRae's brother had taken his pistol away from him on a previous occasion, fearing he might use it, and that three days before his death MacRae had spoken to a close friend about suicide. As for the Special Branch car, Kemp maintained that it had been following someone else (one David Dinsmore, a member of the Scottish National Liberation Army). How Kemp knew any of this he did not divulge.

The dead man's partner, Ronnie Welsh, agreed up to a point with Kemp's diagnosis: 'He may have been drinking as the car ran off the road. What may have gone through his mind is that he already had three drink driving convictions [only one, with another pending, according to Kemp] and with a fourth pending he would have been frightened of the prospect of a custodial sentence.' Welsh's only caveat was that, knowing MacRae as he did, he would have expected him to kill himself indoors, in his Highland bolt-hole, rather than in his car. Welsh did not explain how, with the car out of commission, MacRae would have reached his bolt-hole in order to shoot himself.

In 2005, Fergus Ewing, son of Winifred and a nationalist member of the Scottish Parliament, wrote to the Solicitor-General, Elish Angiolini, requesting a meeting to discuss allegations that MacRae had been under surveillance at the time of his death. Though Angiolini refused to meet him, she did state categorically that MacRae had not been under surveillance.

The public interest in the case could have been satisfied at any stage if the Crown Office had ordered a fatal accident inquiry. The peculiarities of the Scottish system of accounting for unexplained deaths excused the prosecution service from any obligation to hold such an inquiry. MacRae was neither killed in the course of his employment nor was he a prisoner – though he may have feared that he was about to become one – nor was he otherwise in the care of the state. In any of these circumstances an inquiry would have been mandatory; in this case it was at the discretion of the prosecution service. Irrespective of the family's wishes, that discretion could have been exercised in the greater public interest. Thirty years on, the papers that Willie MacRae claimed to have in his possession, if they ever existed, were still missing and the gun that a mortally wounded man somehow succeeded in throwing some distance from his car continued to smell like a smoking one.

II

Unlike the slow burn of the MacRae case, a second death in 1985 exploded at once on to the front pages. In the final minutes of a Scotland-Wales football international at Ninian Park, Cardiff, Davie Cooper scored an equaliser for the Scots from the penalty spot. Newspaper photographers who had been massing round the Welsh bench abruptly moved to the Scottish dugout, much to the irritation of the team manager Jock Stein, who remonstrated with one of them and roughly ushered him away.

With two minutes to go, the referee blew his whistle and Stein mistook it for the end of the match. He rose from the bench, collapsed to his knees and was carried off the pitch and up the tunnel to the medical room. Stewart Hillis, the team doctor, struggled desperately to revive him and heard Stein's last words: 'I'm feeling much better now, doc'. The manager was pronounced dead at the scene while his players, oblivious to what was happening off the field, held on for a draw. The result, in as much as it mattered, was enough to send Scotland into a play-off for the World Cup finals.

One of the Scottish players, Richard Gough, recalled that Stein had been furious at half-time because no-one had told him that the goalkeeper, Jim Leighton, wore contact lenses. Leighton was having trouble with them and Stein replaced him with Alan Rough. 'I remember the feeling of elation when Cooper's penalty went in', said Gough. 'We were celebrating at the end. Then Alex Ferguson [Stein's assistant] came over and said to me: "Big Jock's been taken ill. Keep the boys on the pitch." When we got back to the dressing room, our masseur Jimmy Steel was in tears.' Alan Rough reflected afterwards that, in the days before the game, the manager was not his normal self. He looked unusually pale. 'But his thoroughness of preparation was as good as always', said Rough, 'so we thought little of it'. It transpired that Stein had been prescribed tablets to help him cope with heart disease but had stopped taking them. Hillis, who was

Stein's personal physician as well as the team's, was convinced that if he had persisted with the medication he would not have died.

At the age of 62, his health was failing. Ten years earlier, he was lucky to escape alive from a car accident that drove the steering wheel into his chest. It took him a year to recuperate and when he returned to his managerial duties at Celtic Football Club he was not the man he had been before the crash. 'The snap and the dash were gone,' wrote the sports journalist Kevin McCarra, 'but still he struggled to retain his great reputation. The thought of failure must be all the more intolerable when you have had well over 20 years of unstinting success. Stein fought decline with every resource he possessed.'

Eased out of Celtic, the club he inspired to victory in the 1967 European Cup final, Stein was not so well cast in the often unrewarding role of national team manager. As McCarra tactfully put it, his stewardship of the side thrilled no-one. And when he left his office at the Scottish Football Association for what was destined to be the last match of his career, he may have had a premonition that, in more ways than one, the game was up. 'Before setting off,' said McCarra, 'he uncharacteristically cleared his desk of all outstanding business.' Stein, who had begun his working life as a coal-miner, following his father down the pit, and who never abandoned his socialist roots, was much mourned.

His death cast two long shadows – the first innocuous and absurd; the second darker and more troubling. The first concerned a cross-border row over the award of a Queen's honour for his accomplishments, which only came to light with the release of government papers 40 years later.

In August 1967, a few months after Celtic lifted the European Cup in Lisbon, a civil servant at the Scottish Office, Miss N.C. Telfer, wrote to a counterpart at the Department of Education and Science in London noting that Jock Stein was to be included in the department's list of nominations for the New Year's honours – evidently 'education and science' somehow included football in its remit – but that the department considered OBE 'the appropriate honour'. Miss Telfer clarified with chilly politeness that St Andrew's House took issue with Whitehall's modest evaluation of Stein's merits. 'Since the activities for which it is proposed to recognise Mr Stein are entirely connected with Scottish football,' she wrote, 'we are including him in the Scottish Office List, and in view of the importance of Celtic's achievement in being the first British club to reach the final of the European Cup, we are adhering to our recommendation for a CBE. In our view it would be quite inappropriate to offer Mr Stein an OBE when Sir Alf Ramsay, manager of the English Football Association team which won the World Cup, received a knighthood. The only other Scottish football manager to be honoured in recent years was Mr T. [Tommy] Walker, manager of Heart of Midlothian, who received the OBE in 1960. Heart of Midlothian never achieved international distinction comparable to that achieved by Celtic in winning the European Cup under the management of Mr Stein and we think CBE is the minimum that can be offered him.'

The response from the government's principal adviser on sport, Sir John Lang, was directed not to the relatively humble Miss Telfer but in magisterial fashion to the head of the civil service in Edinburgh, Douglas Haddow, and addressed 'Dear Haddow'. Patronising in tone, it amounted to a yellow card for the awkward squad. Lang claimed to speak for Labour's sports minister, Denis Howell, in being 'inclined' to the belief that, as Stein was the manager of a club side and not a national team, 'a C is rather too high a level for such a person'. The Secretary of State for Scotland, Willie Ross, would have bristled at the suggestion that 'such a person' as a mere sports minister, someone not of cabinet rank, was high-handedly refereeing a Scotland-England game of increasing bitterness. The mood between the two sides was not improved by Lang's suggestion that the chairman of Celtic, Robert Kelly, was 'in lots of ways' more deserving of an honour than Stein, who had been manager of the club for 'only a very short time and has tended to be a man who does not stay in one job very long'. He proposed a CBE for Kelly, an honour that would, he added with grim satisfaction, 'dispose of Stein for a long time to come'.

Haddow – manager Ross no doubt looming over his shoulder – dealt with this English foul with a free kick from just outside the penalty box: 'My Secretary of State is in no doubt whatever that Celtic's European Cup victory is something that calls for recognition in the New Year List . . . We are equally clear that Mr Stein is the right person to recognise at this time. However, we would regard an OBE as quite inappropriate. Our view is that Mr Kelly can wait and we should not be greatly concerned if he has to wait for considerably longer than one or two years.'

In this bad-tempered encounter, England finally prevailed. Fate – or what Lang was delighted to call 'extraneous circumstances'– intervened when four Celtic players were sent off during violent clashes in a match with Racing Club of Argentina. The disgrace was a more than sufficient expedient for the withdrawal of any favours, and the New Year's honours list omitted both Stein and Kelly. Willie Ross claimed that Stein's name was pulled at a late stage because of the 'unfortunate events' in South America.

The following year, 1968, when Manchester United won the same European Cup, the team manager, Matt Busby, who was regarded as a more emollient figure than the abrasive Stein, was immediately offered a knighthood. This exposure of hypocrisy rankled with Willie Ross, who complained in writing to the Prime Minister, Harold Wilson, about the undue proportion of honours for professional football going south of the border. The correspondence came to the notice of that ever-vigilant English defender, Sir John Lang, whose opinion of the Celtic manager was no more flattering than before. Stein, he replied, 'hardly compares with Matt Busby in his service to football, though undoubtedly he is an extremely able manager'. Lang failed to mention – perhaps it did not require to be articulated – Busby's heroic stature following his recovery from the Munich air disaster in which many of his players – the famed 'Busby

Babes' – were killed and he himself was gravely injured. Still, the continuing lack of recognition for Stein felt like an insult to Scottish footballing pride, especially when Lang got his way and negotiated an honour for chairman Kelly in 1969: not the CBE he had first proposed but, rubbing it in, a knighthood.

If Lang felt that this would 'dispose of Stein for a long time to come', he was quickly proved wrong. In 1970, Celtic reached the final of the European Cup for a second time. Willie Ross told Harold Wilson that, if the club won, 'I really do not see how we can avoid an award to Stein, although he made some unfortunate remarks about the refereeing in the Scottish Cup final which Celtic lost'. The phrase 'unfortunate remarks' was a mild version of what happened after Aberdeen's unexpected victory in the cup that year. In a bad case of referee rage, Stein ranted over the decisions of his *bête-noire*, R.H. Davidson, who was suspected of anti-Celtic bias. Davidson, he claimed, had denied Celtic an obvious penalty and awarded Aberdeen a soft one. Stein's biographer, Archie Macpherson, described how the condemnation of Davidson became so loud that 'the Hampden stand trembled'. Ever after, wrote Macpherson, Stein 'would pursue R.H. Davidson, like the posse who kept on the trail of Butch Cassidy and the Sundance Kid'.

The Scottish Football Association rebuked Stein for his behaviour. It could have been another excuse for denying him the honour to which the footballing public believed he was entitled; but the pressure to recognise him was irresistible. A senior civil servant at St Andrew's House prepared a memo acknowledging that he would have to be given something, but added that, the club chairman having had a knighthood so recently, 'I am sure we would have to be content with a CBE for Stein'. A CBE it was. It may not have meant as much to Stein, a man of the people, as it would have done to the many functionaries of the established order who coveted honours and were not above discreetly lobbying for them; and he was never to know how gracelessly and reluctantly it was conceded.

It might never have been conceded if the second long shadow cast by his death had been public knowledge when he was alive. Around the time Miss N.C. Telfer of the Scottish Office was representing Stein's case for a higher honour than a routine OBE, a man called Jim Torbett was insinuating himself into an influential position at Celtic – with damaging consequences for the club and for the reputation of Jock Stein. Though Torbett's creation, Celtic Boys Club, was not formally part of the corporate structure, the directors of Celtic were sufficiently impressed by its potential as a nursery of promising young players to allow Torbett access to the training facilities at Barrowfield in Glasgow. The arrangement worked to Celtic's advantage. Several players did graduate successfully from the boys' club into the senior ranks, if not always at Celtic. But the nature of the club's other function, as a source of sexual gratification for Torbett, was one of Scottish football's dirtier secrets and remained so for many years.

The truth finally emerged at a criminal trial in 1998 when Torbett denied charges of historical child abuse. He was accused of 'shameless and indecent conduct' against three former members of Celtic Boys Club – Alan Brazil, David Gordon and James McGrory – between October 1967 and March 1974. Brazil, a future Scottish internationalist, was 13 when he came to Torbett's notice for reasons not wholly connected to his footballing prowess. In his evidence to the court, Brazil said that, after one training session, he was invited back to Torbett's flat with a group of other boys to eat ice cream and talk tactics. 'I was sitting on the sofa and he squeezed me and put his hand between my legs, touching me. He then kissed me on the side of the cheek'. After the incident, young Alan avoided socialising with Torbett. In his final season with the boys' club, he scored 62 goals – a league record – yet he was one of only two players in the first team who were not signed by Celtic. He wondered why.

'It only happened the once,' said Brazil in a newspaper interview some years after the trial. 'I was strong enough never to go back there again. But a lot of kids look up to a figure of authority and can't get away. There were always six or seven boys who seemed trapped. I was asked in court why I didn't talk about it at the time. But it's not the sort of thing where you go home and say, "Guess what happened to me today? I was interfered with by an older man". How many boys could say that over the dinner table? I wasn't haunted by it, but lots of people suffered psychiatric problems for years.'

A jury found Torbett guilty. Despite the serious betrayal of trust by a man responsible for the welfare of children, he received a lenient sentence: two years in prison, of which he served half. In the immediate aftermath of the verdict, Brazil made an angry statement to the press: 'The people at director level at Celtic Park who knew about this should think shame of themselves for doing nothing about it down the years.' The people 'at director level' to whom Brazil alluded, without naming them, included the chairman Robert Kelly, who in 'lots of ways', according to the government's principal adviser on sport, Sir John Lang, merited a high honour from the state and got one. And although he was not a director, the small group in the know included Stein himself.

A witness at the trial, Hugh Birt, who became chairman of Celtic Boys Club in 1974 after Torbett's departure, testified that Stein told him he had 'booted Torbett out' when he was made aware of the allegations of abuse. But that was the extent of Stein's response to the allegations – and the extent of Birt's. 'I couldn't go to the police without actual proof,' he explained to the jury. 'When I joined I was told by Stein to keep the name of Celtic Football Club clean at all times.' Loyalty to the club was thus paramount, counting for more than any concern for the mental health of the abused boys. The Celtic player Lou Macari, who briefly managed the club in the early 1990s, came to the same view of Stein's justification for colluding in the cover-up. Macari claimed in his autobiography that 'the wish to maintain the good name of Celtic, if that were ever a good enough reason, was the only thing that kept the issue from coming to light at that point'. Macari was informed of 'a string of allegations by young lads whose dreams of playing for Celtic were exploited' – but it took the courage of three of them (Brazil, Gordon and McGrory) to bring Torbett belatedly to justice.

The forgiveness of the clean-living club proved boundless. In 1986, a year after Stein's death, Torbett returned to Celtic as a fund-raiser; and even after his conviction, the club continued to award a lucrative contract, reported to be worth £250,000 a year, to a retail operation, the Trophy Centre, trading in football memorabilia, which was owned by Torbett and included on its board a director of the club. 'This man is a convicted sex offender,' protested one of the victims, David Gordon. 'Why the hell are Celtic still doing business with his company?' There was no answer from Celtic Park. Evidently fully rehabilitated on his release from prison, Torbett had his contract renewed.

In a city of toxic sectarian divisions, there was money to be made out of Celtic's shame. The words 'Big Jock Knew' were printed on scarves and sold outside Ibrox, the home of Rangers Football Club; some of these vile items found their way into the stadium. Rangers supporters chanted the same words, and they were scrawled on walls in Glasgow and even on a bridge over a busy road, yet this slur on the good name of Jock Stein CBE – 'a man who gave his life for his country' according to one of his admirers – was never publicly condemned by Rangers Football Club, or the Scottish press, or the Scottish Football Association. Big Jock did know. That was the problem.

III

In another loss to Scottish football in 1985, though not so consider-able as that of Jock Stein, Hector Nicol took his final bow. 'Scotland's King of Comedy' – there were many rivals for the title – died at the age of 65. The *Evening Times* recorded that he had spent 50 years 'entertaining the world' and had just been honoured at a dinner in

Glasgow to mark his golden jubilee in showbiz. That was pushing it: he had gone to work in a theatre at the age of 15, but only to sell programmes. After a spell as one-third of a hillbilly singing act, the Rodeo Three, he was a straight man to many of the Scottish comics – Jack Radcliffe, Jimmy Logan, Dave Willis, Tommy Morgan, the splendidly named Johnny Victory – before branching out on his own. The turning point in his career came when he appeared at the Ashfield Club, Glasgow, for a one-night stand and was still there five years later. He was a favourite with football clubs, composing a succession of rabble-rousing songs for their fans. 'His bawdy humour disclaimed double entendres,' wrote one of his obituarists. 'He delivered risque jokes in rapid fire volleys, hurling one-liners in torrents at the audiences.' In short, he was filthy. Reputedly he could tell a hundred gags in 10 minutes, most of them blue. But in his private life he wore the mask of tragedy: one of his sons was stabbed to death by a stranger, another choked to death.

In the same year, at the same age, Chic Murray died; a lofty, wistful, bunneted figure, far more subtle than Nicol, a master of the incongruous and the laconic. 'I got up this morning,' he would inform his audience. 'I like to get up in the morning. It gives me the rest of the day to myself.' Or: 'This chap started to talk to me about this and that, about which I knew very little.' Or: 'I believe the minister's going to give a sermon today on the milk of human kindness. Well, I hope it's condensed.' His agent used to say that Murray didn't say funny lines, he said lines funny. But he was not invariably funny as a husband or father; marriage to the long-suffering Maidie, his diminutive music-hall partner, ended in divorce. He claimed to have been turned down for a mortgage on the grounds that he was a vagrant ('That really tickled him,' said his daughter Annabelle). He drank too much, though according to Annabelle he could be an amusing drunk, especially when he was trying to fry an egg. By the end he was a lonely, melancholy figure, hanging out in the BBC canteen in Glasgow, where he was regarded as something of a resident bore. In the Scottish manner, it was only in death that legendary status was conferred upon him.

IV

A third long-standing turn, one for whom Scottish audiences had decidedly mixed feelings, was the poet and controversialist Hugh MacDiarmid, another prodigious drinker. By 1985 he had been dead for seven years, but with the proposal to erect a sculpture in his honour in his native Langholm – the so-called Muckle Toon – he had begun to cause trouble from beyond the grave, which would have delighted him.

His friend Norman MacCaig said at his funeral that, on the anniversaries of his death, Scotland should declare three minutes' pandemonium. Scotland declined to comply with this interesting idea. Chris MacLean wrote in the *Independent* on the centenary of his birth (1992) that 'ripples of appreciation' were more evident than pandemonium. Even the ripples were grudging. Another poet, Liz Lochhead, called him 'the Grand Old Man, mischievous, always playing the devil's advocate, very male, very Scottish, and pretty patronising to women'. She did acknowledge that 'more than anyone else, he made Scots a tongue that could deal with the world's philosophical ideals' and that he 'united the earthiness of Burns with modernist influences'. But most Scots continued to prefer Burns, finding MacDiarmid's braid Scots more difficult to comprehend; and his wayward politics stuck in many gullets. 'He is a very great poet, and I liked him immensely,' said Sorley MacLean – a generous tribute considering that MacDiarmid had once translated some of Maclean's Gaelic poems into Scots and proceeded to publish them without his authority. But MacLean added: 'I never thought his political judgement was sound and I cannot be fundamentally anti-English, as he was.' In similar vein, Donald Dewar said he suspected that few modern Scots knew much about MacDiarmid's political past. 'His poetry was magnificent,' agreed Dewar, 'but I never could take his politics.' What were his politics? He was variously sympathetic to fascism, communism and republican nationalism. Politically he was hardly worth taking seriously. Deirdre Grieve, his daughter-in-law and literary executor, said that he entertained at one point or another almost every political belief it was possible to entertain. In his own words he was to be found 'whaur extremes meet – it's the only way I ken'.

Among the many forked tongues on the centenary, only one commentator played MacDiarmid at his own vitriolic game: the *Glasgow Herald*'s Jack McLean. The poet had written of his disdain for that newspaper: of how a terrible shadow descended like dust over his thoughts, 'almost like reading a *Glasgow Herald* leader'. His opinion of the paper would not have been improved by McLean's contribution to the anniversary celebrations. The 'Urban Voltaire' – a sobriquet with which he had been burdened by his editor, Arnold Kemp – did not write leaders. He did, however, write a column on the leader page, a combustible weekly brew of polemic and personal observation. In the centenary recitation of the poet's qualities he condemned MacDiarmid as 'a thief, a liar, a plagiarist, a coward, a wimp, a snob, scarce a man at all'. It came close to three minutes' pandemonium and would not have taken much longer than that to read – or, perhaps, write.

The town of Langholm affected in the case of MacDiarmid an air of indifference rather than outright hostility, except when provoked, as it easily was. The burgh officials decided they had more pressing business to attend to than MacDiarmid's funeral. Memories in small town Scotland tended to be long, and there were persistent suggestions that Langholm disapproved of a reference in his autobiography (*Lucky Poet*) to a sexual encounter in the local academy involving two pupils, two teachers, and a desk. No matter that the incident occurred in 1904 – it was still remembered in the 1960s when the town refused to make MacDiarmid a freeman of the burgh and chose instead Neil Armstrong, the first man on the moon.

'They'll have to live with him now,' acidly observed MacDiarmid's shrewish wife Valda, as they lowered him to the grave in Langholm cemetery. And, for seven years, they did so quietly – until the Scottish Sculpture Trust commissioned a gifted Borders artist, Jake Harvey of Melrose, to create a permanent memorial to MacDiarmid. It took the form of an open book in bronze, standing 10 feet in height and 15 feet in width. It was a splendid piece, and the trust decided they had just the place for it – a spot on the Langholm to Newcastletown road, a mile east of the town. The townspeople thought otherwise. Objectors claimed that it would be out of keeping with the surrounding countryside and that the view from the site would be severely restricted, if not ruined; the chairman of the Common Riding Commitee complained that it was to be sited at the start of the hound trail. 'It is a hideous thing,' said Councillor Robert Robinson, a farmer from Newton Stewart, 'and this is no place for it.' Robinson must have been speaking from memory, for when he and his colleagues visited the site it was so foggy they could see no further than the end of their noses.

Timothy Neat of the Scottish Sculpture Trust was aghast. The newspapers reported that his voice was 'quivering with indignation' when he gave his reaction to the decision of Dumfries and Galloway Council to reject the planning application. 'This must be seen as a national disgrace. We are not talking about permission for a garage or a shed, but a monument to a major national figure, made by a major Scottish sculptor. The refusal is another example of the Scots spitting in the faces of their own great men.' There was a leader in the *Glasgow Herald* of the pompous sort that had made MacDiarmid's blood boil. On the one hand, Armstrong, whose connection with the town was tenuous, would put Langholm on the map 'perhaps more than MacDiarmid would have done'. On the other hand – there was always another hand – for Langholm to continue to resist recognising the greatness of MacDiarmid 'smells of pettiness'. MacDiarmid, it continued, could be many things, 'but he was never small-minded'.

The *Glasgow Herald* had got that wrong. He was often small-minded, pursuing mean vendettas with awe-inspiring tenacity. He could be an old goat. He could (on the other hand) be charm personified.

The controversy which so exercised the drawing rooms of Edinburgh failed to ignite the readers of the *Glasgow Herald*, whose letters page that week was concerned with the rating system, the high cost of air travel from Glasgow to Wick, the golden jubilee of Clarkston Rugby Club, and a pay review for teachers – not a word about the slight inflicted on the memory of Hugh MacDiarmid, though a passing nod to the memory of R.D. Laing, the Glasgow-born writer and psychoanalyst. In the Muckle Toon itself, a MacDiarmid scholar, Walter Bell, corrected the impression that local opinion was divided on the refusal of the planning application: 'The majority of people in Langholm don't give a damn about MacDiarmid either way. Some people in Langholm would complain about anything.' In the end, the memorial was erected high above the town, at a place called Whita Hill, far enough away for the locals to forget all about MacDiarmid. And in years to come, it was not the poet who would be fondly remembered in Scotland but rather the comedian who got up in the morning because it gave him the rest of the day to himself, and the football manager who did what he mistakenly thought was best for his club.

1986

FRIENDS IN LOW PLACES

I

Peter Heatly, a medal-winning diver turned sports administrator, came up with the ill-starred idea that Edinburgh should bid for the 1986 Commonwealth Games. The offer was promptly accepted, possibly because there were no others on the table. 'It was party time for the Edinburgh bid team,' wrote Brian Oliver, an observer of the subsequent fiasco, 'even if it was hardly a champagne moment.' From the start there were dark murmurings of a boycott of the event in protest at the Thatcher government's refusal to impose sanctions on South Africa over its policy of apartheid; and the world was in the grip of a recession. Who would have wanted to run the risk of hosting a games beset by obvious difficulties both economic and political? In this unpromising scenario maybe only a diver would have taken the plunge.

The Edinburgh financial institutions failed to rally behind the project and potential backers were unimpressed by the performance of the organising committee – a limited liability company chaired by Ken Borthwick, a former Lord Provost of the city. It employed too many staff, sold the media rights for too low a figure, and hired professional fundraisers who were hopeless at raising funds. In the frantic hunt for sponsors, a prominent Scottish businessman was approached at a late stage for a donation sufficient to meet the costs of a particular event. 'How much?' he asked. Reply: '£250,000'. When he responded that a quarter of a million was beyond his resources, he was told that it could be done for £75,000. 'That sum would have been acceptable in the first place,' wrote the journalist Jack Webster, 'but misjudgment on such a scale destroyed the man's belief in their ability to organise a round of tiddly-winks. If he had agreed to the first request, what would have happened to the rest of his money? They got nothing.' The story was typical of the amateur approach.

By late June, a few weeks before the starting pistol, the money was running out and relations between Borthwick's consortium and the Labour-controlled city council had declined from frosty to abrasive. Borthwick implored the Secretary of State for Scotland, Malcolm Rifkind, for a financial lifeline from the government and was briskly rebuffed. The eight directors, who were privately worried about their personal financial liability, made a last desperate throw to avoid the unthinkable embarrassment of receivership: they contacted 37 chairmen of major companies, offering any of them effective control of the event, and such prestige as it conferred, in return for a rescue package.

Only one replied: Robert Maxwell, former Labour MP, millionaire publisher of scientific journals, and for the last 18 months proprietor of the Mirror group of newspapers including Scotland's leading tabloid, the *Daily Record*, whose journalists had recently been embroiled in a bitter dispute with him about a range of issues, including his insistence that their pampered existence – a highly paid four-day week – was no longer tenable. Department of Trade investigators had once denounced him as 'not a person who can be relied upon to exercise stewardship of a publicly-quoted company', and his nickname 'The Bouncing Czech' denoted not only the country of his birth, where he entered the world as Jan Koch, but a cavalier attitude to other people's money. Only beggars who could not be choosers would have chosen Maxwell as the saviour of the Commonwealth Games, and Borthwick was indeed a beggar, a more than usually abject one, when he showed up in London for a make-or-break meeting. 'I think I can help you,' was Maxwell's opening gambit. He then announced that, in this spirit of helpfulness, he required

Borthwick to stand down as chairman at once and that he intended to run the show personally.

Borthwick managed a straight face when he denied that this amounted to a personal humiliation, but his statement to the press betrayed the depth of his naivete. 'No figures were mentioned. There is nothing on paper. I think Mr Maxwell is a gentleman and we simply shook hands and that was the end of the matter. We then had lunch and Mr Maxwell left for Westminster Abbey for Mannie Shinwell's memorial service.'

Maxwell could be called many things, but until that moment 'gentleman' had not been one of them. When the *Daily Record* appeared the next morning it was with a self-serving headline splashed across the front page: '*Record* saves the games', accompanied by a disingenuous claim from the 'gentleman' that he had been personally approached by Malcolm Rifkind to intervene in the debacle. The opposite was true: Maxwell had done the approaching and got nowhere with Rifkind. The terms of the so-called 'deal' being celebrated in Maxwell's own paper were so vague as to be meaningless; Borthwick had returned to Edinburgh with his head on a plate, and with nothing to show for his self-sacrifice but the handshake of a buccaneer.

A few days later, when the new chairman called a press conference in Edinburgh, he was surrounded by a phalanx of aides, including a 'personal assistant' who took an extensive note of the proceedings and such familiar acolytes as Joe Haines, the former press officer of Harold Wilson. Ken Laird, 'bureau chief' of the *Daily Record* in Edinburgh, was introduced as the Games' press officer, while management consultants from Coopers and Lybrand, who had already had a look at the books, were in attendance to underline the gravity of the financial situation. There was £1.8 million left in the bank; a further £2.5 million was urgently required. 'This is like the Battle of Arnhem,' he declared. Any military historians in the room would have been unsettled by the analogy: Britain lost the Battle of Arnhem.

There was a further destabilising statement: Maxwell declared that, whoever plugged the funding gap, it would not be him. Pressed to clarify the exact nature of the guarantee he was offering, he resorted to the usual bombast: 'I don't need to give any guarantee. I and my colleagues are pretty good guarantors and I am well known. If I take on anything then I deliver and I succeed.' So he would not be underwriting any losses? 'If I were to underwrite them, then voluntary effort would immediately stop. Everybody would go home.' He did not anticipate a shortfall. But if it were to happen, 'You can rest assured that I have already contacted the government and the response was satisfactory.' This was news to the Scottish Office, which insisted that it was 'unaware of any approach' and repeated that the Games must be self-financing.

Maxwell, describing himself as 'a nationalised Scot', rounded on the press for rubbishing the Games and for suggesting that he had hijacked them. When journalists pointed out that all they had done was faithfully report the difficulties facing the event, he changed tack: 'Please forgive me if I sound offensive. I was reporting the feelings of the Games people. I have told them that some of it is their own bloody fault.' It was a bravura performance by an actor-manager of the barnstorming school, but the Scottish press – with the unsurprising exception of the *Daily Record* – gave it critical notices. The *Glasgow Herald*'s editorial noted that contrary to the original assumptions Maxwell was putting none of his personal fortune into the venture but was relying on his ability as a fundraiser. The paper added that it said little for the entrepreneurial energies of Edinburgh – 'the UK's second financial centre' – that the Games organisers had 'cast themselves at Mr Maxwell's feet'.

The low comedy of the inaugural press conference turned to pantomime on a second, even more bizarre, occasion when Maxwell divulged that 'the world's greatest philanthropist' was personally backing the Games and that he had flown from Tokyo as a gesture of goodwill. The benefactor in question, Ryoiahi Sasakawa, who stood to attention throughout the press conference, occasionally bowing and praying before the cameras, required the services of an interpreter for his occasional contributions. Although something may have been lost in translation, Sasakawa apparently claimed that he was only 17 years old and expected to live to the age of 200. He said that although he had been imprisoned for three years after the Second World War as a suspected war criminal, he had never been indicted or tried. He disclosed that he was chairman of 50 organisations and founder of the Sasakawa Foundation, a charitable enterprise chaired in Britain by his good friend Robert Maxwell. Later it emerged that Sasakawa was born in 1899, which made him 87 not 17, that he made his vast fortune in rice speculation before the war, and that he had once described himself as the world's richest fascist.

This encounter with the media was no more revealing about the financing of the Games than the first, and when the world's greatest philanthropist was asked to put a figure to his donation, Maxwell cut in and said it would be 'impolite' to question him further. He did, however, add that Sasakawa had 'single-handedly funded the eradication of leprosy' – a non-sequitur not quite in the Arnhem class but of doubtful authenticity. Two decades later, the number of people in the world who were still suffering from leprosy was estimated at 200,000.

Ten days before the off, a second crisis engulfed the Games: they were now facing a boycott as well as a financial black hole. 'Every morning you would wake up and another country had decided not to come,' recalled Peter Heatly. 'It was terrible. You died a little bit every day.' Confronted by demands from black African nations to take action against the regime in Pretoria, Margaret Thatcher refused to budge, maintaining her opposition to sanctions. Nigeria and Ghana were the first to pull out in protest at her intransigence. At that stage, the secretary of the Commonwealth Games Federation, David Dixon, while lamenting that the unity of the event had been destroyed, was predicting that the boycott would affect only 80 of the

3,151 competitors who were scheduled to participate. In the end, 32 nations – and their 1,500 athletes – stayed away. Some checked into the athletes' village unaware that their governments had just joined the boycott; the contingent from Bermuda took part in the opening ceremony before being ordered home.

Chris Brasher, a former Olympic champion, wrote that the Games were 'rudderless and hapless in a sea of disaster' and attacked the stewardship of Ken Borthwick, 'a man who has an amazing ability to score own goals against his own team'. His successor Maxwell, however, was revelling in his new role of Scottish patriot: 'Think of the humiliation to the country if Edinburgh had gone into receivership. I couldn't allow that.' As vague as ever about the money, he was threatening to send Margaret Thatcher a bill for any loss: 'She is a tough lady, but I am a tough hombre.' In one well-publicised economy measure, he invited a number of Commonwealth VIPs to dinner in his private suite and then sent his staff out to fetch a takeaway for the distinguished guests – Kentucky Fried Chicken served from the basket.

Maxwell dished out most of the medals, leaving the mere head of the Commonwealth, the Queen, to distribute what was left, but more than the unity of the event had been destroyed by the boycott. The competition itself was much depleted by the absence of so many competitors. Lennox Lewis, winner of a boxing gold medal, faced in the final a nonentity from Wales, one Aneurin Evans, of whom the BBC commentator Harry Carpenter said on air: 'He really is out of his depth here. If I were him, I'd be running for my life.' Poor Evans finally threw in the towel and was left with an unwanted legacy as the unlikeliest silver medallist in Commonwealth history.

On the penultimate day, the tough lady paid an official visit. When she toured the athletes' village, Thatcher was snubbed by the competitors, who held her personally responsible for the mass boycott. Later, when she arrived at Meadowbank Stadium, a crowd of around 500 anti-apartheid demonstrators were waiting for her and she was pelted with eggs and tomatoes. And when she and her husband, Denis, took their seats in the VIP box, and their arrival was announced over the public address system to the 23,000 spectators, boos and catcalls rang out across the arena, with only a scattering of applause.

In the two hours she spent in the village, she talked almost exclusively to officials and was introduced to only one athlete, the England rower Joanna Toch, an articulate young woman who made no secret of her disapproval of Thatcher's presence. She wanted to know why the Prime Minister had urged athletes not to take part in the Moscow Olympics after the Russian invasion of Afghanistan, yet was now suggesting that politics should be kept out of sport and that there should have been no boycott of Edinburgh. Thatcher replied that the competitors at the Olympics had been allowed to decide for themselves: 'I left you free to choose, dear. I wish to goodness some of the young people who are not here had been left to decide.' She then instructed security to 'get a move on' and brushed past reporters and TV crews, while Toch was taken aside by the England team manager and escorted back to the residences. A Canadian athlete, Nathaniel Crooks, said that Thatcher had 'embarrassed herself' by turning up in Edinburgh, but most of the opposition in the village was unspoken. The athletes, having been warned by their managers not to cause trouble, signified their feelings by making themselves scarce, though one or two were prepared to admit later that they had enjoyed themselves and had been oblivious to the politics. Britain's Sally Gunnell, who won the first of her five Commonwealth golds at Edinburgh, admitted: 'I was just chuffed to be there. I wasn't really reading the newspapers, I had never been to a big event, and I was completely blown away by it.'

For the majority, however, Edinburgh was not a happy experience. Misery was piled upon misery: minority sports such as bowls and shooting attracted more journalists and officials than paying spectators; the performance of the Scottish athletes, apart from the victory of Liz Lynch (McColgan) in the 10,000 metres, was described by one sports writer as 'a pile of dross'; and in the final days incessant rain added to the gloom. The *Guardian*'s Frank Keating summed up the fortnight as 'Games for wellies planned by wallies' while the *Daily Mail* labelled them 'The Disaster Games'. Right to the end, if anything could go wrong, anything did. In the march past of the nations – a rather shorter procession than usual – during the closing ceremony, a super-heavyweight wrestler, Albert Patrick, was carrying the Scottish flag when a gust of wind carried off the cross of St Andrew in front of the Queen. The athletics journalist Doug Gillon wrote that it 'fluttered like a wounded bird before being pursued by a figure of shot-putting proportions' – the 22-stone press magnate. Maxwell's unsuccessful attempts to replace the saltire on its standard, before he rejoined the monarch on the trackside dais, symbolised the comic absurdity of the occasion.

II

In the end the Games were bankrolled by such business associates of Maxwell as David Stephens of Beaverbrook newspapers (so the *Daily Express* too could claim to have 'saved the Games') and Ernest Saunders, CEO of the Guinness brewing empire, rather than by the financial institutions of the host nation. Although it was no excuse for refusing to spare the blushes of Edinburgh and the Commonwealth, the bankers were distracted by problems of their own in 1986. Chief among them turned out to be Ernest Saunders himself.

A native of Austria, Saunders had much in common with Maxwell: he was born with a different name (Schleyer), successfully re-invented himself in Britain, and was popularly known by a nickname. Maxwell boasted two for the price of one: the jauntier 'Captain Bob' – which served him well nine years later when, having plundered the Mirror group's pension fund, he fell to his death off his yacht in the Canary Islands – as well as 'The Bouncing Czech' with its more sinister connotations. Saunders made do with one: 'Deadly Ernest'. Some said it was a tribute to his ruthlessness, another quality he shared with Maxwell; others that he had a habit of droning on at meetings. Unlike Maxwell, he avoided a watery grave. Indeed he was to earn a small place in history as the only person who ever made a complete recovery from pre-senile dementia.

For a while, Deadly Ernest pretended to be Edinburgh's friend. When a Campbeltown-born entrepreneur, James Gulliver, launched a hostile takeover bid for Scotland's most illustrious company, Distillers, Edinburgh decided that it would rather have Saunders, who rode into the capital as a white knight to 'save' Distillers, just as Maxwell was 'saving' the Commonwealth Games. Gulliver, the dynamo behind the Argyll food and retail group which owned the British end of the Safeway supermarket chain, offered £1.9 billion for Distillers, whose products included such household names as Johnnie Walker whisky and Gordon's gin. It was the biggest bid in British commercial history, audacious but well-conceived. Gulliver knew what everyone in the City knew – that Distillers was badly managed. But he was also smart enough to spot that the company was undervalued. The prospect of re-energising a tired brand and creating a world-class company based in Scotland's capital city excited him commercially, for it had the potential to make colossal profits, but it also appealed to his patriotic instincts. Gulliver possessed great entrepreneurial skill and had the knack of choosing as his lieutenants people as driven as he was. He believed that talented Scots should be able to make a name – and a fortune – for themselves without leaving Scotland. But in the battle for Distillers, he suffered from a crippling disadvantage: his lack of close social links with the Edinburgh financial establishment. He was an outsider. He was therefore suspected.

The Distillers' board preferred Guinness; Edinburgh preferred Guinness. But Saunders, to be sure of winning, had to coax key investors into his camp and provide a convincing answer to the critics who objected to control of a blue-chip Scottish company shifting, like so many before it, south of the border. Sensing the need for concessions, he made two significant ones. The first was a promise that the headquarters of the combined Guinness/Distillers Group would be located in Edinburgh. The second was a more personal coup: the signing of Sir Thomas Risk as chairman of his expanded empire.

Risk, the governor of the Bank of Scotland, was a figure of transparent probity and sound practical vision. North Sea oil had created new opportunities for the Scottish financial sector, and Risk made sure that the Bank of Scotland prospered more than most from a period of explosive growth. Assets multiplied; profits rocketed; and Risk was not afraid to innovate, launching Scotland's first electronic banking system. The *Economist* heaped praise on his stewardship, describing the Bank of Scotland as Britain's most admired bank for its marriage of progressive ideas and traditional virtues, yet Risk personally belied his name: he was essentially a rather canny individual. 'Don't bet the bank' was his favourite aphorism – one that he scrupulously observed in his business dealings. A decade later, when the bank merged with the Halifax group to form HBOS, no-one was more dismayed than Risk when his successors did bet the bank with their ruinous lending policies.

Risk had misgivings about Ernest Saunders' offer of the non-executive chairmanship of Guinness/Distillers. Although he had no reason at that stage to doubt Saunders' integrity, he was fearful that his appointment would be seen as tokenism, an empty gesture to Scottish pride. Saunders seemed genuine in his desire to make Edinburgh the powerhouse of the enlarged group and even let it be known that he and his wife were house-hunting in the capital. Such expressions of sincerity persuaded Risk. 'There seems little doubt', wrote the City journalist Robert Martin, 'that it was this commitment [Risk's appointment] that swayed a number of key institutional investors to Guinness. Another was to make Edinburgh the real administrative headquarters.'

In April 1986, victory for Guinness in the takeover battle was hailed in the press as a personal triumph for Ernest Saunders. Risk, chairman-designate, assured journalists that after a long period of uncertainty 'things would be done quickly' – he meant the setting-up of the Edinburgh HQ. But things were not done quickly. Things were not done at all. As soon as he gained control of Distillers, Saunders lost interest in Risk and virtually ignored him. Deeply frustrated, Risk sought an urgent meeting. Saunders declared that he had changed his mind, that he required full executive control of the business and for that reason would be assuming the chairmanship himself. It was a disgraceful breach of trust, made worse by the planting of stories that Risk had somehow been an obstacle to progress. The president of Guinness, Lord Iveagh, claimed that there had been a clash of personalities between Risk and the board, 'which suggests that the consequences of his appointment were not very carefully considered'. The boardroom row existed in Iveagh's imagination. Risk, far from clashing, had been isolated and excluded.

In the fall-out from the notorious 'change of mind', Saunders was supported by his friend the shotputter, who 'threw his weight' – a considerable one, if only in physical bulk – behind the decision. Maxwell claimed that it was not in the interests of the company that Risk should be chairman: 'The real boss would always have been Ernest Saunders.' That was true of many companies led by dominant personalities such as Saunders and Maxwell, but it overlooked the detached guidance and wisdom that a non-executive chairman could offer and the undesirability of giving unfettered power to a CEO.

Outside his own board of nodding donkeys, Saunders had few allies. 'There is not a single institutional shareholder who is not unhappy with the cavalier way that he has handled the situation,' wrote Robert Martin. 'What credence can the investing community give to formal takeover documents? Institutional investors have a duty to put the good name of the financial world before narrow financial advantage.'

There was an early opportunity for the financial world to defend its good name: a meeting of shareholders a few days later, a meeting to be chaired by Saunders, at which he would be proposed – or propose himself – as joint chairman and CEO. Labour's shadow trade and industry secretary, John Smith, got in ahead of the anticipated showdown with a sharp note to the chairman of the Stock Exchange, Sir Nicholas Goodison, accusing Guinness of 'driving a coach and horses through the rules' and suggesting that it had secured Distillers on the basis of undertakings now thrown aside. The *Glasgow Herald* challenged the shareholders to deliver 'as sharp and salutary a rebuke as the board of a public company can receive'. But the shareholders' meeting was a woeful anti-climax: effectively no-contest. In both the proxy vote and on a show of hands, Saunders had an overwhelming majority – around 10 to 1.

'With the expertise of an accomplished politician who knows he has the power, Mr Saunders side-stepped all awkward questions,' reported one journalist in the room. 'Anybody who came to the meeting wanting to find out just how much of the business will be run from Scotland left none the wiser.' Not only the commitment to Risk had been abandoned; the vision of the global headquarters in Edinburgh was also vanishing off the corporate radar. The most Saunders was prepared to offer was the transfer of some unspecified 'central management functions' to Scotland. He added meaningfully that the AGM would continue to be held in London.

His new excuse for breaking promises was that a look at the ledgers, and the shocking details contained within, had made a change of strategy essential. City journalists were scornful. 'It is hard to accept the Guinness contention that it was only when they took over Distillers that they realised how bad things were,' wrote one. 'Distillers' problems were well known. During the bid Mr Saunders kept on about them.' But there was no rebuke – neither sharp nor salutary, simply none at all – from the shareholders. The Scottish victims of the sting, if they felt sore about it, kept their opinions to themselves. Only one voice – Graeme Knox, investment manager at Scottish Amicable – was raised in dissent. 'It certainly does raise doubts about the City's ability for self-regulation,' said Knox after the meeting. 'The erstwhile shareholders of the Distillers' Company, not to say those of Argyll, have been cheated and it is lamentable that Guinness's explanations are so woefully inadequate and question-able.' He went on: 'Distillers' shareholders have been grossly misled by Guinness and abandoned by the ineffectual City authorities and we, who operate daily the dictum of "My word is my bond", are the poorer for it.' Labour's George Robertson backed Knox's principled stand, pointing out that even those institutions that had objected to Guinness's conduct 'simply lay down and accepted it'. The message of the affair, said Robertson, was that 'anything goes in the City and promises are meaningless'. Malcolm Rifkind, who did his mistress's bidding over the Guinness affair as he did over the Commonwealth Games, avoided direct criticism, feebly reiterating that the company had promised to set up a headquarters in Edinburgh.

Risk – the hapless victim of the treachery – was circumspect about its denouement. 'Shareholders,' he said, 'do not want to be surrogate regulators. They do not want that role and it is perhaps unfair to ask them to fill it.' Some City commentators disagreed. They argued that financial institutions, given their enormous influence, had some responsibility for the moral conduct of the companies in which they invested. But this lesson was learned at length and with great reluctance. Twenty-two years later, when the Royal Bank of Scotland came within hours of collapse in the financial crash of 2008 and other banks, including HBOS, had to be bailed out from public funds, only the names had changed. The nature of the problem – the failure to regulate arrogance, recklessness and greed – had not.

By the end of 1986, the hubris of Ernest Saunders was already turning to dust. In the traditional manner of the public figure caught with his pants down, he 'denied any wrongdoing' and announced that he had 'no intention of resigning'. A few weeks later his board, so acquiescent when the going was soft, fired him. It had no alternative after Olivier Roux, the company's finance director, blew the whistle and revealed the existence of a slush fund which had bolstered the Guinness share price and made the takeover terms (£2.9 billion) better than Gulliver's competitive offer of £1.9 billion. Gulliver himself had observed with the deepest suspicion the rise and rise of the Guinness shares, sensed that something rotten was going on, but was powerless to intervene. He never recovered from the blow of losing the glittering prize that ought to have been his, and died 10 years later at the age of 66.

The facilitator of the corruption at Guinness was a New York stock market dealer, Ivan Boesky, who was given a hundred million dollars to set up the slush fund and received a fat fee for his services. Thus armed, Boesky found no shortage of willing investors. A member of the Guinness dynasty, Jonathan Guinness, when he learned that the company had pumped the staggering sum into a limited partnership run by Boesky, meekly accepted the explanation that it was just a 'strategic investment'. Later, when he heard that Boesky was being prosecuted for insider trading, Guinness wondered whether to inform the company's non-executive directors of the firm's 'investment' in a Boesky fund. 'It is always easier to do nothing,' he wrote. 'So I kept my head down.' He was criticised by the *Economist* for his lack of curiosity about the strange goings-on at the business which bore the family name.

At first Saunders suffered no worse than the mild indignity of a Department of Trade and Industry investigation, of the type which had judged his friend Maxwell to be unfit to run a public company. The reaction of the City press to the launch of the inquiry was one of weary cynicism: 'There is little doubt', wrote one analyst, 'that the tactics in the Guinness affair have been employed before'. But the investigation uncovered a story of such criminal deception that in August 1990, almost four years after he was sacked, Saunders came to court on charges of conspiracy to defraud, false accounting and theft in relation to the dishonest share support scheme. He was sentenced to five years' imprisonment, which was reduced on appeal to two and a half, and in June 1991, having served only 10 months, mostly in an open prison, Saunders was released on compassionate grounds, allegedly in the early stages of dementia; he was then able to embark on a new career as a business consultant. In the same year, Sir Thomas Risk, his reputation untarnished by a scandal in which he was blameless, retired as governor of the Bank of Scotland.

Guinness, having swallowed Distillers, itself merged in 1997 with an outfit called Grand Metropolitan and the result was the London-based Diageo, a name invented by a brand marketing consultancy and apparently intended to denote the giving of pleasure. In the depressed industrial town of Kilmarnock, where pleasure came in the shortest of measures, Diageo closed the original Johnnie Walker plant despite protests from across the political spectrum. Among the less tangible assets inherited by Diageo, the advertising slogan 'Guinness is good for you' acquired a new meaning as an ironical commentary on the saga of Deadly Ernest, whose legacy left a distinctively bitter taste, especially in the marbled banking halls of Edinburgh.

III

Further north, on the shores of the Pentland Firth, industrial expansion was also in the air – along with something more sinister. In 1984, the director of the Dounreay nuclear establishment, Clifford Blumfield, had proposed a scheme for expanding the plant. Why not make Dounreay a centre for the reprocessing of fuel from Europe's other fast breeder reactors? It was an idea at the dirty extremity of the industry: to take the most hazardous form of nuclear waste – spent fuel – from the continent and somehow transport it to distant Caithness.

A group of nuclear scientists reacted with undisguised dismay, particularly when it leaked out from official documents that air transport was being considered on the grounds that it offered 'many advantages in providing the necessary security'. The scientists disagreed. 'Anyone familiar with the bleak remoteness of Dounreay's little airstrip, the proximity of a deserted coastline, and the sophisticated ruthlessness of airborne terrorism in the 1980s could read this only with incredulity,' they wrote.

At first the British government was non-committal, but in May 1985, without public consultation, Margaret Thatcher's administration declared its support for the proposal. Later that year the Secretary of State for Scotland announced that the planning application would be considered by a conventional local inquiry with limited powers – so limited that such issues as the method of transportation were ruled irrelevant. The same group of nuclear scientists who had opposed the use of air argued in favour of siting the reprocessing plant 'almost as far from the reactors as it could possibly be' but acknowledged that rationality would have little to do with the outcome.

When the public inquiry opened on 7 April 1986, it had received 2,700 written submissions of which only 12 were in favour of the proposal. A petition opposing it, signed by 12,000 people in the Highlands, was presented to the reporter, Alexander Bell. It was the start of a seven-month hearing in which fate took an influential hand: no-one could have foreseen that within three weeks the credibility of nuclear power would have taken a severe hit, undermining the Dounreay plan.

In the early hours of 26 April, many hundreds of miles from Thurso where the inquiry was taking place, one of the four reactors at an obscure nuclear power station in the Ukraine ran out of control. A power surge created a violent explosion at Chernobyl, the 1,000-tonne concrete and steel roof of the reactor building blew off, and blazing radioactive material was blasted into the atmosphere in menacing chunks. By 29 April, traces of radioactive dust were being picked up as far away as Norway, Austria and the Black Sea. Three days later, blown by the wind, the cloud from Chernobyl drifted over Britain – harmlessly enough, it was thought at the time, as long as there was no rain. It did rain. It rained over Wales and Cumbria, Scotland and Northern Ireland, and over Sweden, Norway and Finland, where the fall contaminated the lichens – the staple diet of the reindeer herds – and in turn the reindeer themselves.

On the hill farms of North Wales, Cumbria and the south-west of Scotland, the sheep were eating radioactive grass and the lambs were soon affected through their mothers' milk. The British government insisted that there was no cause for anxiety. The Secretary of State for the Environment, Kenneth Baker, stated on 8 May that 'the effects of the cloud have been assessed and none presents a risk to the UK.' On the same day, the Scottish newspapers reported that 'a team of scientific experts' who were meeting daily to monitor radioactivity levels in Scotland had come to the same conclusion. The Scottish Office denied that iodine tablets were being distributed to Civil Defence volunteers in an attempt to counter radiation; or rather claimed to have 'no knowledge' of the practice, which was not quite the same as refuting it.

Baker reiterated in a Commons statement that tests had shown radioactivity was 'nowhere near the levels at which there was any danger to health' and that it was 'falling rapidly'. But if these bromides were intended to satisfy the public, they were not completely successful. A Scottish Office hotline was swamped with calls from people demanding to know whether it was to safe to let children out to play and whether clothing worn in the rain should be destroyed. The Scottish Dairy Council maintained, however, that the 'radiation scare' was having no effect on the sales of milk and that although radiation levels were 'slightly higher than usual' they were well below the threshold at which consumers might reasonably start to worry.

At the Dounreay inquiry, one of the few supporters of the re-processing plant, the vice-convener of Highland Regional Council, John Robertson, declined to drink from the jug of water provided for witnesses and instead reached theatrically for a jar of rainwater he had collected from a greenhouse roof three miles from the nuclear plant. 'There has been a lot of talk about Chernobyl and the stuff coming down from the skies,' he told the hearing. 'Just to illustrate my confidence in the cleanliness of Caithness and Dounreay, I'm quite happy to drink this.' He was also happy to share with the inquiry his belief that 'the Highlands do not enjoy the luxury of picking and choosing the economic activities they will or will not accept.'

Robertson's confidence was shaken almost immediately by the discovery, on the foreshore near Dounreay, of a speck of radioactive dust from the core of the Chernobyl reactor. Detected during routine monitoring, it was the first such particle to be found anywhere in Britain. The United Kingdom Atomic Energy Authority (UKAEA), sponsors of the reprocessing plant, hastened to assure the people of Caithness that, even if swallowed, it would cause no harm to health and represented only 2% of the maximum dose of radiation allowed for nuclear workers in a year. If the UKAEA was to be believed, the particle was of no radiological importance. But it was significant psychologically: it had turned up in Scotland, far from the Ukraine; and had done so, inconveniently, on the doorstep of the Dounreay plant. The news sparked rumours of contamination elsewhere. The SNP claimed to have impeccable sources for its allegation that an emergency alarm had been activated at Hunterston B nuclear power station in Ayrshire. The South of Scotland Electricity Board denied that radiation there had reached a level at which respiratory masks or iodine tablets had been issued and further denied that there had been any alarm.

Briefly, the impact of the Chernobyl fall-out on Scotland disappeared from the front pages. The handling of the Dounreay inquiry, meanwhile, vacillated between the petty and the downright obstructive. Penny Boyle, of the Nuclear Reprocessing Concern Group, complained that she had effectively been banned from attending it. One of her goats had died, leaving a new-born kid which required constant attention. She brought it to the Town Hall in Thurso in a basket and kept it there in a room set aside for the objectors. The caretaker told her it would have to go – no animals were allowed in the Town Hall.

A second objector, Frances McKie of the Campaign Against Dounreay Expansion, who was pregnant with her fourth child, made a daily journey across the Pentland Firth from her home in Orkney to question witnesses and present her group's case. 'Frequently alone,' said one report, 'she has been faced with the massed ranks of the United Kingdom Atomic Energy Authority and British Nuclear Fuels' lawyers and officials, with a backroom team across the street, flying regularly to Caithness in chartered aircraft, all at an estimated total cost of more than £1m.' It was an unequal contest, made worse by the contemptuous treatment of Mrs McKie and other objectors. Brian Gill QC, who was representing the three island councils, objectors themselves, protested: 'I am worried greatly that during cross-examination, UKAEA people in the room who were sitting behind this lady were quite ostentatiously laughing at some of the questions and that caused a great deal of upset.' He added pointedly to the reporter: 'I do feel that if they had been more firmly dealt with by you, then a great deal of this could have been nipped in the bid. I think it is terribly important for everybody that there should be no erosion of confidence in the way the inquiry is being conducted.' Bell responded weakly that he had been aware 'on one occasion' of some people finding things amusing. His failure to deal with the virtual intimidation of witnesses discouraged Frances McKie so much that she too stopped attending regularly.

In June there was a disturbing coincidence of events. Despite Kenneth Baker's earlier assurances that no special precautions were required to deal with Chernobyl, it was officially admitted that many sheep had absorbed hazardous quantities of radiation. Farmers over a wide area – at first in North Wales and Cumbria, then in parts of Scotland – were banned from moving sheep and lambs from their land and from taking them to market for slaughter. The order in

Scotland covered Dumfries and Galloway, Arran and Easter Ross and halted the movement of 1.4 million sheep, 17% of the Scottish total at that time of year. It was a drastic step, yet Malcolm Rifkind accompanied it with an apparently contradictory statement – a 'categorical assurance' that there was no reason to stop buying and eating lamb. Labour MPs wanted to know why, if the Secretary of State was satisfied that there was no danger to health, he was imposing the ban; from Rifkind, there was not much of an answer.

The scientific readings of becquerels (units of radioactivity) in milk did appear to give some cause for concern. In the immediate aftermath of Chernobyl, the highest reading in Dumfries-shire was 225 becquerels per litre compared with a normal figure of below 10; in Glasgow it was 40, in Edinburgh 23, in Aberdeen 0.4. The danger point – at which official action had to be considered – was said to be 2,400. In late June, tests in Dumfries and Galloway produced one reading of 1,272 becquerels: an alarming increase on the highest reading only a month earlier and enough to provoke a political response.

Just as the government was adapting its narrative on the risk to health of Chernobyl fall-out, the Dounreay inquiry was hearing evidence of a link between nuclear installations and leukaemia in young people. A Scottish Office study had found that, between 1979 and 1983, five cases of leukaemia in people under the age of 25 were diagnosed within 12 kilometres of the Dounreay plant. Dr Michael Heasman of the Common Services Agency testified that the 'cluster' of cases in an area of low population was more than he would have expected. He said it was conceivable that it was simply a chance occurrence, but he doubted it. Dounreay, he added, was 'out on its own', while the incidence of the disease in the areas around the Hunterston and Chapelcross nuclear power stations he rated 'slightly higher than normal'.

Another witness at the inquiry, John Clokey, an environmental consultant, accused the UKAEA of being cynically selective in its choice of animals and plants for testing. He cited the failure to test mussels near Dounreay. 'There's nothing to stop them being eaten by other sea creatures and passing radiation into the human food chain,' he said. 'But if anything nasty is uncovered, the authority can simply change the species it tests.' Clokey's dim view of the UKAEA's integrity was soon to receive powerful corroboration. At a conference of the British Medical Association, Sir Douglas Black, who had chaired the government's inquiry into leukaemia levels around the Sellafield nuclear reprocessing plant in Cumbria, stated that he had not always been told the truth during his investigation. 'The thing that came out most clearly,' he said, 'was that we were given to understand there was a general level of effluent being discharged which turned out to be five to 40 times higher.'

The report of the Dounreay inquiry appeared in 1988. Although it recommended the granting of outline planning permission, its approval was heavily qualified. The report also recommended that no final decision should be taken until there was further investigation of the leukaemia cluster; it 'tended to support' the hypothesis that there was a link between the incidence of leukaemia and proximity to the Dounreay plant. By then, however, these findings were politically meaningless. In the long interval between the start of the inquiry and the publication of its report, European governments had lost their appetite for nuclear power, Britain had abandoned its fast reactor programme, and there was no longer any prospect of a reprocessing plant in Caithness. The fall-out from Chernobyl was longer-lasting. It was not until 2010 – 24 years after the radioactive rain fell on south-west Scotland – that the last of the restrictions on the movement of livestock was lifted.

THE HAPPY LAND

I

WHEN THE EPISCOPALIAN PRIEST RICHARD HOLLOWAY ARRIVED back in Scotland from a posting in Boston, Massachusetts, he was surprised to find that in his absence Edinburgh had been labelled the 'Aids capital of Europe'. By the spring of 1987, the city was reported to be facing 'an epidemic of massive proportions', according to evidence given to members of a House of Commons Select Committee on a fact-finding tour.

Although the estimate of the number of people in Edinburgh who were expected to be dead or dying of the disease within 12 months – 400 – was a high mortality rate for one city, it fell short of an epidemic, massive or otherwise. Doctors believed, however, that about half of Edinburgh's 2,000 drug addicts were already carrying HIV (the Human Immunodeficiency Virus) and that, as it had been introduced to the city in 1983, earlier than elsewhere, and as the gestation period was between four and five years, the city was on the brink of a health catastrophe – a 'gay plague' as the media unhelpfully referred to it.

As Holloway noted, while the disease was taking its toll of gay men, the fact that the largest group at risk in Edinburgh were intravenous drug users had created 'an irresistible combination of sex and drugs . . . a delicious mix for the puritan mind to obsess about'. He wrote that the traditional prejudices which identified HIV as God's judgement on sinners were more muted in Scotland than in the United States. More muted, perhaps; but in the Christian church far from silent. His clerical colleague, the hardline Roman Catholic archbishop of Glasgow, Thomas Winning, condemned a week-long television health campaign, broadcast on all channels, in which images of tombstones hammered home the government's message, 'Don't die of ignorance'. The television critic Julie Davidson, in her summing-up of the year, said that 1987 would be remembered, particularly by those with a sense of the absurd, as the year of the condom, though she confessed that she had missed the many discussions on the utility of the life-saving rubber.

Whatever his other qualities, Winning was not renowned for his sense of the absurd. He attacked the saturation coverage as 'a lamentable disservice to viewers', claimed that many people were angered and disgusted by it, and insisted that the Christian teaching of fidelity within marriage and chastity outside it 'corresponded to the best medical advice on safe sex'. He found a vocal ally in the clerk to the Glasgow Presbytery of the Church of Scotland, the Reverend Alexander Cunningham, who objected that the campaign had focused on remedies for people 'who want to continue being promiscuous'.

Despite the Edinburgh experience, gay sex occupied many more column inches than dirty needles. The *Glasgow Herald*'s Jack Webster, in one of his more judgmental columns, suggested that 'Mother Nature' was 'attempting some control of promiscuity when all else has clearly failed' and took an incidental swipe at the 'mincing men and screaming lesbians' who were campaigning for gay rights. There seemed to be little attempt on the part of editors, even of respectable newspapers, to control the offensive imagery routinely employed in the reporting of the virus and little regard for the possibility that the use of such language would instill fear among gay men and women and intolerance of homosexuality in the community at large.

But the media could scarcely be blamed for creating a public mood of near-hysteria when the official narrative was so shrill and alarmist. The government's chief medical officer, Sir Donald Acheson, announced that Aids posed 'the biggest threat to health in Britain since the Middle Ages' and proposed draconian measures to deal with it. 'The Government's priority is to make an accurate estimate of the prevalence of the disease in Britain,' he stated, 'even if secret blood tests on hospital patients are necessary.' Secret blood tests would have been a serious infringement of civil liberties, but Acheson appeared to be unconcerned by such ethical niceties.

In the Aids capital of Europe, the panic spread from the streets to the cells of Saughton Prison. Staff reported an incident in which 10 prisoners used the same needle to inject heroin. Some were known Aids carriers. The others, though aware that they were putting themselves at risk, carried on injecting. Paradoxically a police crackdown on drugs in the city had accelerated the spread of the virus by forcing addicts to share needles, while the Scottish Prison Officers Association made the potentially self-fulfilling prophecy that in future prison officers would no longer be held at knifepoint but would be injected by hypodermic needles with blood from Aids carriers. No doubt this intrigued some of the prisoners in Saughton.

One carrier who did use HIV as a weapon stood trial at the High Court in Edinburgh in the spring of 1987. A habitual offender who stole from department stores in order to feed his heroin addiction, he was notorious as the father of one of the first babies in Scotland born with the virus. Giving evidence in his defence, he admitted that at Gayfield Square police station, he had threatened to infect police officers with Aids. He testified that he had somebody on his back, a foot on his neck, and they were beating him; he told them that if they did not stop beating him he would cover them with blood. He was shouting for his medication, which was overdue. They decided to transfer him to the main police station in the High Street. In the van on the way there, one of the officers asked him about the baby who was dying of Aids. There was something about his tone, explained the prisoner, so he leaned forward and head-butted him.

Away from the front line, scientists worked unobtrusively to find a vaccine which might control the spread of the virus. A Scottish veterinary pathologist, William Jarrett, was making optimistic noises about a prototype and thought it might be tested on humans within a year. Jarrett, who had been one of several promising young scientists recruited to Glasgow's new veterinary school in 1949, had established an international reputation for his work on feline leukaemia. A number of cats in a Glasgow household developed a type of lymphatic cancer and Jarrett was asked to investigate. Although cancers of that sort had not previously been thought to be transmittable, Jarrett concluded that the disease must be contagious, eventually discovered the virus responsible, and produced a vaccine against it. As a result, feline leukaemia was virtually eliminated. Excited by the possibility of applying his work on animal diseases to similar conditions in humans, he became a member of the Aids programme of the Medical Research Council and set up a research group. By 1987 Jarrett and his colleagues had developed a vaccine derived, like the feline leukaemia vaccine, from the bark of the Brazilian oak, used by Indians in the Amazonian rain forest as a blood-clotting treatment for wounds from poisoned darts. Trials on monkeys had yielded positive results: it seemed that the vaccine produced antibodies which neutralised the Aids virus. The Medical Research Council declared that there were 'good reasons' to be hopeful. But the optimism was misplaced; when Bill Jarrett died in 2011 at the age of 83, there was still no effective human vaccine to deal with HIV, which had claimed millions of lives in Africa.

In Britain, however, the 'plague' failed to materialise to quite the extent confidently prophesied by such experts as Acheson. A study in 1994, which found that more drug users in Edinburgh were dying from Aids than from overdoses, attracted lurid headlines, but the small print disclosed that the numbers were tiny and the comparison insignificant. Among a group of 202 injecting users, more than half of whom were HIV-positive, there were 16 Aids-related deaths between 1983 and 1992 compared with 15 deaths from overdoses in the same 10-year period. By 2014, the cumulative total of known HIV-positive individuals ever registered in Scotland was 7,384, of whom 1,860 had died. These statistics, while grim and distressing, were thrown into perspective by the number of deaths from heart disease in Scotland: around 18,500 a year every year.

At the height of the Aids outbreak in Edinburgh, the *British Medical Journal* published the results of a study casting doubt on the effectiveness of the government's £20 million health promotion campaign; the Alcohol Research Group at Edinburgh University said that shock tactics in the past had proved unproductive and that such high-profile mass media campaigns were mostly motivated by a political desire to be seen to be 'doing something' about the problem. The fact that the anticipated epidemic was avoided suggests, however, that the year of the condom did have a positive impact.

The occasional celebrity victim kept the media interested long after the original panic had subsided. The first to declare publicly was a gay actor, Ian Charleson, a graduate of Edinburgh University, who was best known for playing the athlete Eric Liddell in the film *Chariots of Fire*. Having been diagnosed with HIV in 1986, Charleson asked that it should be announced after his death that he had died of Aids; it was his way of helping to demythologise the illness. By the end of the decade, the sort of prejudice exhibited in such newspaper columns as the *Glasgow Herald*'s would have been unthinkable.

II

If a sense of the absurd was helpful in coping with the more extreme posturing about Aids, it was essential for an understanding of the spy scandal which implausibly broke over Queen Margaret Drive in Glasgow in the early weeks of 1987. Fifteen months earlier, BBC Scotland had commissioned an investigative journalist based in London, Duncan Campbell, to research and present a six-part television series entitled *Secret Society*.

The choice of Campbell for an inquiry into the inner workings of the British military and political establishments unnerved the board of governors in London. Loathed by the intelligence services for his ability to unearth stories they would have preferred to keep under wraps, he was suspected by an influential member of the board, Daphne Park, a former MI5 agent, of being a 'destroyer' and someone that the corporation should never have employed. She said so frankly at a meeting of the governors in November 1986, but by then it was too late to prevent the imminent train crash.

Campbell had been tipped off about the existence of a spy satellite system code-named Zircon, whose function was to intercept radio and other signals from the USSR and Europe. He would not reveal his source – self-respecting journalists never did – but it was believed to be a former employee of GCHQ, the top-secret signals intelligence agency which had conceived the project. In the summer of 1986, Campbell made a further discovery: that the head of the public accounts committee, Robert Sheldon MP, who was responsible for overseeing government spending, knew nothing of Zircon. Put on the spot by Campbell during an interview for the series, an embarrassed Sheldon accused the presenter of setting him up. Campbell and his producer, Brian Barr, who had been seconded to work on the series from the current affairs unit at BBC Scotland, decided that one of the six episodes should be devoted to Zircon. In doing so, they unwittingly sealed the fate of their ultimate boss, the director-general of the BBC, Alasdair Milne.

Milne had an impressive track record in broadcast journalism, but was less successful as DG; he would not have progressed far in the Diplomatic Corps. Two years before the Zircon fiasco he clashed with the governors over their decision to accede to a request from the Home Secretary, Leon Brittan, not to show a programme featuring an interview with a former IRA chief of staff. It was political interference by a government almost obsessional in its mistrust of the public service broadcaster. Milne believed that the request should have been resisted and resented the ban. With the arrival of Marmaduke (Duke) Hussey, formerly a leading figure in Rupert Murdoch's media empire, as the chairman of the BBC towards the end of 1986, Milne's days were numbered.

Sod's law, a piece of legislation familiar to most people who worked at the BBC, decreed that Hussey's appointment coincided with the completion of the Zircon programme, which was now ready for showing. Hussey made it clear to Milne that the governors were negative about the *Secret Society* series, although they had not yet seen any of the programmes. Nor at that stage had Milne. Behind the scenes, however, the colonel had been consulting his friends in military intelligence. The colonel was the assistant DG, Alan Protheroe, 'short, chain-smoking and highly strung' as Milne wrote of him, a man rarely to be seen without his bleeper. It was not an ironical nickname; he had attained that rank.

On the basis of intelligence received from his contacts in the Ministry of Defence, Protheroe convinced himself that the Zircon episode would damage national security. In December, he wrote to Milne, emphasising the gravity of the situation by having the letter delivered to the director-general's home, and advised Milne that the Zircon programme should not be transmitted. Milne then viewed the series and showed it to the governors, who agreed with Protheroe that the episode must be junked. Hussey informed Milne that it should never have been made. The Christmas holiday intervened, a cheerless one for Alasdair Milne, who had to choose between his journalists and his governors. He chose the governors. When this news reached Duncan Campbell, he contacted the *New Statesman* magazine with the offer of a piece about Zircon. Its publication on 22 January 1987 infuriated the Thatcher government, which promptly slapped an injunction on the magazine and instructed Special Branch to track down the source or sources of Campbell's information. The police questioned the controller of BBC Scotland, Pat Chalmers, for several hours and arrested Protheroe – rough justice for the colonel, who had been so anxious to protect the interests of the state.

Hussey wasted no time in despatching the director-general. He summoned Milne to the chairman's office and informed him brusquely: 'We want you to leave immediately. It's a unanimous decision of the board.' The media statement, in the manner of such communiques, said that the director-general had resigned 'for personal reasons'. For Milne, a proficient piper, there was not much of a lament. The BBC curtly thanked him for his services, and that was about it. The Labour MP George Foulkes claimed all too plausibly that Milne had gone because of political pressure exerted on the governors by Norman Tebbit, the minister closest to the ear of Margaret Thatcher. But not all of her cabinet were pleased by his enforced departure. The Home Secretary, Douglas Hurd, was dismayed that the government's zeal for secrecy, and its hatred of the BBC, had gone so far.

There were immediate moves to subvert the ban. Labour's Robin Cook, having obtained a video copy of the programme, tried to have it shown to MPs in the House of Commons until the Speaker, Bernard Weatherill, ruled that no part of the Palace of Westminster was to be used for the screening. Civil liberties organisations had also obtained copies, however, and arranged public showings in open violation of the Official Secrets Act. The fact that the Zircon project had been concealed from parliamentary scrutiny gave a certain moral legitimacy to these acts of defiance and the threat to national security of showing the programme was in any case grossly exaggerated. If Sir Frank Cooper, former permanent secretary at the Ministry of Defence, had been prepared to speak to Duncan Campbell about Zircon, how secret could it be? Alistair Darling, one of the brighter people on the opposition benches, had a hunch that the row over Zircon was an elaborate blind and that the episode the government really wanted to censor was the sixth and last – a programme about the secret work of cabinet committees. He may have been right. The episode called *Cabinet* was never shown and consigned instead to a BBC vault.

Two days after Milne's departure, the police investigation moved to Scotland and descended into farce. Around 8 am on Saturday, eight detectives from London and Glasgow arrived at the BBC Scotland studios in Queen Margaret Drive with a search warrant granted under the Official Secrets Act. The BBC's lawyers took one look at the warrant and decided to contest it in the Court of Session. Lord Clyde took a second look, sensibly ruled that it was 'too far-reaching and vague' and threw it out. By that stage in the day, Special Branch officers had removed cardboard boxes full of tapes and other material relating to the series. Clyde's judgement meant that all of it had to be returned to Queen Margaret Drive pending the execution of a second warrant. But the second warrant was rejected too: the police had somehow managed to stick the wrong address on the document. So far, the investigation would have done credit to Inspector Clouseau.

It was midnight on Saturday before the third warrant of the long day was finally accepted. It was left to Colonel Protheroe to admit defeat: 'It's quite clear the police are determined to get hold of this material. However careful, however precise, the legal arguments may be, warrants will keep on coming back until a warrant that is entirely waterproof is produced.' The search which had started early on Saturday morning finally came to an end 28 hours later. Brian Barr had his office ransacked and was interviewed twice; the police also raided the house in the west end where Duncan Campbell had stayed during the making of the series. The political correspondent Geoffrey Parkhouse cranked up the story with a report inspired by his Conservative Party sources that 'the leaking of details of the Zircon project is considered so serious that the use of section 1 of the Official Secrets Act, which embraces espionage, may have to be considered'. After a weekend of bungling by the spooks in the works, it felt more than ever like a piece of Boys' Own fiction.

There were surprisingly few howls of derision at the incompetence of the police operation. Donald Dewar confined himself to the comment that it had been heavy-handed and 'slightly bizarre'. But there was near-unanimity about the disturbing precedent. The father [chair] of the journalists' chapel [branch] at BBC Scotland, Harry Smith, said the raid had nothing to do with national security; the government was attempting to censor programmes that it might find politically embarrassing.

In the Commons, David Steel protested that a BBC technician had been phoned at home in the early hours to ask him to help with the search. 'Is the knock on the door in the middle of the night to become part of our society?', he asked the Secretary of State for Scotland. Malcolm Rifkind's response – that the technician had agreed to turn out 'from a sense of moral responsibility' – earned him a raspberry from the other side. Donald Dewar claimed that the raid had been stage-managed by the Crown Office with ministerial authority, and that the warrants had been drawn so widely that they amounted to a fishing expedition 'to see what might turn up'. How, he asked, had the raid been set in motion? What was the role of the Secretary of State? 'It was not a matter for me or for the Government as a whole,' Rifkind lamely informed the House.

No-one ever went on trial for leaking dangerous secrets to Duncan Campbell. The attack on the BBC could have been a clumsy attempt by the security services to cover their embarrassment by harassing those responsible; or it could have been a political witchhunt; or it could have been a bit of both. But the notion that it was a genuine response to a threat to national security looked ridiculous when the Zircon episode was broadcast without fuss in the autumn of 1988. It had been much ado about nothing. And when the Chancellor of the Exchequer, Nigel Lawson, decided to drop the Zircon project to save a little money, it became much ado about less than nothing.

The series producer, Brian Barr, when he died in 2013, was described in an obituary as 'one of those journalists for whom integrity was more important than self-promotional material reward'. But he had celebrity status thrust upon him, if only for a few weeks in 1987. His local paper, the *Paisley Daily Express*, was so impressed that it published a story headed: 'Ex-Paisley choirboy in spy scandal'.

III

Margaret Thatcher won her third successive landslide victory in the general election of 1987, but the dissenting Scots, with a 7% swing to Labour, confirmed their detestation of her political creed, swimming against the strong national tide and inevitably raising serious questions about the stability of the Union.

Thatcher launched her campaign in Perth at the Scottish Tory conference. Bill Henderson, her chief apparatchik north of the border, made the bullish – or foolish – prediction that the Tories would hold their 21 seats and achieve significant gains. 'Labour enters this campaign fighting for its life,' agreed the *Glasgow Herald* in an editorial. The paper was referring mainly to England, where the Alliance (of Liberals and Social Democrats) appeared to be eroding the traditional Labour vote, but thought that 'even in areas like Scotland' poor opinion poll ratings could affect the morale of its supporters. Few gave much credence to the alternative prediction of Donald Dewar that Labour would add eight seats to its tally of 42 – the exact result a month later.

Three factors were influencing Scottish voting intentions. The first was familiar. The pre-election unemployment figures indicated a widening of the north-south economic divide; the number of people out of work in Scotland rose in April to 346,000, while in the UK as a whole it fell. Dewar had worked out that, since Thatcher came to power in 1979, a quarter of a million Scots had lost their jobs. In the spring of 1987, 31% of adults in the worst blackspot – Cumnock and Sanquhar – were on the dole. The second factor was the unsatisfied demand for more autonomy. An opinion poll commissioned by the *Scotsman* confirmed that a decisive majority of Scottish voters not only supported a Scottish Assembly but favoured giving it tax-raising powers to improve public services; even 51% of Tory voters approved of this proposition. When Thatcher came to Glasgow, however, she was adamant in her resistance to devolution. 'No-one ever asks me about it except the media,' she said.

She assured her audience that she was a Disraeli-style Tory, a believer in 'one nation' – an allusion to Disraeli's speech in Battersea in 1872 in which he said that the well-being of the people was the foundation upon which all their happiness depended. In the Britain of Margaret Thatcher, the idea of one nation defined by universal human happiness was ludicrous; no more so than in such places as Cumnock and Sanquhar. But the Prime Minister seemed blind to the geographically patchy nature of her happy land, or may simply have been indifferent to it. If she was aware of the opinion poll in the *Scotsman*, which gave so contrary a snapshot of the national mood, she paid no attention to it.

The relatively poor state of the Scottish economy and the clamour for devolution had been consistent features of politics in Scotland since the Second World War, but the third factor in 1987 was a new and combustible one. Shortly before the election, a bill abolishing domestic rates in Scotland and replacing them with a community charge completed its parliamentary passage and entered the statute book in preparation for the introduction of the new system in 1989. The community charge, which came to be known as the poll tax, would be paid by almost all adults over the age of 18. The only outright exemptions would be granted to people with severe mental disabilities and to the residents of nursing and care homes, while people with severe physical disabilities would be entitled to rebates. Otherwise the charge was to be universally levied, with Scotland the guinea pig for a scheme compelling everyone in a household, no matter how large or how poor, to contribute.

In the final Commons debate on the bill, the Scottish local government minister, Michael Ancram, defended the community charge as 'fair'. On hearing this, a Labour front-bench spokesman, John Home Robertson, told the minister to 'go to hell', which earned him a rebuke from the deputy Speaker for unparliamentary language. Donald Dewar predicted that the people of Scotland would be 'hindered with an unwanted and ill-advised tax'; Robert Maclennan, for the (SDP/Liberal) Alliance, said that it would lead to a humiliating defeat for the Tories in Scotland; the SNP's Gordon Wilson feared that it would cause hardship and distress. Secretary of State Rifkind, who was caricatured by the fiery left-winger Dennis Canavan as governor-general of a semi-colonial junta, had been comprehensively warned.

It was, however, only after the election, not during it, that 'The Scottish Question' – a phrase minted by the *Times* – entered the political lexicon, joining the long-running 'Doomsday Scenario' in which Scotland had several times voted for one party only to be thwarted by England's choice of another. For although the Scots in Margaret Thatcher's 'one nation' were clearly unhappy, the media coverage south of the border made little or no mention of it. On 28 May, a fortnight before the vote, the results of a System 3 opinion poll were delivered to the offices of the *Glasgow Herald* and Scottish Television which had jointly sponsored it. The poll showed that Ancram, the luckless ambassador of the community charge, was almost certain to lose his South Edinburgh seat to Labour. In the Scottish TV newsroom, this had an electrifying effect. Half the items prepared for the early evening Scottish news were ditched and the election package was extended to 20 of the programme's 25 minutes. The professor of politics at Glasgow University, Bill Miller, invited to interpret the South Edinburgh poll, gave a cautious analysis of what it meant for Scotland as a whole, predicting (as Donald Dewar had already predicted) that Labour would win 50 seats and the Tories would be left with 11.

When Rifkind heard about it on his car telephone, he was with Brian Meek, a Tory councillor and journalist. Meek wrote later that Rifkind was 'stunned . . . knocked back in a way I had never seen him before'. The next morning the *Herald* and *Scotsman* gave extensive coverage to the poll, but there was no reference to it on the BBC's *Nine O'Clock News* or on ITV's *News at Ten*, and a week passed before any of the London-based newspapers gave it so much as a nod. Likewise, when a subsequent poll by the same organisation confirmed Miller's view of the looming disaster for the Tories in Scotland and pointed to a strong demand from Scots voters for devolution, the English media ignored it. The *Times* was particularly complacent at that stage, speculating that the Tories had comparatively little to worry about as the SNP was so 'weak'.

The same myopia affected the reporting of Thatcher's visit to Scotland during the campaign; the BBC's man from London concentrated on her attack on the trade unions for the influence they exerted on Labour policy, but there was not a word about the threat to Conservative seats in Scotland; the grilling she received from Scottish journalists went unreported on the BBC and ITN. Alastair Hetherington, former controller of BBC Scotland who was now an academic with Stirling University's department of media studies, wrote that English audiences were left in the dark.

Ancram did lose his seat, as did his fellow junior minister John McKay, who was beaten by the Alliance's Ray Michie, daughter of the legendary Liberal John Bannerman, in Argyll and Bute. The Solicitor-General, Peter Fraser, lost Angus East to the SNP. Tory backbenchers fell like ninepins: John Corrie in Cunningham North; Anna McCurley in marginal Renfrew West and Inverclyde; Barry Henderson in Fife North East; Gerry Malone in Aberdeen South; Alex Fletcher in Edinburgh Central (to Alistair Darling). Labour claimed two especially notable scalps: Roy Jenkins, who had defected to the SDP, in Glasgow Hillhead; and Gordon Wilson in Dundee East.

Although the SNP lost its leader, and performed unevenly elsewhere, the long-term significance of the election from a Scottish perspective lay in a little-reported battle in the far north. 'Can the

Buchan bulldog keep the young pup at bay?', asked one of the *Glasgow Herald*'s constituency reports. The Buchan bulldog, the combative Tory incumbent Albert McQuarrie, required no introduction. The young pup was named as Alex Salmond, 'a 32-year-old Edinburgh oil and energy economist', a rising star in the party (already its vice-chairman), who boasted a strong campaign organisation with 14 branches in the constituency. McQuarrie, 'in typical form', refused to acknowledge Salmond's existence or to engage in public debate with him – or indeed with any of his other opponents. The bulldog was put to sleep by the unimpressed electorate of Banff and Buchan: it was the end of McQuarrie's parliamentary career, as it was of so many others. But the young pup, who was to become a full-grown terrier, soon learned how to bark effectively.

'A defiant Scotland bitterly rejects the decision to return Mrs Thatcher to power for another five years,' reported Geoffrey Parkhouse in the *Herald*. The result must have come as a shock to all those readers and viewers in the south who had depended on the London media for their political news.

'There can be no doubt about it now,' said the post-election editorial in the *Evening Times*. 'We live in a divided Britain. The General Election marks a political watershed in the history of the United Kingdom. Mrs Thatcher has won her place in history. But at what cost. Britain has been rent apart.' The paper added that there were barely enough Tory MPs in Scotland to fill a couple of taxi cabs (the *Evening Times* was not to know that, 28 years later, the sole Tory MP would be travelling alone in the back of a Dumfries taxi). In her moment of greatest triumph, said the paper, Mrs Thatcher stood also in greatest danger: she was on the brink of a constitutional crisis. 'Unless she reacts swiftly, our nation will be propelled down the road of separation – driven there by lack of proper political representation and simmering resentment at the havoc wreaked upon this land by her policies during her last two terms of office.' The piece ended with a warning: 'The Union of 1707 is not writ in stone.'

Malcolm Rifkind's reaction to the humiliation of his party in Scotland would have appealed to those whose sense of the absurd had not been exhausted by the other events of the year. He maintained that there were 'no constitutional problems at all' – even as *sangfroid* this was barely credible – and that there was no reason to believe that home rule had been a significant issue with the voters. There was every reason: he only had to look at the polls. The newly re-appointed Secretary of State resorted to the well-known tactic of blaming the hostility of the Scottish media for the fall in Tory support; the defeated Michael Ancram did likewise. The political correspondent William Clark noted that, although Rifkind was 'all smiles' at his post-election press conference in Edinburgh, there was no doubt that his stature had been diminished.

The STUC's Campbell Christie doubted that the Tories would go ahead with the poll tax – Christie was no soothsayer – and produced a list of 'economic concessions' he believed might be wrung from the government: the safeguarding of the Ravenscraig steel plant; greater funding for such bodies as the Scottish Development Agency; the bolstering of regional policy. The *Financial Times*, voice of the City of London, agreed that Scotland was 'suffering from a drift to the South-East of financial power' and that regional aid had diminished in effectiveness as well as amount.

By the autumn, Malcolm Rifkind had absorbed the shock of the result and seemed on the surface to have learned little if anything from it. Welcoming his Prime Minister back to Scotland, he promised to 'change many of the attitudes and policies which have dominated Scotland for years – and which are responsible for many of our social, economic and industrial problems'. He vowed to rid the country of its 'dependence culture', for which he blamed 'benevolent bureaucrats and paternalistic councils', and to usher in a new era of entrepreneurship, innovation and enterprise. 'Rifkind out to change nation's face' was the friendly headline across one front page. Quite how this re-arrangement of features was to be achieved, he omitted to say.

After her 'morale-boosting' meeting with party workers, who had just been reorganised under a new chief executive (John McKay, straight from his defeat in Argyll), Thatcher emphatically ruled out devolution: 'Scotland is part of the United Kingdom and wishes to remain so. Devolution was not an issue at the election. If it did occur, it would be the first step towards the break-up of the United Kingdom. I stand by the Union.' She was keener to talk to the media about one of her favourite books, *The Wealth of Nations*, from which she claimed she had derived many of her political ideas: 'I have always said that the policies which I espouse, which you call Thatcherism, are really much older than that. They were really started by Adam Smith. He was a jolly good Scot. He blazed the trail and Scots took it all over the world and very successful they were.'

Robin Cook responded with a newspaper article in which he observed that the Conservative Party was seeking psychological comfort for the trauma of defeat by denying the very existence of a Scottish electoral dimension. Not one of the remaining Tories had raised 'a feeble finger' in protest at the Prime Minister's intransigence. He quoted the taunt of the Conservative columnist Brian Meek that if Thatcher invited them to jump in the sea, most would not stop to take off their trousers. But Cook's daring proposal that Scottish MPs of the opposition parties – Labour, SNP and Alliance – should meet in a 'prototype Assembly' in Edinburgh attracted a good deal of scorn. Brian Meek dismissed it as 'pinko bananas' and suggested that 'this great gathering of the socialist clans' should be convened in the Western Isles, where the excitable Dennis Canavan could be taken out for walks. On this note of low comedy, the curtain came down on the 1987 election.

IV

In Margaret Thatcher's happy land, the frustrated electors of Scotland contented themselves with the usual diversions. *Taggart* returned to the screen, 'Britain's top TV cop' having become a money-spinner for his creator, Scottish Television. The new series, the sixth, was shown in 20 countries, including France, where it was adored. Showbiz writer Andrew Young wrote that it contained 'all the essential ingredients – a shoal of red herring, witchcraft, satanism, high and low life in the modern, vibrant city of Glasgow, and all beautifully captured in the camera work of Jim Peters, with the raunchy voice of Maggie Bell blasting over the titles and music by Mike Moran'. Taggart, a tough-guy inspector with lived-in features, was played by Mark McManus, a local actor of no great distinction, as McManus was the first to acknowledge. 'I learned the techniques of acting and applied myself,' he explained disarmingly. It was, however, a piece of inspired casting. When Taggart uttered his thrilling catchphrase, 'There's been a murder', 13 million viewers – including such devoted fans as the Queen Mother – settled down for an hour of undiluted gore and hokum.

McManus, who was a heavy drinker, found personal happiness with Marion Donald, the show's original wardrobe mistress, whom he married in 1990. When she died of cancer three years later, McManus never recovered from the blow and died in 1994 at the age of 59. His character was given an on-air funeral. But it was far from the end of *Taggart* as a programme; the role of investigating officer was inherited by a number of successors until, in 2011, after 28 years and 110 episodes, the series itself was axed, the last of its many victims.

BBC Scotland's hit of the year – indeed of the decade – never achieved the popularity of *Taggart* but earned rapturous critical acclaim. *Tutti Frutti*, produced by Andy Park, was a sharply observed black comedy about a legendary Scottish rock'n'roll band, the Majestics, on its silver jubilee tour. The critic Julie Davidson called it 'moody and magnificent', praising John Byrne's script with its many memorable creations, including a fat man in love (Robbie Coltrane), the luminous Suzy Kettles (Emma Thompson), the band's exploitative manager Eddie Clockerty (Richard Wilson) and his lippy assistant Miss Toner (Katy Murphy). It ran for only six episodes, the same number as *Secret Society*, but unlike Zircon it was long remembered. As light entertainment, it was more fun.

1988

ORDINARY MEN

I

BY THE SPRING OF 1988, MARGARET THATCHER HAD FORSAKEN Adam Smith and gone to a higher place in search of justification for her economic polices. She was now invoking no less an authority on Thatcherism than Paul the Apostle. The Prime Minister emerged in her unexpected new role of theologian in a speech to the General Assembly of the Church of Scotland – the 'Sermon on the Mound' as it was instantly baptised.

It was an address eagerly awaited by the faithful, who were treated in advance to a piece of mischief from the convener of the business committee, the Reverend William Macmillan, who said it was no more than 'probable' that he would stand up, draw the attention of the Moderator to her presence, and invite him to invite her to speak. 'We are not obliged to do so,' he added. When he was asked by a journalist whether the Assembly would expect a political speech, Macmillan replied: 'You can't separate politics from religion. If you say, "Love your neighbour", you are being political.'

It was no mere probability that the Prime Minister would be able to deliver her carefully crafted oration; it was a racing certainty. 'She was dressed in electric blue,' noted the ecclesiastical commentator Stewart Lamont, 'and the air was electric'. He wrote that 'a sustained wave of applause' rose from the Assembly inviting the PM to come down from her seat, and when two young ministers walked forward to protest, 'the applause swelled, warning them their intervention was not wanted'.

Risking the eternal wrath of Stewart Lamont, three more rose to express their dissent. One of them, who wore a kilt for the occasion, represented a parish called Toryglen. Another, the Reverend Paric Reamonn, was attired in what Lamont called 'that quintessentially Tory of garbs, the well-cut tweed suit, which he sported to the Holyrood garden party in the afternoon'. (Reamonn responded that the suit had cost him £5 in an Oxfam shop.) Lamont, dubbing them 'The Infamous Five', said they had 'certainly not learned their manners from Enid Blyton books'. By the end of the affair, however, there was more support for the handful of protesters than for Margaret Thatcher's statement of Christian belief.

She made much of Paul's injunction to the Thessalonians: 'If a man will not work, he shall not eat.' 'Indeed,' she said, 'abundance rather than poverty has a legitimacy which derives from the very nature of creation.' She also recalled Paul warning Timothy that anyone who neglected to provide for his own house – his own family – had disowned the faith and was 'worse than an infidel'. She did acknowledge that 'in our generation, the only way we can ensure that no-one is left without sustenance, help or opportunity, is to have laws to provide for health and education, provision for the elderly, succour for the sick and disabled' – but then came her mantra about the dangers of state intervention and the need for personal responsibility. The tweed-suited Reamonn accused her of using the Assembly for her own political ends and of perverting the Gospel. Lamont hit back scornfully that Reamonn was 'obviously granted a special gift of divining motives of the heart'.

In some newspapers, there was a guarded welcome for Thatcher's attempt to give a theological dimension to her political creed. More than one applauded her underlining of the work ethic, but saw a problem in relating it to her government's programme of social security cuts and its commitment to the community charge, both of which involved a shift of resources to the better-off. Later in the week, the Reverend Erik Cramb, minister of a working-class

Glasgow parish, challenged the Assembly to remember all those excluded from a divided society: 'There can be no doubt that she spoke for those who have a voice, a stake, opportunity, health and vigour. It's not because we are anti-Tory that we speak for the poor, the disabled, the feckless and the vulnerable. That's why we find ourselves in conflict.'

Although the speech was a media sensation for 24 hours, it failed to trigger a longer debate in the Kirk or in Scotland as a whole. The man in the moderatorial chair that year happened to be a learned and widely respected one: James Whyte, professor of practical theology at St Andrews University. 'It's a great pity,' he reflected a year after the event. 'The speech did require a considered answer, but it still hasn't been given one.' Nor was it ever.

Whyte regarded the Prime Minister's reading of scripture as deeply flawed: 'The quotation she used, "If a man will not work, he shall not eat", comes out of a totally different context from ours. St Paul was dealing with a situation where people lay around and did nothing because they thought the end of the world was coming. Paul said, "Look, you can't go on living like that. If you're not going to work, you're going to starve." A totally different situation.' He thought there was very little in the Bible to justify her view that we must use our talents to create wealth: 'The New Testament is about poverty rather than wealth, about giving things away and the dangers of wealth. The truth is, she confuses the creation of wealth with the making of money. Wealth is created by those who take something of no value and make it into something of great value. It's created by craftsmen, by people who work in industry. The shuffling around of shares in order to make yourself a fortune in a fortnight is not wealth creation, it's just making money. She doesn't seem to know the difference.'

Had James Whyte said all this at the time, it would have caused uproar. A year later his comments passed almost unnoticed. But he had already made a gentle point to the Prime Minister in his vote of thanks, presenting her with two reports published by the Church of Scotland: one on the distribution of wealth and welfare benefits; the other on housing Scotland's people.

II

Two days after the Sermon on the Mound, the last obstacle to the introduction of the poll tax in Scotland was overcome by the massive endorsement of the House of Lords. A left-winger from Northern Ireland, Lord (Gerry) Fitt, observed that the rebels on the Government side – Tories opposed to the legislation – had been crushed by an army of peers loyal to Thatcher, at least a hundred of whom he had never seen before: 'Some of them didn't even know whether they were entitled to go into the Lords' guest room for a drink.' One of the Tory rebels in the Commons, Michael Mates, said: 'We sent a signal to the Lords, but they didn't receive it.' Another, George Young, was close to despair: 'We're done for. Now I'm going to devote myself to abandoned children.'

Ron Brown, the Labour MP for Leith, was so incensed by Thatcher's policies – or so driven to drink by them – that in an act of defiance one April evening he grabbed the mace from its place in front of the Speaker's chair. 'Parliament has become a rubber stamp for oppression,' he shouted. But when he tried to rest it on the Government front bench, the precious object fell to the floor. It was a breach of parliamentary protocol, if not exactly the end of the world in the Thessalonian sense, from a serial offender who had been in trouble on many occasions in the past – for such indiscretions as an all-expenses-paid trip to Afghanistan at the invitation of the Soviet-backed government (1981), 'grave discourtesy to the Speaker of the House' (1981), planting what he called 'a fiery cross' on the Speaker's table with the words 'Hands off Lothian' (1981), a breach of the peace outside the Holiday Inn, Glasgow, when he lunged at Margaret Thatcher shouting 'Is this Poland?', for which he incurred a fine of £50 (1982), and a meeting with Colonel Gaddafi in a bedouin tent outside Tripoli only months after the shooting of WPC Yvonne Fletcher outside the Libyan Embassy in London (1984).

Brown was rewarded by his grateful constituents with an increased majority in successive general elections, and had seen off a threat to deselect him as Labour candidate and replace him with Alex Wood, a teacher and Edinburgh councillor. But there was something about the mace incident that irritated even the thick-skinned folks back home. 'We consider that these actions did nothing to further the cause of socialism,' said the chairman of the local constituency party. 'It was a regrettable prank which had little to do with politics and much to do with theatrics.'

'Grovel, grovel, who wrote this rubbish?' Brown demanded when his parliamentary colleagues presented him with the terms of an apology. He refused to deliver it and drafted a defiant alternative version: 'If you want an apology, then so be it. If you apologise to the working class for what they have to suffer, that is fair enough with me. I have many unemployed engineering workers who are willing to repair the mace. They will give you a new one in fact – that is a guarantee.' The Speaker, Michael Martin, MP for Springburn, ruled that Brown had committed three offences: damaging the mace, refusing to apologise properly, and trying to take a BBC employee into the members-only dining room. He was suspended from the chamber for a week. When the Parliamentary Labour Party met to discuss the incident, one member claimed that Brown had 'spent too long in the bar' before grabbing the mace. 'That's not fair, that's not true,' he yelled in response. An overwhelming majority were unconvinced by the protestation and voted to withdraw the whip for three months. Brown somehow managed to convince himself that it was a moral victory.

He celebrated by spending too long in the Commons shower – it made a change from the bar – with a parliamentary assistant named Nonna with whom, it was further alleged, he engaged in 'an amorous romp' observed by envious Conservative MPs. The timing was unfortunate; it coincided with the Prime Minister's address to the General Assembly of the Church of Scotland on the need for personal responsibility. The press found it necessary to record that both Nonna and Ron were naked in the shower, disposing of any remaining doubt that they might have been wearing tweed suits bought from Oxfam. He denied ('strenuously' – political denials were invariably hard-working) the 'sex-in-the-shower' claims and somehow survived that scandal too. His long-suffering wife May 'stood by' him, nursing the constituency in his absence; it was often said that May would have been a better MP.

Eighteen months later, the relationship between Nonna and Ron was exposed fully clothed and in embarrassing detail at Lewes Crown Court. Brown stood trial accused of causing criminal damage at her flat in St Leonard's on Sea, near Hastings, and of stealing a number of items, including two pairs of knickers, which the police recovered from his pockets when they arrested him. Nonna now had a surname: Longden. The court heard that Brown led a double life for three years – sharing a London home with Longden during the week, returning to the domesticity of Edinburgh at the weekend. Longden gave evidence that she was deeply ashamed when their relationship became public and her picture appeared in the papers, and that she had formed an attachment to another man. The jealous Brown went at once to St Leonard's on Sea and smashed 'nearly everything made of glass' in the flat. Four large shards of glass, found among the debris, had been written on; when they were put together they spelled out the word love. According to the prosecution, Brown had paid £600 towards the cost of dental treatment for Longden, 'but only because he caused the teeth to be broken in the first place'. The jury found him guilty of causing criminal damage, but acquitted him of stealing the knickers. The judge, fining him £1,000, said he should be thoroughly ashamed of 'a disgraceful exhibition of bad temper'.

True to form, Brown was unrepentant, joking on the court-room steps that he would have to put the hat round if he was to settle the fine in the six months allowed. 'It is difficult for someone with a Scottish accent and left-wing views to get a fair hearing,' he explained. He and the forgiving May toasted the outcome in champagne and Brown called it a moral victory: another one. But his constituency party thought otherwise. After the trial the tom cat with nine lives finally ran out of luck. He was deselected as Labour candidate for Leith, carrying on as an independent until the general election, when he polled a respectable 4,000 votes but was defeated by an able official Labour candidate, Malcolm Chisholm. He then worked as a taxi-driver, dying of liver failure at the age of 69. Oleg Gordievsky, a colonel in the KGB before his defection to the West, told a Scottish newspaper that his organisation had once attempted to recruit Brown as a Soviet agent: 'The only problem was that we couldn't understand him at all because of the accent. We tried and we tried to figure out what on earth he was saying. We just couldn't understand him. We had to give up because there was no point in talking to someone if we didn't know what he was saying.'

Another Labour MP on the wrong side of his constituency party in the spring of 1988 was the member for Hillhead, George Galloway, who had deposed the fallen darling of Glasgow's west end, the SDP's Roy Jenkins, in the 1987 general election. Voices were so raised at a meeting of the local executive that they could be clearly heard by reporters pacing the corridors of Partick Burgh Hall. 'I am not some kind of patsy,' Galloway was saying, 'and if people want a war then it is a war on two sides – one extremely damaging for all concerned. I have had enough of being smeared and stabbed in the back.' The constituency chairman, Johann Lamont, a future leader of Scottish Labour, could be heard responding that some of the member's comments were 'deeply offensive'.

The immediate source of the problem was a letter from the financial officer of War on Want, Galloway's former employer, documenting expenditure made by Galloway on an American Express credit card while he was general secretary of the charity. The MP claimed the letter was sent to him at the House of Commons; his executive claimed that it was intended for them. Galloway returned the letter to the sender rather than refer it to the executive because, he said, the executive had previously passed on documents to 'scum reporters' in the press. It was nasty stuff in the great tradition of Glasgow Labour politics – though Galloway himself hailed from Dundee, where the Labour politics was even nastier – and the going got rougher still when Galloway confessed to an extra-marital affair and the row could no longer be contained within the family. The vice-chairman of the Scottish Conservative Party, Michael Hirst, called for his resignation. 'People are entitled to a private life,' said Hirst, 'but when personal indiscretions spill over into public life, there should be only one course of action to take.' Hirst himself, some years later, took the 'one course of action', resigning as chairman of the Scottish Tories and as a parliamentary candidate over a personal indiscretion of his own. Galloway, however, was one of the great survivors, and went on to establish himself as a considerable orator – the best in the House in his day according to the political columnist of the *Observer*, Alan Watkins.

A new star was emerging in Scottish politics, rivalling Galloway for forcefulness of expression, if not natural eloquence: Tommy Sheridan, an activist in Labour's extreme left-wing group, Militant, which was recruiting heavily in local constituencies on the back of the poll tax issue. In one of these constituencies, Glasgow Pollok, Sheridan was secretary of the largest ward. At the age of 24 he was also secretary of the Pollok Anti-Poll Tax Union and of the Strathclyde Anti-Poll Tax Federation. The sitting member, James Dunnachie, who sat on one of the larger Labour mountains in Glasgow (a majority of 18,000), was a left-winger himself, a former shipyard worker at Fairfields, mediocre but decent, who took a special interest in housing and campaigned for the rehabilitation of the city's red sandstone tenements. But Sheridan's mobilising brand of radical politics was too strong for Dunnachie's traditional tastes. He wrote to party headquarters claiming that, at an anti-poll tax meeting in Pollok, Sheridan had told the audience to join the Labour Party in order to get rid of elected representatives who disagreed with Militant's 'way of thought'; and that in various incidents, none of which he detailed, Sheridan had tried to bring the local party into disrepute. The party nationally agreed to set up an inquiry into the activities of Militant in Pollok, a move attacked by Sheridan as 'yet another Labour witchhunt'. The atmosphere in the constituency was so bad that an editorial in the *Scotsman* in the early summer of 1988 likened it to Beirut – which only went to show that the author of the editorial had never been in Beirut.

Sheridan's ambition was to have Dunnachie deselected as Labour candidate and replaced by himself. 'I will be fighting Mr Dunnachie,' he acknowledged. 'Poll tax is the main issue of this reselection. Mr Dunnachie says pay it. I say don't pay. If a fair and democratic contest is allowed, then I am confident of victory.' The constituency chairman, Stewart MacLennan, responded wearily that he was 'getting accustomed to the silly stunts of Mr Sheridan'. Militant had identified Pollok as its main hope of dislodging a sitting MP; there had been trouble there before, in 1981, when the then MP, James White, was involved in a bitter struggle with two disciples of Tony Benn, standard-bearer of the left, for the parliamentary nomination. But Dunnachie proved an unexpectedly tough target. His pre-emptive strike, objecting to headquarters about the infiltration of the constituency by extremists, led to the suspension of Sheridan and other Militant supporters, while Dunnachie won the endorsement of 81% of local party members in the reselection vote. The outcome was interpreted by the Scottish press as a triumph for Labour's mainstream. It did no harm, however, to the growing reputation of Tommy Sheridan as a local folk hero.

On 9 July 1988, the Secretary of State, Malcolm Rifkind, had a series of angry exchanges in the House of Commons with two of the SNP's three MPs, Margaret Ewing and Alex Salmond, over the nationalists' policy on payment, or non-payment, of the poll tax. Rifkind had been doing his homework on the SNP's manifesto for the last election. There was nothing in it that gave the party a mandate to urge the Scottish people to break the law by not paying. Ewing rose to insist that the SNP was merely inviting the people to exercise their free will, adding that morally they had every right to question bad laws. Rifkind responded that neither she nor Andrew Welsh – the third of the SNP trio – believed in a policy of illegality but had been forced to support it by Salmond – 'the infant Robespierre' – whom he accused of advocating extremist policies.

It was a bad-tempered day all round. Elsewhere, the chairman of British Steel, Sir Robert Scholey, announced record profits of £400 million, but incensed the steel workers of Motherwell with an incidental statement at a press conference that the Ravenscraig plant was among those 'to be reviewed next year'. Scholey made no secret of his irritation when journalists challenged him about the ominous possibilities of such a review. 'Nothing is forever,' he replied. 'We can give the Craig no more assurances than anyone else.' When he heard the news, the convenor of shop stewards, Tommy Brennan, pointed out that Ravenscraig workers had achieved the highest productivity of any steel plant in Western Europe. 'They have tried their damndest to close us down,' he said, 'but I don't believe any government could stand by and let them do it.' He was mistaken. St Paul had warned the Thessalonians that if a man did not work, he would not eat. Ravenscraig man did work; the figures proved it. But, as subsequent events showed, the text was not to be taken too literally. A man could work, and still starve.

II

Later that day, 6 July, on a calm summer evening 120 miles north-east of Aberdeen, the posturing of politicians suddenly counted for nothing. Shortly before 10 o'clock the first of a series of explosions ripped through the Piper Alpha platform in the North Sea, while more than a hundred of the 226 oil workers on board were asleep. Most of these men died a horrible death, incinerated in their beds. The disaster struck with such astonishing speed that no-one on the platform had time to send a Mayday message; the first alert came from a supply boat, *Lowland Cavalier*, which sent a message to the coastguards at Aberdeen warning of 'a huge explosion' on Piper Alpha. It was 9.58 pm.

A standby vessel, the *Sandhaven*, lay three miles from Piper Alpha. It went straight to the scene. Iain Letham, 27, a deckhand, and two of his mates launched a rigid inflatable fast rescue craft and sped under the burning platform. They managed to rescue four men, but as they retreated to safety they spotted two more who had dropped into the water, and returned in an attempt to save them. 'We got them on board,' said Letham, 'but then there was a second explosion which engulfed the boat in flames. I don't know what happened after that. I just knew I found myself in the water with flames everywhere. Even my hard hat and lifejacket melted. I thought I was going to die. The second explosion happened as people were making their way down ropes and pipes about 100 feet into the water. The impact was colossal. The whole place erupted.' Letham clung to the leg of the platform along with an oilman who had dropped into the sea. Eventually, with flames racing towards them across the water, they swam for their lives to a tug 200 yards away: 'It was bloody hot. Even the water was warm, very warm.' There was no trace of his fellow crewmen from the *Sandhaven* or of the rescue craft or of the men they had rescued.

Jim McDonald, 50, a rigger from Stirling, one of the last men to flee the platform, had been trapped in the accommodation block after the first explosion. 'For about three quarters of an hour we were all sitting inside. Nobody seemed to know what to do. I wasn't going to sit down and get burned to death. I knew I'd be making for the fire, but it would have been useless heading for the helideck. I just forced my way through the flames.' By throwing away the rulebook, he saved his life.

Another of the survivors, Bob Ballantyne, 45, was sharing a cabin with Charlie MacLaughlin, a fellow electrician from Glasgow, and Ian Gillanders, a pipefitter from Nairn. After the initial explosion, he went to the cabin and found Gillanders arranging his socks and underwear and putting clean items back into a drawer; it was his mundane way of dealing with the crisis. Ballantyne begged him to stop. When he didn't, Ballantyne lifted up his copy of Voltaire's *Candide* – a novel about an eternal optimist – and left the room with MacLaughlin. The emergency lighting had gone off and the only light coming into the cabin was from fires licking the windows. Ballantyne, like Jim McDonald, knew that the helicopters would be prevented from landing by the flames and thick smoke, and determined to find his own way out: 'It was like a surrealist painting. Like Salvador Dali's melting watch'. Instinctively, he got hold of a rope and dropped to the level of the deck 20 feet above the sea, where he noticed his mate at the other end of the platform. At that moment there was another huge explosion in which Gillanders, still in the cabin, and MacLaughlin were both killed. Ballantyne swiftly climbed down into the water, where he was picked up by a boat – though not before he found himself stuck in the middle of an oil slick with a ball of flame advancing towards him.

Ron Carey, 45, from Irvine, described the experience as 'either a case of fry and die or jump and try'. He dived from 50 feet 'because I was totally engulfed in the smoke and could see there was clear water below'. When he hit the water, he felt his head being 'cooked' and had to keep ducking beneath the burning waves to cool it. His heavy clothes – he was wearing boots, overalls and a heavy sweater – threatened to drag him down, but he was an excellent swimmer – and lucky.

From a nearby supply vessel, a converted trawler called the *Silver Pit*, men watched helplessly. 'The guys who were killed were waiting to be picked up by boats', said one of the crew, Edward Amaira. 'They were hanging on the ladders waiting. All I could see were the bodies silhouetted in the fire. The safest place to be was the water.' The master of the *Silver Pit*, John Sabourn, said: 'Pieces of burning debris were shooting off like meteors. One piece shot straight towards the wheelhouse windows and I was sure it was meant for me. I remember thinking: "God, if I come out of this alive I will never ever be frightened again". It missed me by feet.'

On board a Sea King search and rescue helicopter based at RAF Lossiemouth, the burning platform could be seen 28 miles away. 'As we got closer,' said Flight Lieutenant Steve Hodgson, 'we appreciated just how huge the flames were. They were absolutely massive. We were flying at 200 feet and when we got there the flames were above us. The glare from the blaze was so bright we could see nothing. We couldn't see if there was anyone on the platform, but even if there had been, we could have done nothing. The heat was so intense we couldn't get closer than a mile.' Squadron-Leader Garfield Parker, captain of a Nimrod from RAF Kinloss, one of the first aircraft on the scene, said he could see the flames raging from 70 miles and estimated that they were 300 to 400 feet in the air.

Dr Graham Page, a consultant at Aberdeen Royal Infirmary, was dozing in a chair at home when the 10 pm news gave the first inkling of the scale of the disaster. He drove at once to the accident and emergency unit, staying there to await the arrival of the injured, while his colleague Dr Alasdair Matheson led a medical team on an Army helicopter taking them to the fire-fighting ship *Tharos*. Around 1 am, as the helicopter was making its approach, the pilot signalled to Matheson to join him. Together they watched a huge ball of fire on the skyline 15 or 20 miles away and saw men leaping 200 feet into a sea of fire. When they reached *Tharos*, which was fighting the flames from a distance of a quarter of a mile, Matheson and his team could feel the heat on their faces. Matheson was surprised that men had survived so well a jump from such a considerable height; he treated only one limb injury. Six plastic surgeons flew to Aberdeen by helicopter from Leicester, where they had been attending a conference, and treated three badly burned survivors and 10 others with less serious burns, mainly to the hands. There were only 61 survivors; 167 men died, including two on a rescue boat.

The Prince and Princess of Wales came to Aberdeen and spoke to the injured in hospital. Among the other visitors to the wards were Armand Hammer, the 90-year-old oilman whose Occidental Petroleum Company owned Piper Alpha, and his consultant, the explorer Sir Ranulph Fiennes. Hammer said later: 'We found out that there was complete darkness. The men were groping around. Everything failed. It was such a tremendous explosion that everything was wiped out.' The company's chief executive in the UK, John Brading, made an early statement in defence of Occidental's safety standards – 'the highest in the industry' – and dismissed comments by the company's former loss prevention manager, Jack Donaldson, that Piper Alpha was the most dangerous platform in the North Sea. But there was a good deal of corroboration for Donaldson's view. 'Piper was synonymous with accidents,' said Jake Milloy, a trade union official. 'People would say, "Piper? Oh, you don't want to go there. That place is ready to go". If somebody had said to me that a platform could fall into the sea, I'd have laughed at them. But the reality is, you're sitting on a bomb.'

Such critics as Donaldson and Milloy spoke in general terms of the vulnerability of a structure which weighed 34,000 tonnes, stood in 474 feet of water, and yet could be destroyed in 22 minutes. But personal testimony was perhaps more powerful. A young woman from Dundee, Linda Anderson, whose boyfriend, Craig Barclay, a 24-year-old welder, was among the victims, said that Barclay had told her in one of their last telephone conversations, only a few days before he died, that he had recently reported a gas leak on the platform and had twice refused to light his welding equipment after smelling gas. Barclay was told to carry out repair work but refused. A safety officer then arrived on the scene and agreed that welding would be dangerous. She thought that her boyfriend's voice on the telephone sounded strained. The dead man's mother, Irene Barclay, said he had expressed worries about gas leaks several times in conversation. 'We just thought it was rig talk.'

Occidental discounted these reports, which were difficult to confirm or deny because both safety officers were killed in the explosion. One of the survivors, Bob Ballantyne – the electrician who had *Candide* at his bedside – was, however, so disturbed by the company's denials that he came forward with his own account of conditions on board Piper Alpha. He told the press that he had smelled gas two days before the explosion. 'I have a very poor sense of smell,' he added, 'so it must have been very strong for me to notice it'. When he and a colleague reported it to their superiors, they were told to leave the area. 'We had a cup of tea and about half an hour later there was a Tannoy telling us work could resume. When we went back they told us there had been gas, but it was now cleared.' Ballantyne, who had worked offshore for 11 years, vowed never to return.

For a while there was an alternative theory about the disaster: the possibility that Piper Alpha had been sabotaged by terrorists. The fact that the living quarters took the brunt of the blasts, and that there had been a change of crew the day before, aroused the suspicions of an authority on terrorism, Professor Paul Wilkinson of St Andrews University, who postulated that a timed device could have been planted in the sleeping block, allowing the bomber to escape before the blast. 'It has long been assumed that oil installations, not just in the North Sea but throughout the world, would represent plum targets,' he said. The truth was less sinister: an accidental leakage of gas which, when it ignited, caused 80 million square feet of gas to explode and burn, releasing energy approaching the scale of the Hiroshima bomb.

A fortnight after the disaster, 4,000 people gathered inside and outside St Nicholas Kirk in Union Street, Aberdeen, for a memorial service relayed by satellite to oilmen working offshore. 'Never before had the city seen a service on such a scale,' said one newspaper report. The city centre was closed to traffic, nearly every shop shut its doors, and the bells of St Machar's pealed out a three-hour tribute to the dead. Andrew Wylie, chaplain to the oil industry, told the congregation: 'The offshore community is a family. How could it be otherwise, when half of every year is spent living at your place of work? And it is tightly knit with a bonding forged through shared hazards, and with a mutual support that can result in a courage quite awesome in its selflessness.' He added: 'Let's be quite clear about the men who died. They were ordinary men doing ordinary jobs, at which they were skilled. It is the location that makes it all so extraordinary.'

On the day of the service, the world's most experienced oil fire-fighter, Red Adair, and his team, were unable to board Piper Alpha because of strong winds. They had faced what Adair called 'a slow, difficult, physically exhausting battle' to cap the burning wells. 'You can do some praying for us,' he had said at the start. Two weeks on, they had succeeded in snuffing out the worst of the leaking wells, but had recovered very few bodies from the sea; 131 were still missing. It took Adair three months to finish the job.

A senior High Court judge, Lord Cullen, was appointed to head an inquiry into the disaster – the deadliest in the history of the oil industry. He made it his business to inspect the wreckage of the platform, seeing for himself an accommodation block which had been recovered from the bottom of the North Sea. His conclusions were damning. A gas valve, removed from pipe-work for overhaul and maintenance, had not been properly sealed; a fitter had failed to tighten bolts on a flange that had been fitted in place of the valve; and when a second oilman put the system back into operation he failed to check it properly, leading to the gas leak that triggered the initial explosion. But Cullen was clear that the disaster could not be attributed simply to a tragic human error. 'As is often the case,' he reflected later, 'such failures are indicative of underlying weaknesses in the management of safety.' He found that these weaknesses took a variety of forms: training and monitoring had been poor; the lessons from a previous accident had not been followed through; evacuation procedures had not been practised adequately; no-one had fully understood the implications of a high-pressure fire for the integrity of the structure.

When Piper Alpha came on stream in the late 1970s, sending crude via a 127-mile-long pipeline to a handling terminal on the Orkney island of Flotta, it was Britain's biggest oil-producing platform, yielding 300,000 barrels a day – 10% of the country's total output. Occidental reacted to a fall in the price of oil – from 30 dollars a barrel in the late 1970s to eight dollars a decade later – by massively scaling back spending on such essentials as safety and maintenance. If it was a disaster of capitalism, it was also a severe indictment of regulation. There were 217 installations in the North Sea at the time, yet the government employed only eight full-time inspectors of these gigantic structures. They were 'inadequately trained, guided and led', said Cullen, and their investigations were 'superficial to the point of being of little use'.

Predictably, however, the main brunt of the political attack was directed at the irresponsibility of the oil industry in general and Occidental in particular. Alex Salmond stated in the House of Commons that the fear of victimisation prevented proper reporting of safety problems on North Sea oil rigs, while Labour's Tommy Graham claimed to know of an industry blacklist of workers who had fought for improved health and safety at work. Another Labour MP, Frank Dobson, narrowed the focus, condemning superficial attitudes and deficient practices on the part of Piper Alpha's management. 'If rules mean anything,' he said, 'Occidental must have broken them and it should be prosecuted.' But despite Lord Cullen's conclusion that there was 'clear evidence of negligence', the Lord Advocate, Lord Fraser, announced three years later that he had not found enough to justify prosecuting the company. What more did he need? It was a shabby decision.

Occidental paid out £66 million to families of the dead, sold off its UK interests, and escaped criminal or civil sanction, leaving many of the dependants angry and bewildered. The body of Ian Gillanders, who was last seen organising his clothes in the cabin, was never recovered. His wife Ann attended the public hearings of the Cullen inquiry and was dismayed by much of what she heard about the casual attitude to safety – including the revelation that the Claymore and Tartan platforms in the North Sea did not immediately shut down production when it became apparent that there was a serious fire on Piper Alpha.

Among the survivors, long-term anxiety and depression led to at least one suicide: that of Dick Common, who took his own life in 1994. He always felt guilty that he, a single man, had survived while a close colleague with a wife and children had perished. 'It never left his mind,' said a friend. 'It was like a nightmare that went on and on.' Many suffered ghastly flashbacks in which they saw, heard and sometimes even smelled the dreadful things they had experienced. The director of the Aberdeen Centre for Trauma Research at Robert Gordon University, Professor David Alexander, who cared for survivors in the burns unit of the Royal Infirmary, believed that it had been a great advantage to have the men together in the same ward, supporting each other. 'What I didn't think enough about,' he said, 'was what it would be like when they got out. For some, it was very hard indeed. Society is sometimes not very tolerant of disfigured people.' Alexander remembered one comment about his patients: 'They shouldn't be out looking like that. It's awful.'

Coping with the grief was made no easier by its extensive radius. The loss of life far out in the North Sea was the equivalent of the toll once extracted by an old-fashioned pit disaster, but with one essential difference: in the mining town and villages, the impact had been felt in close-knit communities which cared for their own. The emotional fallout from Piper Alpha was more diffuse; it affected many communities the length and breadth of Scotland, but inevitably with less communal intensity. Many grieved alone, without the network of mutual help which had given the mining communities such cohesion and strength. Since 1978, the number of people employed in the British sector of the North Sea had risen dramatically – from 12,500 to 28,200. For many men, particularly in the areas of declining or derelict heavy industry, the offshore sector was an alternative source of full-time labour, but at some cost socially and psychologically. Margaret Thatcher, in furtherance of her revolution, had quoted St Paul: 'If a man will not work, he shall not eat'. In order to eat, Scottish man now required to spend long periods away from home, in an alien, dangerous environment, without the comfort of family and friends. It was a lonely life in the new, mobile society; and for 167 men on a July evening in 1988, a lonely death.

In the final days of the year, Scotland was afflicted by a second colossal tragedy, one that went on reverberating for decades. But there has been enough death for one chapter. Lockerbie will be kept for another.

TUCKER'S LIST

I

A FEW DAYS BEFORE CHRISTMAS 1989, A SELECT GROUP ASSEMBLED in Edinburgh. The invitation list included the Secretary of State (Malcolm Rifkind), the Lord Justice General (David Hope) and the Lord Advocate (Peter Fraser, recently ennobled as Lord Fraser of Carmyllie). In the season of peace and goodwill, there was precious little of either; and no call for party hats. The only question to be decided was what to do about Lord Dervaird.

Dervaird – John Murray QC, known to his friends as Ian – had been a judge in the Court of Session for less than two years, taking the title from the name of his family's farm near Glenluce in Wigtownshire. A product of Edinburgh Academy and Corpus Christi, Oxford, married with three sons, Murray was known as a quiet, studious man, happy with civil work but less suited to the rough and tumble of the criminal courts. Earlier in the month, he had exercised unusual leniency in sentencing to only 18 months' imprisonment a man who had raped his children's nanny, a decision that 'caused disquiet in legal circles' according to one report. Soon afterwards, it was Dervaird himself who was causing disquiet.

The three office-bearers were not detained overlong in deciding what to do about Lord Dervaird: he had to go. Hope had earlier invited him to a private meeting in Parliament House, home of the Faculty of Advocates, and informed him of the possibility that 'a certain newspaper' was about to print a story about him alleging 'the supposed use of certain premises for certain purposes'. Dervaird denied that he had used certain premises for certain purposes, but did admit to an 'indiscretion': since his elevation to the bench, he had carried on a homosexual relationship with a certain person and they had been seen together in certain places in London. Rarely had so many certainties been veiled in so much innuendo, though the nature of that innuendo was only officially acknowledged four years later in a wide-ranging report into alleged improprieties in the Edinburgh legal establishment: 'An Inquiry into an Allegation of a Conspiracy to Pervert the Course of Justice in Scotland', by W.A. Nimmo Smith QC and J.D. Friel, regional procurator fiscal.

On 23 December the *Daily Record* reported his lordship's 'resignation' in terms of a mystery. It stopped just short of being a seasonal ghost story, for Dervaird was soon to be professionally reborn as a professor of company and commercial law at Edinburgh University, a role in which his talents may have been more usefully employed. The *Record* hinted at a larger and darker agenda with its suggestion that two other judges had been 'interviewed' about unspecified matters of a personal nature, leaving readers free to speculate. Lady Dervaird, doorstepped at their home in Stranraer, refused to comment, and no reason for her husband's resignation was given in the bald formal statement of his departure – apparently to save him further humiliation and his family further distress. Dervaird had assured the Lord Justice General that his behaviour had not exposed him to the risk of blackmail and that he had not been guilty of criminal conduct. Hope accepted these undertakings, which meant that Dervaird could be despatched relatively painlessly before the fortuitous intervention of the Christmas and New Year holiday. By the time normal service resumed, the resignation of a High Court judge, an event unprecedented in modern times, had vanished from the front pages. But a wider scandal from which the case of Dervaird had emerged, concerning a so-called 'magic circle' of untouched or untouchable lawyers and associates, would not be so easily disposed of: the Edinburgh establishment dined out on it for years.

Its starting point was the criminal prosecution of an Edinburgh solicitor, Colin Tucker, a junior partner in the firm of Burnett Walker WS, on a charge of embezzlement. A routine inspection of the firm's books by auditors from the solicitors' regulatory body, the Law Society of Scotland, in the spring of 1988, had revealed serious irregularities. The practice in such cases was to report the matter to the Crown Office, the procurator fiscal, or the police, depending on the circumstances. In this case, it was agreed to notify the regional procurator fiscal, Douglas Allan. In June 1988 the firm's senior partner, Ian Walker, committed suicide – which the police regarded as proof of his dishonesty. That left Tucker still in the frame.

The policeman in charge of the case, Detective Inspector Robert Leitch, found a note on his desk advising him to contact Douglas Allan. When he went to see him, Allan asked to be kept up to date on the progress of the investigation. Leitch thought the approach slightly unusual. Six days after Walker's suicide, Leitch phoned Allan to inform him that a search warrant had been granted to allow them to retrieve items from Colin Tucker's car. Allan gave an instruction that the firm's offices should not be searched. The police took this as a sign that the regional procurator fiscal was somehow keeping control of the inquiry – 'not that it was wrong, but that it wasn't quite right' as one of the investigating officers put it.

There was consternation at police headquarters that Tucker remained on bail prior to his trial. Detective Inspector Roger Orr, who conducted an internal inquiry on behalf of Lothian and Borders Police into this and related cases, wrote that the decision not to search the offices 'effectively allowed Tucker to continue working and to attempt to defeat the ends of justice by removing evidence beyond the reach of the investigators'. The Nimmo Smith inquiry concluded that there was no evidence to support Orr's claim. Nor, however, did there seem to be any evidence which inescapably refuted it.

Tucker engaged as his solicitor David Blair Wilson who in turn instructed Robert Henderson QC as counsel. Henderson at that time was himself the subject of a criminal investigation into alleged financial irregularities. In December 1985, the secretary of the Law Society of Scotland, Kenneth Pritchard, had written to the Lord Advocate (then Lord Cameron of Lochbroom) expressing concern about 'certain business transactions' in which Henderson had been involved. Cameron at once gave an order that the matter should be urgently investigated and sent a copy of Pritchard's report to the regional procurator fiscal, the same Douglas Allan who was now evincing a special interest in the Tucker case. In January 1986, the deputy Crown agent, Duncan Lowe, wrote to the Lord Advocate: 'The police report when read in conjunction with the earlier material sent by the Law Society makes dismal reading from Henderson's point of view.' He recommended that there should be no attempt to treat him as a case apart. There was then a long delay – unconvincingly put down to pressure of business – in processing the case through the Crown Office's fraud unit. By the autumn of 1989, when Henderson received instructions in the unrelated case of Colin Tucker, his own possible prosecution seemed to be on indefinite hold. Almost four years had elapsed since Cameron's order for an 'urgent' investigation and still Robert Henderson was free to practise at the Scottish Bar and to spread sensational rumours about a judge.

In August he asked his new client to write a potted autobiography, ostensibly so that he 'could get a full picture' of Tucker's life. The story was a lurid one, relating details of Tucker's homosexual relationship with his partner Walker and of their various exploits. The document included many names, of which only one was ever published: Dervaird. After Henderson had read the document, he remarked to Tucker that he had led 'an interesting life'.

Henderson found it expedient to boast of his discovery. He claimed to have 'had a word' about the allegation against Dervaird with the keeper of the Advocates' Library, Brian Gill, a future Lord Justice General. Gill had no recollection of such a meeting. But there was no doubt that, over lunch or a succession of lunches, Henderson confided to other colleagues the existence of the Tucker document and Dervaird's inclusion in it, and may have referred to a 'list' of other prominent people. He then widened the scope of the malice by telling journalists he had information that would 'rock the establishment' and have them 'salivating all the way to the telephone'. There was a suggestion that he had brandished a folder of incriminating material in the foyer of the New Club, the dining club of the city's great and good, in a clumsy attempt to blackmail his lunch companion.

Against this background of poisonous speculation, the trial of Colin Tucker began in December 1989 before Lord McCluskey and a jury. In his defence, Tucker did not dispute that clients' money had been taken but insisted that it had gone to Walker and that he only participated in the embezzlement because Walker had a hold over him; the hold being that Walker had personal information about his sexual life. The jury returned majority verdicts of not guilty. Some observers considered it a perverse outcome, but Nimmo Smith found no evidence that it had been achieved by improper means. The result was a triumph for the gossip-monger Robert Henderson and gave the newspapers a business opportunity to make mischief with that hot property, 'Tucker's List'. At least two papers offered to buy the story, one of them allegedly bidding a six-figure sum, but Tucker spurned all requests.

The police were now intensely interested in the existence of 'the list' and the possibility that it might help to establish a link between senior legal figures and rent boys. They asked Tucker if he knew anything about the rent boy scene in Edinburgh; he replied that he did not. They did not pursue him for the list. Some months later, however, two policemen went to Henderson's house, where they were generously entertained. So much wine was consumed that one of the policemen fell asleep. To the one who was still awake, the QC handed over a typed copy of the list. When Tucker came to hear of this breach of trust, he was appalled. The document was shown to Peter Brown, a detective in the fraud squad, who said later that well-known names had 'popped out' at him. Brown was no more anxious to preserve the confidentiality of the document than Henderson had been; he shoved it in an unlocked desk drawer to which anyone had access and which made leaks inevitable.

An 18-year-old rent boy from Manchester known as Jason entered the plot, selling his story to a newspaper. Jason claimed that one of his first punters in Edinburgh picked him up in a car near Regent Road and went straight to Waverley Station, where he bought condoms. The punter then drove out of the city centre to 'a big house'. As they approached it, the punter instructed Jason to duck down out of sight in the front seat. He was escorted into a book-lined study and told to wait. Jason noticed a framed photograph of the punter on the wall; it showed him wearing 'some sort of long robes'. The punter returned, took Jason to a bedroom, and sodomised him. In its account of the story, the newspaper hinted that the unnamed punter was a judge. If this was true, the judge had committed a crime by having sex with someone under the age of consent (21). Nimmo Smith pointed out that members of the Scottish Bar never wore long robes without a wig, yet Jason had made no mention of a wig. Jason refused to give evidence to the inquiry, so there was no opportunity to ask him if the man in the long robes had been wearing a wig and, if he had, why Jason had not thought to mention it in the first place. The police had been sufficiently impressed by his testimony to put it about that the robes were red and that the house was in Queensferry Road.

In the next instalment of the saga, the police found a 16-year-old boy known as M in a room occupied by Neil Bruce Duncan at 37 Palmerston Place. On 14 January 1990, M had been on weekend leave from a children's home and was returning there by bus when Duncan struck up a conversation with him and persuaded him to go with him to Edinburgh. For the next 10 days, said the Nimmo Smith report, 'Duncan systematically debauched M. He also made it possible for other men to participate in the debauchery by taking him to various houses in Edinburgh.'

Duncan and nine others faced a total of 57 charges. Before their trial, a rumour began to circulate that one of the Crown witnesses – a rent boy – was in a position to point to the trial judge, Lord Sutherland, as one of his punters, that he might be planning some form of outburst during the trial, and that Sutherland's name appeared in a senior police officer's notebook. After a search of the officer's numbered notebooks, no such name was found. Sutherland himself told colleagues that he regarded it as 'incomprehensible' that he should be the subject of such a rumour. Nicholas Fairbairn had once described him as 'a suave, curt, incisive silk with a taste for gin and a mind as sharp as his manner is glib, his cigarettes are many, and his words are few'. His words were fewer than usual in the case of Duncan and his co-accused; he was taken off it for administrative reasons and replaced by Lord Clyde.

A further curiosity occurred: at a preliminary pre-trial hearing, 47 of the 57 charges were dropped and pleas were arranged on the rest, allowing five of the accused to walk free. 'One or two expressed surprise about the acceptance of so many pleas of not guilty,' wrote Nimmo Smith in his report, 'but did not seek to suggest that these decisions could be criticised'. This was an extraordinary reading of the situation. Police officers attending the hearing were aghast at the action of the prosecutor, Thomas Dawson QC, and hurled abuse at counsel as they left the court, while officials in the procurator fiscal's office, having prepared what they considered a credible case, were baffled and angry. William McDougall, who had conducted the precognition of witnesses, told the Nimmo Smith inquiry that such a decision should have been taken at a much earlier stage and Linda Roxton, senior procurator fiscal depute, said she was 'concerned at the somewhat casual manner' in which news of the decision reached her office. Alistair Darling MP, himself a member of the Scottish Bar, wrote to the Lord Advocate – Fraser – asking why, after so thorough and time-consuming an investigation, involving a great deal of public expense, so many charges had been dropped so soon before the trial.

Fraser replied that the 'quality of the evidence' had been carefully assessed by Dawson and that his decision represented 'a proper exercise of the Crown's discretion'.

The policeman Roger Orr rejected this explanation, claiming to have inside knowledge of what actually happened. He wrote to the chief constable that 'Crown counsel arranged a meeting with the various defence agents involved and announced to their surprise that it was no longer policy to prosecute consensual homosexual conduct with persons under 18 years'. According to Nimmo Smith, Orr put it rather more crudely in his evidence to the inquiry: 'Dawson walked into the room and said, "We're not here to mess about with people sticking their cocks up young boys' arses, what we're going to do is this" – i.e. a deal, and I'm told defence counsel were absolutely stunned.' When Nimmo Smith asked the defence counsel if this was true, they all denied it; they also denied that they had been stunned by the abrupt dropping of 47 charges. Nimmo Smith's dismissal of Orr's allegation left what the *Daily Record* might have called a mystery. Either it had taken the forensic genius of Thomas Dawson QC to spot what had eluded the rest of the prosecution team – that the case was too weak to proceed to trial – or there was a more questionable motive. Roger Orr called the outcome 'a deliberate means of preventing possible compromise of prominent public figures by stopping the rent boy witnesses from giving evidence and identifying other homosexual partners'. Nimmo Smith fairly described this as 'a grave allegation', adding that there was not a shred of evidence to support it.

In July the same year – 1990 – the case hanging over Henderson for almost five years was finally dropped. In the opinion of the advocate depute, George Penrose, 'there was not evidence of such cogency and reliability as would justify the very serious allegations that would be involved in the case'. Nimmo Smith agreed that the decision not to prosecute Henderson had been taken 'after an exceptionally thorough investigation and after anxious consideration, by all the most senior people in the prosecution system' and concluded that there was 'no improper motivation' for the decision. Back in 1985, the Lord Advocate of the day, having studied the papers, had ordered an 'urgent' investigation into Henderson's affairs and, a few months later, a senior official in the Crown Office had observed that the case made 'dismal reading' from Henderson's point of view. What had changed in five years? It was another of the many mysteries. But Henderson's star was certainly well-aspected; as was Colin Tucker's.

In the spring of 1991, Tucker entered the dock for a second time in three years, again accused of fraud, only for the trial to come to an abrupt halt after a week when the Crown withdrew the charges against him and his co-accused, Gordon Michael May, and the jury was directed to return not guilty verdicts. Not for the first time in the affair of the alleged magic circle, a high-profile case had gone to court and collapsed. The advocate depute, Alastair Campbell, came to the view that the Crown witnesses were so unimpressive that it would not be in the public interest for the trial to continue; the judge, Lord Milligan, agreed that the case 'wasn't getting anywhere'. Accordingly Campbell phoned the Lord Advocate (Fraser). They both agreed that the only reason for continuing with the case would have been to avoid press criticism. Isabel Clark, the procurator fiscal who was assisting the advocate depute, told the Nimmo Smith inquiry that she was 'extremely upset at the decision to drop the case mid-trial' and objected to the direct communication between Campbell and Fraser and between Campbell and the judge. Campbell's justification was that he made the decision on the basis of the evidence and the evidence alone, and that he would have taken it without reference to the Lord Advocate had it not been for the background of media speculation. Clark continued to maintain that the Crown should have led all the available evidence and that, as she saw it, the advocate depute was 'induced' to take a premature decision.

The police noted that Tucker's co-accused, May, helped to run a night club in Thailand which may have been popular with 'the gay element in the legal fraternity'. Even if this were true, any innuendo that the judge, the Lord Advocate and the advocate depute colluded in a cover-up to protect the good name of their profession was plainly implausible. This case bore all the hallmarks of nothing more dubious than a Crown Office cock-up.

Meanwhile, yet another embarrassment: Douglas Allan, the fiscal who had shown a keen interest in the first trial of Colin Tucker and who was now sheriff of Lanark, was alleged to have attended parties in Palmerston Place, Edinburgh, in the company of David Blair Wilson, the solicitor who acted for Tucker in the first trial, parties at which (as Nimmo Smith put it) 'sexual activities with young men took place'.

The source of the new allegations was disreputable: Stephen Conroy, a former court runner, who served a long prison sentence for fraud. Conroy claimed that he met Allan in a gay pub in Edinburgh called the Laughing Duck, that he danced with him in a disco called the Blue Oyster, that he had dinner with him in the upmarket Howard Hotel. Blair Wilson denied that he had ever been in Palmerston Place with Allan, denied that he had ever met Allan. Allan said that he had never been in the Laughing Duck or the Blue Oyster, that he did not know Conroy, that he generally spent Friday nights with his wife and that he was circumspect in his social life. Nimmo Smith found 'not a shred of evidence' to support Conroy's claims.

Tam Dalyell, son-in-law of the retired judge Lord Wheatley, wrote to the chief constable of Lothian and Borders Police, Sir William Sutherland. 'The basic trouble,' wrote Dalyell, 'revolves around a series of Crown Office decisions on cases investigated by Lothian and Borders Police.' The letter referred specifically to Tucker, the financial affairs of Henderson, and the allegations against Allen [sic]. 'All these cases,' he said, 'have attracted deep disquiet among serious people.' It was as a result of Dalyell's letter that Sutherland appointed Roger Orr to prepare a report. Orr was given a room of his own; his typing was done by someone from Special Branch; no-one else was to have sight of his work. The result was a deeply incriminating document. 'If there is a unifying theme,' he wrote, 'it is the suggestion that Robert Henderson QC, by reason of his possession of Tucker's List, was in effect able to blackmail the Crown and secure that there were either no prosecutions or no successful prosecutions of himself and others whom he sought to favour.' Orr concluded: 'The inference is one of the existence of a well-established circle of homosexual persons in Edinburgh with influence in the judiciary, who may or may not have exercised their influence but who have formed associations which in themselves lay them open to threats or blackmail.' He added that 'homosexuality may well have been used as a means to seriously interfere with the administration of justice.'

Nimmo Smith found no evidence to support the inference in Orr's report; and Orr's superiors, having commissioned the report, let their man hang out to dry. The deputy chief constable, Hector Clark, told Nimmo Smith he had a feeling that 'perhaps there have been too many coincidences' and was prepared to acknowledge that there was 'something to this talk about lawyers and rent boys', but his 'feeling' was not strong enough to advise the chief constable to take it further. Sutherland himself informed the inquiry: 'I don't believe there is any evidence to show there is a high-powered conspiracy.' The response to Tam Dalyell closed the matter: the police would not be pursuing the suggestion of a conspiracy. Nimmo Smith thus had official backing for his sweeping conclusions: that there was no evidence that a conspiracy had ever existed; that there was no evidence of irregularity in the conduct of business in the Crown Office or the Procurator Fiscal Service; and that there was no evidence that any prominent member of the Scottish legal establishment had 'at any material time been compromised by reason of homosexuality or homosexual behaviour'.

Questions remained. 'At any material time': what did this qualifying phrase mean? And the mantra of 'no evidence' – sometimes taking the form of 'not a shred of evidence' – was undermined by the concerns of at least two officers of the Crown – Isabel Clark and William McDougall – about the conduct of specific cases. Likewise did the report of a senior police officer, Roger Orr, count for nothing? Was the resignation of Lord Dervaird irrelevant? What of the evidence of such unimpeachable figures as Kenneth Pritchard of the Law Society and Douglas Lowe, the deputy Crown agent?

The incestuousness of Edinburgh society was never better demonstrated than by the formal presentation of Nimmo Smith's report to the Lord Advocate, who happened by then to be none other than Lord Rodger of Earlsferry, the lunchtime companion Robert Henderson had allegedly tried to blackmail in the New Club – an allegation that Nimmo Smith decided was untrue ('There is no evidence whatever that Lord Rodger is or ever has been in any way compromised'). It was, nevertheless, embarrassing that the recipient of the report should himself have been the subject of rumours that the report's author had felt obliged to consider. Perhaps such an obvious conflict of interest could only have happened in Edinburgh. Perhaps, too, it would only have been in Edinburgh that so many serious allegations against members of the legal establishment were investigated by someone who was himself a member of that establishment – albeit a person of the utmost probity – rather than by some wholly detached outsider.

Among the principal characters in Nimmo Smith's report, the only career forever blighted was that of Roger Orr. Nimmo Smith himself, Thomas Dawson and Lord Rodger were elevated to the bench of judges; Lord Fraser of Carmyllie further distinguished himself by instigating proceedings against the alleged Lockerbie bombers; Douglas Allan was appointed OBE for his services to the administration of justice; Colin Tucker, declared innocent on two occasions, emigrated to London where he was employed by the Lord Mayor, Fiona Woolf, as her 'steward'; Lord Dervaird settled into his new life in academia; Robert Henderson retired to France without ever having tasted prison. When he died in 2012, Lord McCluskey wrote a glowing obituary for the *Scotsman*, lamenting that the life of his friend Bob had been 'cut short' at the age of 75.

Two years later, Henderson's daughter, Susie, revealed to the media the monstrous character of her father – a side unknown to McCluskey and others. Behind the urbane exterior he presented to the world, he was a heavy drinker, a serial wife-beater and a child abuser. She claimed to have been repeatedly sexually assaulted by him from the age of three or four: 'He would say to my mum when he came from the pub, "I'll take Susie for a nap". And that was when he'd do it. He always put a pillow over my head. Another time in the bath he abused me and put my head under the water.' Susie Henderson described how the house was often full of people, many of whom were aware of what was going on. One of them, the oleaginous Nicholas Fairbairn, abused her in front of Henderson, who 'just stood there laughing'. On another occasion Fairbairn raped her; she remembered the pungent smell of his feet. In the Edinburgh of the alleged magic circle, they were not the only things that stank.

II

In comparison with the resignation of Lord Dervaird and all that flowed from it, the second cause célèbre of 1989 was a piece of comic absurdity. The Lord Chancellor (of England), Lord Mackay of Clashfern, who, as previously noted, was not a Tory before he agreed to join Margaret Thatcher's administration, and who owed his original advancement as Lord Advocate of Scotland to the complete unsuitability of Nicholas Fairbairn for this or any other public office, had been a loyal member of the minority sect known as the Free Presbyterian Church. The FP was the remnant of a remnant, a breakaway from a breakaway, whose adherents were often referred to as the 'Wee Wee Frees' in order to distinguish them from the 'Wee Frees' of the Free Church. The Wee Wee Frees were doctrinally the most conservative of Scotland's five Presbyterian denominations and their ministers the most long-winded; a typical sermon lasted an hour.

In his capacity as Lord Chancellor, Mackay attended the funerals of two judicial colleagues, Lord Russell of Killowan and Lord Wheatley of Shettleston (Tam Dalyell's father-in-law), both of whom had the misfortune, from the point of view of the Free Presbyterian Church, to have been Roman Catholics. On the grounds that attendance at a Catholic mass was a sin worthy of excommunication, the southern presbytery suspended Mackay for six months in November 1988; in May of the following year his case was to be heard on appeal at the church's synod.

The over-reaction to Mackay's mere presence at the funerals facilitated the opening of old wounds between the two sects. The eloquent editor of the Free Kirk magazine, the Reverend Donald Macleod, wrote a thunderous editorial denouncing the disciplining of the Lord Chancellor as an example of 'spiritual totalitarianism'. If the trend continued, he said, the Free Presbyterians would find themselves free to attend no other funerals but their own. He went on to accuse them of wishing to legislate on such matters as 'permissible Sunday transport, the length of a woman's hair, the attire of ministers and attendance at extra-denominational meetings' and expressed astonishment that 'a simple social duty' had suddenly acquired such lethal ecclesiastical implications. They were potentially more lethal for a second prominent figure in the church, the Reverend Alexander Murray, a Highland regional councillor from Lairg, Sutherland, who had been suspended for three months and ordered to forfeit a fifth of his stipend for asking a Roman Catholic to say a prayer at a council meeting; Murray was further accused of speaking to the press while suspended.

Among the hardliners, the clerk to the synod, the Reverend Donald Maclean, was the most influential, a man who commanded the utmost respect. The journalists in attendance found him mesmeric: tall, immaculate in black frock coat, hands on hips, looking far younger than his 74 years, with a voice described by one observer as 'a nasal, swooping snarl'. Born in Glasgow of West Highlands stock, he had walked as a child three times a day from his tenement home in the Gorbals to the Woodside district of the city, a 16-mile tramp back and forth, to Sunday worship at St Jude's, the 'Free Presbyterian Vatican' as it was irreverently known, where the congregation regularly numbered more than 1,000. In 1960 he was inducted to the church of his boyhood. 'Maclean commanded the pulpit like the bridge of a battleship, with sweeping gesture and that extraordinary, surging voice,' wrote one admirer, 'and spoke in perfect prose, from minimal notes.' Maclean knew the FP Church inside out: he had been a communicant member since 1937; he had trained most of its ministers; he exulted in its extreme and unabashed form of Presbyterianism; a mere Lord Chancellor held no fears for him. 'When he stood to announce that the synod must now consider the case of Lord Mackay,' wrote one journalist, 'he was awesome.' After three hours of fractious debate in the small whitewashed FP church in Chapel Street, Inverness, there was no agreement.

Maclean said it was very difficult to believe that the Lord Chancellor of a Protestant country with a Protestant Queen on a Protestant throne was under any obligation to attend a papist mass by virtue of his job. He added that it was vital for the church to maintain its 'witness' against the Roman Catholic Church and its mass. 'There is also the question of example,' he continued in full flow. 'Lord Mackay is an eminent Christian . . . There he stood among them, in their idolatrous worship.' Mackay's supporters from his kirk session in Edinburgh maintained that there was a clear distinction between attendance at a mass and participation in it; one speaker reminded the synod that John Calvin himself had made such a distinction. Mackay's minister, the Reverend Angus Morrison, emphasised that there had been no change of doctrine on the part of himself or the kirk session; the issue was whether the Lord Chancellor's presence at a Roman Catholic service at which a requiem mass was said necessarily condoned false doctrine or was tantamount to 'fellowship in sacrilege'. Mackay was not present to hear any of this, but sent a letter to the synod explaining that his attendance had not in any way represented support for the Roman Catholic Church or its mass.

After a further four hours of debate the next day, the synod voted by 33 votes to 27 to dismiss the appeal from Mackay's kirk session and to maintain the suspension until the Lord Chancellor repented. Murray, the Lairg dissident, was informed that he should consider himself still suspended, although he had resumed his ministerial duties on the completion of his three months' sentence. He asked above the din: 'Do I still have a seat on this synod? I have performed a lot of ministerial functions. Are the sacraments I have administered null and void?' He was informed that, had he conducted a wedding (which he had not), the marriage would be considered illegal.

Mackay's supporters let rip. 'It is impossible for me to acquiesce to this decision and it is impossible for my fellow delegates to acquiesce and I appeal to the Head of the Church, the Lord Jesus Christ,' declared his minister. There was then a short discussion on whether it was proper to appeal to the Head of the Church. The assistant clerk, the Reverend Alfred MacDonald of Gairloch, thought not: 'You do not appeal to anyone apart from your own conscience.' The Reverend Hamish Mackinnon of Oban disagreed: 'I have appealed to Christ. The assistant clerk cannot interfere with my appeal to Christ.' At this there was much stamping of feet from the hall and the public gallery. Some left in tears.

A minister from Toronto, the Reverend Malcolm Macinnes, whom the church had once tried to discipline for refusing to wear a dog-collar, told the waiting media that there were elders in the synod who had attended Roman Catholic funerals and that no action had been taken. He had it on good authority that one elder had said to another: 'Keep it quiet.' Before Angus Morrison headed to the telephone to inform the Lord Chancellor of the outcome, he said there was no chance of him trying to persuade Mackay to repent 'as there is nothing to repent'. The church's oldest minister, the Reverend Robert Sinclair, aged 91, predicted that the issue would split the church but he would not be leaving: 'I fought in the First World War. I am not afraid of these boys in there.' Earlier, the venerable Sinclair had told 'these boys' that he had known Lord Mackay since he was a boy himself and that he believed Mackay's conscience was clear. But the boys in there – headed by their disciplinarian prefect, Maclean – were more inclined to heed the inflammatory words of the Reverend Alexander Morrison of North Uist – 'a small, fiery man clad in black jacket and the old-fashioned minister's white bow tie' as he was described by the journalist John MacLeod (son of Donald). 'I've nothing against any of God's creatures,' Morrison had assured the synod. 'But when the Archbishop of Rome kissed the ground on his visit to Scotland he claimed this land as his own. We must make a stand for the truth.'

The two men at the heart of the affair – the clerk to the synod and the Lord Chancellor – emerged from it unreconciled. 'I believe what I did was right and perfectly consistent with my position as an elder,' said Mackay. 'I attended the services in question purely for the purpose of paying respect to my dead colleagues and as a public expression of sympathy to the relatives.' Maclean was unmoved: 'I am not concerned about the public attitude to us, but with the word of God.' Asked if the church would split, he replied: 'I am only the clerk to the synod, not a prophet.' The power of a prophet was not required: it was obvious that the church would split; the church duly split. The following Sunday, 60 members of Mackay's church, Gilmore Place in Edinburgh, met for worship as usual. In the traditional fashion they sat to sing the psalms and stood to pray; Angus Morrison delivered his sermon. Because it was Sunday, he refused to say anything to the press, but it was clear that he and his flock no longer considered themselves part of the Free Presbyterian Church. The same morning in Inverness, several hundred members abandoned their church in Chapel Street – scene of the synod – and flocked to a local school hall to hear Malcolm Macinnes, the rebel from Canada.

The split was soon formalised with the establishment of the Reformed Presbytery of the Free Presbyterian Church of Scotland, which became the Associated Presbyterian Churches (APC). One of its founders, Angus Morrison, later joined the Church of Scotland (and was the Moderator of its General Assembly in 2015). Mackay chose not to join the APC, though he did attend some of its services, as well as services of the Church of Scotland. His elder daughter, Elizabeth, said she preferred the more relaxed atmosphere of an evangelical church near Inverness to the severity of the Free Presbyterian Church in which she was brought up; she explained that the evangelical services were shorter and the hymns were sung to an organ accompaniment – unheard-of in any Free Presbyterian place of worship.

The treatment of Lord Mackay caused bemusement at Westminster. A Tory MP, David Atkinson, put a question to the Prime Minister: 'Do you share the concerns of a great many members of the House that a principal member of the government, the Lord Chancellor, is today being held to account by his church for fulfilling his public duties? Do you agree that is hardly the mark of a church that would call itself Christian or tolerant?' Thatcher would not be drawn, but replied gravely that she had 'very great sympathy' with Mackay. David Steel was frankly incredulous; he said he found it extraordinary that there was still a tiny sect 'as fundamentalist in its outlook as the Ayatollah Khomeini'. It is possible that the clerk to the synod and the spiritual ruler of Iran would have got on rather well. Maclean might, for example, have appreciated the Ayatollah's response to complaints in Iran about a sharp drop in the standard of living: 'I cannot believe that the purpose of all our sacrifices was to have less expensive melons.' Khomeini died in 1989 at 86, Maclean finally expired in 2010 at 95. Both were unreconstructed to the end. 'Bishops!' cried Maclean. 'Who'd want to be a bishop? Bunch of blockheads, the lot of them!' It was noted in a respectful obituary that he had begun his long ministry alongside colleagues who had been ordained in the nineteenth century – the century from which the trial of Lord Mackay of Clashfern had somehow wandered, atavistically, into what passed for a modern Scotland.

III

The young Conservative MP for Stirling, Michael Forsyth, had what it took to be the Ayatollah of Scottish politics. He possessed the necessary inflexibility of doctrine, even if he lacked both the beard and the approbation of his people. In July 1989, Margaret Thatcher appointed the combative right-winger as chairman of the Scottish Tories. It was a blow for Malcolm Rifkind, who would have preferred the moderate Ross Harper, a Glasgow lawyer, until the latter withdrew from politics because of media intrusion into his private life. Only a few weeks earlier, Rifkind had seemingly opened the door to constitutional change by calling at the Scottish Tory conference for 'a genuine dialogue and debate amongst Scottish Unionists of all political persuasions'. But now the Prime Minister had firmly shut the door in her Secretary of State's face. 'Her choice of Mr Forsyth, 34, is a clear declaration that she will brook no dilution of her policies and that she expects them to be taken to the people with more aggression and flair,' said the *Glasgow Herald*. Those on the left of the party – an endangered species – were stunned.

The elevation of Forsyth came as the growing clamour for home rule had found cross-party expression with the setting-up of the Scottish Constitutional Convention, headed by an Episcopalian clergyman, Canon Kenyon Wright. The Convention's principles were enshrined in a 'claim of right' emphasising that sovereignty lay ultimately with the people of Scotland and not with the state; Wright said the claim of right was 'directed against the despotic use of power by an arbitrary government' – which might have been a barbed allusion to the imposition of the widely unpopular poll tax. At the inaugural meeting in the Assembly Hall in Edinburgh on 31 March, Wright delivered a messianic address: 'There will be no turning back.

We will find a way. The forces against us will be strong, the way ahead will be difficult and even dangerous, but we will go on. For what is at stake is the real life of our nation and the values of our community. The stakes are high, but the truth will prevail.'

An unappetising squad of Young Conservatives sporting Rangers' scarves and Union flags chanted 'Scum' as 44 of Labour's 48 Scottish Labour MPs and nine Democrat MPs – precursors of the Liberal Democrats – approached the hall; George Galloway, who was singled out for derision, labelled them lager louts. But in the hall itself, there was the feeling of a dignified, even solemn, occasion. The atmosphere was enhanced by the opening prayer (without which no Scottish ritual of importance seemed to be complete) and by Wright's invocation of a Biblical word – Kairos in Greek – meaning a time; not just any old time, but one ripe with promise. 'We are at Kairos,' he said gravely. 'A time for Scotland.' But Kairos did drag on. George Robertson complained that four hours of debate, without a tea-break, was just too much. 'Who says Calvinism is dead?' he wondered. A reporter from a Japanese newspaper, overcome by the spirit of Kairos, nodded off.

By mid-afternoon, the well-behaved crowd had dwindled noticeably. One of the more alert journalists, Murray Ritchie, noted the absence of splits: 'Things looked ominously constructive.' Chairing duties were shared by the Labour MP for Falkirk, Harry Ewing, and the ubiquitous David Steel, both sweetly reasonable. Since blood on the carpet there was none, the media representatives distracted themselves with matters of incidental interest: the smart striped suit of Brian Wilson, a convert to the devolutionist cause from his implacable opposition a decade or so before; Menzies Campbell, a Liberal lawyer with a permanent air of gravitas, sitting on the floor at the feet of Donald Dewar; the unobtrusive presence of the retired miners' leader Mick McGahey; and the grouse of the Green Party that no crèche had been provided – the nearest thing to a row all day. The Conservatives had boycotted the convention, as belatedly had the Scottish National Party (on the grounds of alleged Labour domination), but at least one Tory turned up anyway – the convener of Dumfries and Galloway Council, John Jameson, who declared that his party's non-participation was 'wrong'.

For grapeshot – the whiff of which gladdened every journalist's heart – it was necessary to leave the hall and hit the phones. 'This is a devolution convention,' sneered SNP leader Gordon Wilson. 'It is rigged so that the Scottish people are given no choice between the options for Scotland's future.' But was it? Was it not in truth something more ambiguous than a devolution convention? Donald Dewar had recently championed the chimera of 'independence in the United Kingdom' without explaining what it meant. 'A notion which is surely ridiculous,' wrote Murray Ritchie. 'Trying to steal the SNP's clothes and even vocabulary when its back is turned is fair political game, but inventing an impossible political illusion is dis-ingenuous to the point of absurdity.' In his speech to the inaugural meeting, Kenyon Wright had only partially succeeded in clarifying the Convention's ultimate objective: 'What we do here today is no narrow nationalism. We have no interest in a little Scotland.' But might he, and they, have had an interest in an independent Scotland somewhat larger in vision? Twenty-five years later, in the run-up to the independence referendum, he acknowledged that he had always seen the Scottish Constitutional Convention as a stepping stone to independence. Whether this was clear to the gathering of like minds in the Assembly Hall, or to the wider Scottish electorate, remains an intriguing question.

On April Fool's Day, two days after the launch of the Convention, the duty of levying the poll tax fell upon Scotland's local authorities. 'We may have to operate the legislation,' said the Labour president of COSLA (Confederation of Scottish Local Authorities), Eric Milligan, 'but we don't have to like it.' The STUC marked the day with a demo in Edinburgh attended by a crowd estimated at 20,000, among whom the SNP claimed to sign up 3,000 supporters for its campaign of non-payment. On the same day, nationalist activists were out on the streets of the cities and major towns gathering signatures. 'The phoney war is over,' said their spokesman, Kenny MacAskill. 'We now have an army of non-payers. The pressure is on the government and already they are getting cold feet because of the complaints they are receiving from all quarters.' (Though the cold feet existed only in MacAskill's imagination.) Jim Sillars stepped up the party's policy of parliamentary disruption with a record-breaking filibuster, speaking for three hours, 43 minutes to an empty chamber of the House of Commons, mainly on the issues he believed were facing the electorate in a forthcoming by-election. But it was not Sillars's friend Alex Neil, the candidate of the party of non-payment, who prevailed in Glasgow Central; Labour, whose policy on the poll tax was compliance with the law, easily won the seat with a trade union official, Mike Watson, who later served a prison sentence for setting fire to hotel curtains, an offence that did not prevent him returning to public life as a junior member of Labour's shadow team in 2015.

Labour, then, was the immediate beneficiary of Margaret Thatcher's intransigence over the poll tax, her stubborn resistance to devolution, and her perverse choice of Michael Forsyth as her party's standard-bearer in Scotland. The SNP, punished for its late withdrawal from the Constitutional Convention and its high-risk strategy on the poll tax, was the short-term loser. But while these old foes would continue to slug it out for the affections of the Scottish electorate, their respective fortunes varying from season to season, the events of 1989 all but finished the Scottish Tories as a major political force. One of Forsyth's predecessors in the job, Michael Ancram, detected the writing on the wall. He said that the Scots felt patronised, that fewer and fewer of them regarded the status quo as acceptable, and that unless Unionism could be re-established as a dynamic option in its own right, the Scottish Tories faced wipe-out and 'the independence train might be unstoppable'. The warning should have been heeded. It was not.

THUNDER IN DECEMBER

I

ALMOST TWO YEARS AFTER BRITAIN'S WORST-EVER TERRORIST atrocity, the fatal accident inquiry into the Lockerbie air disaster opened on 1 October 1990 in a temporary village created in the grounds of Crichton Royal Hospital, a psychiatric institution on the outskirts of Dumfries. The inquiry had its own administrative block, media centre and restaurant. The hearing itself took place in a makeshift courtroom converted from the hospital's recreation wing, a hall large enough to accommodate several hundred journalists and spectators. In making these elaborate arrangements, Sheriff Principal John Mowat had anticipated that many next-of-kin would want to attend, that there would be huge media interest and that members of the public would be competing for any remaining spaces.

In the event, the inquiry was conducted day after day, through the autumn and winter of 1990–91, in a near-deserted auditorium of near-stygian gloom, its heavily curtained windows letting in scarcely a chink of daylight. The bewigged sheriff sat alone on a platform overlooking a congested area reserved for silks and humbler tribunes of the legal profession, as well as a sole non-lawyerly seeker after truth; but beyond that he looked out to row after row of empty seats, more than enough to have accommodated 270 people, equivalent to the number who died at or over Lockerbie when Pan American flight 103 from London Heathrow crashed into the town. In the adjoining media centre, a warren of cubicles and temporary studios, most of the desks reserved for newspapers and broadcasting organisations were never occupied, their telephones lying unconnected. Despite the high level of pre-registration, the international media circus inexplicably failed to materialise.

Perhaps for that reason, the inquiry was rarely mentioned – indeed almost forgotten – in the torrent of subsequent analysis of the Lockerbie disaster. A quarter of century later, it remained the only public examination of the facts ever held on Scottish soil. It is therefore worth examining in some detail what it uncovered, what it failed to uncover, and what it chose not to uncover.

II

Four nights before Christmas 1988, from the window of his house, a police constable, Michael Stryjewski, saw something unusual in the sky. Until that moment, the small Dumfriesshire town, situated in fertile agricultural land close to the Scottish border, had been known mainly for its butter and cheese, and to motorists roaring up the M74 as a road sign to somewhere bypassed. Nothing very remarkable had ever happened in Lockerbie – until 7 o'clock on the evening of 21 December 1988 when an orange glow appeared above the town. 'It seemed to be growing larger and coming downward,' recalled Stryiewki. 'The next thing I saw were shapes falling to the ground. There was a tremendous noise, an explosion, like a miniature atomic bomb, and a mushroom of cloud and flame went upward. I'd say it reached 1,000 feet.' The constable tried to make an emergency call. His telephone was dead.

Ella Ramsden was opening Christmas cards in her living room, half-watching *This Is Your Life* on television, when her dog cuddled up to her and she noticed that Cara's fur was standing on end. Ella had just uttered the words 'What's wrong?' when she heard a noise she found difficult to describe. 'I rushed to my window and looked outside. The whole place was lit up with an orange glow. I'd never seen anything like it. I wondered what was going on.' She was still wondering when there was an explosion in nearby Sherwood Crescent followed by black clouds of smoke. She grabbed Cara and ran to the back door of the kitchen, not sure what to do. All the lights went out and the door refused to open. As she bent down to see if it had been jammed by the mat, the whole house shuddered; unknown to Ella, a piece of a transatlantic airliner had just landed on it. Dirt and dust flew past her, bruising her legs, and she felt that she was being sucked back into the house. 'I grabbed a stew pot from the kitchen and flung it through the glass in the back door. There was an eerie silence outside. I didn't dare scream or yell. So I just said very politely, "If there's anyone out there, will they please come and get my wee dog". Someone heard me and helped us.'

An unnamed man out for a walk had seen a section of the plane twisting and turning in the sky before it settled on Ella Ramsden's house. Such was the randomness of the disaster, many of the 35 students from Syracuse University, returning on flight 103 from semester study in Europe, ended their lives incongruously on Ella's roof and in her backyard in a small town in Scotland of which few if any would ever have heard. People from 21 nations fell on Lockerbie that night.

Bunty Galloway, a neighbour, ran to the front of her own house and saw a boy lying at the foot of her steps close to the road. 'A young laddie with brown socks and blue trousers. Later that evening my son-in-law asked for a blanket to cover him. I didn't know he was dead. I gave him a lamb's wool travelling rug thinking it would keep him warm. Two girls were lying across the road, one of them bent over garden railings. It was just as though they were sleeping'. Bunty was astonished by the number and variety of items in her garden: 'spoons, underwear, headscarves . . . everything'. The dead boy lay at the bottom of Bunty's steps for several days. 'Every time I came back to my house for clothes, he was still there. "My boy is still there," I used to tell the policeman. Eventually I couldn't take it any more. "You've got to get my boy lifted," I told the policeman. That night he was moved.' She never discovered his name, but often thought about her boy.

Another of the eye-witnesses, Ruth Jameson, was at work in the forecourt of the local petrol filling station when she heard a low rumble 'like thunder' just before the sky lit up. 'The noise was deafening. I was absolutely petrified. Suddenly everything started falling down – lumps of plane, bits of seatbelts, packets of sugar, bits of bodies. There were burning pieces all over the forecourt. It seemed to shower for ages, though it was only about five minutes.'

Pearl Lindsay was packing away groceries after a shopping trip to Dumfries when she too heard a sound like thunder. Thunder in December: it felt strange. She stopped what she was doing. The noise got louder and the ground began to shake. It went deathly still – and then there was a terrific explosion. Pearl went in search of Craig, a young man she had been at school with, and eventually found him. He too was wandering the streets. 'Craig wasn't usually a very emotional person, and we didn't normally go around hugging each other. But I couldn't help it and neither could he. As I sobbed onto his shoulder, he replied through tears: "Dinna greet, Pearl, dinna greet". That night in Lockerbie, people who didn't normally bother about each other were throwing their arms round each other, giving each other comfort and reassurance.'

Among the victims on the ground – the 11 inhabitants of Lockerbie who died – were three members of the same family: Joanne Flannigan, 10, and her parents Kathleen, 41, and Thomas, 44, of Sherwood Crescent, the street that took the brunt of the impact. Joanne's body was recovered from a 30-foot crater gouged out of the street when one of the wings and part of the fuselage landed, creating a huge fireball and leaving an overpowering stench of aviation fuel. The bodies of Kathleen and Thomas were never recovered; they may have vapourised. Joanne's older brother Steven, 14, survived by a fluke: 10 minutes before the disaster, he had taken his sister's bicycle to a neighbour in the hope of having it repaired. An older brother, David, who was estranged from the family and living in England, returned to Lockerbie to sift through the wreckage, hoping to find his parents' remains. All he found was a plastic watering can. Both Steven and David died young, Steven when he was hit by a train at the age of 26.

In the agricultural hinterland, the fields of Tundergarth Mains were littered with bodies and debris. It was here that a widely circulated photograph was taken, perhaps the most famous of all the Lockerbie images: of the flight deck section lying on its port side. Among the many smaller pieces, the farmer, Jim Wilson, made an interesting discovery: a suitcase neatly packed with a powdery substance which looked like drugs. He reported it to the police, but not before he had taken a mental note of the name printed on the suitcase.

From all over the world, the media descended. One of the first on the scene, the BBC's Andrew Cassell, knew within seconds that there were no survivors. 'The ambulances gave it away. They were strung out before me – two, three, four abreast – all along one of the country roads leading into the town. Their doors were splayed open in hopeful readiness, their flashing lights casting a flickering blue tinge on the Christmas lights above them. But there was little sign of activity, no paramedics urgently preparing equipment.'

Then came the voyeurs. A Forestry Commission worker was shocked to see lines of cars trying to find a way to the crash site, even after the main road had been closed. He watched in dismay as one man vaulted over the wire fence of a field towards bags of debris collected by a farmer, while his female companion yelled at him from the road: 'Get me a sweater'. He was just as disturbed by the behaviour of press photographers who milled around trying to get better pictures of a corpse on a roof. Angrily he forced his way through them in his van, almost running them over; when the photographers protested, a police sergeant pointedly turned his back on the scene. Most of the images captured by them were never published; even for hard-bitten men on newsdesks, they were too much.

'The visual memory of the locals,' said an Englishman with relatives in the town, 'was of the vast quantity of human flesh littering the countryside, in the gutterings, on rose bushes, in the mouths of dogs.' Dr Gordon Turnbull, an RAF psychiatrist, spent 10 days with the 150 rescuers, encouraging them to talk about the horrors they had witnessed. Strathclyde social workers, sacrificing their Christmas and New Year break, volunteered to help. There was grief on a massive scale to cope with, but also great and growing anger because of the police's refusal to include relatives in the recovery and identification of the bodies. This was the Crown Office's decision, no doubt in the humanitarian interest of sparing families the distress of seeing mulitated remains, but psychologically it may have been profoundly wrong. Rachel Rosser, an academic who had studied the consequences of such a policy on people bereaved by disaster, believed that if relatives were given the option of seeing and touching the bodies, or even partial remains, the incidence of 'pathological grief' could be reduced.

Tom Coker, father of twins Eric and Jason, both Syracuse students, told the inquiry of his strong sense that it was his paternal duty to see the bodies of his sons and participate in the identification and that he had been 'very disturbed' by his exclusion from the process. 'Those carrying out the identification,' he said, 'must bear in mind that each of the people killed was somebody's loved one . . . The twins were my sons, not Pan American's sons and not the sons of the Scottish police.' But the bench took a different view: Mowat said he could 'well understand' that the Crown Office wished to avoid relatives being subjected to the ordeal of picking out one body among all the others in the mortuary. He should have added, however, that once bodies were released for burial, this consideration did not apply with the same force; and yet Tom Coker had to stand helplessly by while executives of the airline had discussions with the undertakers of his sons' funerals.

In the chaos of the moment, the authorities had given no thought to the possibility that a single, well-trained professional, appointed at the start, would have represented the families' needs more skilfully than a multiplicity of officialdom. And if the relatives were not invariably treated with the sensitivity that their situation should have demanded, the same was true of at least one of the volunteers.

David Fieldhouse, a doctor and police surgeon, was watching television at his home in Yorkshire when news of the disaster flashed on the screen. In an act of impulsive altruism, he left the house at once and drove all the way to Lockerbie, arriving there at 10.50 pm. He contacted the police, explained who he was, and offered his services; a police officer was assigned to him. He then worked through the night in wind and rain, searching for bodies, and continued until 4.30 the following afternoon without any stop for rest or food (save for a biscuit). According to the inquiry findings, Fieldhouse 'pronounced life extinct in 58 bodies' – an explicit rejection of the doctor's own firm testimony that he pronounced life extinct in 59.

At around 7 pm on 22 December, he reported verbally to a senior police officer, showed him a map of where he had been working, and told him how many bodies he had dealt with and what he had done about them. He spent the night with a friend in Carlisle, but was back in Lockerbie on 23 December to keep an early appointment near Tundergarth Church with a detective chief inspector of Dumfries and Galloway Police. Although he waited for more than two hours, the policeman never showed up. He was, however, informed by another officer that the bodies he certified had been tagged and that they numbered 58. He never heard what happened to the 59th he had so methodically accounted for.

Fieldhouse was subsequently the victim of a smear. At the fatal accident inquiry, a police sergeant, David Johnston, faced a number of leading questions from the Lord Advocate, Peter Fraser, about one of the bodies found and labelled by Fieldhouse.

'Would this be another example of Dr or Mr Fieldhouse [sic] carrying out a search on his own?'
'It would, my Lord.'

'And marking the body of the person who is dead without notifying the police?'
'That is correct.'

Brian Gill QC, representing some of the bereaved families, also seemed willing to cast doubt on the doctor's integrity.

'Can you tell me when it was that Dr Fieldhouse provided the information [about the bodies he had found] to the Lockerbie inquiry officer?'
'It would be some months later before we were able to ascertain the complete information we had to hand.'
'It is clear, sergeant, that it is scarcely a very satisfactory state of affairs?'
'It was not very satisfactory, sir.'

As the satirical magazine *Private Eye* observed: 'The grieving families were presented with the notion of a slightly deranged surgeon driving up in the middle of the night to certify the bodies without liaising with the police or anyone else and then taking several months to report what he had found.' There was no truth in the allegations. Mowat acknowledged in his report that the doctor had at all times been accompanied by police officers and that when he returned home to Bradford on 23 December he wrote a letter to the police giving a detailed account all he had done over the previous two days. The sheriff called the criticism of Fieldhouse 'undeserved' and graciously thanked him for his services.

But the smear persisted. With cruel timing, Fieldhouse was summoned to a meeting of senior police officers in Wakefield on the fifth anniversary of the disaster (21 December 1993) and peremptorily fired. 'I believe my contract was not renewed,' he said, 'because I stood up for myself at the fatal accident inquiry and was not prepared to condone perverting the course of justice.' His name was finally cleared in 1998, when the minister of state at the Foreign Office, Tony Lloyd, acknowledged in a letter to Tam Dalyell that Fieldhouse had promptly passed on the information about the bodies he had certified but that 'very unfortunately' this fact had been 'overlooked'. Lloyd could not explain why a conscientious doctor had been smeared by police and lawyers at the fatal accident inquiry to the extent that an impression was given that he may not have been a qualified physician. Had the Lord Advocate, Fraser, not known of Fieldhouse's professional status or had he known and smeared him anyway? In the first scenario, the Lord Advocate was incompetent; in the second, dishonourable.

The motive for the attempt to rubbish the doctor's reputation was among the first of the many Lockerbie mysteries. What had Fieldhouse done to attract slanderous innuendo in open court from Scotland's most senior law officer? A possible answer lay in the erroneous official count. Jim Wilson, the farmer at Tundergarth, clearly recalled the name on the suitcase containing what he thought were drugs, yet this name did not appear on the list of Lockerbie's dead. Could the owner of the suitcase have been the 59th body found by David Fieldhouse? If so, who might have been the passenger? While the Yorkshire doctor was selflessly assisting the disingenuous Dumfries and Galloway Police, less philanthrophic visitors were scouring and compromising the crime scene. It was generally assumed that they were agents of the American government.

In 1995 Tam Dalyell put a question in the House of Commons to the Secretary of State for Scotland, Ian Lang:

'Was any dead body taken from the scene, thereby avoiding its inclusion in the official list of those who died?'
Lang: 'No.'

So that, in a word, was that; though only if Lang was in full possession of the facts.

The psychological and emotional scars of Lockerbie would never heal. The physical scars did. In time the town looked much as it had before Christmas 1988. When tourists arrived to gawp, they were surprised to find that there was no longer a crater in Sherwood Crescent. It had been covered up – like so much else about Lockerbie. The politics of the disaster was one enormous crater. After the horrible clarity of all that happened on 21 December 1988, the rest was murky.

III

There were two warnings. On 18 November, five weeks before the bombing, the Federal Aviation Administration in America issued a bulletin containing a detailed description of a Toshiba radio cassette player rigged with a bomb and a barometric triggering device. The bulletin cautioned that the device would be extremely difficult to detect via normal x-ray inspection, indicating that it might be intended to pass undiscovered through areas subject to extensive security controls, such as airports. This became known as the Toshiba warning.

Then, on 13 December, just eight days before the disaster, a notice was posted at the US embassy in Moscow:

To: All Embassy Employees

Subject: Threat to Civil Aviation

Post has been notified by the Federal Aviation Administration that on December 5 1988, an unidentified individual telephoned a US diplomatic facility in Europe and stated that sometime within the next two weeks there would be a bombing attempt against a Pan American aircraft flying from Frankfurt to the United States. The FAA reports that the reliability of the information cannot be assessed at this point, but the appropriate police authorities have been notified and are pursuing the matter. Pan Am has also been notified. In view of the lack of confirmation of this information, post leaves to the discretion of individual travelers any decisions on altering travel plans or changing to another American carrier. This does not absolve the traveler from flying on an American carrier.

The 'diplomatic facility' mentioned in the notice was the US embassy in Helsinki. The caller, a man with an Arabic accent, was specific: a woman flying in from Finland, an unwitting mule, would be carrying the bomb in her luggage. Richard Marquise, head of the FBI's Lockerbie investigation, said the call – the so-called Helsinki warning – was 'totally investigated [after the disaster] and we determined that it was not a credible threat'. Sheriff Mowat accepted that it was a hoax: he dismissed the Moscow embassy notice as 'unofficial and unauthorised', adding that the Helsinki warning should not have been treated as credible 'at any stage'. It was, however, treated as sufficiently credible for the US State Department to alert its employees in Moscow and Helsinki – though not anyone else.

Lisa Parrish, who was living in the Moscow embassy compound at the time, held on to the memo, but felt no sense of indignation that the travelling public made their Christmas holiday plans in ignorance. She pondered how much her government would, or should, reveal of such warnings: 'Is the only humane response to send out widespread alerts, even if they create consternation and fear? Or would that be succumbing to the very "terror" that terrorists intend to foment?' Two days after the disaster, the *New York Times* reported that the American government had cited several reasons for failing to inform civilians, 'including concern that such publicity would only spawn a number of crank threats that could paralyse the air industry'. But the selective nature of the alert, giving embassy employees an opportunity to change their travel plans while keeping everyone else in the dark, angered some relatives of the victims – including Marina de Larracoechea, whose sister Maria Nieves was one of the cabin crew on flight 103. For most of the four and a half months of the inquiry she was the only non-lawyer in a sea of robes and wigs. She was severely critical of the failure to make both the Toshiba and Helsinki warnings more widely available.

An authority on terrorism, Professor Paul Wilkinson of St Andrews University, said in evidence that a threat should be made public only if an airline felt that the threat could not be met by specific security measures. Using the Wilkinson test, either Pan Am was complacent or it was unconcerned: whatever the reason, it decided not to inform its cabin crews of either warning and increased security at Frankfurt Airport only marginally. Mowat found that 'there were good grounds for doubting the efficiency of x-ray alone as a means of detecting explosive devices', yet was satisfied that the limited measures taken at Frankfurt – 'providing as they did for special attention to the baggage of Finnish ladies and their companions', as he quaintly put it – were 'sufficient in all the circumstances'. Though insufficient – of course – to prevent a Toshiba radio cassette player rigged with a bomb from being planted on a Pan Am flight and detonating over Lockerbie.

The Helsinki warning certainly had an impact on bookings. One document placed before the inquiry indicated that 80% of the Christmas holiday traffic from the Moscow embassy either re-booked or tried to re-book with other airlines. The sheriff was unimpressed: 'I do not regard that as concrete evidence that a substantial number of passengers due to fly on flight 103 did in fact cancel their bookings.' This finding hinged on what Mowat regarded as substantial – he left it unquantified. But there was no shortage of anecdotal evidence that some seats were cancelled at short notice and that they were snapped up by students returning home for Christmas. One witness at the inquiry said that, when she attempted to book a student concession on flight 103 the day before departure, she was informed that all the student places had gone. She was one of the lucky ones.

The inquiry report set out the clinical facts of 270 deaths. It found that the device ('a Semtex-type plastic explosive concealed in a Toshiba radio cassette player contained in a Samsonite suitcase') was detonated at around 7.03 pm, 38 minutes after the flight left Heathrow, and that parts of the wreckage landed on Lockerbie 45 seconds later. The opinion of pathologists was that a body thrown from the aircraft at 31,000 feet would have taken two and a half minutes to reach the ground. Most of the passengers died, or were already dead, when they hit the 'soft earth of Lockerbie', as one television reporter described the scene, but the inquiry had to consider the possibility that death was not inevitable in all cases. 'Two passengers had injuries which were less severe than the others,' said the pathologists' report, 'and it is possible that they survived for a short time after sustaining these injuries.' One specialist suggested that, if resuscitation had been provided immediately, the two passengers might have lived. 'Improbable' concluded the sheriff, who issued an unqualified finding that 16 employees of Pan Am – the flight crew – died from multiple injuries 'at or about 1905 hours at or near Lockerbie'; that 243 people – the passengers – died from multiple injuries at the same time and place; and that 11 people – residents of Lockerbie – died from multiple injuries and/or severe burning at Sherwood Crescent. About the primary cause of death there could be no dispute: 'a criminal act of murder'. About the report's other findings, there was scope for endless speculation and argument.

Mowat decided that an unaccompanied suitcase containing the explosive device was loaded on to flight 103A at Frankfurt and unloaded at Heathrow, and that the aircraft which crashed over Lockerbie arrived from San Francisco around noon on 21 December, leaving for New York as flight 103 at 6.25 that evening. So far so clear – in the sheriff's mind at least. But how had the unaccompanied bag found its way to Frankfurt? It had 'probably' arrived there courtesy of an airline other than Pan Am and been 'interlined' to Pan Am without being identified as an unaccompanied bag. 'Probably' was as good as it got.

Mowat found ample evidence to support his judgement that the security arrangements were unsatisfactory: the bags from 103A were taken straight from the tarmac to the baggage container at Heathrow without being counted or checked to see that they corresponded with the bags checked in at Frankfurt. The procedure of then transferring baggage from 103A to 103 after only a routine inspection, despite the Toshiba warning, involved 'a substantial risk' that an unaccompanied bag containing an explosive device would be transferred along with the others. Reliance on x-ray screening alone, at both Heathrow and Frankfurt, 'was a defect in the system of working which contributed to the deaths' and if there had been a positive reconciliation of passengers and bags at Frankfurt, the unaccompanied bag might have been detected and 'the deaths might have been avoided'.

The sheriff did not go quite as far as Brian Gill QC, who attacked the airline's 'reckless and dangerous' practices and accused Pan Am of risking the lives of its passengers and crew by abandoning baggage reconciliation procedures. Expressed in more measured terms, the official verdict was nonetheless a damning one: not only of Pan Am for its casual attitude to the safety of its passengers and crew but of the UK Department of Transport for a less than robust enforcement of its own rules. But in some important respects, the inquiry and the report were seriously flawed.

Early on, it became clear that the proceedings would fall some way short of thoroughness. One of the first witnesses, the farmer Jim Wilson, had relevant testimony to offer the inquiry about the suitcase in his field, a suitcase full of a suspicious-looking substance. He was not asked about it. Had he been asked, his answer would have revealed not only that someone on the flight may have managed to smuggle a large quantity of drugs through security at Heathrow or Frankfurt, but the more sinister fact that the name on the suitcase did not match any of the 259 names on the passenger and crew list. So far as the inquiry was concerned, there was no such suitcase; just as there was no 59th body.

There was a more surprising omission still. It related to the evidence of John Bedford, a baggage handler at Heathrow. In the interline baggage shed for which he was responsible on 21 December, he loaded a number of items upright across the rear of the portable luggage container; he then went for a half-hour break. When he returned he spotted that two additional bags had been placed flat on the base of the container. One, which he described as a 'maroony-brown' hardshell suitcase, 'the kind Samonsite make', was close to the position in which the Samsonite suitcase on flight 103 was located when it exploded. The significance of Bedford's discovery was that all this happened before the arrival of flight 103A from Frankfurt. Who placed them there in Bedford's absence? The obvious answer was his mate Sulkash Kamboj, the x-ray operator, who told Bedford – according to the latter's evidence at the inquiry – that he ran the two bags through x-ray and then put them in the container. Kamboj denied telling Bedford any such thing, insisting to the police, and later to the inquiry, that it was not his job to put bags in the container and that he had not done so on that occasion.

What really happened? It was possible to construct a plausible theory, though with an important prerequisite: an acceptance that security at Heathrow was so lax that anyone posing as an airline employee and equipped with a pass could gain access to the shed and handle baggage. A terrorist masquerading in this way – an insider himself or with an insider's assistance – entered the shed, bringing the Samsonite suitcase with him as a piece of stray luggage; alternatively, the suitcase had been left discreetly in the shed overnight and when the terrorist arrived in the morning he simply picked it up unnoticed by Kamboj. In either version of this scenario, the terrorist handed over the suitcase to Kamboj for x-raying in the normal way; and on to the fatal flight it went, without further scrutiny.

There were two small problems with the theory. The first: what if Kamboj, a stickler for demarcation, was telling the truth? In that case, the terrorist would have had to place the Samsonite in the container himself. Possible, if trickier. Next: What was the explanation for the second additional bag? It seems to have played no further part in the story. Otherwise, the theory held up reasonably well. But there was also a larger problem, and it carried a message fatal to the official narrative. It meant that the Samsonsite suitcase containing the explosive device originated at Heathrow.

Although John Bedford told the police about the suitcase and that its arrival in the baggage shed pre-dated the arrival of flight 103A, and although he repeated this testimony to the fatal accident inquiry, Sheriff John Mowat excluded from his report all reference to the unexplained appearance of the two additional bags, one of which bore a striking similarity to the suitcase carrying the bomb. In that circuitous way of lawyers, Crown counsel had submitted to Mowat that it 'would not seek to discourage a finding that the bag containing the explosive came to Frankfurt as an interline bag'; and it seemed that Mowat was only too ready to accept this explanation, discounting all others.

IV

If the bomb was planted at Heathrow, there was no case for Abdelbaset al-Megrahi to answer. No-one ever suggested that the former Libyan intelligence officer had been anywhere near Heathrow. Nevertheless the prime suspect (along with a co-accused who was acquitted) was brought to trial before a panel of three Scottish judges, sitting without a jury, at a special court in the Netherlands, the neutral venue having been suggested by the professor of Scots law at Edinburgh University, Robert Black QC. Black started with an open mind; by the end of the trial, he was convinced of al-Megrahi's innocence.

The conviction depended largely on the testimony of the chief prosecution witness Tony Gauci, the owner of a clothes shop in Malta called Mary's House. It was alleged that on 7 December 1988, a fortnight before the bombing, al-Megrahi bought some clothes and an umbrella from Gauci's shop, that the clothes were wrapped round the device which brought down flight 103, and that al-Megrahi, a former head of security at Libyan Arab Airlines, collaborated with an official of the airline to breach the security at Luqa Airport and get the device on the first stage of its journey as an interline bag to Frankfurt.

How reliable was Gauci? His credibility took a severe battering four years after the trial in a remarkable newspaper interview with the man who initiated the prosecution, Lord Fraser of Carmyllie. The words attributed to Fraser – he never denied using them – were: 'Gauci was not quite the full shilling. I think even his family would say he was an apple short of a picnic. He was quite a tricky guy. I don't think he was deliberately lying, but if you asked him the same question three times he would just get irritated and refuse to answer.'

When the Lord Advocate at the time, Colin Boyd, read this assessment of the Crown's star witness, he asked Fraser to clarify his opinion of Gauci; others, including Tam Dalyell and al-Megrahi's counsel, William Taylor QC, spoke out more strongly. If Fraser did clarify his opinion, the world was unaware of it. Three years later, however, he gave Gauci a friendlier character reference in a television programme about the Lockerbie case: 'I have always been of the view, and I remain of the view, that both children and others who are not trying to rationalise their evidence are probably the most reliable witnesses and for that reason I think that Gauci was an extremely good witness.' How this statement could be reconciled with his earlier disobliging view of the witness, Fraser did not divulge. But the remarks received little attention, for the story had moved on dramatically: al-Megrahi was now on his way home to Tripoli, released from a Scottish prison on compassionate grounds, having been diagnosed with terminal cancer, after serving eight years of a life sentence for mass murder.

Fraser's re-evaluation of Gauci as 'an extremely good witness' looked ridiculous on close scrutiny. When the Scottish Criminal

Cases Review Commission had a detailed look at the case, it concluded that there was 'no reasonable basis' for the judges' opinion that the purchase of the clothes from Mary's House took place on 7 December; the commission decided that they must have been bought on some unspecified date before then. This was an encouraging finding for the many influential defenders of al-Megrahi, who believed that 7 December was the date of his only visit to Malta. But in 2014, in a three-part documentary for American television, Ken Dornstein, whose brother died at Lockerbie, produced evidence which undermined the case for al-Megrahi's innocence. During 15 years of patient investigtion Dornstein discovered that al-Megrahi had been in Malta in the weeks leading up to the bombing, and that he had company: a Libyan bomb-maker, Abu Agila Mas'ud, who was among those who greeted him on his return to Libya. With that revelation, somehow overlooked by the Scottish prosecutors, the Lockerbie crater got bigger than ever.

Another intriguing piece of evidence – this fragment certainly known to the police – was concealed from both the fatal accident inquiry and the subsequent trial in the Netherlands. A security guard at Heathrow Airport, Raymond Manly, had informed anti-terrorist officers that, shortly after midnight on 21 December, during a routine patrol of Terminal 3, he discovered that a padlock had been cut on the door to the interline baggage shed. It looked to Manly like a professional job. He promptly reported it to his boss, Philip Radley, who went to investigate. Radley found the lock broken in two, which in his opinion would have required 'great force'. He contacted the airport police and recorded the incident in his logbook. No further action was taken: the bags for flight 103 were duly loaded and 17 hours after the break-in the airliner took off, 38 minutes from disaster.

After Lockerbie, Radley too was interviewed by the police, yet neither he nor Manly was called to testify at the fatal accident inquiry or at the trial of al-Megrahi, whose defence had no knowledge of the Heathrow incident until afterwards. It was then that Raymond

Manly, troubled by the memory of the break-in and its possible link to the disaster, finally decided to contact al-Megrahi's defence team – and a newspaper. He spoke to the *Daily Mirror*, which splashed 'Lockerbie: The Lost Evidence' across its front page on a date in history: the morning of 11 September 2001. A second terrorist atrocity – the attack on the twin towers – quickly wiped Lockerbie's lost evidence from the media's radar.

In his interview with the *Mirror*, Manly called the break-in 'the most serious security breach that I came across in 17 years at Heathrow'. He told the paper: 'I believe it would have been possible for an unauthorised person to obtain tags for a particular Pan Am flight then, having broken the lock, to have introduced a tagged bag into the baggage area. A terrorist who wanted to put a bomb on that plane would have gained access to the perfect place. The luggage would not be checked again before being loaded on the plane.' Having given a statement to that effect at the time, Manly heard nothing more from the police. When he inquired, he was told that no-one knew about his statement; it seemed it had been lost. 'I find that just incredible', he said. 'My statement has disappeared and so has the padlock. No-one can even tell me if it was tested for fingerprints'.

This testimony formed part of the grounds for an appeal against al-Megrahi's conviction. But the Raymond Manly who appeared in court cut a pathetic figure. He performed poorly, informing the bench that because of an accident he was under medication and that he felt like vomiting. 'He looked very frail and behaved in a highly emotional, at times even aggressive manner,' noted Dr Hans Kochler, the UN observer at the hearing. Kochler thought the unimpressive quality of his evidence – he was confused, for example, about the way in which the padlock was attached to the door – might have been counter-productive. The judges had little hesitation in dismissing al-Megrahi's appeal, rejecting the theory that the bomb was introduced at Heathrow by describing it opaquely as 'a theoretical possibility' rather than 'an actual possibility'. Kochler regretted that it had not been possible to obtain any information about the medication the witness was taking or the nature of the accident that had made the medication necessary. If there was an innuendo in this observation, it was never amplified.

One question above all others continued to haunt the prosecution: its insistence that the suitcase with the bomb inside it was carried on flight 103A from Frankfurt. In that case, whatever happened to the suitcase which appeared mysteriously in the baggage container at Heathrow before flight 103A from Frankfurt had arrived? A police officer, Derek Henderson, carried out a meticulous search of the baggage strewn across the fields, houses and gardens of Lockerbie and found nothing resembling the maroony-brown hardshell suitcase of the Samsonite brand. The only suitcase of that description was the one blown to pieces by the bomb inside it – the one allegedly introduced in Malta for onward transmission to Frankfurt. How could it have been introduced in Malta if it made its first appearance during John Bedford's teabreak? It made no sense. But by then nothing about Lockerbie made sense.

Post-Scottish devolution and the election of an SNP government in 2007, Dr Jim Swire, father of one of the victims, pursued the unresolved question of the Heathrow break-in with the justice secretary, Kenny MacAskill. Swire wanted to know if the Crown Office knew about it all along. The police at Heathrow Airport had known about it; the Metropolitan Police had known about it; it was barely credible that the Crown Office had not known about it. Swire proposed that as Mowat's inquiry was denied all knowledge of the break-in, the fatal accident inquiry should be re-opened or a new one established. The question was not answered; the suggestion was not taken up. But in 2012, the chief constable of Dumfries and Galloway Police finally admitted that his force, too, had known of the Heathrow break-in and not shared this knowledge with the public inquiry.

V

The average age of the passengers on flight 103 was only 29. Some good came from the loss of so much glittering youth. Each year, for example, Syracuse University appointed 35 Remembrance Scholars – the number of its students who died at Lockerbie – with a remit to create projects in their memory; on the 10th anniversary of the disaster they made a remembrance quilt.

The parents of Flora Swire, with the help of Nottingham University where she studied, established a memorial fund to support medical students who, like her, were working towards their PhD. Full of vitality and creativity, Flora was a young woman of many talents, an accomplished pianist and guitarist, sculptor and writer. When the flight came down a few hours before her 24th birthday, she was looking forward to joining her boyfriend in the United States for Christmas.

Another of the many stories: Helga Mosey, 19, who had been enjoying a gap year in America, was returning there after a pre-Christmas break with her parents in Lancashire; a gifted musician and singer, she had been expected to study music at Lancaster University. At 9 pm on 21 December, a family friend telephoned her father, John Mosey, with the news that there had been a plane crash in Scotland. When Mr and Mrs Mosey switched on the television and saw the words Pan Am flight 103 on the screen, 'we put our arms around each other and asked God to help'. They used compensation payments to build a home in the Philippines for abused and abandoned children and to finance similar projects around the world. John Mosey preached forgiveness, quoting *Romans* chapter 12, verse 21: 'Don't be overcome by evil, but overcome evil by doing good.'

He saw his daughter for the last time when they parted at Heathrow Airport. He remembered the smell of apple shampoo on her hair.

THE CLIMATE OF OPINION

I

SOUTH RONALDSAY IS THE FOURTH LARGEST OF THE ORKNEY ISLANDS ('The Orkneys' as unwary journalists still occasionally refer to them, much to the irritation of the locals). Reached by a causeway known as the Churchill Barrier, which was built as a naval defence in the Second World War, South Ronaldsay is one of the older human settlements in the British Isles. In 1958 a Neolithic chambered cairn containing 16,000 human bones was discovered there; archaeologists believe that it was in continuous use for at least a thousand years. A burnt mound, the Bronze Age equivalent of a kitchen oven, was found nearby.

More recently, in the late seventeenth century, South Ronaldsay was said by a contemporary observer to be 'abounding with People' and there were attempts, not hugely successful, to start a lead-mining industry. By the nineteenth century it had become a centre of the herring fishing industry – until that too proved to be a short-lived balm for the traditional ills of an island community. In the closing years of the twentieth century, although South Ronaldsay was no longer abounding with People, the indigenous population of around 1,000 had been augmented by incomers.

The same movement was taking place on other Scottish islands and was sometimes the cause of simmering resentment; the natives had an uncharitable way of lumping together the new faces as 'white settlers'. Many were seeking refuge in retirement from the stresses of urban existence, only to discover that isolation brought its own problems; others to pursue a simpler, 'alternative' way of living; some in the hope of escape from personal crisis or unhappiness. A few had more suspect motives, believing that a remote location, seemingly far from the attentions of the police and the social services, would place them under the radar of scrutiny. But as the newcomers to South Ronaldsay were to discover, there is nowhere less anonymous than an island.

II

The W family – husband, wife and 14 children – appeared in South Ronaldsay in 1985; the following year a 15th child was born. Like all the other families involved in the Orkney child abuse scandal, they were newcomers from England. No sooner had the Ws arrived than rumours reached the social work department in Kirkwall that several of the children were being abused by their father.

In March 1987, Mr W was sent to prison for seven years for a catalogue of sexual and other abuse described in court as 'sadistic and horrific'. This – a conviction for serious criminality – was the starting point for the media whirlwind which swept South Ronaldsay in the early weeks of 1991, yet it was seldom referred to in the subsequent coverage. In 2014 the novelist Will Self, in what purported to be an informed analysis in the *New Statesman* magazine, was intent on debunking the more extreme claims, but had to concede: 'A local woman told me that some of the children of the W family had indeed been abused physically.' It should not have required local gossip to have the facts of that abuse confirmed – they had been a matter of public record for 27 years – but Self's ignorance could be explained, if not excused, by the consistent lack of media focus on the cruelty inflicted on the W children. The fact that abuse did occur within a South Ronaldsay family failed to suit the media's narrative and so was airbrushed from the record whenever possible.

In 1990, one of the W children, a few weeks short of her 16th birthday, alleged that she was the victim of an inter-sibling sexual relationship. It was not the first suggestion of sibling abuse in the family. 'They [the Orkney social work department] tried to look for evidence of sibling sex abuse and they failed,' alleged one of the W children in a television interview in 2013. This was factually incorrect: the social work department, far from concocting the story, had been advised by the children's school that one of the children, the 15-year-old, had confided to a teacher what had happened to her. Had the department failed to act in the child's interests, it would have been damned for gross complacency; it did act – securing a place of safety for the girl in a children's home – and was damned anyway. The household was in disarray: the father in prison; one of the older children in care; the mother struggling to cope. The innuendo that the social work department then acted alone and randomly in launching an investigation into the other allegations of sibling abuse was also incorrect: from the start it was a joint investigation with the police. Although that fact was conveniently overlooked in almost all the media reporting, it did not escape the disinterested attention of Lord Clyde, the judge appointed to review the Orkney case.

A fieldworker from the social work department, Lynn Drever, and a police officer visited the house. Clyde acknowledged that communicating with the W family had never been easy. On previous visits, social workers had found Mrs W surrounded by people she called her friends – a close-knit circle which included two parents known only as Mrs T and Mrs M, as well as Mrs McKenzie (wife of the minister of the parish) and the local GP. On this occasion, the informal support group included the minister himself, the Reverend Morris McKenzie. Drever asked them to leave. The hostile clergyman replied that reasonableness was not what he expected of social workers – but did leave. After the meeting, the police and the social workers agreed to seek place of safety orders for all seven children under the age of 16. Six of them were removed from school, one of them running back into the classroom before a social worker, Mary Finn, led her out by the hand.

The seventh, a girl, was found in McKenzie's manse after a journalist had alerted the director of social work, Paul Lee, that she had 'taken sanctuary' in the parish church. At a children's hearing the next day, Mrs T and Mrs M and the minister's wife again supported Mrs W; according to Clyde their conduct was 'obstructive' and the social work team leader, Susan Millar, had 'considerable difficulty' in obtaining possession of the child. She was eventually taken away to the mainland to join her siblings. When the children were medically examined, there was evidence of 'chronic penetrative abuse' of three of them; in two cases, the abuse had occurred after their father's imprisonment. Such facts were not allowed to get in the way of the media's sympathetic coverage of the family's supposed persecution and their condemnation of the social workers for 'dragging' a child out of her classroom, an incident Clyde decided had been over-dramatised in the telling. Mrs T and Mrs M, and the McKenzies, went on supporting Mrs W and had no difficulty persuading the media to back their campaign to have the children returned.

The social work department was hard-pushed. Paul Lee had been in Orkney only a year and had no direct practical experience of sexual abuse cases. Susan Millar, the team leader, who was living in the islands only because her husband's work had taken him there, had a low opinion of Lee; she was critical of what she saw as his lack of serious commitment, his lack of consideration for herself and her team, in the critical area of child care. And, like many social workers, she was facing an impossible workload. As the scandal was breaking, she wrote to Lee handing in her notice. That left a fieldwork staff of five: Drever, Finn, Charlie Fraser, Julie Lee and Michelle Miller. Lee decided that an experienced extra hand was required to deal with the crisis and secured a secondment from the Royal Scottish Society for the Prevention of Cruelty to Children (RSSPCC).

On 6 February, the woman from the RSSPCC, Liz MacLean, and a police constable, Linda Williamson, conducted an interview with one of the W children, eight-year-old M, who testified that 'Morris' was the central figure in a group of about 18 people. 'Unprompted' according to Clyde, M said that Morris 'makes us run into a circle and he stands in the middle' – apparently to the musical accompaniment of Kylie Minogue and Michael Jackson. She then quickly drew a hook-like object coming from Morris's arm and described how he wore a long, black cloak with a hood over his head and a black mask over his eyes.

'What happens?' she was asked.

'He hooks you when you're dancing,' she replied. 'When he hooks you he pulls you in towards you.' She added that she didn't want to talk about 'the dirty stuff'. But later in the interview she said that Morris 'put his willie into Maggie's fanny'. She giggled, and they asked her how he did it. She said: 'Lying down'. She then pleaded with MacLean and Williamson not to tell anyone. She said: 'My dad will kill me.' They comforted her. She pulled a doll into herself, stood still, and said: 'Don't tell my mum.'

Williamson's initial instinct was not to believe what she was hearing. The words 'My dad will kill me' changed her mind. She told the Clyde inquiry that she was shocked by what emerged during the interview. She recognised names being given by M – the names of both adults and children – and informed her superiors. A chief inspector's first reaction was to call it 'an isolated story by a small child, insufficient for criminal proceedings, but to be taken seriously'. Six days later, another of the W children corroborated the story and said she had been hooked by Morris. They asked her how, if Morris had a long cloak on, he got his willie out. 'With the zip,' she replied indignantly, making a pulling motion with her hand. She was asked if there was a name for Morris and she said: 'You could call him Master.' A third child, a boy, separately interviewed, said they all went into a field at a quarry at night time. Everyone danced around Morris until he hooked someone. Sometimes they all dressed up as cowboys. 'I don't look, I don't look,' he said. The 'big people' drank wine.

If the W children were to be believed, other children were involved and other children's parents. MacLean did believe them. She believed they had communicated enough to indicate penetrative abuse and that action had to be taken. Back at the social work department, there was a sense of shock – coupled with an acceptance that the children had had no access to each other for some weeks, which seemed to give credence to their separate accounts of events at the quarry. Susan Millar consulted Dr Linda Hamilton, senior clinical psychologist on Orkney, and according to the latter's testimony (disputed by Millar) claimed there was 'enough evidence to sink the *Titanic*'. Millar was suffering from stress and overwork; she had tendered her resignation; she had just heard the news of a death of a member of her family; now she was having to cope with the possibility that organised sexual abuse was taking place on South Ronaldsay, abuse involving not only the W children but nine other named children from four other families. She admitted that she was operating 'on automatic pilot' – and it showed. There was not enough evidence to sink the *Titanic*, there was not yet enough to sink a rowing boat, yet she decided, with Paul Lee's approval, that all the named children should be removed under place of safety orders. It was the evening of 13 February.

The police's evaluation of the material was more cautious. They too noted that the information had come from the children separately and that there was a significant degree of corroboration. A senior detective who studied the drawings was struck by such spontaneous repeated details as a cloak with a hood and the headlights of a car. He and his colleagues were coming to the view that the adults who appeared to be implicated should be detained and interviewed.

At social work headquarters, however, events were moving more swiftly. On 14 February, the field workers were informed of developments, reacting with a mixture of shock, horror and pity. Mary Finn was reported to have found the news 'difficult and painful to absorb because of the number of children and adults involved and the nature of the abuse described', while Charlie Fraser accepted that the children were in immediate danger and should be removed to places of safety. Lynn Drever, who had met such resistance in the W household, was reassured by the undertaking that the parents would be questioned by the police. Only Julie Lee came close to uttering dissent; she was unhappy that questions about the techniques employed in the interviews were discouraged. But having only recently joined the department, she felt she had to defer to the management. Paul Lee voiced his suspicion that the supporters of the W family knew more than they were saying. Susan Millar, reminded that the sources of the allegations were three children who came from a background of significant abuse, insisted that abused children were no less likely than other children to tell the truth. All possible objections were being swept aside. By the end of the meeting, the decision to intervene was a foregone conclusion.

There were alternatives. The police could have searched the quarry or carried out discreet surveillance of the parental homes. Equally, they could have interviewed responsible people in the area, including a councillor and a headteacher, to find out what, if anything, they knew or suspected. None of that was done. The social work department, rather than relying on the assessment of Liz MacLean alone, could have arranged for the children to be independently assessed by a child psychologist. That was not done either. Instead there was a rush to judgement – and precipitate action.

After the meeting, Paul Lee promptly sent a fax to his fellow directors of social work in all of Scotland's regional authorities appealing for help. He said he needed experienced back-up staff to come to Orkney for a week from 25 February, that they would be 'involved in initial interviews', and that separate placements would have to be found for each of the children. He added that, as feelings were likely to be running high on Orkney, it would not be possible to accommodate them on the islands. Lee recognised that separating the children 'could be upsetting' but that it was in their best interests. Not only were the children to be kept apart; they were to be denied all access to their parents and deprived of all personal possessions. Liz MacLean and Susan Millar both strongly advocated this policy, MacLean arguing that it would give each child 'time and space on his own to reflect and talk, to feel safe, to expose any fears or concerns and thus facilitate a disclosure'. Millar detected a risk of a dominant older sibling putting pressure on a younger child to 'close down' and maintained that this risk was all the greater in cases of organised abuse.

Whatever the wisdom of this strategy, two serious errors had already been made. Susan Millar had informed Liz MacLean's employer that the parents were not only being arrested and questioned, but charged and imprisoned. Only later did the RSSPCC learn that all the police envisaged was a six-hour detention period. Further, Lee had given the impression in his round-robin to the social work departments that the volunteers would have an important role beyond merely accompanying the children to the mainland. No such role was contemplated for the outsiders: they would be left to discover for themselves that they were mere facilitators. Among the six Strathclyde social workers who agreed to go to Orkney, Rena McCarry had the clear understanding from a meeting with Susan Millar in Glasgow on 21 February, six days before they were due on the islands, that the police had evidence of considerable strength, enough to convict the parents, and that she and her colleagues would be fully briefed about the families as soon as they arrived. Another of the Strathclyde workers, Maureen Hughes, said that had she known in advance the limitations of the role required of her, she doubted if she would have gone.

After the public and media outcry about the removal of the W children from school, Paul Lee decided that the next evacuation should be carried out as covertly as possible. 'A sudden, simultaneous and secret operation', as Clyde put it. 'It was desired to minimise any risk of local support frustrating the removal . . . It was felt that the most likely occasion when all the children and their parents would be together would be at home in the early morning.' The strategy was a public relations disaster. A 'dawn raid', as it would inevitably be labelled, would only fuel public indignation and media outrage about innocent children being forcibly taken from their parents without proof of guilt. Though it was hard to see what other strategy would have worked – short of not removing the children until the allegations had been more rigorously examined.

On 25 February, the mainland social workers – one from Central Region and another from Lothian as well as the Strathclyde contingent – flew to Orkney. Lee was so obsessive about maintaining the subterfuge that he insisted on splitting the group between two separate flights. When they finally got to Kirkwall Airport, Rab Murphy from Strathclyde put through a call to inform the social work department of their arrival. There was little response. Later, when Murphy managed to speak to one of the Orkney field workers on the phone, she told him that a meeting scheduled for the afternoon had been cancelled and they were not to attend until 11 o'clock the following morning. Surprised by this discourtesy and the lack of urgency, the group were left to kick their heels at their hotel in Stromness.

When the meeting did take place, it was over in 45 minutes. Rena McCarry recalled the atmosphere as 'hostile' and the mainland workers quickly sensed a barrier between themselves and Susan Millar, whose manner struck them as cool and inflexible. For want of anything better to do, the visitors went sightseeing. In the afternoon, after Liz MacLean had given a brief outline of the statements made by the W children, one of the mainland workers expressed suspicion that all the allegations had been made within a short time to the same two people. Clyde recorded in his report that MacLean had a disconcerting habit of airily changing the subject when such awkward questions were raised. When she was asked what form of penetration had occurred, she replied that it had been 'just the usual type'. She dealt unimpressively with other questions about the validity of the disclosures. Maureen Hughes tried to test her skills as an interviewer by asking about the kind of details which would have been significant to a child: What was the exact location of the last incident of abuse? What were the weather conditions? Was the grass wet? Hughes and the others were unconvinced by MacLean's response. The seasoned Rab Murphy was left doubting the professionalism of her work and the substance of the information she had obtained from the children. The presentation seemed to him 'flimsy'.

'The mainland workers returned to Stromness feeling a deep concern about the removal of the children,' wrote Lord Clyde. 'They had hoped to be assured of the justification for the place of safety orders, but they were not. Some of the workers were very close to saying that they would not take any further part. They felt that they could not remove the children with conviction of the correctness of that action.'

That evening, a further meeting was hurriedly convened in an operations room at social work headquarters known as the bunker. It was crowded – there were about 50 people there, some of them standing or sitting on desks – and the mood was confused and unhappy; the discussion, such as it was, achieved nothing. Rab Murphy stayed behind for a private conversation with Paul Lee, Susan Millar and Liz MacLean. It was 10.30 pm. The meeting degenerated into a slanging match, but not before Murphy had reeled off the main concerns of the mainland workers: the dearth of information they had been given, the misunderstanding about the nature of their role in the operation, the refusal to give them access to the transcripts of the interviews with the children, the splitting-up of the siblings, the ban on personal possessions – a radical departure from normal practice – and the overarching question of whether the removal of the children was justified in the first place. An exhausted Susan Millar, buckling under the pressure, responded angrily that the mainland workers should have voiced these concerns earlier. How could they have done? They had come to Orkney in good faith; they had been misinformed; and now they faced an intense dilemma, morally and professionally. In time they were to receive scant sympathy from Lord Clyde, who condemned them for 'failing to recognise the dangers of inter-authority co-operation'. It would have been more reasonable to argue that they recognised the dangers well enough, but that they were left in an impossible situation.

Rab Murphy made a late-night telephone call to his boss in Glasgow and listened to meaningless words of sympathy. The workers had been cut adrift, left to wrestle with their own consciences. At 11.30, they sent a message to Paul Lee: they would assist in the removal of the children, but only because the alternative – leaving the Orkney staff to do it themselves – would be more damaging. By the time the social workers got to bed, nine children on South Ronaldsay were within six hours of being removed from their homes.

III

At 6 am on 27 February, Paul Lee and Susan Millar joined the teams gathering at Kirkwall police station. Rab Murphy asked Lee if there was the usual document for parents to sign, consenting to the medical examination of their children. There wasn't; nor had there been any discussion of what was to happen if the parents withheld consent. In this state of unpreparedness, with even the ages of the children uncertain, the social workers and the police boarded a cavalcade of cars and set off for South Ronaldsay over the Churchill Barrier. Lee and Millar returned nervously to their offices to await developments, while field staff not directly involved in the operation brought sweets, drinks and toys to three 'safe houses' where the children were to be taken pending their departure for the mainland.

When four social workers and five police officers arrived at the house of the B family, it was 7 am and daylight. The team were taken aback by the discovery that two of the three children – the daughters

WB and EB – were living in a caravan in front of the house and that only SB, the Bs' eight-year-old son, lived in the house itself. When Mrs B answered the door, and the police explained why they were there, she began shouting. WB, aged 13, emerged from the caravan in her dressing gown. Her mother hugged her, continuing to hurl abuse at the social workers: that they were evil, that they were not taking her children away, that nothing of a sexual nature had happened in the house, and something to the effect that 'this isn't like other parts of the parish'. WB slipped into the house and locked herself in the bathroom. Her younger sister EB, aged 11, was wakened by the screams of her mother. Two of the team entered the caravan and asked the bewildered child to get up; they helped her to dress and took her out to one of the cars. Mrs B went after her, trying desperately to hold on to her, until a police officer and a social worker pulled her away. EB finally got into the car.

SB, the boy, who had been sleeping in his bedroom in the house, was found on the staircase, having been wakened by the commotion. Rab Murphy urged Mrs B to be calm in order to minimise the trauma, but she would not let her son go, and the police finally had to pull him by the wrists from her grasp. Murphy put his arms on the boy's shoulder and walked with him to the car. One of the police officers then fetched a tool and was about to break down the bathroom door when WB opened it. She said she would rather have been removed from school than from home. Lynn Drever, one of the Orkney social workers, explained that the decision had been taken to avoid publicity, to which WB responded that the neighbours would see what was going on. She added that her parents would not harm her and that she was worried about her mother's health.

Mrs B told Murphy that the children were not to be medically examined as the experience would traumatise them. She predicted that she would not see her children again. Murphy replied that this would be decided by the children's hearing. One of the police officers – a man – could bear it no longer and told Mrs B that she would see them again and would get them back; he was criticised by Clyde for 'an understandable observation but an inappropriate one'. In the car, the children were told that they were going to a place of safety 'because we know that something bad is going on'.

Mrs B was now alone with the police. After they searched the house, they took her to Kirkwall for questioning. She was brought back in a highly distressed condition around 4 pm and ran upstairs screaming for her mother, who had been dead for 21 years. In desperation she phoned a neighbour, who came round to see her. She tried to phone her husband, who was working away, but was too distressed to be able to explain coherently what had happened. The neighbour broke the news to him. That evening, she was joined by a number of people in the neighbourhood and someone suggested that she should contact the press. She promptly did.

Similarly distressing scenes were witnessed in three other houses on South Ronaldsay that morning. At the house of the H family, the door was answered by Mrs H in her nightclothes. A social worker explained briefly that the children were believed to have been abused. Mrs H called on her husband, who was upstairs in bed recovering from a brain tumour – a fact unknown to the social workers. As husband and wife shouted insults at the group and threatened them with violence, their nine-year-old son PH, upstairs in bed, heard the raised voices and went at once to the bedroom of his sister TH, aged eight, and told her that the social workers and the police 'want to take us'. A police officer offered a little comfort: he said they were going away on an aeroplane and that they should treat it as an adventure. The children were allowed to say goodbye to their pet budgerigar and rabbit before being escorted out to the cars around 8.30 am. Mr H sat quietly at the kitchen table downstairs, pale and shaking, staring ahead, evidently resigned to his situation. After the children had gone, he stirred himself, telephoning his MP, his GP, a local councillor, the local paper (the *Orcadian*), and the Reverend Morris McKenzie.

The M parents were small farmers, former teachers, and Quakers. When they opened the door to the conservatory, they were confronted by a group of eight people. A policeman in plain clothes explained that they were investigating allegations of lewd and libidinous practices. Mr and Mrs M reacted with incredulity, saying the allegations were ridiculous. A social worker was next to speak – with the news that place of safety orders had been obtained for the two children, SM, aged 15, and JM, aged 11. Mrs M replied: 'Oh, so you have come.' She added that her younger son had asked if they would be taken away because of the family's support of the W family. She then went upstairs to rouse the children. Mrs M told the boys that she and their father were being accused of doing naughty and sexy things to them. The older boy swore and stormed off; the younger one stood in the hall looking sad. When the parents suggested that the boys should take something with them – a toy or a book – the request was refused. As they were taken to the cars, Mrs M hugged both boys and asked them to act with dignity.

Mr and Mrs T were Jewish and had lived in Israel until 1984. They had two children: a boy, BT, aged 12, and a girl, MT, aged eight. Mr T was a skilled artist, designing and making jewellery. The entire family were asleep when two social workers and five police offices arrived at the house. Mr T was so angry that he had to be restrained. In response to a police sergeant's reference to child abuse, Mrs T asked who was doing it. The sergeant replied that her name was on the warrant. Mrs T said to her husband: 'They are accusing me of child abuse'. Mr T was shown a copy of the place of safety order, and wanted to be left with a copy, to see a summary of the reasons, but he was not allowed to take a copy in his hands or to keep it. One of the social workers sought consent to have the children medically examined and Mr T said he would like to phone Dr Broadhurst, the local GP, and have them examined by him. When it was explained that it would have to be done by a police surgeon, the parents would not consent.

Mrs T was accompanied by a police officer and a social worker to a bedroom which the children were sharing. BT, who was lying on his bed weeping, said that it would be like the case of the W children and he would never see his mother again. MT seemed quite calm, very white and still; she neither wept nor spoke. Later she clung to her father and cried. He hugged her and asked her to find a hairbrush. He started to touch her hair and Mrs T took over and plaited it. Mrs T asked her husband in Hebrew whether he had some small things to give to the children. The children chose pendants from his workshop, one with the design of a dolphin for BT, the other of a seal for MT, which they were wearing when they left. No details about the children – such as their Jewish faith or their vegetarian diet – were noted down; the social worker Mary Finn briskly assured Mrs T that they knew very well how to look after the children. Finn refused the children breakfast and they were not allowed to take any books or teddy bears. At the Clyde inquiry, MT said the worst bit about the experience was leaving the house. She felt she was 'beyond tears' – a remarkable statement from one so young.

During the police's search of the house, which took three and a half hours, Mrs T found her daughter's glasses and said that MT would need them for reading. She was informed that she would have to take them to the social work department. The couple were then driven to Kirkwall to be interviewed.

At one of the safe houses – the hostel of Kirkwall Grammar School – the children were finally given breakfast. Mary Finn told MT that what was happening was not her fault and that the police would not hurt her parents. She explained that MT and her brother were going on a plane to Inverness, where they would be taken to people who would look after her. MT listened carefully but said nothing. She took off the pendant which her father had given her and dropped it in her pocket, but later put it on again. Rena McCarry spoke separately to BT, who was adamant that his parents had done nothing wrong. On the way to the airport he became visibly distressed to the point of being physically debilitated; McCarry described the walk to the aircraft as 'awful'. He broke down completely when the plane took off, in marked contrast to the controlled behaviour of his sister. At Inverness, where they parted, MT displayed no sign of emotion and did not kiss her brother goodbye.

Later that day, once all nine children were off the islands, the police visited the church and manse of the Reverend Morris McKenzie. As someone called 'Morris' had featured so prominently in the allegations of the W children, an earlier search of the premises might have been helpful to their investigation. They removed a number of items, including a black cloak with circular clasps depicting a lion's head, which was hanging openly on a peg in the vestry. McKenzie explained that he used it for funerals. They also found animal excrement, a brownie uniform, a broken cross and some animal masks, all of which – with the possible exception of the excrement – might have aroused the suspicions of more vigilant examiners, particularly as brownie uniforms were said to have been used in the alleged sexual entertainments at the quarry; but Clyde was content to accept that they were innocent exhibits. Most incriminating of all, they found a rubber hot-water bottle in the minister's bed. On it was written the name of one of the W children and the words 'the big boy'.

Around 9 am, the local councillor, a Mr Annal, had telephoned the (Aberdeen) *Press and Journal* and the *Orcadian* with a tip-off that a terrible blunder had been perpetrated. There was no need; the parents, supported by McKenzie, had already contacted the media. Before long, the words 'ritualistic' and 'satanic' were being used to describe the alleged abuse in terms which not only rejected the allegations but ridiculed them. 'The source of these descriptions remained obscure,' noted Lord Clyde. They had never been used by the social work department, but they might have been an invention of sub-editors hundreds of miles from Orkney, whose casual stereotyping was designed to ratchet up a juicy story with the capacity to run and run. As it did.

Soon the papers were full of more general stereotyping inspired by the scandal. As Samantha Ashenden observed in one of the few sceptical assessments of the case: 'Mothers were depicted as providing a natural source of warmth and love, but also common sense and standards of discipline in child rearing, to be measured against the potential harm of thoughtless or trendy social workers.' South Ronaldsay, which had its fair share of dysfunctional families, was simplistically depicted as a law-abiding, God-fearing community rallying together in support of the rights of parents and in defiance of interfering social workers who had 'snatched' their children in what one newspaper (the *Times*) called 'a frightening intrusion'. Another, the *Mail on Sunday*, attacked 'the untramelled power' of social workers and suggested that the Orkney intervention was not only illegitimate, but politically motivated to destroy the institution of the family. The Church of Scotland was publicly critical of the operation, emphasising the rights of the child, but seemed to be less concerned with the welfare of the child, which the media likewise chose to ignore.

The full truth of what happened, or did not happen, on South Ronaldsay may never be known. The parents, with the exception of the father of the W children, rightly enjoyed then, and rightly continued to enjoy, a presumption of innocence. Some or all may have been completely blameless. But the default position of those who unquestioningly denied the existence of child abuse was based on two misconceptions. The first was not strictly accurate: that none of the children complained of having been abused. It requires no special powers of psychological insight to understand why abused people – especially abused children – would not complain: the powerlessness of their situation, coupled with the potency of such emotions as shame, embarrassment and fear; and in the case of South Ronaldsay, the added factor of social and geographical isolation, the relative lack of contact with adults outside the immediate family circle. When one of the W children, having reached the age of 39, finally summoned the courage to speak out, she described how her father used to beat her and her 14 brothers and sisters with sticks and rubber pipes, how he would make them stand in a bin full of nettles, how he treated one of her brothers like a dog, keeping him chained and not allowing him into the house; but none of this behaviour, which went on under the noses of a community subsequently celebrated in the national press as an exemplar of family life, was the subject of complaint from the victims themselves. The child who spent his formative years chained like a dog did so uncomplainingly. Even when the W case came to light, and the father went to prison, still there was a reluctance on the part of journalists, and of many in public life, to acknowledge that sometimes evil functioned within families. The deniers pointed to the implausibility of organised abuse taking place unseen on an island whose landscape made everything visible; yet a child kept in chains outside the family home – somehow that was invisible.

The second misconception relied on the outcome of the medical examinations of the nine children, which took place – despite the lack of formal parental consent – as soon as they were removed from Orkney. The results were negative and the same conclusion was drawn: just as abuse could not have taken place because no-one had complained of it, so abuse could not have taken place because there was no sign of it. For years afterwards, those who sought to rubbish the allegations leaned heavily on the medical evidence – or lack of it – without troubling themselves to read the small print. In cases of very recent penetrative sexual abuse, it was more likely than not that evidence of it would be detected, but a study by the Royal College of Physicians found that many girls showed no physical symptoms after a week and that acts not involving penetration usually left no clinical signs.

Paul Lee, when he was informed of the results of the tests, refused to withdraw the place of safety orders on the grounds that they proved nothing. It was a foolhardy decision, for a storm of protest was breaking over Orkney, and over the country as a whole, about the removal of the children. The mainland social workers returned home, shaken by an experience they had found uniquely harrowing and dismayed that no charges had been brought by the police. They left behind a community in a state of hysteria.

On 5 March, there was a meeting of the children's panel. A crowd gathered outside in support of the parents and one of the local social workers, Michelle Miller, had abuse hurled at her as she left the building. Inside, the atmosphere was fraught. The children's reporter, Gordon Sloan, who had been seconded from Strathclyde, threatened to demand the ejection of a friend of the parents for disrupting proceedings, and when the panel granted a warrant for the continued detention of the children, the mood turned uglier still. Three hundred people attended a public meeting in the village of St Margaret's Hope on South Ronaldsay to vent their fury at the social work department. The anger was directed mainly at Susan Millar, who was told that she was no longer welcome in the community.

The hostility cut both ways. From all over Britain, 3,000 letters were sent to the children via the department; none was ever forwarded. Even letters from parents were not sent on. A teddy bear was returned to one set of parents, who discovered that the stitching had been tampered with, while another was sent back an Easter egg which they claimed had been broken into to see if something was concealed inside. The irrationality on both sides fuelled an aggressive media campaign in which the social workers were personally demonised.

Orkney, one of the smallest local authorities in Britain, was ill-equipped to deal with the barrage of media interest. The chief social work adviser to the Secretary of State for Scotland, Angus Skinner, came up with the idea of recruiting an experienced press officer dedicated to the task, and Nicholas Clayton was appointed. Clayton, boxed in by the restraints of official confidentiality, found it impossible to match the free flow of information and gossip between the media and the parents. He was not long in the job before he realised how concerted was the local campaign to discredit the social work department. The media not only knew the identities and the telephone numbers of the four families; they were frequent and welcome visitors to their homes. Clayton was unhappy that newspapers routinely reported the story in a way which enabled the children to be easily identified – but he had to accept that, in Orkney, the normal rules of reporting of cases involving children no longer applied.

On 25 March, the children's panel met for a second time and renewed the warrants for a further 21 days. 'The agitation and disorder were difficult to control,' wrote Clyde. 'The chairperson had difficulty in being heard.' Gordon Sloan again objected to the behaviour in the room; the parents put it about that he was 'tyrannical and arrogant', a character reference eagerly picked up by the media but which came as a surprise to his colleagues back in Glasgow.

At social work headquarters, there were signs of institutional meltdown. Four of the field workers – Mary Finn, Michelle Miller, Julie Lee and Lynn Drever – sent a memo to Paul Lee expressing their dissatisfaction that they were being kept in the dark about the whereabouts and welfare of the nine children. Susan Millar stepped in with a sharp rebuke, indicating to her underlings that they were not to criticise or question senior management and that what was required of them was complete trust. It was whistling in the dark. In the department, as in Orkney as a whole, trust had broken down.

Through all of this, eight of the nine children were living with foster carers (the ninth, one of the older boys, was placed in a residential school). Over a period of four weeks, they were repeatedly interviewed, some as many as 10 times. Clyde considered this excessive. The children of the B family, who were being fostered in Lanarkshire, never wavered in their insistence that nothing untoward had happened to them; one said the story had been invented by people with a grudge against the English. One of the M children alleged that his removal was part of a vendetta by the social work department. The testimonies of three of the children were more disturbing. At one of his interviews, nine-year-old PH introduced the name Morris

McKenzie. At a later interview, he talked about big people hurting little people, drawing figures to show areas of the body where a girl could be hurt. On a third occasion he returned to the subject of Morris McKenzie, saying that he took his belt to him when he did bad things. He spoke of a gathering of adults and children and of a girl being hurt by adults; he gave the interviewers their names. His younger sister TH, aged eight, said that a bad man she called the prime minister had hurt her botty; she said she and her parents had gone in a car to a field, where the prime minister was in the middle of a circle of people, pulling little girls into the ring and hurting their botties.

MT, aged eight, related going to 'the meadows' with adults. She drew drawings of a circle with a man in the middle wearing a cloak which had a button with a silver lion's head on it. She also drew a stick and said that the man pulled children from the ring and danced with them. The interviewers asked MT what a little girl who was pulled in might be feeling. MT replied that she would be feeling very sad and hurt and would say, 'Stop doing that to me.' At a later interview, she returned to the subject.

Lord Clyde challenged the methodology of the interviews. He felt that leading questions were too often asked. Without access to the transcripts, it is impossible to give an objective view of this judgement. But two facts were inescapable: three out of nine children did testify to abuse and at the centre of each of their stories was a figure either named or identifiable as the Reverend Morris McKenzie, the parish minister who kept a hot water bottle in his bed with the words 'the big boy' on it and who had a black cloak with clasps depicting a lion's head hanging in his hallway.

The case came to the sheriff court on 3 April and was brought to a swift and sensational conclusion when Sheriff David Kelbie dismissed the proceedings brought by the children's reporter as incompetent, ruled that there was no need to hear any evidence, and indicated that the children should be returned to their parents.

Gordon Sloan was driven to despair by the outcome and decided that there was no longer any justification for detaining the children. He continued to believe that it would have been in their best interests to remain in places of safety and had intended to produce the evidence of the W children in support of that conviction. But now that an adult had made it clear from the bench that he did not believe the W children – in effect that they had been fantasising – Sloan was pessimistic about the prospect of getting them to give evidence in court. The sheriff became the new hero of the hour, a people's champion. Among the flattering profiles, he was depicted by the *Scotsman* as 'the man who campaigns for a better world', a family man, someone of 'humanitarian principles', with an interest in ecology and public transport, a supporter of Scottish nationalism.

Now that a court had found in their favour, the parents and their supporters moved at once on the social work offices where Susan Millar, Paul Lee and Nicholas Clayton were discussing the terms of a press statement. A TV crew prevailed on the marchers to stop briefly for better pictures; and then the crowd went on marching – straight into the department and unimpeded into Paul Lee's office. 'They were abusive, aggressive and assertive,' wrote Clyde in his report. The camera crews clambered on to chairs in order to obtain a vantage point of what amounted to a gross invasion of a public building. Susan Millar tried to phone the police but Mrs M violently restrained her from doing so. The police who had somehow failed to spot the significance of vital clues in their search of the minister's manse now failed to come to the rescue of beleaguered social workers. Millar and Clayton abandoned the office, leaving the parents with Lee, who agreed to do what he could to have the children returned by nightfall.

Unknown to the parents, however, not all the children were keen to go home. During his stay with his foster mother, nine-year-old PH had acted out disturbing plays involving religion, violence, bloodshed and sex. One of these dramas involved a minister who wore a black coat and a hood; PH referred to the minister's wife and said that costumes were kept in the minister's kitchen. He gave his carer a detailed description of the minister's house and said it was filthy – a view shared by the police. His sister, eight-year-old TH, when she heard she was returning to Orkney, went into a fit of rage. She smashed her doll on the ground, started sucking her thumb and seemed to the foster carer to be shocked and bewildered. She said she did not want to go home and stood like a wooden doll refusing to get dressed. She left the house in tears and, at the airport, began speaking in baby talk, 'very different from the quiet and retiring person she had been at her placement'.

When eight-year-old SB was told he was going home, his foster carer was taken aback by his response. She expected him to be excited, yet he seemed subdued. He asked her if it meant that all the bad things would not happen any more. The foster carer was lost for words. She immediately got on the phone to a child psychologist, who advised her to listen carefully to what SB had to say. The boy then began to tell her of events in the quarry, demonstrating with the use of soft toys how someone – a person he named – handled him sexually. He added that he was worried about certain 'games' at home. The foster mother found the occasion 'very upsetting' and contacted a social worker, Susan Brown, who in turn spoke to the Orkney social work department to see if SB could be retained in his place of safety pending further investigation. The answer was no: the boy must return with the others. The parents, armed with Kelbie's decision, were now in a position to dictate the hectic pace, in which a second's delay was a second too long.

A senior social worker at Strathclyde, Philip Greene, in a telephone conversation with Paul Lee on Orkney, questioned whether the children should return immediately, pointing out that the existing warrant still had some time to run. He also pleaded with Lee for discharge medicals, if only for the protection of the foster carers. Lee flatly vetoed the idea and explained that there was no time to waste.

There wasn't. A party was being organised at Kirkwall Airport. The principal guests had to be assembled and put on a plane. Any other course of action was unthinkable. Unthinkable even to Lord Clyde, who managed to defend the extreme haste with which the return to Orkney was facilitated on the grounds that 'the prevailing climate of opinion' made it necessary. In the end, a High Court judge, whose first concern should have been the welfare of the children, felt obliged to bow to the demands of the mob, adding that, although a renewal of the place of safety orders would have been theoretically possible, it would have created 'an even greater public outcry'. So what if it had? Did the rule of law count for so little?

The aircraft from Glasgow carrying four of the children landed at Inverness to pick up the five who had been fostered in Highland Region. It was raining heavily when the flight finally touched down at Kirkwall. Philip Greene had asked Paul Lee to arrange somewhere at the airport where the children could be reunited with their parents in peace and quiet. That was not possible either; Lee said there would be no Orkney social workers in attendance. The terminal building was packed with jubilant parents and supporters and with the many journalists who had played such a notable role in securing the children's release. A piper was playing and the place was bedecked with bunting.

A police officer came on the aircraft and advised Greene, who had accompanied the children, not to leave it – which the social worker took as a warning for his own safety. He ignored it. He and a second social worker from Glasgow, Paul Hersee, escorted the children into the building. The handover was a shambles: it seemed that nobody was in charge. The crowd surged forward and engulfed the children and the two social workers from Glasgow were left standing. The children had been removed in the early morning of 27 February. It was now the afternoon of 3 April. After five weeks, they were on their way home.

IV

It was not quite the end of the affair. The children's reporter, Gordon Sloan, successfully appealed to the Court of Appeal, which delivered a withering verdict on Kelbie's decision. It found that the sheriff had allowed himself to form views about the case – his opinion, for example, that the W children had been 'coached' into giving the desired answers – 'that would have made it impossible for him to bring a fair and balanced judgement to the issues'. The way was open for the case to be referred to a different sheriff and for the evidence to be heard. Sloan decided not to pursue it further – which, as Clyde said in his report, left unsettled the one question most people wanted answered: were the parents innocent or guilty?

What followed was utter capitulation. On 1 May, the Crown Office announced that there would be no further criminal investigation in relation to the nine children. In July, it was decided at a case conference to remove the children from the child protection register, despite the objections of the police. By then Susan Millar had left the employment of Orkney Islands Council, her professional reputation ruined partly by her own poor judgement at a time of crisis but also by the cruelty of the media coverage. At the height of the hysteria, there was a television camera peering into her office window. Her colleagues also had to endure invasions of privacy. Charlie Fraser, one of the field workers, was portrayed as a Christian zealot fighting satanism and was followed by TV crews when he ventured out of doors. Another, Lynn Drever, discovered that her religious affiliations were being investigated. Paul Lee received many abusive telephone calls.

Lord Clyde acknowledged that the relentless publicity had kept the public hostility alive, and that the social work department regarded the television and radio coverage as particularly ill-informed, sensational and upsetting, but he offered no formal condemnation of the media excesses – and was surprisingly restrained in his comments about the campaign of ridicule and abuse heaped on the social workers by the parents and their supporters. He said only that the campaign 'did not help towards constructive dialogue'. Nor, beyond reporting the incidents, did he have any criticism of the circus at Kirkwall Airport or of the earlier storming of the social work offices, the act of violence which took place there, and the lack of protection given by the police to its victim. Like so many others, the judge allowed himself to be swayed by what he called the 'prevailing climate of opinion'.

The attack on the Orkney social workers widened into a more general attack on their profession. 'Sack the lot and start again, after the latest shameful indictment of our arrogant, incompetent social workers,' was the headline over a *Daily Mail* piece by Professor David Marsland, a sociologist who himself made the news some years later when he proposed the compulsory sterilisation of people he deemed 'mentally and morally unfit'. An academic closer to home, Professor Alastair Bissett-Johnston, a specialist in family law at Dundee University, delivered a lecture suggesting that the treatment of the nine children by the social workers had been a form of abuse in itself, 'regardless of whether sexual abuse occurred or not'. The implicit equivalence between two forms of abuse – one characterised by what he regarded as overbearing questioning, the other by sexual penetration of young children – went unchallenged; indeed was generally approved.

Twenty years later, the *Daily Record* reflected on the Orkney saga. 'Today,' it wrote, 'many of those involved are either dead or have no desire to talk about the episode'. Morris McKenzie was dead; Sheriff David Kelbie was dead; Lord Clyde was dead; and no-one seemed to know what had happened to Paul Lee, Susan Millar and Liz MacLean. But most if not all of the parents, as well as the children themselves, were still alive – yet the paper was unable to persuade any of them to talk. The *Record* maintained that the allegations had been 'ridiculed as completely false' and wondered why it was still called a child abuse scandal when no abuse had occurred; the raids had been the result of allegations by a single child whose 'relative' – an oblique reference to the father of the W children – had been jailed for incest – no mention of the 'sadistic and horrific' catalogue of abuse for which he was actually sentenced; and 'despite intensive questioning, none of the children seized said they had been abused'. The *Daily Record* was far from alone in its disinclination to adopt a more open-minded approach to the case; an article in the *Guardian* in 2006 dismissed the allegations as 'lunacy' and said that Sheriff Kelbie deserved the public's gratitude for throwing them out.

One expert witness told the Clyde inquiry that the sheer scale of organised networks of abuse 'naturally induces a sense of horror and repugnance in professionals and lay persons alike, which can lead to a collective denial of the problem'. Susan Millar, in her evidence, said that the first step towards a solution was for society to realise that the problem existed. But it was many years before society did. It took the malevolence of celebrity exposed by the Savile scandal, followed by Alexis Jay's landmark report on the sexual exploitation of girls in Rotherham, to change cultural attitudes towards allegations of child abuse.

1992

THE TRAMPLED BAGPIPE

I

No figure in post-war Scotland was more demonised than Black Bob, known in polite circles as Sir Robert Scholey, chairman of the British Steel Corporation (BSC). Many assumed he had acquired the sobriquet on account of his butchery of the Ravenscraig plant in Motherwell. After his death in 2014 at the age of 92, one of his obituarists offered a a more innocuous explanation: Geoffrey Goodman wrote in the *Guardian* that Scholey had acquired an early habit of wearing a black protective helmet when moving around the steelworks in his stewardship. For the avoidance of any remaining doubt, the Scottish press coined an alternative nickname: Son of Frankenstein. Scholey, a blunt Yorkshireman, was immune to such insults; the more the Scots hated him, the more he revelled in his reputation.

He was a frustrating enemy for another reason: no-one knew more about the industry than Black Bob, immersed in it from birth as the son of a Sheffield steelworker. When Margaret Thatcher appointed him to the chair of the loss-making nationalised corporation in 1986 with a brief to return it profitably to the private sector, his detailed knowledge, gathered over 40 years at the sharp end, was unrivalled.

Brutally cutting the workforce from 250,000 to 52,000 in less than two decades, he converted an annual loss of £1 billion in 1973 (the year he joined BSC as chief executive) into a profit of £800 million by 1990. By then he had succeeded in making Britain the lowest-cost steel producer in Europe, as well as the most profitable

– and without the state aid lavished on its European competitors. The transformation was achieved at immense human cost, yet the attempts to paint him as a typical product of the new profit-obsessed managerial class over-simplified the stereotype. Far from being a pet functionary of the Thatcher revolution, Scholey never cared much for the lady and fiercely resented the interference of all politicians, whose meddling he dismissed as 'social messaging' – an art in which he never pretended to be skilled.

In the saga of Ravenscraig – a word almost as popular in Scottish front-page headlines as sex and death – the tensions between Black Bob and the vote-catching politicians simmered for years before they finally boiled over in the run-up to the 1992 General Election. He had a clear strategy for the industry. Unfortunately for Scotland, it never included Motherwell, the home of Scottish steel.

In 1957, when Colvilles opened the Ravenscraig plant – 'a vast and complex new works' involving the excavation of four million cubic yards of earth and the building of miles of new roads – the Scottish press was impressed by the scale and ambition of the project. 'The question is often asked how long will the growth in the demand for steel continue,' mused one commentator at the time. 'No conclusive answer can be given but it has to be remembered that the steel industry itself is just 100 years old . . . The new industrial age now entered following the discovery of atomic energy makes it essential to keep an open mind about where saturation point will lie. It certainly seems a long way off.' A question less often asked was why the government, exercising its considerable powers to direct new industry, directed it in this case to a site so far inland. The basic strategic error – the location itself – bypassed, publicly at least, the Secretary of State for Scotland, John S. Maclay, who described the creation of Ravenscraig as 'the single most important development in the diversification of the Scottish economy'.

By 1966 the plant was reported to be 'blasting away at full steam', producing a high-quality product with a loyal, dedicated workforce. Only 18 years later, Black Bob – who had consistently maintained that Ravenscraig was too far from its markets – made a first attempt to close it. He made a second attempt in 1986, a third in 1988. Each time he was thwarted by the ability of a pugnatious trade union convener, Tommy Brennan, to maintain cross-party support for its survival.

In the spring of 1990, Scholey prepared for a new pre-emptive strike and adopted bold tactics in going public with it. Labour's Donald Dewar and Gordon Brown walked into his office for a prearranged meeting to seek reassurances about the future of Lanarkshire steel production and left stunned by Scholey's disclosure not only that he intended to close the hot strip mill with the loss of 770 jobs but that he proposed to spend £83 million on a new plant in Wales. A deeply embarrassed Secretary of State, Malcolm Rifkind, who claimed to have known nothing of the plan, immediately deplored the decision and called on the company to think again: 'As we would with any other major employer in Scotland, we shall seek to persuade British Steel to reconsider in the interests of both the company and the workforce.' Even the Thatcherite ideologue Michael Forsyth, in the last months of his brief reign as Scottish Tory chairman, was caught off-guard, agreeing that the Motherwell workers deserved to be supported. As on so many occasions before, there was no hint of a breach in the political consensus; and the Scottish media were once again propelled into a spasm of patriotic fury.

'Black Bob Scholey, the flint-like boss of British Steel, today disembowelled the Scottish steel industry before the very eyes of our senior politicians,' thundered the *Evening Times*. 'It was a breath-taking snub administered by a man who cares not a fig for Scotland, and is hell-bent upon moving all steel production south of the border. It was also a massive snub for Malcolm Rifkind. He too had beaten a path to Bob Scholey's door – with a compelling economic argument for investing in Scotland . . . Mr Rifkind, if he values his political hide, must now search out another investor who is prepared to take Ravenscraig off Scholey's hands and keep it going as a viable concern.'

The Labour MP for Motherwell North, John Reid, accused the Secretary of State of being slow off the mark and said he had been pressing him for a year to meet Scholey: 'The least he can do is make it plain to everyone that if Ravenscraig goes he will go as well. It is a matter of honour.' This went beyond the usual rhetoric of opposition politicians, for Rifkind's predecessor, George Younger, had warned Thatcher that he would quit if the plant closed. 'The Government does not run strip mills and it does not run industries' was Rifkind's response – an indication that he would not be putting his job on the line even if the shutdown of the strip mill was followed by the closure of the entire plant. Thatcher had assured a television interviewer, Kirsty Wark, that she had a soft spot for the Ravenscraig workers because of their help during the miners' strike in allowing coal to enter the works in defiance of the pickets, but the spot turned out to be nothing more than a passing blemish on the Prime Minister's implacable features. Within 24 hours of Scholey's announcement, she compounded Rifkind's misery by 'slapping him down' at a cabinet meeting, emphasising that there was no chance of the Government exerting pressure on British Steel over a purely commercial decision. 'Rifkind's position is now untenable,' said George Galloway, Labour MP for Hillhead. 'It was hanging by a thread after the poll tax debacle and that thread has now snapped.'

The *Evening Times* returned to the attack: 'All Scotland must fight for Ravenscraig. Far too much is at stake for us to permit our steel industry to be slowly bled to death.' The paper proposed two alternative solutions. The first – to bring so much pressure to bear that the Government ordered Scholey to reverse the decision – was unrealistic, particularly as a weakened Secretary of State had hurriedly amended his position and was now claiming that Ravenscraig no longer played a crucial role in the Scottish economy. The second sounded more plausible: it repeated the earlier suggestion that a consortium should be found to run the plant independently. Ravenscraig's workforce had 'consistently broken every production record in the book . . . Think how they would respond to a new management which has faith in them.' The Conservative MP Allan Stewart, a former industry ministry, supported the idea: 'It's a perfectly good Tory solution. It's a market economy solution.'

An economist, David Jenkins of the Bank of Scotland, predicted that the closure would have a significant wider effect: 'Ravenscraig feeds a number of other industries with raw materials and markets. You will also remove a major sphere of influence which helps to attract other companies.' The CBI in Scotland estimated that, in addition to the jobs directly at stake, 2,000 more were at risk in related companies. These were serious losses, especially in Lanarkshire where unemployment, although it had been halved in the past three years, still stood at 11%; and they would become more serious still if the whole complex were to close – as eventually it did. But the headline figures obscured the diminishing contribution of steel production, which accounted for only 2.5% of Scottish manufacturing output, and the fact that Ravenscraig was no longer a mass employer of labour in the same league as Ferranti (with 6,000 employees), Rosyth dockyard (with 5,300) and Rolls Royce (with 4,900). Such comparisons were seldom made; nor was there much appreciation of the depressed state of the global market for the product. It was undeniable that BSC had not fought determinedly enough for its share of North Sea oil business, much to the dismay of Alick Buchanan-Smith who, when oil minister, was struck by the corporation's failure to grasp the opportunities on its doorstep. By 1990, however, the campaign to save Ravenscraig had become a test of national pride rather than a case fought on commercial grounds.

The flight from rationality was evident in a succession of emotional utterances. The leader of Scotland's Roman Catholics, Cardinal Gordon Gray, protested in a letter to the *Scotsman* that there was 'no morality in the marketplace'. One of the union leaders, George Cole, called for 'holy hell to break loose in the streets of Scotland'. The SNP prophesied that 'people power' would reverse the 'industrial genocide' and the party's most eloquent tribune, Jim Sillars, said that no other nation in the world would take the humiliation lying down, 'especially from a colonial government they never even voted for'. Strathclyde Regional Council's leader, Charles Gray, announced the setting up of an all-Scotland 'council of war' and offered to fund research into ways of securing Ravenscraig's future under a new owner. The notion of a Scottish consortium had disappeared into the nearest blast furnace, but rumours were said to be 'sweeping Westminster' that several potential Japanese buyers were lining up to submit bids. In the way of such rumours, no bid ever materialised.

Holy hell failed to break loose in the streets, and the shadow Secretary of State, Donald Dewar, seemed to be making a conscious effort to lower the temperature when he opened an emergency debate in the House of Commons: 'We on this side try to avoid the doomsday argument and try not to proclaim that the end is nigh. Too many people in Scottish politics see disaster as a political opportunity privately to be welcomed, even if publicly deplored.' Dewar was unable to resist a dig at the beleaguered Rifkind for his tactless observation at a press briefing that the job loss was 'not dramatic in itself, although disappointing to those affected' – an insensitive choice of words even if it contained an awkward germ of truth.

The battle for Ravenscraig – it tended to be fought in militaristic terms – divided the press neatly along territorial lines. The Scottish tabloids circulated 'Save Ravenscraig' car stickers and posters, while the *Scotsman* appended a special tag, 'Save the Craig', to every item it published about the story. 'Ravenscraig became a totem pole in Scottish politics,' wrote BBC Scotland's industrial correspondent Maurice Smith. 'The newspapers bellowed support.' In the bellowing, however, professional detachment was sacrificed to patriotic propaganda, leaving little room for scepticism. Smith claimed that if a reporter had a story critical of British Steel, facts were less important than with any other news story. One source at BSC told him: 'When the Scottish press rang, you wondered sometimes whether to bother even following up their inquiry. There was a real sense in head office that the paper knew what they were going to publish anyway, no matter what we said.'

South of the border, the press greeted the closure of the strip mill as the inevitable consequence of commercial realism and heaped scorn on the Scottish reaction. The London *Evening Standard* led the chorus of derision: 'The Scots, who have become subsidy junkies as successive governments have tried to bribe them with ever larger handouts, at the expense of the comparatively little-subsidised English taxpayer, will no doubt wail like a trampled bagpipe at the removal of British Steel's financial support for Ravenscraig.' This well-worn mantra bore little relation to the facts. In the south-east of England, public subsidy of transport had risen from £387m in 1990 to £669m in 1992, while a staggering £2.2b was being invested in London's underground system – 'ever larger handouts' dwarfing the relatively modest sums available for the development of a vulnerable economy in the land of the trampled bagpipe. The editorial's assumption that the Motherwell plant was being heavily subsidised was also mistaken, no doubt wilfully. Ravenscraig was not losing money and nor was it inefficient; the rate of production – 2.33 man hours per tonne – was as good as any in Europe. It was closing because Scholey could see no future for it.

By the end of 1990, some of the principal characters in the Ravenscraig story had been written out of the soap opera: in September, the Tory establishment moved against the abrasive Forsyth, who relinquished the chairmanship but continued to exercise an influence on Scottish politics as a minister of state (and later as Secretary of State); Thatcher was the victim of a somewhat larger coup orchestrated from within and in November left Downing Street in tears; and the new Prime Minister, John Major, moved Rifkind from St Andrew's House to the relative sanctuary of a UK department, replacing him with the low-profile Ian Lang. But the story itself had some way still to run; and in the early months of 1992 Ravenscraig returned to the headlines with a bang.

II

True to form, Black Bob's way of marking the forthcoming General Election was to announce the closure of the remaining plant at Motherwell. Bloody-minded to the last, he was retiring in July 1992 and supposedly wished to avoid any pressure being put on his successor to keep steel-making in Scotland alive, particularly if the outcome of the election turned out to be a Labour government.

From the Scottish Tories' point of view, the timing – a few months before the first post-Thatcher election – could not have been worse. Their president Michael Hirst accused Scholey of delivering 'a slap in the face' to the workforce by not giving the bad news personally. Labour's George Robertson said that BSC had failed in its duty as a public limited company: 'Why did he [Scholey] not have the courage and decency to face those people who rose to every exhortation to deal with the challenges put before them?' The manners of Black Bob were an incidental distraction; in Tory ranks there was undisguised panic at the likely political fall-out of an accelerated closure, while Labour was entitled to worry that the decision had handed its nationalist enemy a trump card.

Donald Dewar, opening yet another Ravenscraig debate in the Commons, revealed that when he met the Secretary of State for Trade and Industry, Nicholas Ridley, to discuss the crisis, the notoriously dry-eyed minister had been 'disastrously frank'. Ridley said that he had done nothing because the Scottish Office had not asked him to do anything, adding that 'the search has always been for a face-saving formula'. This inevitably raised questions about the competence of the new Secretary of State for Scotland. According to Dewar, the sole contact at ministerial level between British Steel and the Scottish

Office in the six months before the announcement boiled down to one meeting on 6 January 1992, when the decision was already a *fait accompli*. A report in the *Sunday Mail* produced a different timeline: the paper claimed that Ian Lang was informed on 20 December that an announcement would be made on 8 January and did nothing to influence the outcome. Papers released long afterwards (in 2010) confirmed that Lang did know as early as 20 December but that, far from doing nothing, he mounted a desperate rearguard action to persuade Scholey to change his mind. He told Scholey that the public would view the closure as 'a further example of discrimination against Scottish plants' and a 'betrayal' of Scottish workers and urged him to seek an alternative. Lang had one half-positive idea to offer: that the plant could be left 'ticking over' until the market improved. Scholey, who would have regarded such an appeal as another example of social messaging, was unmoved.

Among the epitaphs, there was sympathy for the workforce, whose professionalism had always been in sharp contrast to the juvenile behaviour of the car workers at the Linwood car plant, which had closed in 1981 after years of dismal industrial relations. A Tory MP, Bill Walker, said that the workers and their shop stewards had been nothing less than magnificent: 'Today, they are paying the terrible price for world over-capacity in steel-making and the lack of demand. They are also paying the price, I believe, for the mistakes made by politicians in locating the plant so far from the deep water port of Hunterston.' Jeremy Bray, the Labour MP for Motherwell South, was generous in his praise: 'They have worked hard and loyally, they have learned new skills, developed new methods, pioneered new technologies and triumphed over disaster. They have acted intelligently, with foresight, courage and integrity. They have achieved unequalled levels of performance.' Although most of the speech sounded like an admission of defeat, Bray rallied with a tentative proposal to use Ravenscraig as a demonstration plant for a new process called thin slab casting. He believed that firms in America were ready to examine

the possibility and visualised a consortium of at least three steel man-
ufacturers taking over the plant.

An American firm did send a study team to Lanarkshire to establish whether its pioneering German-designed thin slab technology
could be adapted to a traditional mill like Ravenscraig, and were duly
feted by Scottish Enterprise, the Government's new development
agency. Nothing came of the idea, just as nothing had come of the
much-touted Scottish consortium, or of the Japanese bidders whose
interest had so recently had 'rumours sweeping Westminster'. There
would be no thin slab casting at Ravenscraig. There would be no
'ticking over' in the Micawberish hope that something would turn
up. There was nowhere left for the steelmen to go. The *Financial
Times*, which in 1990 had been one of the newspapers clamouring
for closure, sounded rueful: 'There was never a community more
deserving of EC and UK government help in rebuilding the local
economy. Ravenscraig's workforce has every right to expect politicians to move whatever bureaucratic obstacles stand in the way of
measures to stimulate the creation of jobs in industries more suited
to the periphery of Europe.'

Defiant to the last, the angry man of the SNP, Jim Sillars,
maintained his default position on any threat to national dignity:
full-throated indignation on behalf of the people of Scotland. Donald
Dewar had rejected the nationalists' assertion that a steel industry in
Scottish ownership would soon have order books overflowing with
oil money: 'There is no escape in myth-making about the North
Sea market. Structural steel, tubes and plates for the North Sea are
not required in sufficient quantities to breathe life into the SNP
headlines.' Sillars would not accept it. He took particular exception
to a critique in the *Herald* – which had dropped Glasgow from its
masthead – deconstructing the SNP's case that Ravenscraig could
have been saved by a combination of state ownership and a vigorous
exploitation of the oil market. Sillars was so incensed that he and
the party's oil spokesman, Iain Lawson, called a press conference

and distributed a nine-page statement rebutting the article point by point. It amounted to a personal challenge to the impartiality of the author, the paper's economics editor Alf Young, who had once worked for the Labour Party in Scotland as a research officer. His fellow journalist, the Labour MP Brian Wilson, rose to Young's defence: 'An attack on the right of one journalist to analyse and comment freely is an attack on the freedom of the entire Scottish media to do likewise.' Young himself said he would not be losing any sleep over it, but the paper's editor, Arnold Kemp, was reported to have told Alex Salmond that he 'wouldn't care to live in an independent Scotland run by you people'.

As it happened, the cause of an independent Scotland had just secured an influential new supporter in the unlikely form of the Australian media tycoon Rupert Murdoch. A few days before Black Bob's pre-election bombshell, Murdoch's tartan flagship, the Scottish edition of the *Sun*, had rubbished the plant's viability in an editorial stating firmly that 'only socialists' would throw money at it. But the narrative was about to change. On 23 January 1992, the same day as MPs fell over themselves to thank the doomed Ravenscraig workforce for their services, a paper formerly noted for its shrill Thatcherite sympathies underwent a startling conversion with a front page dominated by a giant saltire and the splash headline: 'Rise now and be a nation again'. The *Sun* said it had been thinking 'long and hard' about what form of government would best serve Scotland's future, and had come to 'the inescapable conclusion' that its destiny lay as an independent nation within the European Community.

An alternative, more cynical view was that the *Sun* had been thinking long and hard about its own future and had come to the inescapable conclusion that its destiny north of the border lay in support for the Scottish National Party. In December 1991, at a meeting chaired by Murdoch, two pipers bedecked in tartan had introduced a presentation by the paper's Scottish editor, Bob Bird, making the case for a separate political identity for the Scottish edition. Chris McLean, the SNP's press officer at the time, put it frankly: 'It made obvious commercial sense. If you want to undercut your rival [the Labour-supporting *Daily Record*] and win young working-class readers, supporting independence is a very good way of going about it.'

The paper's Scottish political editor, Andy Collier, went about it with some relish in a statement of intent: 'The political and economic union with England is now nearly 300 years old. It has served us well in the past, but as links with Europe strengthen, that union is becoming more and more unnecessary. The time has come to break the shackles. To collect our own taxes. To run our own lives. To talk to other nations of the world on our own behalf. For too long – 300 years too long – we have thought of ourselves as a second-class nation, somehow not worthy or capable of being an independent state. This is nonsense. With independence, Scotland could be one of the wealthiest small nations in Europe.' And there was a great deal more in the same spirit: 'We are a very different people to the English [Collier, an Englishman himself, spoke with some authority on this subject]. But, over centuries, we have shared common ties and spilled blood on the battlefields of the world together. Our marriage to each other has become so bitter and difficult it is now beyond salvation. What both parties need is an amicable divorce so they can be close friends again.'

The news of the metamorphosis – there seemed to be nothing more important happening in the world on 23 January 1992 than the political opportunism of the *Sun* newspaper – spread in self-parodic fashion from page 1 to pages 2, 3, 4, 5, 6 and 7. Two Scottish professors gave a patina of scholarly respectability to the occasion: Geoffrey Barrow of Edinburgh University ('1603 and all that . . . how the Scots got mugged') and David Bell of Stirling University ('Without oil we're fine, with it we're rich'). A full-page spread headed 'Here's tae us, Wha's like us?' boasted that Scottish brilliance was the 'envy of the world', naming William Wallace and Mary Queen of Scots, both of whom had their heads chopped off, as well as two notable tax exiles, racing driver Jackie Stewart and the SNP-supporting film actor Sean Connery, neither of whom had been decapitated at the time of writing, as examples of Scottish brilliance. There was no mention of David Hume and the other giants of the Edinburgh Enlightenment whose dazzling intellects had truly made Scotland the 'envy of the world' at a time when, according to Collier, the Scots were wallowing in self-disgust as second-class citizens. The SNP declared itself 'delighted' by the *Sun*'s commitment and the columnist who had been hired in 1989 as an alternative to the diet of right-wing populism – 'Big Jim Gives It To You Straight' – found himself catapulted to the heart of the paper; the 'Big Jim' of the slogan being none other than Big Jim Sillars.

Elsewhere in Kinning Park, the Glasgow headquarters of the Murdoch operation in Scotland, the editor of the *Sunday Times Scotland*, Gerry Malone, a former Tory MP, exercised his right to be different. Malone wrote that 'the voice of the bar-room cretin' – possibly an oblique reference to his close colleagues in an office nearby – had entered the debate on Scotland's constitutional future. The *Sun*'s conversion had been 'vacuous . . . spurred by petty resentments and braggadocio that make better-tempered Scots cringe'. Long ago declared extinct in other newspapers, the word braggadocio lingered on in the high-dependency unit of the *Sunday Times Scotland*. Malone developed his theme: 'This new-found macho tartan posturing is typical of a Johnny-come-lately to any cause. What is depressing is the thought that somebody knows it reflects the views of readers and will add to sales. But not much to the growing debate over what constitutional future beckons.' It was not great writing, but it may have been a little brave to say it at all.

Big Jim continued to rage. It was what he did best. The urbane Ed Pearce, in a *Guardian* piece not long before the election, had written of Scotland: 'She may be surprised at how easily and comfortably we let her go . . . Nobody is murdering or persecuting the Scots, no matter how much the more wrought nationalists might like that. But there is a serious risk that Scots, remembering Wallace and forgetting Hume, will opt for the triviality of a little state.' Big Jim dismissed Pearce as boring and irrelevant: 'The days of being patronised, lectured to, bullied and insulted are over. Opinion in England counts for nothing. It is what we believe about ourselves that is proving decisive. We'll soon be saying goodbye to Pearce.'

The constituents of Glasgow Govan, who had voted for Sillars in a by-election in 1988, would soon be saying goodbye to Big Jim himself. How this reversal came about was part of the narrative of the 1992 General Election, an event of many surprises and no little hubris.

Ahead of polling day on 9 April, victory for Labour under its prolix leader, Neil Kinnock, and a strong showing by the SNP were widely and firmly predicted. Kinnock may have thrown it with a triumphalist rally in Sheffield before the tiresome formality of the election itself, but the unexpectedly poor performance of the nationalists was harder to account for. The SNP had its new best friend, the *Sun*, noisily on its side, and was expected to benefit electorally from the Ravenscraig closure. Its vice-chairman for publicity, Alex Neil, spoke catchily of Scotland becoming 'Free by 93' and the party had the most professional of the party political broadcasts, employing such ambassadors of pop culture as the singer-songwriter Pat Kane to woo the youth vote. In comparison, the *Daily Record*'s five-page special on the costs of independence – 'How much will it cost you to go it alone?' – felt dour and defensive.

The result was a morale-sapping anticlimax: the general view that the SNP would take 25% of the vote and win a dozen seats proved wide of the mark. It did hold the three seats it won in 1987, and Dick Douglas, who had defected from Labour in 1991, managed to retain Dunfermline West, but it made no gains – and the loss of Govan was a heavy blow. Sillars denounced his fellow Scots as '90-minute patriots', an allusion to the fickleness of the Tartan Army. The Scottish Tories, whose extinction had been gleefully anticipated, attracted 26% of the vote, held two seats – Ayr and Stirling – they had been tipped to lose, and gained Aberdeen South from Labour. It was not exactly the 'great watershed in Scottish politics' that Ian Lang had prophesied, but it was not at all bad. By the end of the night, there was no need for John Major to book the furniture van.

The post-mortem was prolonged and almost comically self-regarding. The journalist David Kemp, who a week before the election had detected 'a real vision of a possible future', wittily confessed to *Herald* readers that he and his colleagues had been suffering from Babbity's Syndrome, a debilitating condition caused by over-exposure to a fashionable bar named Babbity Bowster in Glasgow's Merchant City. It was a favourite watering-hole of journalists. 'A highly civilised milieu, with an excellent cross-section of Scotland's chattering classes,' wrote Kemp. 'Unfortunately, self-delusion appears to flourish in the atmosphere I have described. I know, for I too am a regular . . . Brigadoon had come alive once again, and it was intoxicating. There was such an air of certainty. The Tories were going to lose almost everything . . . it was all nonsense, of course.' Another *Herald* columnist, Ian Bell, a Scottish republican sympathiser, thought that 'we chatterers in the central belt should do a little more travelling and much less talking.'

The despair spilled over into the influential weekend broadsheet, *Scotland on Sunday*. The BBC's Maurice Smith wrote that the paper's two pages of post-election commentary by regular columnists Joyce McMillan, James Naughtie, Kenneth Roy, Allan Massie and Muriel Gray set the tone of post-election coverage, articulating, with the singular exception of Massie, a mood of 'collective frustration'. In Smith's judgement, the *piece de resistance* was the spiky Gray's. 'We messed up,' she wrote. 'We split our vote . . . England had already made up its mind to carry on travelling the roller-coaster to Hell, and when the land of the Union Jack boxer shorts makes up its mind, we have no choice but to thole it.'

The sourest patriot of all may have been the able Murray Ritchie, who, disenchanted by his native country, exiled himself in Brussels as the *Herald*'s European editor. In an interview with the *Sunday Times Scotland*, Ritchie admitted that, with many other journalists, he had 'failed to listen to the voices from the street', but added the slightly contradictory observation that Scottish politics was mostly a charade, lent credibility by 'a loose alliance of journalists and politicians, all motivated by career advantage'. Gerry Malone responded that, although Ritchie was leaving, it was 'not without one last whinge against the wicked Scots'.

Donald Dewar's reaction to the election defeat was to call for a referendum on devolution. The suggestion met with a lukewarm reception. In Babbity Bowster's, where the chattering classes sought consolation in large glasses of dry white wine, there might have been a feeling that devolution was now too distant a prospect to be seriously contemplated. Against most expectations, the Conservatives were back in power for another five years, allowing such forces of darkness as Black Bob to hasten the closure of Ravenscraig; it was brought forward three months, to July. Big Jim fulminated in his *Sun* column that 'no sooner have we bottled it at the general election than British Steel – the company whose boss openly boasted about thrashing the nation – takes a quick knife to Ravenscraig.' Scholey had not boasted about thrashing the nation. After an hour of questioning about the Motherwell plant at his company's annual general meeting in 1991, he had merely said: 'I think we've thrashed the Scots thing for long enough.' There was a difference between changing the subject at a meeting and thrashing a nation, but the phrase stuck. It became the stuff of another Ravenscraig legend: the last one.

III

Four years later, when the huge cooling towers at the abandoned plant were blown up, Tommy Brennan and some of the other union men gathered in a car park to watch the spectacle. A journalist approached him. 'Tommy,' he said, 'this must be a sad day for you.'

The reply was unexpected: 'No, it's not. I'm quite happy to see them come down because it means we can start doing something with the site. They're no longer any good to us.' Gradually there emerged a new Lanarkshire economy based on electronics, engineering and distribution – industries that the *Financial Times* doubtless regarded as more suited to the periphery of Europe. Brennan was happy to give journalists a tour of the faceless new factories and call centres.

The transition was difficult and only partially achieved. Many felt that the cultural identity of Motherwell had been destroyed; that the steel men had done real jobs and that the new alternative – menial labour in some non-unionised, low-paid factory – held little appeal. A study by researchers from Sheffield Hallam University found that unemployment in the town, officially 9%, was closer to 27% if the figure was extended to include all those on disability who were not claiming unemployment benefit. In many families, women were the new breadwinners.

There was an acute sense of loss. Jim Maxwell, a crane driver at Ravenscraig, was 46 when the plant shut. He found it hard to adjust: 'I couldn't settle and flitted from job to job. I'd been there 20 years and missed the camaraderie.' He drifted back into heavy industry, working for a demolition contractor. Frank Roy, another ex-Ravenscraig man, eventually went into politics as Labour MP for Motherwell and Wishaw: 'I had been a steel worker for 14 years and suddenly I had no livelihood. I felt very bitter. We had lost a good, modern production plant. I wanted to get as far away from steelwork-ing as possible.' John Potter, chaplain at the plant for 20 years, spoke of collective as well as personal suffering: 'The people had worked so hard to build up a modern steel-making facility in the hope that they would have something to pass on to the next generation, and that hope was denied. Ravenscraig was a comprehensive employer of people. It needed managers, engineers and computer experts, but also drew on a large pool of semi-skilled workers who were relatively well-paid. You wonder what has happened to the people who didn't have the cerebral skills. I think they may have been gently discarded by society.'

When the *Guardian*'s Stephen Moss visited the site in 2001, he looked into a hole in the ground. The only sound came from birds circling overhead. He wrote: 'Nature, with a bit of help from a £40m clean-up, has reasserted itself, and this monument to Scotland's industrial past has been buried. Literally, as 40 years of industrial waste now lies beneath the site in sealed containers.' To Moss, the town appeared bleak and forbidding; he searched in vain for such simple signs of prosperity as a civilised coffee shop. 'There are two views of what has happened,' he wrote. 'One sees it as a release from an industrial past that had become inhibiting: closure really was closure, the end of one era, the beginning of another . . . The other believes it was a disaster and argues that the effects are still being felt, economically and psychologically.' He asked several of the evangelists for the new economy what had replaced the old sense of community founded on steel. Either they looked at him blankly or they used one word: diversity. As Moss observed: 'But that is an economic definition; they had no notion of how the community now saw itself, what it believed in, how it cohered.' He might have added that what was true of Motherwell was true of post-industrial Scotland as a whole.

THE RUTHLESS SCOTS

I

ON APRIL FOOL'S DAY 1993, THE NEW CHAIRMAN OF GREATER Glasgow Health Board celebrated his first day in office with a call to the sick people of the city to overcome their ill-health by growing their own fruit and vegetables. The fact that many of the sick people lived in cramped flats in high-rise blocks, without access to gardens or allotments, had escaped the limited analytical ability of the new chairman, whose name was Bill (William S.) Fyfe and who lived in a large house with its own swimming pool in the relatively leafy burgh of Ayr. One newspaper reported that the man now fronting the largest health board in Britain, with a budget of £700 million and 32,000 employees, was asking the disadvantaged citizens of Glasgow to 'dig for victory'. As it turned out, the only hole the announcement created was one that the chairman went on digging for himself.

Fyfe was one of two natives of New Cumnock, a small mining community in Ayrshire, who rose to prominence in the 1990s. His father, the local GP, had played some part in the heroic rescue of trapped miners from the depth of Knockshinnoch colliery in 1950, an event which inspired John Grierson's film, *The Brave Don't Cry*. Young Bill was 15 at the time and a pupil at fee-paying Dollar Academy; skipping university, he embarked on a number of business ventures with patchy results – the last, a printing company, went bust. He was too devoted to his alternative interest, Conservative politics, ever to have made it as an entrepreneur; by his early thirties he was a councillor in Prestwick, graduating to a seat on Ayr County Council.

There was nothing remarkable about any of it. But he had the good fortune to be that rare beast, a relatively bright, youngish Tory in local government, and with the coming to power of Margaret Thatcher in 1979 he was ideally positioned for advancement. He secured a paid job as chairman of the small Ayrshire and Arran Health Board, and when the notion of a more businesslike NHS gained traction in the early 1990s, the Secretary of State, his friend Ian Lang, propelled him into a role for which he was ill-equipped by ability or temperament. He gave him the sickest city in Europe to run.

Fyfe took pride in his appearance. The media noted his im-maculately coiffeured hair and his diamond-studded signet ring. But when he marched into the Bath Street headquarters of Greater Glasgow Health Board, it was with tackety boots. He made it clear that he would be a hands-on chairman. And he was a chairman with a mission: nothing less than a revolution in the bureaucracy of the health service, whose noble post-war ideal the Conservative govern-ment perceived to be tired and in need of reform. Fyfe set himself up as the man for the job, espousing a concept which he described as 'Scottish Health plc', a term heavily suggestive of the mores of capitalism. He swiftly earned a reputation as the 'arch apostle of market-led health service management', in which people of business skill and experience, rather than medical practitioners, knew best. At that stage, no-one was inquiring too deeply into the chairman's own business record.

In pursuit of its agenda, the government had decided several years earlier to encourage hospitals to apply for conversion into self-governing trusts. It was a divisive move. Most doctors and nurses opposed it, fearing that it would create a two-tier NHS and lead to an increasingly privatised service; successive opinion polls showed that it was unpopular with the public; the opposition parties hated it. Impervious to all opposition, Lang pressed ahead. In December 1991, he approved applications for trust status from the Foresterhill group of hospitals in Aberdeen, the Royal Scottish National Hospital at Larbert (which specialised in treatment of mentally handicapped patients), and the South Ayrshire group of hospitals. The last application was the most significant politically: it was delivered by the then chairman of the Ayrshire and Arran board, Bill Fyfe, confirming his growing status as a favourite son of St Andrew's House and a hot tip for promotion. Fyfe had said that 'self-governing trusts will happen only with the doctors' approval and only if they are convinced that patients will benefit.' The doctors of South Ayrshire were not at all convinced: 50 of the 59 consultants voted against the opt-out scheme, leaving Fyfe to find some other justification.

In Aberdeen, the resistance of the medical profession was even more pronounced: two consultants in favour of trust status; 87 opposed. In November 1991, a month before the Secretary of State rubber-stamped the Foresterhill application, the Tory leader of Aberdeen District Council, Mike Hastie, said he could not believe that the government would push through the scheme: 'It would be an act of sheer folly and I do not believe Mr Lang is capable of that.' But he was.

During explosive exchanges in the House of Commons, the shadow secretary of state, Donald Dewar, accused Lang of betraying the NHS. He claimed that the hospitals were being 'forced out of the mainstream of the health service' and objected in particular to the inclusion of a hospital for dealing with the mentally handicapped, 'by no stretch of the imagination a candidate for the market mechanism'. The local MP, Dennis Canavan, said the Larbert application had been opposed by 96% of the staff and 'virtually the entire community'. The Labour MP for South Ayrshire, George Foulkes, wondered why Lang was 'arrogating to himself the claim to know more about patient care than all the professionals' and objected to the 'handing over of public assets to a few of his Conservative cronies, a form of legalised theft'. Malcolm Bruce, for the Liberal Democrats, complained that the Tories were 'turning a caring service into a business' and said the public had no confidence in the type of managers that Lang proposed to put in control of the trusts, whom he characterised as 'Tory Party stooges'. Lang coolly reiterated the familiar line that the service would continue to be 'free at the point of delivery' and that the aim of the scheme was to provide 'greater autonomy, greater local flexibility, greater local ownership and decision-making'. It mattered little that so few in the NHS had any appetite for the dish on offer.

Lang was displeased that none of the original applications for trust status came from Greater Glasgow. The general manager, Laurence Peterken, had abandoned a successful business career to join the NHS and seemed the ideal man to pioneer a market-led health service. At his first press conference, however, he 'swept aside any suggestion that he was a government hatchet man'. So it proved, much to the consternation of his political masters in Edinburgh, who suspected that over the years Peterken had gone native. St Andrew's House decided that Sir Thomas Thomson, a distinguished medic without the business pedigree now deemed essential, should be replaced as chairman by someone who could deal with the Peterken problem. Fyfe, the 'Tory stooge' selected for the assignment, found the problem tougher than he ever imagined. In Peterken, a former fighter pilot every bit as abrasive and single-minded as himself, the brash Ayrshireman finally met his nemesis.

Although he was not due in the office until April, Fyfe was actively plotting as early as February, clear in his understanding that his initial brief was the removal of Peterken. In a series of meetings, for which he was later able to produce documentary evidence, he had discussions with the solicitor to the Secretary of State and the director of personnel at the Scottish Office, at which the only item on the agenda was the Peterken problem. Some progress was made – enough, anyway, to justify a letter from a senior civil servant to the Treasury in August asking for approval for a pay-off to the general manager of around £185,000. The Treasury rejected the proposal, ruling such payments irregular or even unlawful, and the back-pedalling civil servants then had to explore with Fyfe the possibility of alternative employment for Peterken. It was barely conceivable that all this had gone on without the knowledge and authority of ministers. Officially, though, it had. Meanwhile, back at the office, Peterken had launched an internal inquiry into Fyfe's expenses claims. It had become a dirty war; and the sick people of Glasgow – whose best interests were ostensibly being served by it – still showed no inclination to grow their own veg.

In early November, the chairman peremptorily fired the general manager without notice and in the latter's absence. Did Fyfe have any authority for doing so – or did he temporarily take leave of his senses? Either way, it was sensational; it was the brutal politics of the commercial boardroom; it was not how things were done in the public sector, even in the more aggressive market-led NHS that Fyfe had come to personify. Fyfe, who was essentially a maverick, may have acted on impulse, though it seemed unlikely, even for him. Later, when he gave evidence to a parliamentary select committee, he insisted that his actions were 'approved at the highest level at all times'. His friend – perhaps now erstwhile friend – Ian Lang equally emphatically stated to parliament that Fyfe had been told repeatedly that 'he could not and should not seek to terminate Mr Peterken's employment and make the offer of a financial settlement to him'. The health minister Lord Fraser – formerly of the Lockerbie inquiry – declared that the first he knew of the sacking was after the event.

Whatever the truth, it was Fyfe himself whose future was now on the line. He had lost his favourite son status; he had become an embarrassment. A fortnight after Peterken's departure, the chief executive of the NHS in Scotland, Geoff Scaife, wrote to him: 'The confidence of ministers in the running of GGHB under your chairmanship has been severely shaken.' It was an invitation to resign, but Fyfe declined to take the hint. It was left to the non-executive board members, who had played little if any part in the machinations, to deliver the *coup de grace*. They convened to review the case and decided that it had been a botched job: the correct procedures had not been followed and Peterken was entitled to take the civil action he had been threatening. That threat had been withdrawn as a condition of offer of his new job, in a specially created and unadvertised post in the NHS central management, at the same salary as he had enjoyed in Glasgow (£86,000 pa). Fraser admitted later that he was given it in order to avoid having to settle a hefty compensation claim.

After eight turbulent months in the air, Peterken the pilot had achieved a soft landing, while Fyfe, the navigator of Scottish Health plc, was crashing to earth. He received an ultimatum from his own board: clear your desk by 4 pm and leave the building. He did, but with only 19 minutes to spare, and only after informing the *Evening Times* that he had no intention of quitting. For a senior public figure, it was the most humiliating exit imaginable; there had never been anything quite like it.

The scandal raised a political storm. George Galloway made one of his turbo-charged interventions in the Commons, demanding to know 'how much longer the Secretary of State can pretend that he and other ministers had no knowledge of the grisly details of this affair'. George Robertson, who had succeeded Donald Dewar as shadow secretary of state, asked: 'Does the Secretary of State appreciate that his total silence over the past five weeks is both significant and deeply suspicious? Who is telling the truth in this sordid tale: Bill Fyfe – the Secretary of State's personal nominee last year for running this giant quango – or ministers of the Crown, with whom ultimate responsibility for this shambles lies?' Lang avoided a direct answer, but stated firmly that Fyfe had been 'an architect of his own downfall'. By then the architect lay severely injured in hospital, having crashed his car on the Fenwick moor on the way home one evening. He disappeared from public life and in a sad epilogue three years later was declared bankrupt over a debt of £66,000. To the end he maintained that he had been cast as a fall guy. He died in 2015 in Ayr Hospital, which he had once delivered to a grateful government as the first of Scotland's NHS trusts.

II

The exhortation of W.S. Fyfe left the sick city of Glasgow unmoved: the people resolutely declined to dig for victory. Indeed the early 1990s marked the beginning of a deterioration in their health relative to urban populations in the rest of Britain. If you had the misfortune to be born in one of the many deprived areas of Glasgow, you could expect to have a shorter life than someone born in one of the many deprived areas of other major cities. A sociological conundrum known as 'The Glasgow effect' defined the unexplained health disparities between Scotland's largest city and anywhere else of comparable size in the UK. The high mortality rate, first spotted around 1980, of people between the ages of 15 to 45 was particularly striking and contributed to the city's bleak life expectancy. Epidemiologists found it difficult to account for: why did the Glasgow poor suffer more wretched health and die earlier than the poor of, say, Birmingham, Manchester or Liverpool?

A consultant surgeon at Glasgow Royal Infirmary, Harry Burns, had observed something interesting about his patients. When he operated on someone from the east end, he discovered that, typically, the wound he had opened would take at least a day longer to heal than it would have done had the patient lived in one of the more prosperous districts of the city. There was an obvious answer: people in the east end smoked more, drank more, and ate the wrong food. Even if they wanted to eat well, they were defeated by their environment; a 1993 study ironically entitled Glasgow Healthy City found that deprived areas had fewer reasonably priced outlets for fresh food and that, to obtain good value and the proper nutrition, poor people had to travel: so healthy diets cost more. But the obvious answer was not necessarily the whole answer. Harry Burns arrived at the conclusion that junk food, alcohol abuse and excessive smoking were symptoms of a deeper malaise.

'As a doctor at the Royal,' he said, 'I never once wrote a death certificate saying the cause of death was living in a horrible house or unemployment. People die of molecular disease, such as proteins coagulating in arteries and causing heart attacks and strokes. Yet we know that poor social conditions lead to poor health and premature deaths'. He was so disturbed by the condition of the poor in his own city that he embarked on a new career in public health. In 1990 he was appointed director of health at Greater Glasgow Health Board and was still there when the new chairman issued his notorious cure-all prescription.

Harry Burns had been profoundly moved by the 1971 Glasgow rectorial address of Jimmy Reid on the theme of alienation. The trade union leader had compared the high-rise blocks to filing cabinets in which the problems of society were hidden away, and had spoken passionately about the fate of the people living in them, 'victims of blind economic forces beyond their control'. This helped to shape Burns's subsequent thinking on the nature of the underlying ill-health of Glasgow and the west of Scotland, which he identified as a loss of social cohesion triggered by the wholesale closure of traditional industries such as shipbuilding, mining and steel, the subsequent break-up of well-established communities, and their dispersal to anonymous peripheral estates. He came to believe that the ability to attain good health depended in part on whether people felt in control of their lives and that in Glasgow they had lost control of them. There was some evidence to support this hypothesis: a study by the Glasgow Centre for Population Health, found for example that Glaswegians were less likely to go to church, join clubs, or take part in community activities than people in the rest of Scotland. But there was an inherent weakness in the argument. De-industrialisation, with its baleful social consequences, was not a phenomenon unique to Glasgow. It was keenly felt in the cities and towns of the north and midlands of England and in many other parts of Europe, yet without impacting so severely on the health of the people.

Burns went on to become chief medical officer for Scotland, enjoying considerable influence as a thinker and policy-maker and helping to inform a more preventative approach to public health; by 2014 he was bemoaning the breakdown of the family, claiming to find evidence of stress in the brains of pre-primary children, and calling for early intervention in the lives of teenage girls 'before they get pregnant'. It was unclear how these methods were expected to give people more control over their lives – the starting point of the doctor's inquiries – and it felt like a long journey from the compassionate spirit of Jimmy Reid's rectorial address. Despite the efforts of Harry Burns and others to understand it, 'The Glasgow effect' lingered on, equally resistant to the over-simplifications of a health board chairman and the alarming remedies of a public health specialist.

A possible explanation, not widely discussed, lay in the grotesque inequalities festering in the city. The conferring of the accolade 'European City of Culture' in 1990 meant comparatively little in artistic terms; many of the events during the year would have taken place anyway. But it meant a great deal in terms of prestige and public relations; it became part of the successful re-packaging of Glasgow as a mecca of contemporary style and edgily fashionable tourist destination. A visiting journalist from Paris noted the vast amount of money lavished on removing the 'coat of industrial grime' and sent back a despatch to *Le Monde* lauding how Scotland's most populous conurbation had been given a makeover and was now a city of art and high culture. In reality, this second city – the new Glasgow – did not amount to much. It extended the length of smart Buchanan Street, branched out into the former mercantile quarter, and reached affluent tributaries of the west end and the south side. But it left the first city – the old Glasgow – virtually untouched. A short taxi ride from the high-end shopping arcade known as Princes Square, the unwary visitor from *Le Monde* would have stumbled into Springburn, which once built railway engines for the world but had been reduced to a ghetto of high unemployment, deprivation and stress. The two cities co-existed in close physical proximity, one morphing into the other with surprising abruptness, but there was little attempt to explore the resentment that the old city, starved of material possession, might be feeling towards the new – or its damaging implications for the psychological health of the excluded majority.

III

In Scotland as a whole, the social statistics of the year pointed to a society in rapid and fairly dramatic transition. Fourteen years earlier, only 10% of births were to unmarried parents; by 1993 the proportion had risen to 27%. In 1993, one in 12 of the babies born in Scotland were to mothers under the age of 20; and of those mothers eight out of 10 were unmarried. One in every four marriages ended in divorce, and half the divorces involved at least one partner under the age of 21. The number of children living in one-parent households had doubled in a decade and one-parent families accounted for one in six of all families. A Scottish Office report pointed out that some children were having to cope more than once before adulthood with the emotional and practical trauma of parents separating or divorcing.

The changes in the structure of the family were accompanied by a spectacular growth in the provision for formal education. Although secondary school rolls were falling, many more pupils were staying on beyond the compulsory minimum leaving age of 16. The number of students attending further education colleges rose by 50% between the mid-1980s and the early 1990s, and by 1993 more than a quarter of young Scots were entering higher education.

When Scottish writers put a human face to these statistics, the results were seldom edifying. A young journalist, Andrew O'Hagan, recalled for an essay in the *London Review of Books* his upbringing in an unnamed Scottish new town (Irvine). He described in graphic detail the commonplace torture of children, including some inflicted by himself and his friend Heather, aged six, during their walk to school. Their target was a boy called David, fragile and ginger-haired, who was expected to walk straight, carry the bags of Andrew and Heather and speak when spoken to. If he failed in any of the tasks allotted to him, he would be slapped or hit with a ruler. One morning, on top of an out-of-the-way railway bridge, they 'practically skinned the screaming boy's legs'. The kids who did the bullying in Irvine had their own way of walking – 'dragging our feet, hands in our pockets, heads always lolling towards the shoulder'. Andrew and his friends carried sticks and could never have enough matches for their minor acts of arson. 'Most of our games, when I think of it, were predicated on someone else's humiliation or pain,' he wrote. 'It made us feel strong and untouchable.' But he added the incongruous caveat that the torturers led double lives – for they also celebrated first communions, sang in the school choir and played in football teams.

The article, whose context was the recent murder in Liverpool of six-year-old Jamie Bulger by two older boys, ensured its author instant notoriety. Some correspondents in the magazine wondered if O'Hagan was suggesting that children murdering each other was somehow normal. The director of social services for Croydon observed that, having waded through the catalogue of beastly and criminal behaviour, he was not at all sure what point O'Hagan was trying to make. 'Why?' was never asked. No insight was offered; nothing constructive offered. The reader in cultural studies at the Open University in Edinburgh, Angus Calder, charged into the controversy with what he called 'a modest proposal': the state schools – 'Bastilles of learning' – should be abolished and the community should provide free schools as it provided free libraries for citizens who wanted them, and these free schools should be generously funded. Calder was not quite done with his mischief: the 'unfortunate' school teachers should be relieved of responsibility for the behaviour of schoolchildren and their intellectual and moral progress, and the community should 'face up squarely to the inherent badness of its own young'. Nothing came of the idea of non-compulsory, community-run free schools;

on the contrary, the school leaving age was extended to 17 and, in the Bastilles of learning, children were required to sit more exams than ever.

One of the lessons of O'Hagan's story was that statistics really did lie. The participation of the Irvine torturers in a range of wholesome extra-curricular activities would have earned them the approval of social scientists and directors of health, in welcome contrast to their counterparts in Glasgow who risked premature death by playing no part in the community and devouring too many of the deep-fried Mars bars of popular mythology.

In 1993, the annual Scottish Crime Survey included questions about drugs for the first time. It found that the most frequently reported, cannabis, had been taken at least once by an impressive 24% of respondents in the age group 16 to 29; amphetamines, valium and LSD by between 2% and 5% of the sample; ecstasy, solvents and cocaine by 1 to 2%; crack cocaine and heroin by less than 1%.

It took a work of fiction, introduced that year at the Edinburgh International Book Festival, to give a voice to the small minority of Scots, mostly young, who were addicted to the hard stuff: *Trainspotting* was launched to international acclaim. Set in Leith, the port of Edinburgh, where its author grew up, the novel charted the dysfunctional lives of a small group of heroin users and their friends. Irvine Welsh, the son of a dock-worker, had left the local Bastille of learning at 16, worked for a while as an apprentice repairing TV sets, headed to London and played guitar in various bands. For a while he was close to destitute and lived in a succession of seedy bedsits. By his early 20s, he was 'seriously addicted' to heroin, thieving and scrounging, 'disintegrating from within'. A bus crash in which he was injured may have saved his life: instead of blowing the compensation money – £2,000 – on drugs, he invested it in a mortgage for a flat in Hackney. In the late 1980s he returned to Edinburgh to the respectable work of a training officer with the city council's housing department, and began writing *Trainspotting*. The result caught the attention of

Robin Robertson, editorial director at the publishers Secker and Warburg, who decided to take a chance on it. Just before the launch, publisher and author sat together in an Edinburgh pub wondering how they could promote it; Welsh thought of sending anonymous letters to the *Scotsman*, condemning the book for besmirching the good name of the city. There was no need: *Trainspotting* was a more or less instant global hit and the film adaptation, released two years later, made Welsh richer than ever. In the year of the Scottish independence referendum (2014) he was living in Chicago with his second wife, reflecting on his first novel's cult status as 'a rite of passage book for kids to read', and espousing the cause of Scottish independence from afar, as many expat Scottish celebrities did.

The crude, unrealistic demotic of *Trainspotting* somehow translated brilliantly to the cinema, Ewan McGregor's voiceover setting a blistering pace in the opening narrative: an invective against the consumer society culminating in an affirmation of heroin as a lifestyle alternative to starter homes and DIY. In a later scene set among the hills, there was a hint of authorial political commentary when one of the characters wailed: 'It's shite being Scottish. Ruled by effete arseholes, and all the fresh air in the world won't make any fuckin' difference.' The young audiences who flocked to their local Odeons to see this nasty stuff lapped it up – at many screenings there was the unusual sound of applause as the credits rolled at the end – and the metropolitan critics gave it rave reviews. The *Observer*'s Philip French, who detected some arcane connection to the work of Chekhov, thought the script had the 'unsentimental ruthlessness of much recent Scottish writing' – either a high compliment or a grim commentary on Scottish writing, depending on one's point of view. Either way, Welsh was hailed in the *Scotsman* as 'the most successful Scottish writer ever', leaving unanswered the question of who might have been the second most successful.

Welsh, whose life had once 'disintegrated from within' because of heroin addiction, nevertheless felt that drugs were misunderstood:

'The main issue for me is that so many people are using them negatively, to get as far away from the horror and dullness of straight mainstream life as possible, rather than positively, as life enhancers.' The Scottish Crime Survey indicated that the overwhelming majority of young Scots had never used hard drugs and were more likely to be seen wielding a paintbrush in a starter home than injecting themselves with heroin; and of those who did use heroin the results were more often fatal than life-enhancing. But at least *Trainspotting* bore a more than passing resemblance to the actuality, unlike the Oscar-winning *Braveheart* (1995), a bizarre take on the life of William Wallace so riddled with inaccuracies that history teachers feared for the effect on their pupils. One educational writer, Frank Adams, called for a national curriculum 'which is relevant to a society that can celebrate the doubtful history of *Braveheart* and yet, for many, live in the stark reality of *Trainspotting* at one and the same time'. The all too plausible theory that *Braveheart* ignited nationalist fervour and anti-English feeling could never be proved, though it continued to be as endlessly debated as the national curriculum.

IV

Among the unsentimentally ruthless Scots, the ability to work hard and make money, once hard-wired into the national character, was no longer much in evidence. The relentless drain of talent, mainly to London, had been so long a feature of Scottish life that it may have diminished the gene pool; yet the native entrepreneur was not quite an extinct species. In 1993, while the first of the New Cumnock men took over the chairmanship of Greater Glasgow Health Board, the second opened a sportswear shop: Tom Hunter was on his way.

Hunter had left the village in the late 1970s to study business at Strathclyde University. The mines had closed and the family firm – a grocery – had closed with them: there was no future in New Cumnock. With a little help from his father he started selling cheap clothes and shoes from the back of a van; he specialised in such lines as the shell-suit, often voted the ugliest fashion item of all time and a particular favourite of the disc jockey Jimmy Savile. Only five years after opening the first store, Hunter sold his company to a competitor for £252m. He was uncertain what to do next; his financial advisers urged him to forsake Scotland for the tax haven of Monaco. Instead he stayed in his native Ayrshire and, inspired by the example of Andrew Carnegie, announced that he was giving most of his money away; this extraordinary commitment to philanthropy topped the BBC's *Nine O'Clock News*. He went on to establish himself as a world-class benefactor, launching one project in association with the former American president Bill Clinton, though the crash of 2008, in which he lost some of his great fortune, stalled the full extent of his ambition.

For the humble garment with which he started out, there was no way back. The unhealthy people of Glasgow, whose diet worried the first of the New Cumnock men so much, found something more flattering to wear, while fans of *Trainspotting* may have wondered what happened to poor, pregnant June, who looked 'like a pile ay crumpled bones in that hideous shell-suit'.

FOG OVER THE MULL

I

ON 1 JUNE 1994, A FLIGHT LIEUTENANT WITH RAF SPECIAL FORCES in Northern Ireland, Jonathan Tapper, received an instruction for the next day. He was to transport a group of 26 VIPs – senior members of the intelligence and security services, as well as civil servants from the Northern Ireland Office – from the military air base at Aldergrove, 18 miles north of Belfast, to Fort George, near Inverness, for what the media called 'a top secret conference'.

There was nothing unusual about the mode of transport, a Chinook helicopter, even if it meant that many of the people leading the war against the Provisional IRA were travelling together. This was normal practice in the hostile conditions of Northern Ireland at the time; it was reckoned to be the quickest and most effective way of moving senior people around. Whether it was the safest soon came to be keenly debated. Nor was there anything unusual about the purpose of the flight. The high-level group from the British Army and the Royal Ulster Constabulary periodically met outside the province; the conference at Fort George, an eighteenth-century fortified garrison visited by James Boswell and Samuel Johnson on their tour of the Highlands, seems to have been an annual event.

The only unusual feature of the mission was Jonathan Tapper's reluctance to fly. Twenty-eight years old, a skilled and experienced pilot whose psychological assessments and personal files gave no cause for concern, Tapper would not have taken lightly his decision, the evening before the trip to Scotland, to phone his boss, the deputy flight commander, with a request. He explained that it had been some time since his training in the new Chinook model, the HG2, which was being introduced in Northern Ireland, and that consequently he felt ill-prepared for the flight.

There might have been more to it. Serving aircrew were anxious about the transition to the HG2, the preparations for which were described later as 'rushed, fraught and chaotic', and about mysterious technical faults during tests. For the Scottish sortie, Tapper would have preferred to pilot the HG1, which he knew and trusted, and asked the deputy flight commander if this would be possible. He was told that the one remaining HG1 in the province was not available and that he would require to fly the HG2.

On 2 June (according to one of the official reports of what happened that day) Tapper and his crew carried out 'routine troop movements' in Northern Ireland before the final assignment of the shift – the flight to Fort George on ZD576. But the phrase 'routine troop movements' disguised the arduous character of his working day; by the time he picked up the 25 VIPs – fate decreed that one of the 26 dropped out at short notice – he had been on flight duty for more than nine hours, with a four-hour round trip to Scotland still to face; had he been alive to complete the mission he would have required special authorisation for the journey home. Did fatigue contribute to his own death and the deaths of his co-pilot Rick Cook, two other crewmen, and all 25 VIPs? It is a largely unexplored possibility.

Pilots planning a flight have a choice of operating under visual flight rules (VFR) or instrument flight rules (IFR). Under VFR rules, the pilot must be able to operate the aircraft with visual reference to the ground; flying through cloud is therefore forbidden. If the weather is bad, and visibility poor, the regulations require the pilot to switch to IFR. Tapper opted for VFR – a slightly surprising choice considering that the weather over the southern end of Kintyre, which would be his first sight of the Scottish mainland, was notoriously changeable and often affected by fog and low cloud.

With its human cargo of some of the best brains in the province, ZD576 took off from Aldergrove at 4.42 pm. Eight minutes later, it was seen flying low over Carnlough on the Antrim coast and out over the north channel in the direction of the Mull of Kintyre. At 4.55 pm, a member of the crew tried to contact Scottish Air Traffic Control (Military) at Prestwick. No-one answered the call and the crew made no attempt to repeat the message, which investigators took as a sign that it was non-urgent. It was the last communication from the aircraft.

At about the same time as the call to Prestwick, a yachtsman in the area saw the helicopter flying 'at a steady speed straight and level below the cloud base at an estimated height of between 200 and 400 feet, about two nautical miles west of the Mull of Kintyre lighthouse'. The yachtsman noted that cloud and hill fog covered the land mass of the Mull. There were, however, conflicting accounts of the state of the weather at the critical moment. The yachtsman was inconsistent in his testimony, but the lighthouse-keepers were firm in their recollection that the fog was too thick to enable them to see the helicopter – they could see nothing. An alternative view within the RAF was that the cloud may have been more broken than the eyewitness impressions indicated. There was no certainty about any of it – though also no reason to doubt the lighthouse-keepers.

One of the crew manually changed the waypoint of Tapper's selected route to waypoint B (Corran, near Fort William). At that point, the navigation computer should have presented Tapper and Cook with a 'steer left' direction. Instead, inexplicably, the aircraft continued to fly towards the terrain of the Mull. A few seconds after the waypoint change – about 15 seconds to disaster – it was flying at a height of only 468 feet above sea level, plus or minus 50 feet. The difference made no difference. Whatever the precise height, it was well below safety altitude. The helicopter then began to climb dramatically at a groundspeed estimated at 150 knots. It was too late to avoid a rocky outcrop on the side of Beinn na Lice, 810 feet above sea level. After its first impact with the hillside, it continued airborne for around 200 metres, executing violent manoeuvres until it landed upside down and broke in two, shedding both engines. All 29 on board were thrown from the aircraft, incurring fatal injuries, and the fuel tanks ruptured, causing a horrific fire which destroyed about 80% of the wreckage. It was the RAF's worst accident in peacetime – if the long years of civil war in Northern Ireland qualified as peacetime – as well as an incalculable loss to British intelligence.

The BBC reported: 'The explosion scorched surrounding heather and gorse as the helicopter was turned into a huge fireball. The bodies of the dead are being taken to a temporary mortuary in Machrihanish air base.' In the same report, the possible causes were named as pilot error, instrument failure, mechanical collapse, even birdstrike. On the night of the disaster, it would have seemed inconceivable that the actual cause would never be determined.

The RAF's ground-fighting corps sent an initial team of six – later augmented to 60 – to the crash-site. One of the first to arrive, Paul Ashley, recalled the trauma of the assignment: 'We had trouble landing as the cloud was so low and there was limited space to put the aircraft on the ground. When we were dropped off, the police took us to a tent that had been erected on the night of the crash. The mist and smell of aviation fuel made it feel like something out of a film. It was a horrible, sad place to be. It was one of the worst experiences of my life. But the worst was when they allowed the families to visit the site. A woman with shoulder-length blonde hair wearing a short red coat stopped by our vehicle. She said: "Thank you and please thank everyone for me." That did it for me. I had to walk away so as not to show the tears running down my cheeks. I will never forget those words.'

Ashley and his colleagues stayed five days in the tent: five days of intense speculation in the media. Had it been an IRA spectacular? Had the Provisionals somehow managed to shoot down the aircraft in a terrorist coup of coups? This theory was quickly and emphatically ruled out, but short of sabotage the disaster posed many questions beyond the official theory that it was simply a tragic accident caused by poor visibility in bad fog.

II

Specialists from the Air Accidents Investigation Branch (AAIB) combed the site for clues, but it was a frustrating and dispiriting task. They found no hint of an on-board explosion or a pre-impact fire; they could detect no major loss of electrical power; so far as they could tell, the navigation equipment appeared to be operating normally; there were no signs that the rotor or other systems had malfunctioned. But the investigation was severely hampered by the destruction of most of the forensic evidence in the fire and by the absence of a cockpit voice or flight data recorder – the so-called 'black box' – for which there was no legal requirement on this type of aircraft. The expert leading the investigation, A.N. Cable, told a House of Lords select committee: 'The evidence was remarkably thin . . . we spent a great deal of time trying to find evidence'.

His report – perhaps the most reliable of the many official documents about the crash – included an important statement that 'the pre-impact serviceability of the aircraft could not be positively verified' but that 'no evidence was found of malfunction that could have contributed to the accident' (apart from a minor inconsequential fault). If that nuanced conclusion had been respected, the relatives of those who died might have been spared years of gratuitous additional grief. No-one was more upset than Cable when a sentence expressed in clear enough language was misrepresented or ignored by people in high places.

The RAF promptly established an internal board of inquiry with a brief to determine the cause of the accident. Unsurprisingly in the circumstances, they were unable to identify a definite cause, but decided that 'the most probable cause' was the selection by the crew of an 'inappropriate rate of climb' insufficient to overfly the high ground on the Mull of Kintyre. RAF regulations provided that 'only in cases in which there is absolutely no doubt whatever should deceased aircrew be found negligent'. It was a uniquely high standard of proof, so high that it too became a source of confusion and mis-understanding, and the board of inquiry decided that the evidence fell far short of justifying it. The board were 'reasonably certain' that ZD576 was flying fast at low level close to the southern end of the Mull, but in the absence of a black box, and since all the witnesses were dead, 'they could not know how or why the crew got into that situation or what they were intending to do about it'.

Regrettably, that was not the end of it. The board's finding was subject to scrutiny by two 'reviewing officers' of the highest rank in the service, air marshals Sir John Day and Sir William Wratten, whose first reaction was to invite the board to reconsider the question of human failings. So the board did – reporting back that, although it was likely that Tapper had made an error of judgement in the at-tempted climb over the Mull, it would be 'incorrect to criticise him for human failings based on the available evidence'.

Day and Wratten vehemently disagreed. Exercising their right to amend the verdict, they condemned both pilots for 'negligence to a gross degree'. Day found it incomprehensible that two trusted pilots should have flown a serviceable aircraft into cloud-covered high ground. In his view there was no doubt that Tapper had allowed the helicopter to proceed at high speed and low level directly towards the Mull, despite the obvious dangers; Cook, who was presumed to have been handling the aircraft (although there was no proof of this), should have recognised an unsound and potentially dangerous course of action. They should have been ready to take decisive steps to ensure the safety of the aircraft and its passengers – either by slowing down or by switching to instrument flight rules and climbing to safety. Day, an experienced helicopter pilot, said that the finding of gross negligence was the hardest he had had to make in his RAF career. He based it on what he regarded as unarguable evidence that the pilots 'consistently and on purpose' flew into cloud, contravening at the waypoint change the most fundamental rules of flight. He was unable to explain their actions. He found them 'just incredible'. And he was critical of the board of inquiry for failing to carry out 'a robust, non-emotional analysis' of serious failings.

His colleague, Wratten, was just as emphatic. He maintained that the Mull of Kintyre was 'completely covered in cloud from a height of about 300 feet upwards' and that, in those conditions, the pilots' clear duty was to divert away from the bad weather or climb to safety. Such action was 'instinctive to every pilot'. In the prevailing weather conditions, it was 'entirely contrary to the pilots' training to be flying so fast and so close to high ground'. He too found it impossible to account for their actions, but added the damning observation that it was 'more often experienced pilots who are tempted to carry out risky manoeuvres'.

There were two main problems about this indictment of Tapper and Cook. The first was the assumption by the air marshals that the Chinook was, in their word, 'serviceable'. Cable, the man from the AAIB, had been at pains to assure the board of inquiry that he did not intend the key sentence in his report to mean that the absence of evidence conclusively proved that there had been no technical malfunction. He reminded the inquiry that a single fault in several systems of the Chinook could result in a catastrophic failure of the aircraft. He regarded it as self-evident that it was impossible to prove beyond all doubt that no malfunction had occurred and pointed to concerns about the digital electronic control system during tests. Despite these heavy qualifications, the reviewing officers went on to base their findings on a judgement – it could be no more than a judgement – that ZD576 was functioning normally at the time of the accident, a belief that seemed to stem from a misreading of the key document.

Many years later, when he was called as a witness at Lord Philip's independent inquiry into the case, Sir John Day adopted a somewhat cavalier view of the AAIB report: 'That's just the way they write them . . . every single Air Accidents Investigation Branch report will have those kinds of caveats in them because the wreckage is always such that there is going to be something missing.' When Philip suggested that he had dismissed the possibility of a malfunction of the kind envisaged by Cable, he said: 'Fair enough if you look at it like that, but what I am saying is that any AAIB report into an accident would have said the same thing and my judgement was that they were negligent at the waypoint change.'

The second problem led directly from the first. Cable's expert assessment had created a reasonable doubt about the cause of the accident, and it was a doubt that should have precluded any finding of gross negligence. Instead the reviewing officers dismissed the doubt and made a presumption of negligence, ignoring the imperative that 'only in cases in which there is absolutely no doubt whatsoever should deceased aircrew be found negligent'. The words 'absolutely' and 'whatsoever' left no room for compromise. This was a standard of proof very much higher than the standard of 'beyond reasonable doubt' which applied in the criminal courts; and it was a form of words unfamiliar to most lawyers. Sir John Day took the precaution of seeking legal advice before he came to review the board of inquiry's findings, but the advice was flawed. As Philip observed: 'It introduced a reference to RAF policy which could be interpreted as an assertion that the standard of proof meant what the RAF wanted it to mean.' The poor briefing might have explained the subsequent inflexibility of the air marshals, though it could never justify it.

Within the RAF, there was a strong feeling that two airmen who were no longer able to defend themselves had been unfairly blamed for an accident the cause of which was far from obvious. The standard of proof had not been met – the extreme finding of gross negligence fell well short of satisfying it – yet there was now a stain on the reputation and character of the dead men. Philip heard that opinion throughout the service found the outcome 'repugnant'.

Among serving aircrew there was also deep unhappiness that the board of inquiry consisted of senior officers who had command and control of the flying operations which they themselves were investigating. The lack of independent scrutiny was a glaring defect – and the top brass, for their own reasons, were reluctant to address it.

III

When the board of inquiry's report was submitted to the Secretary of State for Defence, it was with a striking lack of candour. Malcolm Rifkind, who had been promoted from the Scottish Office two years earlier, was not told at the departmental briefing that there had been a serious difference of opinion between the board and the reviewing officers; nor was he informed of the exceptional standard of proof required before a verdict of gross negligence could be delivered. Rifkind felt he had no alternative but to accept the report, though he did so with great sadness. Only 11 months later, in May 1995, did he learn that when he made this decision he had not been in full possession of the facts. By then, there was considerable unease outside and inside the RAF about the injustice of the verdict and a feeling that the families of Jonathan Tapper and Rick Cook were being subjected to a cruel ordeal.

In defiance of reason, the Ministry of Defence maintained an intransigence at least equal to that of the reviewing officers. For years it continued to insist that Tapper and Cook were 'undoubtedly in control of the aircraft' at the change of waypoint and that it was not possible for a catastrophic technical failure to remain unnoticed in flight. As they approached land, they should have been aware that their visibility was about to reduce significantly and should have taken appropriate action. The factual evidence 'pointed compellingly to a controlled flight into terrain'.

The change of government in 1997 brought no immediate change in the official narrative despite growing public clamour. The

Scottish MP John Reid was appointed minister of state for the armed forces in Tony Blair's first administration. He informed the House of Commons defence committee in 1998 that he had 'reviewed and scrutinised the circumstances of the crash with a sceptical and compassionate eye, and had found no grounds for over-ruling the board's findings'. Reid might as well have left his compassion at home before reaching this illogical conclusion. Malcolm Rifkind, now in opposition and more than ever anxious that there might have been a miscarriage of justice, approached his successor as defence secretary, Geoff Hoon, with an appeal that the case be reopened. He argued that the reviewing officers had reached their conclusion on the basis of judgement rather than fact and that, although the possibility of gross negligence could not be ruled out, there were many grounds for doubt and the pilots were entitled to the benefit of it. Hoon turned him down.

Reid and Hoon had been persuaded, or had somehow persuaded themselves, to disregard the verdict of a fatal accident inquiry in Scotland (at Paisley Sheriff Court in 1996) that there were insufficient grounds for finding the pilots guilty of gross negligence. The position of Reid and Hoon became increasingly isolated, even risible, when the public accounts committee of the House of Commons, having conducted its own review in 2000, decided that a technical malfunction may have contributed to the crash and exposed the conflict of interest in the RAF's handling of the inquiry. The committee questioned the perceived objectivity of the two reviewing officers, who were among those responsible for keeping the Chinook fleet operational. This anomaly had somehow eluded the sceptical and compassionate eye of the minister of state for the armed forces, but it was no longer eluding parliament. The following year, after yet another inquiry, the House of Lords agreed that the verdict of gross negligence could not be justified.

Painfully slowly, the case against Tapper and Cook unravelled – even in the hierarchy of the RAF itself. One of the air marshals on the board of inquiry, Andrew Pulford, came to regret including any reference to an 'error of judgement'. Pulford said that 'the degree of doubt as to what happened was such that it was unsafe to go into the question of human failings at all, or to try to quantify the degree of error'. He speculated that the pilots might have found themselves in 'a goldfish bowl' while flying over the sea: a condition in which there was no visibly discernible horizon. In that event, their situational awareness might have been compromised, raising the possibility that they became disorientated. They should then have slowed down. But in the absence of any record of what the pilots actually said to each other, it was impossible to know what happened. Was there a failure of communication – or even a disagreement? We would never know. But when Pulford's theory was put to Sir John Day, he was unimpressed. He conceded that the crew may have flown into cloud 'inadvertently' – a marked improvement on the earlier 'consciously and on purpose' – but if that had happened they should have taken decisive and immediate action.

Wratten, likewise, vigorously defended the original finding. He wrote a piece for *Scotland on Sunday* accusing the pilots of putting their passengers in grave danger, 'solely through failing to exercise the skill and judgement of which they were capable'. And when he faced Jeremy Paxman on the BBC's *Newsnight* programme, he showed an ability to trade blows with a hostile interviewer:

Wratten: 'As far as my colleagues and I are concerned, there is no doubt at all. There wasn't then. There isn't now.'
Paxman: 'But that simply can't be true.'
Wratten: 'Well, perhaps you could explain why.'
Paxman: 'Because there is plenty of doubt.'
Wratten: 'And what is that doubt?'

Paxman went over the familiar ground, accusing the air marshal of 'arrogance', a fault sometimes levelled at Paxman himself. Wratten, in his return of serve, resented his interrogator's suggestion that he would jeopardise flight safety in the interests of operational capability.

> Paxman: 'I think the implication is that you were predisposed to find in terms of pilot error because that would keep the Chinook fleet operational . . . It would be like the Concorde disaster being investigated by the boss of Air France'.

A furious air marshal responded that this was 'an extraordinary allegation, which impugns the integrity not only of my colleagues and me, but also of the chief executive of Air France'. He hinted that the chief executive might have something to say about it.

> Paxman: 'The problem is that the accusation against these two men, who are of course in no position to rebut the allegation, is one effectively of manslaughter, no?'
> Wratten: 'Absolutely not. Absolutely not. It is of negligence . . . And failing to discharge their duty of care.'
> Paxman: 'Are you untroubled by this?'
> Wratten: 'Untroubled is a word which doesn't fit easily in a tragedy of this proportion.'
> Paxman: 'Yes.'
> Wratten: 'It is rather unfortunate that you chose to use it.'

The air marshal got slightly the better of the encounter, forcing Paxman into a tight corner though failing to capitalise on the interviewer's ignorance of the law: there was no such crime in Scotland as manslaughter.

Apart from the suggestion, strenuously denied, that their finding of gross negligence had been motivated by operational pragmatism – the need to keep the Chinooks airborne in the continuing battle against the IRA – rather than by considerations of fairness to the dead pilots, Day and Wratten were acutely aware of the public interest in the case. Day feared that, if they had not found the pilots culpable, they would have been accused of 'ducking the issue'. The way he saw it, he had to get the decision 100% right: he could not be too lenient or too harsh and he sincerely believed that the decision was 'the only honest one'. Wratten too was aware of the risk of a whitewash. These admissions confirmed the error of expecting senior officers to serve as impartial adjudicators. While sitting in a quasi-judicial capacity, when they should have been concerned with the evidence and the evidence alone, they allowed an extraneous factor – a concern about how their decision would be received – to influence the decision-making process. That in itself should have disqualified them from the process.

In 1999, a trade magazine, *Computer Weekly*, published the results of an investigation into the Chinook's engine control system. It revealed that, from the start of the upgrade from HG1 to HG2, warning lights would come on, forcing crews to embark on a series of distracting checks – only to discover that there was no apparent problem. Sometimes the engines were in danger of going out of control as the computer system pumped in too much fuel. On other occasions, the opposite happened: the engines would run down. The irregularities left no trace, baffling and disconcerting crews. Might this have been in Jonathan Tapper's mind when he made the call to his commander on the last night of his life?

Ten years later, a second incriminating piece of evidence was leaked to the *Daily Telegraph*: on the day of the crash, a memo to the Ministry of Defence from the military aircraft testing establishment at Boscombe Down in Wiltshire had challenged the reliability of the computer system controlling the Chinook's engines and requested 'in the strongest possible terms' that the RAF should cease HG2 operations until the software programme was thoroughly checked out and verified. Despite this, not only did the flight to Scotland late that afternoon go ahead; the report of the RAF's board of inquiry failed to mention the memo. There were only two possible explanations: the Ministry of Defence unaccountably neglected to forward the memo or the board of inquiry, having received it, attached no special significance to it.

Finally, in 2011, the new Secretary of State for Defence, Liam Fox, ordered an independent inquiry into the accident and appointed a Scottish judge, Lord Philip, to chair it. He was assisted by three privy counsellors: Michael Forsyth, Helen Liddell and Malcolm Bruce. They did a thorough job, producing a report of admirable clarity: the conduct of the original RAF inquiry had been unfair to the deceased aircrew; Rifkind had not been able to make an informed decision; the Ministry of Defence, on a matter involving the reputation of men who died on active service, had adopted an 'extremely regrettable' stance; there could be no certainty about the serviceability of the aircraft and, according to RAF regulations, certainty was what was required; the aircraft had been experiencing a number of malfunctions, the causes of which were not fully understood; neither of the pilots had a record of recklessness – so why would they act in a way contrary to their instincts and training? Day and Wratten had been unwilling to engage in constructive discussion; the debate surrounding the finding of gross negligence had become both polarised and protracted; the loved ones were continuing to suffer distress. The panel's recommendations could not have been more plainly stated: the finding of negligence should be set aside; the Ministry of Defence should offer an apology to the families.

In a statement to the House of Commons in July 2011, Liam Fox accepted the report in full and undertook to give a personal apology to the families. Mike Tapper, the father of Jonathan, said that Day and Wratten should apologise, while Chris Cook, the brother of Rick, told the media that a dreadful wrong had been righted. It had: but it had taken 17 years to wear down the British establishment.

On the internet – the new conduit for fantasists and accusers of all kinds – one fanciful theory succeeded another: the helicopter had been shot down by a surface to air missile, probably launched by Irish republicans; it had been trying to avoid 'a fixed, fuzzy obstacle that they needed to get close to' (this from someone who claimed to be a member of the Royal Navigation Institute and who went on to assert that it had been sabotage and an inside job); and the 'coroner' – there was no such post in Scotland, just as there was no crime of manslaughter – had covered up the fact that everyone on the helicopter had died of gunshot wounds to the head. Aviation experts came up with a more prosaic explanation: that ZD576 had suffered a temporary 'overspeed', forcing it to climb on to the Mull as the pilots fought to bring down the engine speed.

On 31 August 1994, the day of a breakthrough in Northern Ireland, Jonathan Tapper, Rick Cook, their colleagues Graham Forbes and Kevin Hardie, and their 25 distinguished passengers had been dead for almost three months. The IRA declared a ceasefire; the many years of violence were almost at an end.

IV

It was a year of social reform as well as peace: the lowering of the age of consent for homosexual acts between consenting adults from 21 to 18, a measure affecting the whole of the UK. But if it took years to correct individual injustices – as in the Tapper/Cook case or in the earlier scandal of Patrick Meehan – it took a great deal longer to improve the lot of oppressed minorities, especially in Scotland.

Progress on advancing sexual freedoms was not so much gradual as near-glacial. In 1967, when the Wolfenden report recommended that consensual sex between adult men should be decriminalised, the only dissenting voice on the committee was a Scot, James Adair, a Kirk elder and former procurator fiscal, who went on to deliver an inflammatory speech to the General Assembly of the Church of Scotland. Adair claimed that, if the Wolfenden proposals were adopted, it would no longer be illegal for 'perverts to practise sinning for the sake of sinning' and predicted that homosexuals would soon be soliciting vulnerable youths in the streets. The Assembly, clearly impressed by the supposed threat to public morality, voted against Wolfenden by a large majority.

The influence of the church was often cited as one of the main reasons for the long delay in enacting the committee's recommendations in Scotland. It was only in 1980, with the passing of the Criminal Justice (Scotland) Act, that private homosexual acts between consenting adults were finally decriminalised – 13 years after similar legislation was introduced in England and Wales. But the Kirk, an easy target for blame, may have reflected a wider public hostility to homosexuality. In the immediate aftermath of Wolfenden, when the *Daily Record* sought the views of the man and woman in the street on 'THAT' report, it encountered a set of prejudices remarkably similar to those of Adair's. A canteen worker told the paper that 'nothing could be more degrading' than homosexuality; a young shop assistant said that 'innocent people must be protected against these vile creatures'; a member of the armed forces called for 'this disgusting action to be stamped out'. Any hope that the sample might have been unrepresentative was undermined by a readers' poll in which 85% of respondents declared their opposition to Wolfenden – in contrast to a similar poll in England and Wales which found that only 51% opposed it.

In practice, gay men in Scotland were no longer being prosecuted for having sex in the privacy of their own homes. In 1976, the Lord Advocate, Ronald King Murray, stated that in the preceding 10 years there had not been a single prosecution of that kind. But the fact that a succession of chief law officers had exercised their discretion not to prosecute failed to dispose of the issue: as Lord Wilson of Langside (Lord Advocate, 1967–70), pointed out during a House of Lords debate, a future Lord Advocate, a less enlightened one, might take a different view of a law which continued to criminalise homosexual behaviour. A historian of the gay movement, Jeffrey Meek, wrote: 'It appeared not to be in the public interest to prosecute homosexual acts committed in private, even if corroborating evidence existed, as it would serve little more purpose than exposing private and intimate details of the lives of

Scottish homosexuals to public scrutiny. Linked to this was the consistent lack of desire to reveal the ubiquitous nature of homosexuality in Scottish society for the fear that it would encourage further deviation from any heterosexual ideal that was supported by legal institutions, religious institutions and the popular press in Scotland.'

Homosexual acts in public places did continue to be prosecuted occasionally, and in the post-Wolfenden years unattached gay men in Scotland tended to lead furtive lives. Another scholar of the gay movement, Bob Cant, recalled stumbling on a pub in Dundee, the Glass Bucket, close to the bus station, which was unofficially recognised as a gay pub in the early 1970s. On the street outside, 'a lot of ashamed, isolated men tramped up and down, night after night, torn between desire and terror', while inside 'conversations were struck up between men who had previously given every indication of being strangers . . . There was a steady choreographic flow of men as they moved around the pub to position themselves next to other men with whom they imagined they might have something in common.' So foreign was the concept of 'coming out' in this part of Scotland, Cant was convinced that, if anyone had asked the bar staff whether the Glass Bucket was a gay pub, they would have denied it.

Robin Cook's amendment to the Criminal Justice (Scotland) Act, which brought Scotland belatedly into line with England and Wales, was not approved without resistance. The Secretary of State, George Younger, said that although the government would remain neutral on the question, there was no reason why the laws of Scotland and England should be identical, described Cook's amendment as 'not ideal' and insisted that it should be fully discussed; in the end, although 203 MPs voted for the amendment, a stubborn minority of 80 voted against. When the House of Lords came to discuss it, there was more than a hint of old prejudices dying hard: a former Lord Provost of Glasgow, Myer Galpern, equated homosexuality with alcoholism and proposed medical research into the causes in an effort to 'relieve these people of what their indulgences are and what their practices are'. Reflecting on the debates of 1980 a generation later, the journalist David Torrance wrote in near-disbelief that 'for the first three years of my life, what I would become – or rather how that identity would manifest itself – was still deemed "criminal" within the eyes of Scots law'. Torrance added that when he asked his gay friends when private homosexual acts ceased to be criminal in Scotland, there was general astonishment that it was as recently as 1980.

The change in the law had little immediate effect on attitudes. The Criminal Justice (Scotland) Act was not quite dry on the statute book when the *Scotsman* revealed the existence of a Grampian Police handbook attacking the morality of gay men: 'It is a sad reflection on modern society that there are still to be found in our midst persons who are so lewdly disposed that they will stoop to the most revolting and almost unbelievable acts of indecency . . . Consequently no effort is ever spared by the police to suppress this insidious form of evil whenever and wherever it may occur.' The convener of the Scottish Homosexual Rights Group, the lawyer Derek Ogg, said the document was encouraging police officers 'to treat a huge minority of Scottish citizens as alien, evil and morally inferior'. It would have seemed inconceivable then that, in the lifetime of Derek Ogg and David Torrance, Scotland – Scotland, of all places, with its deep-rooted antipathy to homosexuality – would by the early years of the twenty-first century have become one of the most gay-friendly nations in the world.

LIVES OF THE YOUNG

I

KELLY HOLLAND, 17, LEFT HER PARENTS' HOUSE IN HAMILTON ON 20 June 1995. Early next morning, she was spotted by a police patrol 'wandering through the gardens of King Street shouting and wailing, sort of incoherently'. When the police approached, Kelly shouted 'Fuck off and leave me alone'. They arrested her and took her to Hamilton police station. Underneath the sleeve of her sweatshirt, which she was clutching tightly to the palm of her hand, there was a piece of broken bottle. She was charged with breach of the peace, resisting arrest and possession of an offensive weapon, and then put in a cell, where she knocked the glasses off a policeman's face and struck him twice on the neck and shoulders. Three days later she killed herself in Cornton Vale Prison, Stirling.

Until the age of 14, Kelly had been a bright, motivated girl; and then something happened; something never explained. Her father recalled: 'She would be very unpredictable. She would be sitting having her lunch and two minutes later she would go out a window. Never the door, always a window for some reason. I found her sleeping in doorways, in bus stations. And when you found her it was like she didn't realise she had been away. I used to say things like "Where have you been?" "Naewhere." "Where are you going?" "Coming hame." It was as if she had done nothing wrong.'

In 1992, she was detained – sectioned – under the Mental Health Act in Hairmyres Hospital before being transferred to a psychiatric unit in Livingston. She absconded and was found in Newcastle with a paracetamol bottle containing 100 tablets. No longer considered clinically depressed or suicidal, she was discharged from the unit and resumed her erratic life. 'She has been traumatised in some way and is bothered with a deep-rooted anxiety which she is unable to share yet,' concluded a social inquiry report in October 1994. 'She would never give you any information,' said her father, 'she kept everything to herself.' A social worker, Allan English, found it difficult to engage her in conversation or to make any progress with her. 'I never found she displayed any extreme emotions. I don't think anyone had any definite explanation as to why she was behaving like that.'

Kelly was arrested many times, mostly for breach of the peace, and was a frequent visitor to Cornton Vale, Scotland's only women's prison. Two weeks before her death, she faced yet another court appearance for conducting herself in a disorderly manner by attempting to throw herself out of the first-floor window of a house. The police put it down to drunkenness, but the procurator fiscal depute at Hamilton, Stewart Cassidy, decided not to prosecute. 'As a person without any medical qualifications or experience, I was just concerned about her mental welfare, given the nature of the evidence against her.' Instead, he referred her to a doctor.

The police casualty surgeon who examined her, Dr Michael O'Keefe, found her quiet, co-operative and polite. Kelly had no memory of the events of the previous night, but was able to inform him that she had been drinking – two bottles of Buckfast and two bottles of cider. She said she had no intention of trying to kill herself. 'Kelly said she was too old for all this. Those were her exact words. She was 17 years of age, and she'd been in trouble with the police for several years.' O'Keefe formed the opinion that she was not certifiable under the Mental Health Act, but that she had an immature personality with addictive traits. He decided that she was suffering from a personality disorder.

Only briefly, if at all, did this deeply vulnerable girl ever receive the therapeutic care and treatment that might have saved her life. By the night of her final arrest, she was an enigma – to her family, to her social workers and to the medical profession. To the police, however, she was simply a persistent nuisance. One of the arresting officers on 20 June, Graham Rankin, 26, told a fatal accident inquiry into her death that he had no cause to believe that Kelly was in any way disturbed; they had had dealings with her in the past 'and she was always quite aggressive towards the police'. Asked what training he had been given to identify individuals exhibiting signs of a psychiatric condition, he replied: 'No training whatsoever.'

Another of the procurator fiscal deputes at Hamilton, Maureen Sinclair, shared her colleague Stewart Cassidy's acute concern and was aware of Kelly's suicidal tendencies. Anticipating that she would be remanded in custody, Sinclair telephoned the police with an unusual request: she asked the police to alert the prison authorities to the fact that Kelly was a possible suicide risk. The duty police officer at Hamilton Sheriff Court, Adam Angus, had no recollection of speaking to the fiscal and suggested that she must have spoken to someone else. If he had spoken to her, and he was satisfied that the information was 'not just a hearsay comment', he would have raised a special risk form, which would have accompanied the prisoner into custody. But the system broke down at once: there was no special risk form; in the end, neither of the humanitarian gestures of the prosecution service at Hamilton counted for anything.

After her arrest, Kelly spent the rest of the night and the whole of the following day and night in police custody before being taken to court at 8 am on 22 June. By then she had been alone in a cell with virtually no human contact for 32 hours. Just as Maureen Sinclair predicted, she was remanded to Cornton Vale Prison to await sentence. She finally arrived there at 6 pm on 22 June.

A prison officer, Carol Anne Mercer, described the procedure: 'The police bring them in, take the handcuffs off them. One of us checks the warrants and another officer checks them bodily to see if they have anything in their pockets. They are then placed in a cubicle. Once they've been strip-searched they are given the chance of a bath or a shower. Once that has been done, the nurse officer has usually arrived and one by one they start seeing the nurse officer as well. In between times they get offered a cup of tea and a sandwich.'

That evening there were 10 arrivals, of whom half were judged to be in need of regular observation in their cells. There were four levels of observation according to the perceived degree of risk: every 15 minutes, every 30 minutes, every 60 minutes, and SSS (strict suicide supervision). If a special risk form had been attached to Kelly's warrant, as Maureen Sinclair had requested, she would have been placed automatically on SSS (also known as 'Triple S' or 'sui'). After the nurse officer, William Rock, saw Kelly Holland he made the following note: 'Alcohol abuse. Two to three bottles of wine and Budweiser approximately two days ago. Very quiet and apprehensive. Previous history of attempted suicide. Fifteen minutes obs. meantime. States that she is not going to harm herself.'

For each new inmate, a door card was attached to the cell door. It was colour-coded by religious affiliation: green for Roman Catholics, white for Church of Scotland, pink for Church of England (the policy made no provision for smaller denominations or for atheists). The card contained the prisoner's name, date of birth, date of admission, details of any psychiatric or medical reports, and on the back a note of the charge or charges against the prisoner. When a prison officer, Gloria Graham, went to reception to escort Kelly to the remand block, she turned the door card over. 'I said to her, "My, haven't you been busy?", and she said, "Yeah, I know." I then asked her how she was feeling and she said "A bit gutted", and when she was last in the prison and she said "Only a few weeks ago". By that time we had entered the remand block and I asked Kelly how old she was and she replied that she was only 17.' Graham saw no special significance in the remark about being gutted; it was a term prisoners often used.

Kelly was allocated Cell 2, Unit 3, in the remand block, also known as Romeo, and transferred to the supervision of a second officer, Pauline Mitchell, who left her chatting to a fellow inmate, Arlene Elliot. Mitchell next saw Kelly at lock-up time, around 8.45 pm. 'She was in the kitchen getting a cup of tea for going to her room. She was joking and laughing with the rest of the girls.' Fifteen minutes later, now in her cell, Kelly asked Mitchell for a pen and a light. Mitchell thought she seemed fine: there was no reason to believe that there was anything wrong with her. Karen Minty, a prisoner, shouted over to her from the cell opposite to ask if she was all right. 'She just said yes. You can't really have a conversation. I heard him [a prison officer, John McFadyen] speaking to Kelly. He just sort of poked his head through the hatch and asked if she was all right, and she said yes, she was all right'.

It was McFadyen's responsibility to check Kelly every 15 minutes. On two or three of his 'obs', he noticed she was writing a letter. He didn't 'actually physically see her crying', though he reported that her eyes seemed slightly red. On a further visit around 12.30 am, she was lying on her bed, apparently asleep. Fifteen minutes later, he checked her cell again and saw a silhouette at the window. 'It was a particularly hot night, and I thought she was just getting some air from the window. I asked Kelly was she okay, was everything okay, shone a torch in, and that's when I noticed the ligature from the top half. I immediately realised the enormity of the situation.' He was asked at the inquiry if there was any sign of life. 'There was none. I was looking for a wee bit, a gasp, anything, but there was nothing.' Looking around the room afterwards, one of the prison nurses, Colin MacLeod, noticed an envelope on top of Kelly's bed. In all probability it had been concealed under the pillow and disturbed during the attempt at resuscitation. The letter was a farewell note to her parents in which she said she had never felt so alone and that she was crying, that she couldn't stop crying.

A prisoner across the yard, Ethel Arkley, 18, who was tossing and turning, unable to sleep, got out of bed to open the window and saw Kelly hanging – suspended by a white bedsheet – in the cell directly opposite. McFadyen was holding her up. Other officers arrived and Arkley heard someone saying that Kelly had been a silly girl and 'We'll need to get an ambulance'. She saw two officers giving her mouth-to-mouth resuscitation. Then an officer closed the hatch and she could no longer see anything. Later she was moved to something resembling a padded cell for what was left of the night. It was bare except for a mattress. She was stripped of her normal clothes, put into Bermuda shorts, given valium, and told to go to sleep and not make a fuss. When she was unlocked at 6.30 the next morning, there was no mention of Kelly Holland's death. She was seen by a doctor, who said he would give her a 'sleeper' (prison argot for mogadon). Ethel Arkley was not too sedated to observe that, for several days afterwards, 'everything was being done bang on time, really efficient . . . then on Sunday they went to church and had a service for Kelly.'

II

Arlene Elliot – the girl with whom Kelly Holland was seen chatting on her admission to Cornton Vale – was the same age as Kelly – 17 – and, like her, a habitual offender. On 2 May 1995 she had been seen by the prison psychiatrist, Dr Margaret Morrison. 'She gave me a two-month history of auditory hallucinations, of hearing voices. She said they were usually pleasant, then they became derogatory and then imperative. They told her to harm herself by pulling her hair and by punching her abdomen. She said that she had a recent stomach upset with vomiting and she said this had been as a result of the voices. The voices had told her that she was fat and that she should vomit. They had threatened to kill her if she told anyone and she also believed that people were looking at her and laughing at her . . . I found her to be very distressed and disturbed. I concluded that she was suffering from a psychotic disorder'.

There were striking similarities with Kelly's story. Arlene too was 14 when an abrupt change in her personality transformed her from a quiet, churchgoing girl with an interest in the cello to someone rootless and unpredictable. She too would disappear without warning – but in her case for weeks at a time. 'I felt she was a young girl who probably didn't know where she was going or where she wanted to be,' said her social worker, Marie Moran. 'Quite a pathetic young girl.' Her mother, Roseanne McKay, was clear about the root of the problem: 'Drugs. God knows what she was into. You could just guess, actually. She was snorting heroin. Injecting it at the end, I believe. She was always talking to herself, with a faraway look. We thought it was the drugs.'

Margaret Morrison learned that Arlene had been taking up to £100 worth of heroin and up to 30 temazapan capsules a day, depending on what money she had available, and that she also consumed LSD, amphetamine and ecstasy on a more occasional basis. Morrison placed her on strict suicide supervision because of the obvious risk that she would harm herself, and contacted Dr Robert Hunter, consultant psychiatrist at Gartnavel Hospital, with an urgent request that he should examine her; it was Morrison's opinion that she was detainable under the Mental Health Act.

Hunter and a senior nurse from Gartnavel arrived at the prison by prior arrangement around 4.30 pm on 10 May and were surprised to be told at the gatehouse that they were not expected and that the prison was closing down for an hour and a half or longer. He testified to the public inquiry: 'I said to her, well, I think it's very important that you let us in, we've made this effort, we need to get in, and she said, well, I don't think you'll get in, but I will go and see what I can do, and we had a seat for perhaps 15 minutes or so. She then called us back and said, no, we can't let you in, it's the prison regulations, you understand.' Hunter left without seeing Arlene Elliot. On the same day, a medical officer at the prison noted in her records: 'Arlene is now very much more settled. The voices no longer tell her to harm herself or others. However, she has had her hair cut in order that the voices cannot make her pull it out.' She remained in prison, where her condition seemed to improve; Margaret Morrison now regarded community care as a more suitable option.

Arlene was released from Cornton Vale later in the month, only to be sent back on 30 May – remanded on a minor shoplifting charge. The nurse officer, William Rock, who testified that he had been under too much pressure at the time of her re-admission to read her medical notes, contented himself with the impression that she seemed 'fine' – a favourite word of prison officialdom – and put her on low 'obs' (every 60 minutes). A consultant clinical psychologist, Dr Kevin Power, criticised Rock's complacency at the screening interview: 'I see very little point in having information available that is not taken into consideration when arriving at a judgement.'

Arlene resumed her habit of sleeping a great deal. The prison officer Pauline Mitchell saw her asleep in her cell just before lunch-time one day, but it caused Mitchell no particular concern. She explained that many of 'the girls' went to bed during the day and that about three-quarters of them were medicated in some way. The drug administered in Arlene's case was largactil – 'enough to knock a horse out' according to a fellow inmate. Margaret Morrison agreed that it would have made her feel sleepy and expressed dissatisfaction about the daily routine of remand prisoners. 'Much of the time is spent doing very little', she said. The street chat in Cornton Vale was that if you were put on largactil you ended up a zombie.

Just after midnight on 23 June, Kelly Holland committed suicide. Arlene was understandably distressed by the news. Later that day, one of the prison medical officers, Dr Alexander Stuart, received a report that she was over-sedated. He confirmed that, at that stage, she was on largactil of 125 milligrammes three times a day and diazepam of 10 milligrammes three times a day, but insisted that the drug was 'actually helping her psychotic symptoms'.

'On the 23rd of June?' he was asked at the inquiry.

'On the 23rd of June.'

'But then she commits suicide on the 26th of June?'

'I can't comment in terms of her psychotic symptoms, those were being treated.'

On 23 June, Margaret Morrison interviewed Arlene for the last time. They discussed her feelings about Kelly's death. 'She took a fatalistic view,' said Morrison. 'She used an old Glasgow term, "What's for you will no' go by you." That was the term she used, which was what gave her comfort. She felt that SSS was a form of punishment, that it would be very restrictive to her. She knew that she would be placed in a stripped cell and that she wouldn't have access to her friends.' Morrison considered that SSS would have been counter-productive – that it would have caused a deterioration in her mental state – and so placed her on 30-minute observation. The next day she was taken off all observation.

On the warm afternoon of 26 June, some of the remand prisoners were allowed out to sunbathe. 'Arlene came into the office to ask for some suntan cream,' recalled Margaret Reilly, a prison officer. 'We had a bit of a laugh and a joke between us. Arlene had her T-shirt tucked up inside her bra and her bottoms tucked down trying to get as much sun as possible, and we were joking about her getting quite brown, and she just seemed pretty happy at that time'. Early that evening, according to another officer, Moira Grattan, she was 'in and out of her room, dealing with washing . . . I remember her in the sitting room, hanging up clothes. I believe she was getting ready for a bath.'

Around 7.30 pm, Ethel Arkley – who was still recovering from the trauma of witnessing Kelly hanging – went to Arlene's cell. The door was closed and she got no response. She looked through the spyhole.

'And what did you see?'

'I seen Arlene, I opened the door into her room, I just seen Arlene's face blue and then opened the door further to see if I was seeing things and . . .'.

'What position was she in when you saw her?'

'A nightdress was hanging round her neck.'

'Nightdress hanging round her neck?'

'Yes.'

'And you thought her face was blue?'

'Yes. I froze when I opened the door and I looked at her face.'

'Did she seem to be breathing?'

'No.'

'Did you notice anything else about her physical appearance, her face or anything of that sort?'

'Her eyes were pretty white.'

'And what was your reaction?'

'I was frightened and I started panicking. I ran down the bottom of the hall and I say to Miss Granton, "Miss, miss, miss," but she walked away from me. I put my hands on my head and shouted, "Somebody help me, Arlene's hung herself." Then Miss McMurtrie came running down from Unit 6.'

'And what happened after that?'

'One of the nurses came along and shut the door, and the prisoners came along, and one says what's wrong, what's wrong with Arlene? and I said Arlene's hung herself and Anne Dodds grabbed me and took me to my room.'

'Took you to your room?'

'And I started crying and officers locked us up.'

After a second suicide within three days, the regime at Cornton Vale faced intense media scrutiny. Arlene Elliot's mother denounced a system in which troubled 17-year-old girls were locked up with murderers: 'It's wrong, totally wrong, from the bottom to the top . . . There should be something done about it.' As witness after witness testified, very little was done about it. Rock, the nurse officer, was sent on a suicide prevention management course; prison officers might have read a booklet on the subject with more care than before; one or two said they had gone on training days. The hospital wing, built in the mid-1980s as a response to the AIDS scare but hardly ever used, remained mothballed. And the depute governor, William Low, giving evidence to the inquiry, could not remember whether the death of Arlene Elliot had even been discussed by the prison's medical review board.

When he was asked if he had implemented any changes in the light of the two suicides, Low replied: 'Basically, no.'

'Did you come to the conclusion, then, that no change to the regime was required?'

'The regime as it was seemed reasonable.'

After hearing the evidence, Sheriff Principal John Maguire found that both deaths had been caused by the deliberate acts of the deceased. If Arlene Elliot, 'a person of considerable vulnerability', had been maintained on strict suicide supervision after Kelly Holland's death, she might not have committed suicide. 'However, there is nothing except hindsight to suggest that the doctors' decisions were wrong.' In the case of Kelly Holland, 'a disturbed girl', he said he did not think that confusion among police officers about the issue of a special risk form had anything to do with her death. None of the police officers dealing with her case in Hamilton had thought her a suicide risk. The sheriff concluded that there were no defects in the system, nor any reasonable precautions which could have been taken to prevent the deaths of Kelly Holland and Arlene Elliot. He made no recommendations.

How could the sheriff have come to such a perverse finding? How could he have supported so inadequate a regime?

As he pointed out, the police in Hamilton did not regard Kelly Holland as a suicide risk. What he did not point out was that two members of the procurator fiscal's department took the opposite view. One dropped a charge of breach of the peace alleging that she had attempted to throw herself out of a window; another was so concerned about her suicidal tendencies that she called the police and asked them to alert Cornton Vale Prison by the issue of a special risk form. Whoever received this request forgot or neglected to contact the prison, but there was no suggestion that the person responsible was ever disciplined. It was just another day in court.

Kelly's father expressed disbelief that his daughter was kept on 15-minute observation. It seems more likely that she was observed every 15 minutes but that the duty prison officer failed to realise the significance of her red eyes as she wrote what turned out to be a suicide note. Prison officers in Stirling, no less than police officers in Hamilton, were largely untutored in suicide prevention – was this not 'a defect in the system'?

Arlene Elliot, who had attempted suicide more than once, seemed 'fine' to the nurse officer, Rock, when she was admitted on 30 May. Only in cross-examination did it emerge that he had not read her case-notes in full before placing her on 60-minute observation. Sheriff Principal Maguire sounded mildly perturbed by this disclosure when he heard it in evidence, but evidently the lax screening procedures did not amount to 'a defect in the system'.

A few weeks earlier, Arlene's state of mind was so poor that Dr Morrison decided that she should be sectioned under the Mental Health Act. But when the consultant psychiatrist from Gartnavel Hospital arrived to assess her, he was refused admission to see the patient. Did such bureaucratic inflexibility not represent 'a defect in the system'?

The inquiry's resident psychologist, Dr Power, who was allowed to sit through the evidence before giving an expert summing-up, concluded that, short of shackling prisoners to their beds, nothing could be done to eliminate the risk of suicide. There were, however, occasional hints that a safer and more therapeutic regime might have been possible. Dr Morrison considered that prisoners at risk should be cared for by nurses in a prison hospital rather than observed by officers in a stripped cell. Prompted by her evidence, the inquiry should have grasped the opportunity to recommend the opening of the Cornton Vale hospital, both as a 'reasonable precaution' and as a humane reform.

Instead, the inquiry implicitly supported the degrading conse-quences of strict suicide supervision. In the case of Arlene Elliot, a teenage schizophrenic was stripped, forced to wear humiliating clothing, put in a cell furnished by a mattress on a concrete floor, denied personal belongings or the most basic creature comforts, and incarcerated in total isolation. When Prison Watch, the UK prisons watchdog, referred to a country which stood 'virtually alone internationally in using the archaic stripped cell and the 15-minute observation system for suicide risk inmates', he was speaking of Scotland. The inquiry report made no criticism of the practice; nor did it have anything to say about the shaming inhumanity of a penal policy which remanded girls as young as 17 to an adult prison when they were of no danger to anyone but themselves.

Shortly after the deaths of Kelly Holland and Arlene Elliot, two more inmates of Cornton Vale took their own lives. In the face of this succession of self-inflicted deaths of girls and young women for whom the state had a duty of care, the chief executive of the Scottish Prison Service insisted that there was no crisis. There was something worse: a barbarity with no place in a civilised society.

III

While Kelly Holland and Arlene Elliot, their lives already wrecked by drink and drugs, aimlessly wandered the streets of Lanarkshire between their frequent visits to prison, two unemployed 19-year-old youths, Andrew Dick and John Nisbet, went in search of cheap thrills to the seaside. The Pavilion (or 'Piv'), an old-fashioned dance hall close to Ayr beach, once the setting for nothing riskier than adolescent sexual fumbling, had been appropriated as a rave venue called Hanger 13.

Andrew and John lived in two of the most deprived places in the west of Scotland: Andrew in Possilpark, a desperately poor ghetto of Glasgow; John in the post-industrial village of New Cumnock.

On 30 April 1994, the two lads headed independently to the regular weekend rave in Ayr; and for a few hours the grimness of being out of work in Possilpark and New Cumnock could be forgotten.

John was accompanied by Gillian, a year older than himself, also unemployed, also from New Cumnock. On the bus to Ayr, a journey of 40 minutes, Gillian drank a full bottle of Buckfast, a cheap wine produced in Devon at a monastery of the same name, by men of God ultra-sensitive to criticism of their product. Inside Hanger 13, she took an ecstasy tablet. She explained that it had a special marking, that of a dove, 'a wee white dove', and that it made her feel happy. Her boyfriend John Nisbet, who had not been drinking on the bus, made up for it at the rave, swallowing one and a half ecstasy pills.

Another of the New Cumnock contingent, Brian, explained to the fatal accident inquiry how it worked at Hanger 13. If you wanted 'stuff', you tended to buy as a group, each member contributing his share – a 'whip-round' as the sheriff, Neil Gow, jauntily put it. Someone was delegated to approach a dealer. There was never a dearth of dealers. That night, the go-between returned with nine Es at £13 each: a single transaction worth £117.

Brian swallowed one pill, another an hour later. They made you want to dance, and you became hotter and hotter; and before long you were making your way to the bar for a bottle of water – another £1; and once you'd drunk your water you took the empty to the Gents and filled up from the tap; and that kept you going for the rest of the night. Unless you were John Nisbet, who didn't keep going. He was ill-advisedly dressed for the occasion in a fluorescent orange jacket and a baseball cap, with joggers under his trousers. His friends warned him that, if he insisted on wearing all that clobber, he would be unable to withstand the heat. Later in the evening the stewards found him sitting alone, legs crossed, shaking and sweating, speechless, drifting into unconsciousness. They dragged him into the bracing air and called for an ambulance. It was 12.30 am. 'I found a young gentleman being supported by two security guards', noted the ambulanceman. 'He was quite delirious. He was throwing himself about and could not be restrained.'

Inside the hall, Andrew Dick was high on drugs, though not yet in a state of collapse. His mother had understood that Andrew was going clubbing in the city. Unknown to her, he and his friends had hired two taxis to take them the 30 miles to Ayr. They arrived at Hanger 13 around 10 pm, instructed the taxis to wait, and agreed to rendezvous outside the venue at 2 am for the journey home. The economics of the jaunt, for a group of mostly unemployed young people, were baffling. A share of the taxi would have cost each of them £20, admission to the rave £9, a bottle of water £1, and (say) one E, £15 – a total of £45 a head; though probably more, depending on the number of Es bought on the premises.

One witness recalled Andrew Dick's excitement as he waited in the queue to be lightly frisked for drugs. He was 'happy, jumpin' aboot, couldnae wait to get inside' – for his fix of ecstasy. Within a few hours, he was 'fu' o' it, no' in a stable way, fu' o' drugs, just walkin' aboot hissel'. At 2.25 am, a second ambulance had to be called. 'Patient unconscious,' reported the paramedics. 'Possible drugs. We found him outside, propped up against a wall. We tried to rouse him, but there was no way we could get any response.'

It had been a busy night at Hanger 13. Clare, a 20-year-old student from Paisley, had to be hospitalised with convulsions after taking half a tablet. Scott, 21, was told by his regular supplier that demand was so high he had sold out. He got the stuff from someone else – the first person he asked. When he returned home, his fingers became tingly, he began to hallucinate, he felt sick. They took him to hospital and put him on a heart machine; all this on one E. Had he taken ecstasy since? Yeah: a few times.

Dr Leo Murray, head of the accident and emergency unit at Ayr Hospital, was called from home to attend to John Nisbet. He found that the patient's pulse was extraordinarily fast, that he wasn't responding to pain, that he was very hot, and that his brain wasn't functioning properly. Suspecting ecstasy, Dr Murray contacted the national poisons service for advice. Two hours later, Andrew Dick arrived: 'an exact re-run'. John died at 11.30 am on Sunday morning; Andrew lingered until 11.30 pm that night. On Monday, Helen Dick called the police to report her son's apparent disappearance.

When Leo Murray graduated in 1979, he had never heard of ecstasy. By the mid-1990s, its use was commonplace; according to one survey at least 10% of young people in the age-range 14 to 19 took it as a dance drug and mood enhancer. Murray decided to accompany the ambulance service to a rave – not Hanger 13 – to observe the phenomenon for himself. He saw hundreds of people with widely dilated pupils. As he explained to the inquiry: 'If we're jumping around at a rave in a high ambient temperature, and we've just popped a pill, and we're not replacing fluid, there comes a point at which the body's ability to control its temperature at 37 degrees fails. Our system breaks down with profound results. We start to bleed spontaneously. Clots develop all over the body. We're wrecked.'

Among young people themselves, there was a growing acknowl-edgment of the risks. Lucy from Clydebank wrote to the clubbing magazine *M8*: 'The experts have told us of the dangers and a lot of us have experienced them. What do you do when you're so overjoyed dancing but you find you can't really breathe properly. Your legs start to feel rubbery and you need to take a five-minute break. You are so hot and no matter how much you drink, you can't cool down. You start to panic, which makes your breathing worse and causes your racing heart to pump even faster. What kind of happiness is this?'

IV

Four months after the deaths of John Nisbet and Andrew Dick, Hanger 13 was still open and more popular than ever. On 20 August 1994, Derek Hamilton celebrated his birthday by organising a bus to take himself and 14 friends, including Andrew Stoddart, from the Lanarkshire village of Rigside to the rave at Ayr. In the local pub, where the group met, Andrew asked 18-year-old Craig if he would share an E and Craig agreed, on the understanding that it was normal to take an E before a rave. Andrew swallowed his half while waiting in the queue outside Hanger 13.

Inside the hall, he spent £45 on three more tablets and showed them to his girlfriend Clare, a non-user. He took the first with water; then another; Clare said she didn't know what happened to the third. Later, Andrew complained of not feeling well; his legs were sore and he was having difficulty controlling them. She called a steward and he was dragged outside. She couldn't tell whether he was conscious. Another of the Rigside crowd, Lorraine, 18, heard someone say that he would be 'OK in a few minutes', that he was just dehydrated. 'It was as if he was having a fit,' said a third witness. 'They got him out of the building and round the corner to a play park. He lay on the ground and they tried to resuscitate him. He was sick. They turned him over on his side. It was raining heavily. They called an ambulance.' Dr Leo Murray received him in A&E: 'Clinically this young man was dead when he arrived. I was struck by the fact that his muscles were rigid. We tried to stimulate an already dead heart. There was no response. He felt hot to the touch. I declared him dead at 1.20 am.' Three hours later, after the police had noted the names of everybody inside Hanger 13, the party from Rigside was driven the short distance to Ayr police station and informed that Andrew Stoddart was dead. He would have been 21 on Christmas Day 1994.

There was an extraordinarily thorough police investigation, led by Detective Inspector John Corrigan. He and his team did a full count: there were 1,288 people in attendance that night, including 39 staff, of whom the police failed to trace only 80. All the others were systematically questioned in an inquiry which consumed 10,000 police hours – 'one of the largest investigations ever conducted in this area', as Corrigan assured the fatal accident inquiry. And the analysis was impressive: it disclosed, for example, that more than half of the paying customers had travelled from outside Ayrshire, some from as far afield as Tayside, Galloway, Lothian and Borders, even four from England; and that, despite the door check, 17% were under-age, including some as young as 13 and 14. Most revealingly of all, the police estimated that 25 people at Hanger 13 were dealing.

From the statistics provided by this admirable police work, it was possible to extrapolate others. The gate receipts, based on an attendance of 1,249 at £9 a head, amounted to more than £11,000. Multiplied by 52, this yielded an annual revenue for the Saturday rave ('dance night' as the management preferred to call it) of almost £600,000. But if the police were accurate in their assessment of the number of dealers, and in their expert view that 50% of those attending bought ecstasy tablets, and if each of the punters bought just one E at an average cost of £13, the illegal revenue on a Saturday night at the Piv exceeded £8,000 – more than £300 per dealer. Multiplied by 52, this produced an annual illicit revenue of £421,000, making drug dealing at Hanger 13 one of the more profitable local businesses. There was no suggestion that the management or its employees were implicated.

The proprietor, Christine Ridha, was closely questioned by Jack Drummond, uncle of Andrew Stoddart, who represented the Stoddart family at the inquiry. Drummond asked her whether it was fair to charge customers an extra £1 for water, having charged £9 at the door.

> Ridha: 'I have no problem with that.'
> Drummond: 'We've heard that water is essential.'
> Ridha: 'I am supplying an entertainment venue, not a place for taking drugs. I have to pay for my water, and I think the price is reasonable.'

Sheriff Gow agreed that it was proper to charge for water. He wondered about the ventilation of the premises, but suggested that a full air-conditioning system would be expensive. Ridha responded that the possibility of such a system was being considered.

> Gow: 'Dancing in a warm atmosphere is part of the scene, I suppose? They don't expect to be dancing in the freezing cold?'

The sheriff appeared to be doing the witness's work for her. But one of the stranger features of the case – the partial failure of the water supply – went largely unscrutinised. Several witnesses had referred to it, one testifying that 'the water was turned off in one of the toilets' and that 'the pressure wasn't strong in one of the others'. The management agreed that there was 'a problem one night' (the night Andrew Stoddart died), but added that it was a failure of the public supply. The Crown failed to call an official of the water department to substantiate the complaint. Nor did it produce expert witnesses to testify to the quality of the ventilation. When the procurator fiscal suggested to the manager, Ridha's son, that 'outside the hall is what they [the stewards] consider a cool area', he got a nod in response.

Drummond, in his summing-up, criticised the lack of a cool environment, the ease with which drugs could be obtained, and the inadequate stewarding of the large crowd (only 20 stewards for 1,249 customers). But the sheriff's determination, published in February 1995, was another example of Scottish judicial cop-out: Gow decided that most of the matters raised 'should be left to the discretion of the management' and made no recommendations. The local Tory MP, Phil Gallie, a well-known zealot on questions of law and order, actively supported Hanger 13 in its campaign to stay open, claiming that its presence in the community prevented the drugs problem from being driven underground; he even turned up as guest of honour at a 'Save the Hanger, Save the Scene' night.

It seemed there was no limit to the wilful blindness of the authorities to the wretched lives of many young people, in prison or out of it. It seemed there was no end to the collective complacency. What would shake official Scotland out of that complacency? Would anything? Then something did.

1996

ONE OF US

I

Thomas Hamilton, a 43-year-old organiser of boys' clubs, spent the last afternoon of his life in the house of Agnes Watt, 64, whom he had been brought up to believe was his sister. Their close relationship appears to have been unimpaired by the revelation that Watt was not his sister but his mother. They kept in touch by telephone and he visited her regularly. He was with her on Tuesday 12 March 1996, arriving around 2 pm, leaving four hours later. Watt noticed nothing unusual about him; he was the same as always. He had a bath – he had no bath in his own house, only a shower, which he disliked – and something to eat, and they had a talk: 'a blether' as Watt called it.

When Hamilton was three years old, his parents divorced and he was adopted by his maternal grandparents. He moved with them from Glasgow to Stirling, where he attended Riverside Secondary School and got a job as an apprentice draughtsman in the county architect's office. From the age of 20 he was self-reliant, setting up a DIY shop known as Woodcraft, which traded profitably for some years in Cowane Street, Stirling; and soon after opening the shop he became an assistant Scout leader in the town. Briefly he was to all outward appearances something of a model citizen. By the late 1980s, however, his world was collapsing: the business had folded (a victim of cut-price DIY chains, perhaps), he had been blacklisted by the Scouts as a suspected paedophile, and his adoptive mother had died, leaving him to share a house at 7 Kent Road, Stirling, with his adoptive father, James. Registered unemployed, he was dabbling in freelance photography and trading in cameras, while pursuing his twin recreations: boys and guns.

'Thomas was always a very calm person, certainly in the house,' his adoptive father recalled. 'There were never any moods or tempers. He never showed any violence at home, he never raised his hands to me at any time. I never knew Thomas to ever have a girlfriend and he never went out socialising. Never went dancing or out drinking. I don't think that he ever drank, and he never smoked. He had his own friends to visit at Kent Road, but I never took any interest. I don't know who they were. When they came they would either go into Thomas's bedroom or into the living room and I would go into my bedroom.'

'They didn't get on,' admitted Agnes Watt, who was living else-where in Stirling. 'You see, my daddy drinks and he used to come in and Tommy would be in his bed and he would wake him up and start arguing with him.' By 1992 the relationship had deteriorated to such an extent that the adoptive father went to the council for help; they offered him sheltered housing. 'The reason I moved out,' he said, 'was that Thomas began to take over the whole house. He moved all my personal possessions and items of furniture into my bedroom, some pictures I had on the wall, and my telephone and other personal items. I just could not be bothered with it all and Stirling District Council arranged for me to move. I did occasionally see Thomas in the streets of Stirling or in the Thistle Centre [a local shopping mall], but we just ignored each other and walked on. I never stopped to speak with him.' From August 1992, Thomas Hamilton lived alone at 7 Kent Road.

Although he was long ostracised from his adoptive father, Hamilton was clearly still bothered by him. He was the subject of the afternoon 'blether' with Agnes Watt on 12 March 1996. When she was questioned later, Watt had little to say about their final conversation, but insisted that talking about James had not upset or annoyed 'Tommy' in any way. Agnes Watt waited for him to phone in the evening, which he invariably did after one of their meetings. But there was no call. She wondered why.

Hamilton, a serial complainer, had been busy in the preceding few days. He had sent a letter personally addressed to the Queen at Buckingham Palace signed 'Your Obedient Servant, Thomas W Hamilton'. It began: 'I understand you are Patron of the Scout Association and in that capacity I would like to make you aware of my long-standing complaint [against the association].' The complaint was undeniably long-standing; it went back 22 years. At a meeting with him in 1974, the county commissioner, Brian Fairgrieve, formed the impression that Hamilton had a persecution complex and delusions of grandeur, that his actions verged on the paranoid, and that his moral intentions towards boys were dubious. Fairgrieve wrote to Scottish Scout headquarters: 'While unable to give concrete evidence against this man, I feel that too many "incidents" relate to him such that I am far from happy about his having any association with the Scouts.' Fairgrieve went on to mention two occasions when he took boys – 'favourites' – with him on expeditions to Aviemore and they all stayed together overnight in his van. 'The lack of precaution for such activities,' wrote Fairgrieve, 'displays either irresponsibility or an ulterior motive for sleeping with the boys.'

Kicked out of the Scouts, Hamilton responded by setting up his own sports clubs, 15 of them during the period 1981–96, in Central, Lothian, Fife and Strathclyde regions, for boys between the ages of 7 and 11. They tended to be held on school premises that Hamilton rented from local authorities. The respectable choice of location may have conferred, in the minds of parents, a certain legitimacy on the project, particularly as Hamilton promoted his clubs, through leaflet drops, in a fairly professional way.

In the small commuter town of Dunblane, seven miles from Stirling, a 10-year-old boy, Malcolm Robertson, attended the local High School for one of Hamilton's clubs. One evening, Malcolm failed to show up and Hamilton wrote to him demanding an explanation: it had the whiff of a personal reprimand. The boy's mother was incensed by the letter and phoned Hamilton. 'He is in the Cubs, he goes to school, he goes to a swimming club,' she told him. 'If he is absent from them, they don't write to him, they write to me as the parent.' There was not much response: Hamilton remained strangely calm.

The boy's father, George Robertson, shadow secretary of state for Scotland, decided to visit the club unannounced with a friend and fellow parent: 'We were both struck very quickly by the bizarre nature of what was going on. There were a large number of small boys in shorts stripped to the waist being bossed around by two or three middle-aged men, swaggering around in a very military-type way. It looked like the Hitler Youth.' The Robertsons decided that their son should not return. The next night, Hamilton turned up on the door-step asking to speak to Malcolm. George Robertson ordered him to leave with the parting shot: 'I don't have to give you reasons why a 10-year-old boy is not coming back.' He was concerned enough to contact the local MP, who happened to be his Tory opposite number, the Secretary of State for Scotland, Michael Forsyth. 'Confronted by Mr Forsyth's questions about what precisely I was talking about,' said Robertson, 'I found myself in the same difficulties that so many other people had: that it was difficult to put your finger on what people felt was wrong with Thomas Hamilton.' Forsyth was aware of the rumours about Hamilton, but also aware that Hamilton felt he was being judged by innuendo rather than hard fact. In that sense, the story had not moved on since 1974, when Brian Fairgrieve had been 'unable to give concrete evidence against this man'.

Hamilton polarised opinion in the town. He had his supporters, local people who believed that he was doing a good job with the boys, keeping many off the streets. But the headteacher of Dunblane Primary School, Ron Taylor, was never a member of the Hamilton fan club. He was disturbed by reports from parents of Hamilton's practice of taking photographs of children in swimming trunks:

there was a suggestion that the photographs, though not indecent, were inappropriate. Taylor's response was to say that he had heard a number of allegations and was unsure about them, but that from what he had heard he would not send his own children to the club. The parents seemed grateful for this advice.

One day Hamilton came to the school bearing leaflets, and asked Taylor to distribute them. Hamilton complained that members of the school staff had been 'driving parents away' from his club and asked Taylor to 'perhaps disabuse them of the idea that I am a pervert'. Taylor gave a neutral response and, when Hamilton had gone, binned the leaflets. Later, he received a letter from Hamilton claiming that 'teachers at Dunblane Primary School have contaminated all of the older boys with this poison, even former cleaners and dinner ladies have been told by teachers that I am a pervert'. On 12 March 1996, the day that Hamilton had the 'blether' with his mother, Taylor received a copy of his letter to the Queen complaining that he was unable to walk the streets of Stirling for fear of being ridiculed by his enemies in the Scout Association and elsewhere.

When Hamilton was not firing off letters to all and sundry, he was firing actual shots at specific targets. He was first granted a licence to carry firearms in 1977 – he was 25 at the time – citing as his 'good reason' – the requirement in the application form – his membership of a gun club. His interest in guns was dormant for long periods, but in 1996 it revived with a vengeance. In January that year, he attended the range used by the Stirling Rifle and Pistol Club. Although the office-bearers noted that his shooting was reasonably good, one or two were surprised by the unusual rapidity of his firing. On 2 March, at a shoot in Largs, he again fired very rapidly; with one pistol he expended 12 rounds on a single target and was told that this was out of order. A club member, whose female cousin had come along for the ride, gave Hamilton a lift home to Stirling. When he got out of the car, the woman said: 'That is a right weirdo, that one. He talks about guns as though they were babies.'

In another incident early in 1996, James Gillespie, a friend of Hamilton, called at Kent Road. 'He was cleaning his revolver at the time,' said Gillespie, 'and he asked me if I had any kids would I allow them to attend his club. I said no, I wouldn't. He pointed the revolver at me and fired it with a blank chamber. I got a fright. I was holding a cup of coffee. I called him a stupid bastard and threw the coffee at him and walked out smartly and that was the last I saw of him.' When he was asked later why he would not have allowed any child of his to go to one of Hamilton's clubs, Gillespie replied: 'I thought he was too military.' Did anything else give him the impression that Hamilton might be dangerous? 'Just the idea of having guns in the house in the first place, too many for anybody to have in the house at the one time. I think at one stage he had a machine gun.' Gillespie decided not to report the incident to the police; he knew that Hamilton would simply have denied it.

On Thursday 7 March, a nine-year-old boy attending the club at Dunblane High School was surprised to be taken aside by Hamilton: 'We did the usual games. In the middle of football, Mr Hamilton sat me on a bench to speak to me. He asked me the way to the gym [of Dunblane Primary School] and the way to the hall. He asked me what time certain classes went to the gym. He asked directions about how to get to the gym once he was in the main hall and where the stage was.'

The degree of premeditation was confirmed around the same time by his visit to a van hire firm in Stirling. The receptionist, Karen Gillies, vividly remembered her brief encounter with Hamilton: 'He unnerved me quite a bit. The way he spoke. Very slowly, very clearly, precisely, but with no emotion or expression. There was just nothing, nothing in there. You couldn't have held a conversation with him.' In the end, the only conversation he had was with his mother. By then, the evening of 12 March, the letter to the Queen had been delivered, the white van had been hired and paid for, and Thomas Hamilton knew where he was going in the morning. Sixteen children – Victoria

Clydesdale, Emma Crozier, Melissa Currie, Charlotte Dunn, Kevin Hasell, Ross Irvine, David Kerr, Mhairi MacBeath, Brett McKinnon, Abigail McLennan, Emily Morton, Sophie North, John Petrie, Joanna Ross, Hannah Scott and Megan Turner – and their teacher Gwen Mayor also knew where they were going in the morning. They were going to school as usual. So was Hamilton.

II

It was a bitterly cold morning: the killer had to scrape ice off the van before he drove the short distance to Dunblane. He arrived at 9.30 and parked beside a telegraph pole in the car park of the primary school. He promptly took out a pair of pliers and cut the telephone wires at the foot of the pole, disconnecting the adjoining houses though not the school itself. Armed to the teeth with weaponry and ammunition, he crossed the car park and entered the school unobtrusively by a door next to the toilets of the gymnasium.

The school day had started half an hour earlier with an assembly for primaries 1, 2, 3 – including primary 1/13, a class of 28 pupils, Mrs Mayor's class, which then excitedly changed for gym. Mayor had a meeting to attend and had arranged for a part-time PE teacher, Eileen Harrild, to stand in for her. Both teachers, with a classroom assistant Mary Blake, were in the gym for the start of the period when they became aware of a figure coming through the door. Harrild turned and saw a man a few feet away. He was wearing a woolly hat and ear muffs with his hand extended. He had a gun in his hand. She was about to ask him what he wanted when he took a couple of steps and began to shoot, indiscriminately and very rapidly. She put up both arms to protect herself, and was shot at once. She managed to stumble towards an area used as a storeroom, was joined by Blake and some of the children, who had also been shot, and there the little party hid while the shooting continued in the gymnasium. Then there was silence: 'everything seemed to be very quiet'.

Mary Blake described the scene in the storeroom: 'I thought this was the end. I thought if he came round the corner we would all be dead. One child kept saying, "What a bad man". They all kept saying they were sore. One boy had a hole in his arm and was holding it . . . I was trying to keep the children quiet, I was shushing them. I could feel blood running down my neck, and I had a great deal of pain in both legs. The shooting stopped for a short time, and the children were wailing, and I heard a buzzing sound in my head. Then the shooting started again for a few seconds and then stopped again. I remember asking Mrs Harrild if she was all right and she said, "He got me in the chest", but her arm was also injured. We felt so helpless. I couldn't do anything for the children. I couldn't move.'

In the space of three or four minutes, between 9.35 am and 9.40 am, Hamilton fired 105 rounds with a 9mm Browning self-loading pistol, most of them in the gym, although he also fired shots towards the library cloakroom and into a classroom. Standing over the children, he fired at point-blank range, killing 16 of them; he also shot dead Gwen Mayor. Thirteen of the survivors were wounded, six seriously.

A student teacher, David Scott, who was in the art class with a view into the gymnasium, witnessed the denouement of the horror: the suicide of Thomas Hamilton: 'He turned the gun on himself, close to his face, holding the gun in his right hand . . . I then heard a shot. The man's head went slowly backwards with a jolt, his knees folded and he landed on the floor on his back'. The pathologist who conducted the post-mortem, Professor Anthony Busuttil of Edinburgh University, described the discharge into the mouth from a hand-gun as 'a characteristic elective site for self-infliction of such an injury in persons committing suicide'. He declared that death would have been instantaneous.

Ron Taylor, who was in his office elsewhere in the school, had heard a noise, assumed that workmen were in the building without his knowledge, and felt mildly irritated about it, when a member of staff interrupted a telephone call with the news that something dreadful had happened in the gym. The headteacher put down the phone, sprinted down the corridor, burst into the gym, and was confronted by 'a scene of unimaginable carnage, one's worst nightmare'. The air was thick with a bluish smoke and the smell of cordite. Taylor ran back to his office to call the emergency services. He and the janitor, John Currie, then moved through the gym. There was a gun beside the body of Hamilton and he told Currie to kick it away, which Currie did. He also removed the revolver from Hamilton's hand and threw it aside.

At 9.57 am, responding to a call at 9.43, the first ambulance arrived. At 10.15 am, the injured left for Stirling Royal Infirmary. Around 11 am, a specialist scenes of crime officer, Malcolm Chisholm, examined the body of the murderer. He discovered that Hamilton had four holsters strapped round his waist, with 743 rounds of ammunition at his disposal. Close to the body he found a Smith and Wesson revolver with black customised hand-grips, a second Smith and Wesson, and two Browning self-loading pistols. The police descended on Hamilton's house. When Agnes Watt phoned, hoping to speak to her son, it was a police officer who answered.

Parents started to gather outside the school around 10 am, closely followed by the media. By 11 am, a radio reporter was claiming as the result of a police tip-off that 12 people had been killed. This was news to the parents, who knew nothing apart from hearsay and rumour. There was a severe problem of identification, partly because the one person – Gwen Mayor – who knew all the dead children was herself dead but also because a strategic error was made before the injured children were removed to hospital: the police, apparently out of sensitivity for their feelings, decided not to ask them for their names. The process of elimination was made more difficult still by the lack of communication between the hospital and the incident room at the school; little or nothing was heard from Stirling Royal Infirmary for some time, intensifying the distress and frustration of parents. A police officer could have been sent to the hospital to extract essential information, but this simple expedient seems not to have occurred to the high command, including the chief constable of Central Scotland Police, who were dealing with the emergency.

After the trauma they had just endured, the injured children were deprived of the presence and comfort of their parents. Instead of taking immediate steps to reunite parents and children, the police decided to assemble all the parents – irrespective of their status – in a house close to the school. The house was not big enough to accommodate all of them, and the group spilled over into the grounds, where Superintendent Joseph Holden, the officer responsible for family liaison, addressed them within earshot and sight of the journalists and prurient hangers-on who were observing the scene from just over the garden wall. He took the first of his 'conscious decisions': not to mention fatalities until he was sure of his facts. He did, however, undertake to go to the school and ask his colleagues what they knew. Having confirmed that it was Gwen Mayor's class, Holden returned to the house and announced that the parents of children in 1/13 were being moved to a second house in the vicinity. Still there was no mention of fatalities.

'And all of this having to take place under the eye of the media, which was increasing in number by the moment, is that right?' he was asked by counsel at the subsequent public inquiry.

'Yes,' he replied.

'We are now inside the second house,' counsel continued. 'All the parents of Mrs Mayor's class had come with you?' – 'Yes.'

It was 11 am. The children and their teacher had been dead for almost 90 minutes.

'What did you feel it appropriate to tell them at that stage?'

'I felt it appropriate that I tell them what I knew at that point, and what that was was that a shooting incident – a man had entered – sorry, I think I said a person – I am not sure – a man or a person had entered the gymnasium and had discharged a firearm and that there had been fatalities and injured – seriously injured.'

'On that being said to the parents, did any of them appear to have any information as to the number of children who might be dead?'

'Yes. A man, or a male person, which I assume was a father, immediately said that he questioned – or he asked me to say that there was 12 dead, 12 deceased. And I asked him "How do you know that?", and he told me that a radio broadcast – either he had heard or he had been told that a radio broadcast had numbered the dead as being 12.'

'Looking back at the situation with which everyone had to cope that morning, did it make matters any more difficult for all those involved that the members of the media may have been in the position to broadcast details of numbers killed and injured before the relatives were being informed of what had happened?'

'Yes. I mean, I was quite shocked at the statement made by what I assume was a father, and it certainly didn't make my job – I didn't know that information, that information could have been correct, and I didn't want to deny it. I just didn't know, so it did make my job much more difficult at that point.'

The next 'conscious decision' was not to inform parents that their child was dead until the whole ID process was complete. Apart from confusion between two children, the process was complete at 12.04 pm. Half an hour later, the parents were moved from the second house to the school, again in full view of the media, and taken to the staffroom. A policewoman called out the names of the known survivors and asked their parents to leave the room. For the others the waiting continued.

'Can I ask you, Superintendent, so that we all understand this. At that stage were any steps taken to inform the parents that there was this continuing uncertainty about the identities of those who had been killed and those who had survived?'

'I did not specifically instruct that, and I did not do it myself. I took the view that I should be trying to get that information, and I was within the incident room doing that.'

'What I want to ask you about is why the problem that medical and other staff were experiencing in identifying victims wasn't conveyed in general terms to the parents as an explanation for the delay which was undoubtedly building up?'

'There are two comments I would make. One was we felt that with every minute that went by we would get information that we could go and give those parents. The second was that, rightly or wrongly in hindsight, it wasn't felt appropriate or of any help to go in and say while the uncertainty continued.'

According to the police, the first of the bereaved parents were informed at 1.45 pm, the last around 2.30 pm. One family claimed, however, that they were still waiting for information as late as 3.30 pm.

The testimony of Gwen Mayor's family tended to support the 3.30 theory. When her daughter Esther arrived at the school she was put in the staffroom with the parents. So poor was internal communication that, when Mayor's husband arrived, he was taken to the library and left there on his own for half an hour until he threatened to go out and speak to the media. Only then did the police officer on the door reluctantly concede that 'the worst case scenario has occurred': it was his way of saying that Gwen Mayor was dead. At 2.45, Esther finally learned that her father was elsewhere in the school and father and daughter were re-united. She insisted that 'a significant number of parents' were still in the staffroom at that time. When this was put to Holden, he replied: 'I can't comment on that.' The man in charge of the investigation, Detective Chief Inspector John Ogg, said he found it 'difficult to believe' that parents had waited so long for news, but admitted that he was not in a position to contradict the claim. And no wonder: for, although the parents requested access to senior officers, neither the chief constable nor his deputy, both of whom were in the building, came to see them.

If the police operation was a shambles, the political response was more adroit. The Secretary of State for Scotland, Michael Forsyth, no longer required evidence to support the rumours about Thomas Hamilton: he had it all now, in blood, grief and anguish. The morning after – 14 March 1996 – he met the Lord Advocate, Lord Mackay of Drumadoon, to discuss the events at Dunblane. Later that day, Forsyth sent a memo to the Prime Minister, John Major, recommending a judge-led inquiry: 'The Lord Advocate and I consider that the judge may find it necessary to address questions relating to the way in which firearms legislation is applied in practice, about security of school premises, and about the supervision of voluntary youth workers. I think we have to allow these matters to be exposed to public scrutiny, and I have confidence that, providing the right judge is selected, we need not fear any over-reaction on his part.'

Only 24 hours had elapsed since the brutal murder of 16 small children and their teacher, and the Secretary of State was concerned about the possibility of 'over-reaction', whatever that meant. Lord Cullen – apparently a judge who could be relied upon not to over-react – was appointed later that very day. On 21 March, Forsyth hosted a 'supper' at Bute House, the residence of the Secretary of State, for Lords Cullen and Mackay to discuss the terms of the inquiry. The official note of the meeting included the revealing statement: 'Lord Cullen said he would find it helpful to be kept in touch with developments in government thinking on relevant issues and hoped it would be possible to have regular meetings on policy issues.' From the start, then, there was some doubt that the judge-led inquiry was truly independent of, and aloof from, the political machine; but this doubt did not surface publicly for many years, until the release of official documents, by which time Dunblane was becoming, to all but the permanently grief-stricken, a distant memory.

A week or so after the Bute House gathering, with worldwide media interest in the massacre intense, Lord Mackay sent out a notice to editors warning them to cease their investigations – otherwise they could be held in contempt. In contempt of what, though? The judge-led inquiry was not a criminal trial; the only conceivable accused – Thomas Hamilton – was dead. The inquiry had the formal status of a tribunal. To Mackay it made no difference: legitimate and continuing press interest in the circumstances was somehow in danger of preju-dicing the non-trial. The Crown Office added a Kafkaesque flourish to the communique: editors must not publish or broadcast the nature of his lordship's instruction.

The *Scotsman* bravely disobeyed the latter oppressive order with a spirited piece by Ian Bell, who wrote that 'the very sorts of people Lord Mackay seeks to protect – police officers, councillors and local authority officials – have taken cover behind Cullen. It seems the public's interest, and the public's right to know, are to be allowed only one representative. Such are the number of potential witnesses to the long, squalid career of Thomas Hamilton, indeed, that the media need hardly now dare speak to anyone.' If only Bell had known the full extent of the audacity – that the judge leading the inquiry, the integrity of which had to be preserved at all costs, had already asked to be 'kept in touch with developments in government thinking on relevant issues'.

It was in this atmosphere of mutual mistrust that the Cullen inquiry began its work in the Albert Halls, Stirling, on 29 May 1996.

III

In the early stages of the inquiry, there were unexplained oddities, in-cluding the decision not to call two of the main witnesses – Scott, the student teacher, apparently the only person who saw Hamilton shoot himself, and Currie, the janitor who accompanied the headteacher through the gym after the massacre.

Among the other curiosities, a disagreement between the police officer leading the investigation, John Ogg, and the headteacher, Ron Taylor, about the initial call to the emergency services was never resolved.

Ogg was asked: 'And we have the call to the police by Mr Taylor, a 999 call?'

'It wasn't a treble nine call.'

'From the school at 9.41?'

'Yes, but it wasn't a treble nine. It was an ordinary call.'

'An ordinary call at 9.41?'

No answer.

Taylor's lawyer sought clarification: was Ogg sure that it had not been a 999 call? Ogg explained that it had been received at the main switchboard, whereas 999 calls came into the control room.

'And is there any log of that?'

'Yes, we checked.'

But Taylor was equally emphatic. When he was asked what he did when he ran back to his office from the gym, he replied: 'I then dialled 999.'

'Are you clear in your mind it was a 999 call?'

'In my own mind I am clear about that because I had never dialled a 999 call before and I didn't have the number of the local police station to dial.'

And there it was left: a matter of no great moment, except as an indication of the relaxed approach to conflicting evidence. The log could have been produced in an effort to resolve the difference in testimony; the log was not produced.

Equally baffling was the failure to probe Eileen Harrild's impressions from the storeroom. She was asked when help started to arrive; how long was it after Hamilton stopped shooting? She gave the surprising reply that 'I think possibly it was more towards the end of the shooting.' The implication was that someone may have entered the gym before Hamilton shot himself. If that was true, who might it have been? The possibility was not explored.

The star witness – if only as the personification of official complacency – was the depute chief constable of Central Scotland Police, Douglas McMurdo, who was responsible for signing off 4,634 firearms and shotgun certificates – a staggering total considering that Central was one of Scotland's smaller police authorities. He was grilled for several hours, emerging from the ordeal bloodied but relatively unbowed. Only by quoting from his testimony at some length is it possible to appreciate how Hamilton functioned in plain sight in respectable society for so long.

'Have you had occasion to refuse an application for the grant or renewal of a firearms certificate?'

'On a number of occasions, yes.'

'Did you ever revoke any?'

'I did indeed.'

'And revocation was a power you had?'

'Indeed it was.'

'When did you first encounter or learn of the existence of Thomas Hamilton?'

'This is in July 1988. He was running a summer camp in Inchmoan Island [Loch Lomond] . . . There was a camp started on the 3rd of July of that year, and one of the lads who had been camping on the island spoke to his mother on his return and expressed his dissatisfaction with the camp.'

Responding to a report from the boy's family, two police officers were despatched to Inchmoan, but no action was taken.

'How did you find out about all of this?'

'It was reported to me eventually, I think probably by Mr Hamilton complaining about our, as he saw it, intrusion into something which was none of our business.' The complaint took the form of a handwritten letter to the chief constable rebutting the various allegations.

'These are things like some boys not enjoying the camp, not being allowed to return home early, not being allowed to phone home?'

'Yes.'

'Not liking the food?'

'Yes.'

'Not being allowed to know the time?'

'Yes.'

'Parents not being allowed to visit?'

'Yes.'

'Not being allowed to wear long trousers most of the time?'

'Yes.'

'And doing exercises in which they had to keep their tummies in?'

'Yes.'

There were more sinister allegations: that as the scantily clad boys performed particular movements, Hamilton recorded them on film or video so that he could watch at home, that he bullied and swore at some boys while inviting others – his favourites – to rub suntan into his body and sleep beside him. The choice of an isolated location made it easier for Hamilton to impose a regime of strict controls and to deprive the children of basic freedoms. Many features of this behaviour would come to be known as grooming, a word not yet in the lexicon of child abuse.

Seven months after the police's visit to Loch Lomond, McMurdo renewed Hamilton's firearms certificate. Fully aware of the allegations, he did not consider them serious enough to revoke the certificate. In November 1991, following a second incident at one of Hamilton's summer camps on Loch Lomond, the head of Central Scotland Police's child protection unit, Detective Sergeant Paul Hughes, sent a damning memo to his superiors recommending that Hamilton should no longer be allowed to carry guns: 'I am firmly of the opinion that he is an unsavoury character and an unstable personality. I would contend that Hamilton will be a risk to children whenever he has access to them and he appears to me to be an unsuitable person to possess a firearms certificate. It is my opinion that he is a devious and deceitful individual who is not to be trusted.'

Colin Campbell QC, representing the families of the dead children, wanted to know McMurdo's opinion of the memo: 'Does it describe a person who is fit to be entrusted with firearms?'

'I think you have got to look beyond the actual memorandum to the evidence on which Mr Hughes bases his opinion'.

'Before you go on to that, can I ask for an answer to my question?'

'Which is?'

'Does it describe a person who is fit to be entrusted with firearms?'

'No'.

'So your view would be that Mr Hughes is describing an individual whose firearms certificate, if he had one, should be revoked?'

'I'm not saying that at all . . . The whole memorandum from Mr Hughes was an impression. An impression. A gut feeling. A sixth sense or whatever. It did not have any evidence to substantiate these remarks at all.'

McMurdo again decided to take no action. He was so unmoved by the memo that he felt no obligation to interview Hughes: 'I knew all about the case . . . I didn't need to speak to him.'

'Were you aware of an incident in the summer of 1992 where children were running away overnight from the camp at Dunblane High School?

'As I recall that, they were got wandering about at 10 o'clock in the evening or something.'

'Yes?'

'That is when he held the camp actually within the school.'

'You were aware of that incident?'

'Yes, indeed.'

It is unclear whether the depute chief constable knew of a report by a children's reporter after the 1992 summer camp that a tragedy involving children in Hamilton's care was 'almost waiting to happen'. He was certainly informed of an attempt by his own force's child protection unit to obtain a warrant to search Hamilton's house, mainly for indecent photographs. McMurdo was asked: 'What was the decision of the fiscal on that one?'

'I don't think we got one.'

'Well, you got a decision but you didn't get a warrant.'

'Yes.'

In February 1995, an application from Hamilton for the further renewal of his firearms certificate landed on McMurdo's desk. It came unattached – there was no accompanying note of caution or qualification from his junior officers.

'So when it came to dealing with this application, was it just a piece of paper amongst a number of other pieces of paper that you just signed automatically?'

'I don't sign anything automatically.'

'So what attention did you give to the certificate before you signed it?'

'I read through it and signed it.'

'Any chance that the name of the individual would not mean anything to you when you were dealing with the renewal and you had no other material in front of you?'

'You are joking. Thomas Watt Hamilton I think was pretty well known to me by that time.'

Pretty well known, yes; but not well enough to alter McMurdo's judgement that Hamilton was a fit person to own guns.

'How did you apply your mind to it?'

'I thought about it, but there was absolutely nothing that I knew about Thomas Hamilton that would prevent me from signing the certificate and I doubt if there would be many people who would know any more about him than I did.'

'Now I recognise that we don't live in a police state, thank goodness, and that you have to have reasons to make decisions which revoke a certificate or an entitlement a person has.'

'Yes'.

'But by February 1995, had things not got to such a pitch with Hamilton that you ought to have been collating all the information available on him, studying it again and reconsidering it before you made your decision?'

McMurdo responded by detailing the complaints against Hamilton before concluding: 'There was nothing there to suggest that this man would in any way be dangerous with a firearm.'

'There were a number of complaints made by parents about what they perceived as inappropriate conduct towards their children?'

'Things almost had reached a witch-hunt by that time. Rumours were circulating about the town but there was nothing at all in the photographs we looked at. There was not one we found that was in any way indecent.'

'We know that, at the police intelligence system, there was a card, an index card, which classified him as "homo" and then the letters "indch", which is suspected indecency towards children. So it went that far as far as police intelligence was concerned, did it not?'

'Intelligence I am not proud of. Intelligence [that] does not add up to much, I'm afraid.'

Later he gave this assessment of Hamilton: 'He was somebody you wouldn't take to. He was not a personable sort of individual. He could perhaps be described as a bit effeminate but that is all you could say about him.'

'Bitter and petty-minded?'

'He could certainly be bitter in certain circumstances, yes.'

'Was he somebody who was in your view fit to be given the let of local authority premises?'

'Well, that was a debate that went on as well.'

'Can you answer yes or no, please?'

'Well, I know the council looked on this very carefully and their view was that there was not sufficient evidence to take it away.'

Hamilton did business with four councils. McMurdo was not asked to say which of them he had in mind, but the fact that

Hamilton was promoting boys' clubs on school premises a week before the massacre shows that local authorities were as loath to take action against him as McMurdo himself was. Hamilton had been the subject of three police investigations (1988, 1991 and 1992), two indictments of his character by a child protection officer and a children's reporter, and innumerable complaints from parents, including a senior politician. Under the law, he could have been banned from holding a gun licence on the grounds of 'intemperate habits or unsound mind'. McMurdo took a narrower view of the legislation: serious defects of character were insufficient to withdraw a certificate; it required a criminal conviction. As Colin Campbell QC put it: 'The dead hand of a purely administrative system, incapable of independent judgement and unwilling to exercise the quasi-judicial function expected of it, failed to prevent the use of a gun by Thomas Hamilton.'

Campbell, in his summing-up, argued that it was a preventable tragedy: 'But for the culpable failure of Central Scotland Police, it is probable that the events of 13 March at Dunblane Primary School would not have occurred.' Was it also a predictable one? George Robertson, from his personal dealings with Hamilton, had 'no indication that he was bottling up any ferocious, murderous instincts' – a sentiment genuinely shared by most of the people in Dunblane with whom Hamilton came into contact. But it was a sentiment based on an incomplete knowledge of the facts.

By the end of the inquiry, there should have been no doubt that a mountain of testimony was pointing to the conclusion that Hamilton combined a sexual interest in young boys with an irresponsible use of guns; yet the junior counsel for the Crown, Iain Bonomy, in his closing speech to Lord Cullen, delivered a surprisingly equivocal verdict: 'Such evidence as is before you that he was a pervert in the sense of abusing children you may consider to be not entirely reliable. There is, however, clear evidence that he was odd, eccentric and creepy . . . on the other hand he ran well-disciplined or regimented activities for boys . . . the signs are that most boys did not feel threatened by his behaviour.'

The 'well-disciplined' clubs had invoked comparisons with Hitler's youth movement, and the suggestion that most boys were unthreatened by his treatment of them was not borne out by the consumer reaction. Typically the attendance at his clubs dwindled sharply after a few months: from as many as 70 to as few as a dozen. Hamilton's response was to close down and start again elsewhere, in this way establishing a succession of such ventures in different towns and villages across central Scotland. If – setting aside the murder of 17 people – the worst to be said about him was that he was 'odd, eccentric and creepy', it was not saying very much.

The thriller writer Frederick Forsyth wrote many years later that the Cullen report was 'one of the weirdest documents the Scottish establishment has ever produced'. It may not have been weird, but feeble it certainly was. Douglas McMurdo, who left Central Scotland Police soon after the massacre, was reprimanded for failing to act on the memo of his child protection officer; according to Cullen he 'should have made further inquiries'. It was the mildest of criticisms, but at least he was obliged to account for his actions. The same could not be said of the procurator fiscals who repeatedly decided to take no action against Hamilton; Cullen decided that it would be 'inappropriate' to expect them to defend their decisions publicly.

The judge had heard, and no doubt considered, a rebuke for the police from the junior counsel for the families, Laura Dunlop, who deplored the long delay in informing the bereaved parents that their children were dead. 'It is a form of torture,' she said, 'to be kept waiting in the knowledge that something terrible has happened without having details of what or to whom.' She added that it was 'particularly unfortunate that the parents of the injured children were not able to be with them in the first few hours' and stated firmly that the parents' request for someone senior to come and speak to them should not have been denied.

These failures of emergency planning and simple humanity should have been worth a chapter in Cullen's report. Instead the judge chose to overlook them. It was an inexplicable omission, helping to fuel the long-standing anger and bitterness felt by grieving parents and confirming that little if anything had been learned from the bureaucratic insensitivity apparent eight years earlier in the immediate aftermath of Lockerbie.

Worst of all, Cullen passed up an opportunity to influence meaningful legislative reform. Colin Campbell had uttered an impassioned plea on behalf of the families 'that never again should we tolerate the possibility of crimes such as this being carried out with legally-held weapons'. After all he had heard of the suffering at Dunblane, Cullen remained unconvinced of the need for fundamental change: 'The banning of multi-shot handguns would have a very damaging effect on the sport of target shooting and would give rise to claims for compensation and adverse effects on the economy.' A year later, the new Labour government did what Cullen should have recommended: it banned handguns. Few cared about the effect on 'the sport of target shooting', and the endangered economy survived somehow.

After the inquiry, the authorities unwisely decided to put a closure order on the Dunblane papers: thousands of pages of official reports and documents were to be locked away for 100 years. This provoked a succession of wild claims fuelled by access to the internet: the police knew that Hamilton was about to go on the rampage; the masonic order was implicated in the scandal; Hamilton had friends in high places and may have been supplying them with boys. In 2003, bowing to political pressure, the Lord Advocate, Colin Boyd, announced that, owing to 'exceptional circumstances', he was releasing the papers into the national archives. The suspicion that they would contain the names of leading figures in the Scottish establishment proved to be unfounded, and there was nothing to substantiate the more extreme theories.

But if Hamilton acted alone, he was no 'loner' – the shorthand term routinely conferred on him in newspaper reports. The loner excludes himself from society; the loner is an outsider. Hamilton mixed in the community; he even mixed with several police officers. He may have been 'a bit of a creep', 'head-down', 'a very shy person' and 'far too polite', before he turned his gun on the children of Dunblane, but there was no avoiding one profoundly upsetting fact: the perpetrator of the massacre was one of us.

A MOST SATISFACTORY RESULT

I

THE JOURNALIST FROM THE *SCOTSMAN* EXPECTED TO SEE SOME DULL specimen on a lab bench. He reported back to his readers that instead he found a delightful, lively animal, bursting with personality, who bounded over, jumped and pushed her head into his hand. It was Dolly the Sheep's first date with the media.

She had been born eight months earlier, on 5 July 1996, but it was not until late February of the following year, and the publication of a paper in the science journal *Nature*, that the world's first successfully cloned mammal was unveiled to the world at the Roslin Research Institute near Edinburgh. Scientists had inserted DNA from a single sheep cell into an egg and implanted it in a surrogate mother. The result was Dolly, an exact genetic duplicate. Why Dolly? 'She is derived from a mammary gland cell and we couldn't think of a more impressive pair of glands than Dolly Parton's,' explained the leader of the research team, Dr Ian Wilmut, in a reference to the famously endowed American country and western singer.

The BBC enthused that the sheep's birth was being heralded as 'one of the most significant scientific breakthroughs of the decade, although it is likely to spark ethical controversy'. The nature of the breakthrough was that Dolly proved you could turn the genetic clock back: take a differentiated cell, reactivate its silent genes and make the cell behave as though it was a recently fertilised egg. It captured the public imagination as few scientific discoveries had done, though the intense fascination with Dolly took the Roslin scientists by surprise; she soon became a worldwide phenomenon.

As the Institute acknowledged on its website years later, a clone – the idea that there might be a copy of any one of us lurking around – had long been a strand in science fiction, 'and the prospect that it might be possible to clone a human being excited a lot of speculation and interest'. At the time, however, Wilmut was at pains to play down this aspect of the research, describing human cloning as not only illegal but repugnant. His assurances failed to satisfy animal rights activists and pro-life lobbyists, who would sometimes object to his appearance on public platforms. In March 1997, only a few weeks after Dolly's existence had been revealed, Wilmut addressed a hearing of the US Senate's public health and safety sub-committee: 'I understand why the world is suddenly at my door. But this is my work, it has always been my work, and it doesn't have anything to do with creating copies of human beings. I am not haunted by what I do, if that's what you want to know. I sleep very well at night.' Subsequently, he and his colleague Keith Campbell wrote that the debate on human cloning had been 'merely a diversion and one we personally regret and find distasteful . . . we did not make Dolly for that. Still less did we intend to produce flocks of identical sheep.'

In a newspaper profile, Wilmut was described as balding, bearded and unassuming, a man fond of walking the mountains, curling and sipping Scotch whisky. He seemed an unlikely target of occasional bomb threats. Nor would he have appreciated a further spasm of publicity in 2011 when four former employees of the Institute petitioned the Queen to have him stripped of the knighthood he had been awarded for his services to science. They claimed that Wilmut had not planned, designed or carried out the experiment which created Dolly, that he had obtained unfair advantage, and that he was not entitled to the honour. Wilmut himself had consistently and openly acknowledged that Keith Campbell deserved '66% of the credit' for Dolly. Nothing came of the petition and the press hinted that one of the signatories – Campbell was not among them – might have held a personal grudge against Wilmut. There was nothing unusual about scientists falling out over questions of credit and attribution, but going to the Queen about it was something new.

Dolly did not enjoy a long life. At birth the animal technicians looking after her were delighted. She presented as 'a normal, vigorous lamb, standing and sucking unaided within minutes' and her progress was apparently so encouraging that the scientists decided she should be allowed to breed. They selected a small Welsh mountain ram and between them Dolly and her mate produced six lambs; the first, Bonny, was born in the spring of 1998, they had twins the following year and triplets the year after that. In the autumn of 2001, however, after she had started to walk stiffly, X-rays confirmed that Dolly had arthritis. She responded well to a course of anti-inflammatory treatment; the symptoms cleared up after a few months. But in a sheep only five years old, it was an unusual development, arousing suspicions that cloned animals were destined to age prematurely. These suspicions appeared to be confirmed in February 2003 when a scan disclosed that tumours were growing in her chest: Dolly had a form of lung cancer, a common enough disease in sheep, particularly a sheep who had been kept indoors as she had – for security reasons. She was put down before she could regain consciousness; Dolly was dead at the age of six. Stuffed, she went on to a form of immortality as an exhibit in the Royal Scottish Museum.

Roslin stated that it did not believe her death was related to her having been cloned and that intensive health screening had not revealed any abnormalities which could have resulted from advanced ageing. The critics were unconvinced. Dr Patrick Dixon, a writer on the ethics of human cloning, pointed out that she was not at all old by sheep standards – many sheep lived to the age of 11 or 12 – and that the nature of her decline, particularly the early onset of arthritis, would have a huge impact on the possibility of producing a cloned human baby. The science correspondent of the *Guardian*, James

Meek, wrote: 'She was a copy. And, like most copies, she faded a little bit quicker than the original. She was barely 40 in human terms ... The premature death of Dolly supports the views of scientists in Japan and the US who maintain that all cloned animals are born with health problems.'

A new theory emerged. Dolly's genetic mother was six when Dolly was cloned. Could it be that the real age of clones was their own age since birth – plus the age of the genetic donor? If this speculation was correct, then Dolly did not die at the age of six; she was in effect 12+. Whatever the explanation, a little of the gloss had come off the original discovery that what scientific orthodoxy had deemed impossible was achievable in the shape of a breathing, bleating sheep. Ian Wilmut decided in 2007 not to pursue the form of cloning which produced Dolly, as a result of which the dream – or nightmare – of human cloning receded. Twenty years after her birth, the Roslin Institute's verdict was that, although the practical implications of cloning livestock seemed 'relatively limited', there had been a long-lasting benefit in the change of perception about biology.

II

Even if Roslin had gone on to produce a human clone, it would have been too late to save the Conservative Party in Scotland. By May 1997 there were no Tory MPs left to clone: the Scottish party was obliterated in the General Election that swept John Major out of Downing Street and Tony Blair into it. Among the ministers who lost their seats were Ian Lang, Malcolm Rifkind and Michael Forsyth. Forsyth would have defied any attempt to produce an exact genetic duplicate.

Two senior Tories failed to reach even the starting blocks of the election campaign. The member for the supposedly rock-solid Conservative seat of Eastwood, Allan Stewart, stepped down when allegations about his private life surfaced in the *Sunday Mail*. Two years earlier, Stewart had resigned as a junior minister over a criminal conviction for breach of the peace – a relatively unusual offence in douce East Renfrewshire. After 'a normal Sunday lunch – with a gin and tonic and a glass of wine', he had wandered out to inspect the felling of trees on the M77 dual carriageway and was confronted by an environmental group protesting at an extension to the road. Stewart's response was to brandish a pickaxe; again, not something that happened every day in Eastwood. 'I picked it up,' he explained to the court, 'first of all to avoid anybody else picking it up and secondly in possible defence. There was then a robust discussion – I felt scared. The situation was extremely unpleasant.' He was fined £200 and promptly suffered a nervous breakdown, but kept his seat.

It was common knowledge in the party that the MP had a drink problem; his friend Ross Harper, a former president of the Scottish Tories, alluded to it in an article in the *Independent*. 'Those who knew rallied round to help,' he added. But then the *Sunday Mail* got hold of a story that Allan Stewart and a Mrs Knight, both married to other people, were staying together at his south London flat having met as fellow patients in a private clinic: 'Those dark days in the exclusive clinic saw the beginning of a special friendship. But last night, the link which has developed between the pair was shrouded in mystery.' All the key phrases of tabloid innuendo were there: 'dark days'; 'exclusive clinic'; 'special friendship', 'last night', 'shrouded in mystery'. Knight – affectionately known as Bunny – 'fled to her secluded Perthshire farmhouse' (there being no possibility that fugitives from the *Sunday Mail* ever walked in a normal fashion), where 'her husband of 19 years, Ricky, was waiting'.

Ross Harper saw nothing remarkable about any of this. He conceded that 'a relatively elderly woman whom he had met at the clinic was staying at his house' but denied there was any suggestion of an improper relationship. ('With alcoholics who are undergoing treatment, a problem shared leads to a problem solved.') Bunny was 47.

Allan Stewart, who had survived the pickaxe incident, failed to survive the special friendship with Bunny; he had to be replaced as the candidate for Eastwood, where the idea of two friends innocently sharing a flat in south London was too daring to be acceptable in Newton Mearns, even in 1997. The chairman of the Scottish party, Sir Michael Hirst, would have been the obvious replacement in such a plum seat. But then, just as abruptly, he too was gone. An opponent or opponents in his own party, whose motives were never satisfactorily explained, leaked a story, true or false, about a homosexual relationship. Before the newspaper had time to print it, Hirst wrote to the Prime Minister that 'as a result of a past indiscretion in my private life, I feel that my position could become untenable'. A bitter Hirst took to BBC Radio Scotland to declare that 'the poison has been spread far, deep and wide' by a tiny group in the party. Suspicion fell upon a former MP who had reportedly once said that Donald Duck would make a better parliamentary candidate than Michael Hirst, but when she was challenged by the press, she denied there was any conspiracy to do him down. Whoever it was, Hirst felt that he, she, or they had 'wrought terrible damage on the party'. He might have been right. Soon there was not a Tory in the land still in a job.

III

John Major, his campaign derailed by a succession of personal scandals of which Hirst's was a fairly mild example, deluded himself that he might still be able to produce a trump card. The card in question – the future of the Union – was more trick than trump. His warning that Labour's plans for a Scottish parliament and a Welsh assembly would mean 'the end of a thousand years of British history' was not only arithmetically but constitutionally unsound. Politically, too, it was a loser. The prospect of a thousand years of British history going down the drain left the voters of England unimpressed, while in Scotland these alarmist noises may have been counter-productive.

Scotland returned 56 Labour members, including its first Muslim MP, Mohammad Sarwar, and its first wheelchair-bound MP, Anne Begg.

Not for the first time, the SNP's dream of a historic breakthrough came to nought. The dream had been based on an assumption that Tony Blair's preoccupation with winning marginal Tory seats in England, and his perceived lurch to the right, would alienate Labour supporters north of the border. It was a miscalculation of the popular mood. The nationalists did reasonably well, winning six seats, three more than in 1992, but it was some distance short of a breakthrough, historic or otherwise.

On the morning of 2 May 1997, Tony Blair awoke as master of all he surveyed – commanding 419 seats in the House of Commons and a majority of 179, and with Celtic Britain expunged of all Conservative influence. Yet he had become Prime Minister only by the intervention of fate or what older-fashioned religious folk called the will of God: the sudden death of his predecessor as leader of the Labour Party, John Smith.

On the evening of 11 May 1994, Smith had addressed a fund-raising dinner in the Park Lane Hotel, London, attended by 500 well-heeled sympathisers, many from the business world. The Labour MP Margaret Beckett, who was present, recalled the climax of his speech: 'The opportunity to serve our country – that is all we ask.' Smith returned to his flat in the Barbican, where at 8.05 the following morning he had a massive heart attack. He never regained consciousness. A fortnight earlier, he had visited the A&E department of St Bartholomew's Hospital in support of a campaign to save it from closure and was shown round by a consultant, Mike Besser. It was there he was pronounced dead at 9.15 am, despite the efforts of Professor Besser to resuscitate him.

It was Smith's second heart attack. The night before the first, in October 1988, he had complained of chest pains at his home in Edinburgh and was prevailed upon to cancel a flight to London the next morning and go instead to the city's Royal Infirmary for a check-up. He had an ECG and was examined by a doctor. 'Whatever it is, we don't think it is your heart,' the doctor said. Smith collapsed more or less at his feet and was briefly unconscious before spending three days in intensive care. He appeared to make a full recovery and embarked on a vigorous dieting regime. He began climbing in a serious way, managing 108 of Scotland's 284 Munros (mountains over 3,000 feet) and reducing his intake of food and wine, though he was never quite able to shake off his reputation for conviviality. He had been renowned as the life and soul of the party – the sleeper train from Euston back to Scotland on Thursday nights after the parliamentary week was invariably livelier for his presence. But he did succeed in losing weight, shedding around three stones from his 15-stone frame: he had been far too heavy for a man of his modest height. When he returned to the House of Commons in January 1989 he was a diminished figure, though only physically. His political stock continued to rise.

After the unexpected loss of the 1992 election, the shadow chancellor was the obvious choice to succeed Neil Kinnock, although it was widely acknowledged that Smith may have contributed to the defeat by proposing modest tax increases, a thought anathema to middle England, wherever that was. The party elected him by an overwhelming majority. In his maiden speech he tore into John Major as 'the devalued Prime Minister of a devalued government'. He combined his forensic skill, first honed as a star of Glasgow University debating, with a sharp and often caustic wit. At the Labour conference later that year he branded Major and his chancellor Norman Lamont as 'the Laurel and Hardy of British politics' and in June 1993 he made a funny speech blaming two recent misfortunes on the incompetence of the Tory government. He said it was no wonder 'that we live in a country where the Grand National does not start and hotels fall into the sea'. He was, then, something of a card as a public speaker, though less effective on television, where it mattered more. And, in his two years as an effective Leader of the Opposition, he had earned general respect, even affection, as a politician of unusual integrity in a sea of mostly Conservative sleaze. He was said to embody the qualities of a bank manager, which later ceased to be any kind of compliment. The elder statesman of the Liberal Democrats, Menzies Campbell, a contemporary at Glasgow University, said he 'had all the virtues of a Scottish Presbyterian but none of the vices'.

His death stunned Westminster: there was genuine sadness at the death of a decent man. John Major delivered a well-judged tribute in the House of Commons, saying that he had always thought of him as an opponent rather than an enemy, and recalling with gentle humour that he and Smith 'would share a drink: sometimes tea, sometimes not tea'. That night a medical drama on BBC TV, appropriately entitled *Cardiac Arrest*, was cancelled to make way for an extended *Nine O'Clock News*. His close friend Donald Dewar spoke at his funeral in Edinburgh: 'The people know that they have lost a friend.' Outside Cluny Parish Church, a large crowd stood silently in an icy wind as the coffin of Labour's lost leader was carried down the steps to the hearse, onward to Iona for burial. 'John Smith showed people that there was a style of politics, a type of politician, with which they could identify,' wrote Neal Ascherson in the *Independent*. 'He had seemed at first bustling, ambitious, lawyerly – much like the rest of them. But then it was seen that he was angry about selfishness and unfairness, that he meant what he said.' Ascherson added that John Smith loved Scotland 'extravagantly' and that his most important unfinished business was the establishment of a Scottish Parliament within the UK: 'He was convinced that this would strengthen the Union.'

Two of the mourners, the principal contenders for the crown of heir apparent, were caught by the cameras walking together in the church grounds. Tony Blair and Gordon Brown had already talked about the succession, indeed may have have done so in general terms within minutes of Smith's death. In a television interview in

2010, Brown was asked if he believed he would be Labour leader after Smith. 'I thought that would be possible,' he replied, 'and the first person I phoned when I heard John had died was Tony.' Brown introduced the conversation by imparting the news: 'Look, Tony, you may not know this, but despite the fact it's not been announced, John unfortunately has died.' There was then a short exchange about 'sorting things out'. At that stage, Brown was still the senior partner in the relationship and may have seen himself as the natural successor to his fellow Scot. 'I believed I could do the job,' he told Piers Morgan in the same interview 16 years later. 'I believed that I'd got the experience and built up the experience to do it.'

In the days after the funeral, however, it was not Brown but his sidekick Blair who emerged as the bookies' favourite. On 31 May, the two men met in Granita, a restaurant in Islington, north London. The encounter was to acquire almost mythical status as the occasion when the terms of the agreement for the leadership were hammered out and Brown agreed to stand aside. But it was not without its oddities, the most obvious being the choice of venue. The journalist Allison Pearson happened to be dining with her husband in the same restaurant that evening: 'It was extremely clattery, open-plan, small tables, with absolutely no sense of privacy.' She noticed Blair sitting by himself, ignored by the other diners, whose attention was focused on the real celebrity, an actress in the BBC soap opera *EastEnders*. On her way to the lavatory, Blair said hello and the second oddity occurred: he asked Pearson, someone he had never met before: 'What do you think we should do?' She took this to refer to the general direction of party policy; only later did it occur to her that he might have been referring to the more personal question of the leadership. 'I heard footsteps behind me,' said Pearson. 'I assumed it was Cherie [entering the restaurant]. Then I turned round and saw Gordon with an aide.' The aide was Ed Balls, who left quickly, leaving Brown and Blair on their own. They talked for about an hour. It was not much of a dinner.

Afterwards, both men dismissed its significance: 'Oh,' said Blair, 'we'd done all our business by then, anyway.' Indeed the deal appears to have been brokered a few days earlier at the Edinburgh home of Nick Ryden, a friend of Blair. Ryden said: 'Tony Blair was staying and Gordon Brown turned up. There was wine. There was whisky. And there was a takeaway number for the Indian restaurant. I went to the pub and left them to it.' At 1.30 in the morning Ryden was finally allowed back into his own house and gave Brown £30 for a taxi home. In his absence, Brown may have extracted what he came to regard as an unambiguous undertaking that he would be in full control of economic policy in the next Labour government and that, at some stage, Blair would step down as Prime Minister and make way for him. Brown should have got it in writing. The terms of the agreement – whether they were decided in Edinburgh or in Granita's restaurant was ultimately beside the point – were to prove more elastic than Brown had ever expected and caused serious friction between the Prime Minister and his strong-minded Chancellor.

IV

The first Labour cabinet for 18 years was packed with Scots to an almost embarrassing extent: seven out of 22 (eight if you counted Blair himself, who was born in Edinburgh): Gordon Brown, Chancellor; Derry Irvine (Lord Irvine of Lairg), Lord Chancellor; Alistair Darling, Chief Secretary to the Treasury; Robin Cook, Foreign Secretary; George Robertson, Defence Secretary; Donald Dewar, Scottish Secretary; Gavin Strang, Minister for Transport. From a Scottish perspective, though, only one of these appointments counted: Donald Dewar, the only politician who had accompanied the body of John Smith to its final resting place, had the job of delivering the devolved parliament that both believed would strengthen the Union. And he set about it with characteristically dour determination.

The outcome of the second referendum on Scotland's constitutional future was never in much doubt: the only question was whether the Scots would turn out on 11 September 1997 in sufficient numbers to demonstrate a genuine commitment to the project. They did, though only just: a poll of 60% was good, but not great; one and a half million electors stayed at home on the momentous day. Of those who did vote, 74% endorsed the setting up of a Scottish Parliament and 63% approved giving it tax-raising powers; the most enthusiastic supporters of devolution were West Dunbartonshire and Glasgow, the least enthusiastic East Renfrewshire (of pickaxe notoriety) and Orkney.

The two most significant features of the result were that all 32 of the electoral regions backed the proposition – the devolutionists could thus claim an all-Scotland consensus – and that, if there had been a 40% hurdle to overcome, as there was in 1979, it would have been overcome. Literary allusions came thick and fast the morning after. The SNP leader Alex Salmond turned T.S. Eliot's on its head with his boast that Scotland had voted 'not with a whimper but with a bang', while BBC Scotland's political editor, Brian Taylor, preferred Yeats ('All changed and changed utterly'). Tony Blair arrived by helicopter in the park next to Holyrood Palace and was greeted by Donald Dewar. 'A satisfactory result, I think,' said Dewar. Blair smiled and nodded. 'Yes, most satisfactory,' confirmed Dewar. And off they both went, up the Royal Mile to a victory celebration in Parliament Square, next to the building where the Scottish Parliament had adjourned 290 years before. 'The settled will of the Scottish people', John Smith had repeatedly called devolution. And it felt settled enough that afternoon, as a band of female drummers entertained the crowd.

It was not settled for long. Even as Tony Blair was assuring his supporters that the overwhelming vote would cement rather than break up the Union, Alex Salmond was delivering what one newspaper called 'an apocalyptic prophecy': an independent Scotland in his lifetime. As Salmond was only 42 at the time, in a country with a male life expectancy of 77, the nationalist tribune and well-known betting man was predicting independence no later than 2032. Although that seemed to be erring on the side of pessimism as this book was being written in the autumn of 2015, the Salmond prediction was dismissed as fanciful, even absurd, in the immediate aftermath of the referendum. The leader of the Scottish Liberal Democrats, Jim Wallace, pointed to devolution in Catalonia: 'Those countries that have devolution have proved successful because they meet the will of the people.' By September 2015, Catalonia was clamouring for independence from Spain; so much for the soothsaying powers of Jim Wallace. Donald Dewar too seemed to regard his 'satisfactory, most satisfactory' result as an all-time clincher; it had 'settled once and for all the arguments about Scotland's desire for some form of home rule'.

Once and for all? In Scotland, just as in Catalonia, devolution settled nothing. The judgement of John Smith, author of the settled will theory, was proved to be mistaken, perhaps fatally so for the long-term prospects of his party. Of the rest of his political legacy, little remains but fruitless speculation about what might or might not have happened had he lived. Wyn Grant, professor of politics and international studies at the University of Warwick, believed that a Smith premiership would have been a cautious one: that he would have swithered on Britain joining the euro and concluded in the end that there were too many uncertainties to do anything but defer a decision; and that he would have been more reluctant to commit Britain to intervention in Iraq. Under Smith, Labour would have won easily in 1997 and with a smaller majority in 2001 but, thought Grant, might have lost in 2005 – 'It would then have been the Conservatives who would have been in office during the global financial crisis and taken some of the blame that went to Labour'. Only one thing was certain about the Smith premiership that never was: he would have given Scotland its own parliament, with the many unintended conse-quences which flowed from it.

V

On 31 August, Diana, Princess of Wales, and her boyfriend, Dodi Fayed, were killed in a car accident in a Paris tunnel. Her car was being driven by a chauffeur who had been drinking and who may have been distracted by the attentions of the paparazzi. Diana, who was not wearing a seat belt, was heard groaning 'Oh, my God' and 'Leave me alone' before she lapsed into unconsciousness, severely injured beyond hope of survival.

Her estranged husband, the Prince of Wales, was with the rest of the royal family at Balmoral when the news broke. The old house – subsequently demolished and replaced – had been privately purchased by Prince Albert, consort to Queen Victoria, along with the rest of the estate, and Victoria adored it. 'All seemed to breathe freedom and peace,' she wrote, 'and to make one forget the world and its sad turmoils.' But for a few days in the late summer of 1997, the sad turmoils of the world permeated even the jealously guarded summer retreat of the British monarchy. Charles had the task of imparting the news of their mother's death to their children William and Harry. Later that morning, it looked like business as usual: the Queen led the royal party to Crathie Church for Sunday worship and there was no outward exhibition of mourning.

Back in London, the Prime Minister was as shocked by the news as the rest of the country. His press adviser, Alastair Campbell, heard him intoning on the telephone: 'I can't believe this, I just can't believe it.' Unlike the palace courtiers, however, Tony Blair had his wits about him and was instantly connecting with popular sentiment; or, as Campbell later put it, 'He was straight on to the ramifications.' Without delay Blair made the first of the apparently impromptu yet subtly crafted statements which helped to define the relaxed style of his premiership in its opening phase. He spoke of Diana as 'the people's princess'. There was no reason to doubt the sincerity of the phrase, but it was so clever – it came conveniently in the form of a ready-made headline – that most journalists assumed that Campbell, a former tabloid journalist, had coined it. As Campbell confirmed later, it was Blair himself. In an instant, he had captured what many people were thinking about the glamorous yet accessible Diana, dead at 36 after an unhappy marriage to a man who was in love with someone else.

At Buckingham Palace, the royal standard was not flown at half-mast; it was not flown at all. This correctly reflected the protocol that it was flown only when the Queen was in residence; and the Queen was still in Scotland, observing a period of silent mourning and unwilling to expose her grandchildren to the crowd, despite the immense media pressure on her to return to London. 'Where is our Queen? Where is her flag?' splashed the *Sun*. A reporter from the *Washington Post*, Dan Balz, wrote that the public felt 'a modest contempt for a royal family that was clearly out of touch', but to some it felt more visceral and threatening: an outbreak of mass hysteria. 'It was like the Nuremberg rallies,' wrote the publisher Carmen Callil. The *Guardian*'s Jonathan Freedland likened it years later to 'a new totalitarian state of the emotions'. Whatever it was, it was easily fixed: the monarch did return to London and made a live television broadcast from the palace.

In the film *The Queen*, which fictionalised the events of that week, she and Tony Blair are reflecting on the possible damage to the reputation of the monarchy. 'Quite suddenly and without warning, it will happen to you,' the Queen says out of the blue. 'It will, Mr Blair.' And so it did, over Britain's participation in a war that long-dead John Smith might have been canny enough to avoid.

1998

CAUSE CÉLÈBRE

I

ONE FRIDAY NIGHT IN FEBRUARY 1998, EIGHT ASIAN YOUTHS AND four non-Asian youths – commonly described as white youths – confronted each other outside a chip shop in the Shawlands district of Glasgow. Two of the white youths ran off, leaving twin brothers Colin and Craig Gilmour, 17, to defend the honour of their tribe, as they understood it. The three main protagonists – the Gilmours and 15-year-old Imran Khan – were pupils of Shawlands Academy, Scotland's largest multi-racial secondary school, in which 800 of the pupils were white and 600 Asian; one in 10 of the teaching staff was from an ethnic minority background – the highest proportion of any school in the country.

Apart from any educational merit it may have possessed, the school was a notorious focal point of racial disturbances. Six years earlier, after a white prefect reprimanded an Asian pupil, 30 Asians descended on its gates and, wielding baseball bats and sticks, charged through the assembled children. It was called a riot. Two years before that, in 1990, a teacher was accused of racially abusing a child. The British National Party regarded it as a fertile recruiting ground, distributing leaflets. Andrew Johnson, an academic at Strathclyde University, accused the school of complacency, claiming that racially motivated gang violence had been a reality in Glasgow for years, that young Asians felt they had to group together to defend themselves, and that white racists, tooled up and ready for a fight, headed for Shawlands on a Friday night. But it was not until February 1998, and the incident outside the chip shop, that a life was lost: that of Imran Khan.

The Gilmours had been expelled from Shawlands Academy for racially abusing Asian children in the playground. Khan, though, was little better: he looked older than his years, was considered the leader of his gang, and had a local reputation as a bully. As the *Daily Record* put it: 'White kids meet Asian kids, knock lumps out of each other, then go and get chips'. But it went far beyond chips that night. The familiar ritual was complicated by Khan's suspicion that it was the Gilmour brothers who had mugged him for his jewellery. 'Are you the boys who took the rings off me?' he challenged them, as he took a run at the pair. An Asian eye-witness recalled: 'I thought I saw a knife flashing in the hands of one of the twins. It was so fast I never saw what happened to Imran.' In the unequal contest – the Gilmours with their knives, the enemies with only belts or bottles – Khan fell bleeding. He was taken to the Victoria Infirmary, where he appeared to be making a complete recovery from his stab wound and punctured lung. Both had healed when, eight days after the attack, he died of multi-organ failure as the result of an infection.

Was he killed by the Gilmours or by the medical profession? When the case came to trial at the High Court in Glasgow, Frank Mulholland, summing-up for the Crown, did not dispute 'the glaring deficiencies in Imran's medical care', but begged the jury not to lose sight of 'the vicious knife attack that put this boy in hospital'. The jury acquitted Colin Gilmour of murder but convicted him of attempted murder by stabbing Khan four times in the back with a flick knife. The judge, Lord Kirkwood, ordered him to be detained for seven years. The murder charge against his brother was dropped on the fifth day of the trial, though he was sentenced to two years' detention for slashing another Asian youth in a separate incident.

The verdict sent a clear message about the jury's thinking: that the neglect of the doctors in failing to treat the infection, rather than the actions of the Gilmour twins, was responsible for the death of

Imran Khan. Lorraine Gilmour, the brothers' mother, told the media that the murder charge had been pursued for political reasons: 'The Crown were afraid the Muslim community would say it was a racist decision to drop the charges and so they allowed the trial to continue.' Whatever the explanation, the verdicts and relatively lenient sentence imposed on Colin Gilmour did nothing to ease the racial tensions in the community. Demonstrators in support of the Khan family marched through Glasgow protesting at what they saw as the injustice of the outcome, while the headteacher of Shawlands Academy had already resigned, claiming she had been falsely accused of racism.

Beyond these immediate reactions, there was a longer-term problem: one of denial that racism in general existed in Glasgow or that particular incidents were racially inspired. Both the prosecution and defence in the Gilmour trial somehow managed to persuade themselves that there was no racial dimension to the attack – how, in the face of overwhelming evidence to the contrary, they could have reached such a conclusion was baffling – and the trial judge went along with them. He said there was nothing to suggest that it was a racist assault and that the case 'again demonstrates the dangers inherent in young men going about with knives'.

An editorial in *Scotland on Sunday* set out a dissenting case: 'Lord Kirkwood is, of course, perfectly entitled to draw his own conclusions . . . However, we should guard very carefully against rushing too readily to accept the view that racial tension played no part in this tragedy. "No racism here" is a glib slogan, but it is little more than that. Furthermore, it is a perception which is not shared on the streets of Glasgow's south side. There is a widespread belief there, notwithstanding the judge's and counsels' comments, that racist motives played a significant part in this affair.' A 14-year-old non-Asian boy in Shawlands, interviewed by a journalist, put it more plainly: 'They hate us and we hate them.'

Within the Muslim community, there was a reluctance to admit to the scale or character of the problem. A Labour councillor,

Bashir Maan, who was perhaps its most articulate leader, preferred to play down the racial element in the routine street and playground violence, while acknowledging profound cultural differences: 'Many Muslim parents keep their children away from white children and that creates a situation where the two groups are completely separate. Then you've got people who do not understand each other's cultures and who, because they are not encouraged to mix, fall naturally into two very different camps. Many Muslim parents are convinced that, if their children become friends with white children, they will fall into bad ways. They believe their youngsters will get involved in pre-marital sex, drugs and drinking.'

Asian families were first attracted to Scotland in the 1950s and 60s by Glasgow Corporation's recruitment drive; they came to do such essential work as driving the buses and staffing the hospitals. For a while, in a period of relative prosperity and full employment, they seemed to co-exist with the indigenous Glaswegians amicably enough; but by the late 1980s second-generation Asians were affected by racism and poverty in some of the most deprived areas of the city. The cultural divide, and the absence of any coherent attempt to bridge it, created a breeding ground for trouble. A survey by the Scottish Ethnic Minorities Research Unit in 1987 found that more than half of Indians and Pakistanis in Glasgow had suffered racial attacks on their property and that 82% of women had been subjected to racist abuse.

A decade later, in the wake of the Khan case, the aggression was nastier and more threatening. Two weeks after Khan's death, three white youths in Shawlands menaced a 53-year-old woman, Kishawar Noor, with a knife and pulled her to the ground. 'We are told the city does not have a race problem,' said her son, Mohammed Shahid. 'This is not true. We suffer daily from abuse, mostly verbal.' Few of these incidents ever attracted the attention of the police or the local media; the attack on Kishawar Noor only became known within the context of a newspaper piece about the death of Imran Khan. The official line persisted: the illusion that Scotland, unlike England, was a harmonious multicultural society. 'I wanted to believe that Scotland did not have the same problem as the rest of the UK,' said Harris Beider, chief executive of the Federation of Black Housing Associations, after a comparative study of racial attitudes in Belfast, Cardiff, London and Glasgow, 'but we found exactly the same sort of harassment in Glasgow as in Hounslow. It does not usually result in a brick through the window or murder, but it is a daily occurrence, even for young kids.' Beider believed that the statutory agencies had failed ethnic minorities in Glasgow and that victims of abuse were let down by the indifference with which their complaints were dealt with.

Racism was not exclusive to Glasgow: it was more generally prevalent in urban Scotland and especially in such pockets of racist intolerance and crime as the Muirhouse scheme in Edinburgh (another stomping ground of far-right activists) and Maxwelltown in Dundee. In these cities, too, there was an unwillingness by the authorities to recognise racism for what it was. In January 1989, two refugees from Somalia, Axmed Abuukar Sheekh and his cousin Abdirizak Husuf, were assaulted by a crowd of soccer casuals outside a pub in Cowgate, Edinburgh, having been racially taunted inside the premises. Husuf fled for his life, but Sheekh died in hospital of stab wounds. Of the two men who stood trial for his murder, one was acquitted while the other was convicted only of assault and received an 18-month prison sentence. The conduct of the case, and its unsatisfactory judicial result, outraged the ethnic minority community, and there were street protests about the refusal of the police to record the murder as racially motivated and the failure of the court to provide proper interpreting facilities for Husuf during the trial. Six months later, as a result of public pressure, the police did belatedly agree that the attack had been racially motivated, but by then serious damage had been done to community relations in the city.

The 'pervasive myths' about racism in Scotland were laid bare in a paper for the Scottish Executive: 'The Scots can't be racist because they've been oppressed by the English'; 'There aren't many black people living here'; 'They look after their own, they stick to themselves'; 'They're all rich because they run all the shops and restaurants'; 'Their children do well in our education system and are over-represented in universities'. In a second paper, published in the journal *Scottish Affairs* in 2000, Elinor Kelly, an honorary research fellow at Glasgow University, alluded to the 'gulf in experience and understanding' between people in positions of power and influence in Scottish society and the victims of racial abuse. 'This gulf,' she wrote, 'may be based on disbelief that there can be anything in Scotland which bears any resemblance to the horrors unleashed by the regimes of Hitler and Milosovic.' Between the mass slaughter of civilian populations in Europe and random acts of racial abuse and violence in Scotland, no reasonable parallel could be drawn. By then, however, the atmosphere had been further poisoned, and with it the language of public discussion, by a high-profile murder in Lanarkshire: the case of Surjit Singh Chhokar, who – in a further disturbing parallel – came to be known erroneously as 'Scotland's Stephen Lawrence'.

II

Stephen Lawrence was 18 years old, British-born, living in south-east London, an A-level student with ambitions to be an architect, when he was murdered in an unprovoked racial attack while waiting for a bus on the evening of 22 April 1993. The police investigation was not only botched but corrupt. A public inquiry chaired by Sir William Macpherson found that police officers failed to give first aid when they reached the scene, failed to follow obvious leads, and failed to arrest suspects. A BBC programme alleged that one of the officers took money from the father of one of the chief suspects in exchange for obstructing the investigation. A subsequent report for the Home Secretary by Mark Ellison QC found circumstantial evidence linking an alleged corrupt police officer with involvement in the murder of a private investigator. It was only in 2012 that two of the assailants were convicted of Lawrence's murder.

It is in this context that the case of Chhokar – and the many attempts to relate it to the Lawrence case – should be viewed. Chhokar, who was 32 at the time of his death, was an Indian citizen who came to the UK as a child, his father having arrived a few years earlier. The family dynamics were complicated. Chhokar was separated from his wife Sandeep (Sandy), with whom he had two daughters, had been in a relationship with a local woman, Elizabeth Bryce, for six years and was cohabiting with her in Wishaw, while his wife and children lived in the nearby village of Law. Sandy, who loved her husband and hoped for a reconciliation, had no contact with her husband's parents, who seemed to hold her responsible in some way for the breakdown of the marriage.

On the morning of 4 November 1998, Chhokar and Bryce drove from her house to Chhokar's flat (which he continued to rent, despite cohabiting with Bryce) to collect his fortnightly girocheque from the state. He discovered that the flat had been broken into and that the cheque was missing. They went straight to the job centre in Wishaw, where Chhokar was informed that it had been cashed earlier in the day by one Andrew Coulter, who was known to both of them. Coulter had convinced the staff in the job centre that Chhokar had given him the cheque and asked him to cash it at the post office.

At around 11.30 that night, Chhokar returned from his work as a waiter at an Indian restaurant in Bellshill – an employment apparently compatible with his receipt of state benefit – and parked his car outside Bryce's house. Bryce heard shouting from the street, looked out of the window, and saw her boyfriend being assaulted by three men. She ran out of the house and shouted, 'Fuckin' leave him alone, you bastards' and 'Andrew Coulter, I'm getting the fuckin' polis for you'. The men ran off, leaving Chhokar to stagger across the road to his car, where he collapsed. 'I've been stabbed' were his last words.

A high-ranking police officer, the divisional commander Sandy Forrest, decided to visit the crime scene. He was conscious that the incident had occurred 'in the post-Lawrence era' and was anxious to show an example to his junior colleagues about the handling of potentially racist attacks. When he arrived in Wishaw, however, Forrest formed a preliminary view that it had not been racist. 'As far as I was aware,' he said later, 'this was not an incident of a black person being set upon randomly by three white youths . . . It was about a fallout over a giro cheque and a threat to go to the police.' The motive, thought Forrest, was essentially revenge. But this was only his initial impression; the police inquiry was still in its early stages.

Early the next morning Forrest was surprised to hear from Susan Dean, a public relations officer at Strathclyde Police headquarters, asking him to clear a press release more or less ruling out racism as a factor in the crime. Forrest recalled: 'I said under no circumstances should that draft press release be released. I said that I disagreed with the decision . . . I phoned Kenny MacIver [the officer in charge of the inquiry] and he was adamant that he did not want the press release to go out in that way . . . He was outraged. Susan Dean's argument was that the details of the deceased were already in the public domain, press speculation was already to the effect that the crime was racially motivated and that we should point out that it did not appear to be. She argued that if we did not issue the press release, the media would speculate.' Dean, a civilian, got her way: the statement was issued. The episode would have made an interesting case study of the influence of corporate public relations departments, their symbiotic relationship with the press, and their power to overrule senior operational management, even in matters of life or – as in this case – death.

Dean was probably correct in her judgement. Only the premature timing of the announcement was wrong. The more the police probed the circumstances of Chhokar's death, the less likely it seemed that racism was at the root of it. The only piece of evidence indicative of a racist motive was the statement of a local man, James Rooney, who told the police: 'About three or four weeks ago I was in the park next to the community centre. There were other people there, but I'd be lying if I said who they were. Anyway, Andy Coulter said to me, "Did ye hear about it, that black bastard Chhokar raped a bird behind Almas?" [a local restaurant]. I said no, I never heard about it. He seemed angry, a bit upset about it, but he never said any more about it. He never mentioned it to me again.' The rumour was untrue. Chhokar had a criminal record, but he had never raped a woman behind Almas; besides, Rooney's evidence was inconsistent – he later admitted that the remark may have been made, not three or four weeks before the fatal assault, but as long as a year earlier. It was not much to go on. With so long a time-lag, it would have been difficult for the Crown to argue racial aggravation – especially as the police had neglected to ask members of Chhokar's family whether he had ever been subjected to racist attacks from his three assailants or anybody else in the local community. Chhokar's sister, Manjit, did ask the police if he had been assaulted 'because he was a black man' and was told that 'it would not appear to be anything like that'. Sandy, the dead man's widow, volunteered that most of his friends had been white and that he was 'Westernised', adding that, although the Lawrence murder was racist, she did not believe that her husband's murder fell into the same category.

Sandy, who emerged as a voice of sweet reason, essentially a dignified and conciliatory figure, received scant reward for her co-operation. At a formal interview with an official of the procurator fiscal's department before the first trial in the case, she was asked personally intrusive questions about her relationship with her husband. She was asked if he had ever abused her. An office-bearer of an organisation known as PETAL, which represented victims of murder, was present at the interview. 'I got the feeling', said the woman from PETAL, 'that if Sandy had not been coloured it would not have happened in that way.'

Two successive trials ended badly from the Chhokar family's point of view. In the first, a man called Ronnie Coulter was convicted by a jury of assaulting Chhokar – a disconcerting reprise of the jury's finding in the Edinburgh case – and was set free when the Crown failed to move for sentence. Dashan Chhokar, the dead man's father, found this leniency incomprehensible. There had been no attempt during the trial to explain to him what was going on, and no attempt at the end of it to explain that Coulter had been found guilty of a simple assault not involving a weapon, that he had already served three and a half months in prison on remand, and that the Crown considered that further detention would have been excessive. But it was not the unexpected release of Coulter that finally propelled the case into public prominence for the first time so much as the provocative statement to the jury by the trial judge, Lord McCluskey: 'Ladies and gentleman, a young man was murdered in a public street by one or more of persons whose identity has been freely discussed. For reasons that I cannot begin to understand one, and only one, of these persons was placed in the dock and charged with the crime.' McCluskey had no right to question the independent judgement of Scotland's chief prosecutor, the Lord Advocate, as the Lord Advocate, Hardie, indignantly pointed out. The media seized on this public row and within hours the Chhokar case had been promoted to the status of a *cause célèbre*.

'Someone killed my son,' said Darshan Chhokar. 'Yet, whoever it is, they are not in jail.' Sister Marjit commented that 'it looks like something has gone wrong in the court system.' And the family now had an articulate ally in a young trainee solicitor with a knack for publicising his causes. 'Aamer Anwar, a race campaigner who was once beaten up by Strathclyde police officers, described the Chhokar case as totally unacceptable,' reported one newspaper. It continued to quote him: 'This shows that the Crown Office is in a total mess and sends out a green light to racial attackers. Stephen Lawrence's attackers are still out on the streets, and so are the killers of this man.' The equivalence with the Lawrence case was thus implanted in the public mind, and in the very week that Macpherson published his indictment of the Metropolitan Police. The policy officer of the Scottish Commission for Racial Equality, Mike Conboy, backed Anwar's reading of the case: 'It is appalling to say the least that you have got an Indian man dead, attacked by three white guys, and no-one is being held responsible for it. There is a tremendous amount of work to do in Scotland to ensure that our criminal justice system is up to scratch in recognising and dealing with racially motivated crime. How is the black community supposed to have any confidence in justice?' The next day, Chhokar's sister kept up the media pressure, suggesting that the Crown Office had 'not bothered bringing three men to court because my brother was a Sikh . . . Was he less important?'

In this inflammatory atmosphere, it was left to a Detective Sergeant Duffy to maintain liaison with the family. He was shown into the living room of the Chhokars' house and found that someone he had never met – Anwar – was there too, in his capacity as spokesman for the newly formed Chhokar Family Justice campaign. According to Duffy, Anwar 'kept going on about race . . . I kept saying that race was not an issue.' Duffy felt that Anwar's presence was reasonable – 'If I had been in the same position as the family, I would have wanted someone to ask questions for me' – but that nothing he said satisfied Anwar. He returned to the office and told his bosses that he had been 'ambushed': that it had been a meeting with the campaign rather than a family liaison meeting. A one-sided account of the meeting found its way into the following morning's *Scotsman*, which reported that it had 'ended within minutes after Aamer Anwar asked for more detail about why the police investigation discounted racist motives for the attack'.

In the second trial a year later, Andrew Coulter entered the dock along with his co-accused David Montgomery, both charged with murder. After the much-publicised organisational failures of the first trial – a failure to keep the family informed of arcane court procedure as well as the familiar lack of interpreting facilities – the Crown Office pulled out the stops to accommodate the family's every wish. Aamer Anwar allegedly said: 'It was the same people involved in the two trials. I think they realised that the shit was going to hit the fan and they over-reacted. They were going round and getting glasses of water for the family. It was funny to see how far you could make a fiscal depute go to help somebody.' This comment was attributed to Anwar by Raj Jandoo, an advocate commissioned by the Lord Advocate to conduct an independent inquiry into the case, and was included in his report. Jandoo accused Anwar of treating family liaison with derision.

Even if his attitude was derisive, it was not far from the truth. Left in the first trial to fend for themselves in the alien environment of a process they could barely comprehend, the family now found themselves consulted at every turn. Throughout the second trial, before and after each sitting, there was a meeting between the Chhokars and Alan MacDonald from the Hamilton procurator fiscal's office, with Anwar performing the dual roles of interpreter and family spokesperson. No request for practical assistance was too much – including a microphone for one of the counsel (Derek Ogg) whose voice the official courtroom interpreters had difficulty in picking up.

The atmosphere was nevertheless tense and often emotionally charged. As Jandoo observed: 'While the trial was running in court, another drama was being played out elsewhere in the building.' He claimed that Anwar repeatedly complained about the conduct of the prosecution case by the advocate depute, Sean Murphy, and that, late one afternoon, Anwar turned on MacDonald: 'Jesus Christ, what is he [Murphy] like? The whole prosecution is incompetent.' MacDonald – an evangelical Christian – immediately left the meeting in protest. 'I was appalled,' he told Jandoo. 'I hear a lot of swearing, but that offended me . . . I had been trying to be sensitive to them [the family and Anwar] and so would expect them to be the same for me.' At another meeting, Mrs Chokkar, the dead man's mother, started to cry. The couple could not understand why the men in the dock were laughing and why the dreadful manner of their son's suffering and death was not coming across in court as they would have wished.

Anwar sensed that the case was going badly for the prosecution and, according to Jandoo, blamed it on Murphy, calling him 'a hopeless choice', pointing out that he was 'not even a QC' and that it 'looked as if he was training on the job'; Chhokar wanted to know why no-one was letting Murphy know that he was 'screwing up'. Most of this reached the ear of the beleaguered advocate depute, who believed that it was not the strongest case evidentially but that, if it went to the jury, the Crown would have fulfilled its duty. It did go to the jury, which acquitted Montgomery of murder and found Andrew Coulter guilty of assault. He was sentenced to 12 months' imprisonment. 'If this had been India or Pakistan,' Chhokar was reported as saying after the verdict, 'I would have been forced to avenge my son. Our hands are tied here.'

The Crown Office asked a senior procurator fiscal, Elish Angiolini, to review its handling of the case. Her approach to the assignment was later described by Jandoo as 'utterly informal . . . not a sound basis for any kind of report, however provisional'. She arranged to question Alan MacDonald in a tearoom. 'It was only when I thought about it afterwards that it troubled me,' he admitted. 'She didn't say whether or not it would have a bearing on my career. She didn't indicate whether the report might lead to disciplinary proceedings.' The informality extended to contacting the advocate depute in the first trial, Frances McMenamin, by mobile phone while McMenamin was on a train. It was generally assumed that Angiolini's report was for internal consumption only. When the Lord Advocate decided that it should be made public, no-one was more shocked than Angiolini herself – with the possible exception of Frances McMenamin, who was 'stunned' to find it all over the newspapers and dismayed that she had not been sent a copy in advance. Nor, however, had anyone else.

McMenamin, although she had led the prosecution case at the first trial, had no more than casual contact with the family. She recalled: 'I came out of the back door of the court one lunchtime with papers and I saw Mr and Mrs Chhokar and who I thought was their daughter. I think they were waiting for someone and I nodded to them, but I did not say anything. I did acknowledge them and the daughter smiled back . . . My next contact was on the Thursday. I had parked my car and was heading into court. I was not wearing my wig or gown. Mr and Mrs Chhokar were leaning against a wall outside the court. I was aware of the fact that I hadn't spoken to them at all during the course of the trial. I stopped and said, "How are you coping with everything?" I don't remember them saying anything in response, but they nodded to me . . . My impression was that perhaps I was intruding on their grief.'

Angiolini's report included an explanation from McMenamin that, while it was her usual practice to speak to relatives of the deceased during a murder trial, 'circumstances peculiar to this case made such communication difficult'. The Crown Office decided that it would not be 'appropriate' to disclose what these circumstances were, though by imparting them privately to the family it must have known they would be public knowledge soon enough. A few days later, a broadsheet newspaper carried another of the many stories favourable to the Chhokars: '*Scotland on Sunday* can reveal that the Crown Office attempted to cover up the reasons why a prosecutor snubbed the Chhokar family . . . We can reveal that the problem was that McMenamin was also dealing with a VAT fraud in which Chhokar's father, Darshan, was a potential witness and she feared a conflict of interest. The case involved the evasion of whisky duty worth £1.6m and in July last year three men were sentenced to a total of 11 years in jail. Darshan Chhokar was not called to give evidence.' There was nothing new about the alleged 'cover-up': the Crown Office had already acknowledged that it would not be making the reasons public; Frances McMenamin, even if she feared a conflict of interest, had not 'snubbed' the family, but had made two attempts to acknowledge them, in her own words out of 'sheer human decency';

and the newspaper's story omitted to mention that the Crown Office had considered putting Darshan Chhokar in the dock in the VAT case before deciding that he should not face prosecution.

In a second sequel to the saga, Raj Jandoo's report covered the same ground as Angiolini's but more extensively and thoroughly. His starting point was philosophical. He asked himself what was meant by institutional racism. His answer was that it occurred 'wherever the service provided by an organisation fails – whether deliberately or not – to meet equally the needs of all the people whom it serves, having regard to their racial, ethnic or cultural background'. Using that definition as his benchmark, he decided there had been institutional racism in the Chhokar case. He specified 'the failure of the police to consider racial aggravation as a factor in their investigation of the crime', as well as miscellaneous failures of the procurator fiscal's office: to acknowledge that the family might have difficulty in dealing with correspondence in English, to realise the need for interpreters, to maintain liaison with the family during the first trial. He was critical too of the ignorance about Sikh funeral customs and the reluctance to release the body for cremation, which caused the family needless distress.

Most of this was fair; but in his condemnation of the police Jandoo went too far. Their investigation was exemplary in its efficiency – as he had to acknowledge. The divisional commander, Forrest, promptly on the scene, was sceptical that the crime was racially motivated but careful not to rule out the possibility. The early press release was an error of judgement, but not one for which the investigating team could be blamed. The witness Rooney recalled a conversation in which the words 'black bastard' were used, but this was the only evidence pointing to a racial element in the crime and Rooney was not exactly a model of consistency. The strong belief of the deceased's wife that it was not a racist crime, indeed that most of her husband's friends were white, was impressive. Should the police have asked others in Chhokar's circle if he had ever been racially abused? Probably. But it was unfair to conclude that they 'failed to consider racial aggravation as a factor'. Acutely conscious of public sensitivity over the Lawrence case, they did consider it – before coming to the not unreasonable conclusion that inflamed tempers in a dispute about a girocheque provoked the fatal attack.

Even if that conclusion was mistaken, it did not imply dishonour on the part of the police. There was no delay in arresting the suspects. There was no attempt to impede the investigation. There were no murky pay-offs to protect the guilty. In short, there was no corruption. For all these reasons, the claim, all too readily put about by the media, that Sirjut Chhokar was 'Scotland's Stephen Lawrence' was going too far; yet it went on disfiguring public discussion of racism in Scotland for many years.

III

In a concurrent *cause célèbre* involving the police, media hyperbole again played a part in sustaining public interest. The *Mail on Sunday*, talking up the story, called it 'one of the most damaging scandals in British judicial history' involving 'political intrigue and a cover-up that reaches to the very heart of the Scottish establishment'. The case of Shirley McKie, though never in danger of living up to such extravagant billing, was an intriguing detective mystery in its own right – and acquired a deeper significance for raising doubts about the reliability of fingerprint evidence in criminal trials.

McKie, a 35-year-old detective constable, was a member of the team investigating the murder of a reclusive spinster, Marion Ross, who was stabbed to death at her bungalow in Kilmarnock in 1997. A construction company run by a man called Asbury had recently built an extension to the house, which gave the police their first lead: McKie and her sergeant were instructed to track down the workmen. Asbury informed them that his grandson David, who worked for him, had vanished and left a suicide note. When the young man's bedroom was searched, McKie found a biscuit tin containing £1,400 in cash; and when fingerprint experts examined the tin they identified one of the prints on it as the murdered woman's. One of Asbury's prints was found on a gift-tag attached to a parcel in Ross's house.

He did not commit suicide. Instead he returned to Kilmarnock to face a charge of murdering Marion Ross. Asbury had no record of violence, and apart from the two fingerprints, for which there might have been an innocent explanation, the case against him was relatively weak.

Police sealed off the bungalow and imposed a system of controlled access. Shirley McKie, a junior officer, was not permitted to enter the house beyond the porch, yet among the 428 fingerprints examined by a specialist team at the Scottish Criminal Record Office (SCRO) in Glasgow, one – labelled Y7 – was identified as her left thumbprint. It was found halfway up the door-frame of the bathroom. When a superior broke the news, Shirley McKie was so upset that her vehement denials could be heard in other parts of the building. She maintained that it could not be her thumbprint because she had never set foot in the house. There was some surprise at her response; one senior officer wondered why she was making such a fuss about a relatively unimportant matter and felt she was over-reacting. She was sent home and her long ordeal began. The received wisdom was that fingerprints never lied. McKie's father Iain, a retired superintendent, was as convinced of their infallibility as any other police officer, yet equally convinced of his daughter's integrity and innocence.

McKie was, however, known to the Scottish Criminal Record Office. In an earlier case, her fingerprint had been found on a plastic bag, an important piece of evidence. She insisted she had been wearing latex gloves when she handled it. SCRO officers suspected her of lying – and even when it was demonstrated that fingerprints could show through latex gloves, they were not completely satisfied. The Director of SCRO, Hugh Ferry, regarded Y7 as significant for two reasons: its proximity to the body and the fact that, so far as he was concerned, McKie had form. Chief Inspector William O'Neill, head of the fingerprint bureau, was told that she had 'done something similar before'. Did this influence, perhaps subconsciously, the examiners' judgement in the identification of the print from the Ross house? Was it lurking somewhere at the back of their mind? A senior judge from Northern Ireland, Sir Anthony Campbell, who was commissioned by Scotland's justice minister to conduct an inquiry into the case in 2008, considered this theory and rejected it.

Detective Chief Inspector Stephen Heath was so taken aback by the strength of McKie's denial, and by its serious implications, that he gave instructions that the veracity of the print should be checked. He did so reluctantly: it was the first time in his 20 years with the police that he had questioned an identification. 'He felt he was taking a big step in raising these issues,' wrote Campbell. 'As far as he was aware, the identification of a fingerprint had never been wrong. One of the core beliefs that was drummed into you was that no-one has the same fingerprints.' The print was re-photographed and, 'because of the gravity of the matter', rechecked by a larger group of experts. SCRO sent back word: it was hers. They were categorical about it.

A distraught McKie tortured herself with various implausible theories about how the print might have got there. Had she experienced some mental blank and forgotten that she had entered the house? Another disturbing possibility grew in her mind – that the print had been planted by colleagues. When Heath heard this, he felt so undermined and depressed that he thought of resigning. It implied that there had been a conspiracy by Strathclyde Police to pervert the course of justice in a murder trial. The attitude of senior officers towards her hardened; her closest colleague – in police argot her 'neighbour' – distanced himself. Sir Anthony Campbell, when he came to review the case, was not surprised by the growing hostility towards her at the time: 'There is no evidence that the police were "out to get" McKie. Nor is there any evidence of any conspiracy involving the police and SCRO falsely to identify fingerprints in the case. The evidence is that the police went out of their way to have SCRO check the identification and methodically examined the explanation that she advanced.' He also rejected an innuendo that became common currency in the media's view of the case: that the fingerprint experts may have colluded in identifying the print.

David Asbury stood trial for the murder of Marion Ross. McKie, giving evidence on oath, repeated that the fingerprint could not be hers because she had never been in the house. In his address to the jury, the advocate depute accused McKie of lying. He told the jury that she had done something like this before (a reference to the plastic bag) and that she had dug herself into a hole. He described her as a rogue policewoman who had added an unnecessary burden to the case. 'Fingerprint evidence is irrefutable,' he added, 'and this is not an exception.' It was the most damning indictment of a police officer imaginable, so bad that it overshadowed the outcome of the trial: Asbury was convicted and sentenced to life imprisonment. The verdict was overturned on appeal.

Disgraced and humiliated, Shirley McKie faced the prospect of a long prison sentence. In the spring of 1998, she was arrested at dawn, taken to Kilmarnock police station, strip-searched, and charged with perjury. While on bail awaiting trial, she scoured the internet in the hope of finding someone – anyone – who might be able to clear her name. She stumbled on two respected fingerprint experts in the United States, David Wertheim and David Grieve, who agreed to look at the case. They spent many hours comparing the fingerprint on the door frame of the bathroom with an imprint of McKie's left thumb and decided that they were made by different people. In Wertheim's opinion the mark on the door frame had been made by a right thumb. McKie broke down with sheer relief. It was only three weeks before the start of her trial, in which she was to be represented by one of the sharpest defence lawyers in Scotland, Donald Findlay. 'From that point,' wrote Anthony Campbell, 'both prosecution and defence were dealing with a situation that was unique, at least in Scotland.'

In his address to the jury, Lord Johnston made little attempt to conceal his feelings about the case. Why, he asked, would McKie continue for two years, in the face of mounting pressure and in an isolated and lonely position, to deny any involvement with the fingerprint? The jury took only 90 minutes to acquit her. The judge then delivered a warm tribute from the bench, expressing his respect 'for the obvious courage and dignity which you have shown throughout this nightmare . . . I very much hope you can put it behind you. I wish you all the best.'

McKie left the dock believing that the nightmare was over and that she would be able to return to work, to a job she loved. But it was made clear to her that there would be no way back; she was deemed medically unfit for service. Even the trial from which she walked away exonerated, Lord Johnston's praise ringing in her ears, returned to haunt her. A passage critical of her in Anthony Campbell's report dwelt on her answer to a prosecution question about whether, in the run-up to the trial, anyone apart from the American experts had looked at the disputed fingerprint. McKie replied that she didn't know. As Campbell pointed out, the truth was that someone else – a fingerprint specialist – had looked at the print, that he had identified it as McKie's, and that she was aware of this. Campbell said that her incorrect answer in court 'did not necessarily lead me to approach with scepticism her earlier and consistent denial that she entered the house in Irvine Road beyond the porch area.'

Media interest in the case continued long after she was formally cleared. By early 2006, when a retired senior police officer, Brown, was pursuing his own informal inquiries, nine years had elapsed since the discovery of Marion Ross's body. Brown had a meeting in his house with a journalist from the *Sunday Mail*, Marion Scott, and two fingerprint examiners from SCRO. Scott mentioned 'rumours' – among them that McKie had been in the house; that she had not been in the house, but that her fingerprint had been planted by a jealous colleague; that there had been some kind of sexual liaison in the house; and that she was a 'murder ghoul'. Brown's hunch was that McKie opened the door and said something like, 'I'll have a quick look.' Campbell found no evidence to support any of these rumours and speculations.

The inquiry also heard of a conversation among police officers on dock duty at the High Court in Paisley. One had allegedly said to another: 'That bitch will get us done, it was me that let her into the house.' When he was asked why he had done it, he replied that it was because he fancied her. The officer in question, when he gave evidence to the inquiry, claimed that it was someone else who had admitted letting McKie into the house. The identify of that person, if he existed, was never discovered. Brown hinted in evidence that several people knew the name of the guilty party but that no-one was prepared to divulge it because they all feared for their jobs. There was no proof of any of it, but the many innuendos and smears neverthe-less found their way into the official record.

Campbell, after a painstaking review of the fingerprint evidence, decided that the SCRO examiners had made a genuine misidentifi-cation. It was an extraordinary error that permanently blighted their careers. He further determined there was no evidence that McKie had ever entered the house. Once more she was exonerated. There were echoes here of *The Winslow Boy*, Terence Rattigan's play, based on real events, about a naval cadet falsely accused of stealing a postal order and the long campaign to clear his name. Scotland's own Winslow Girl never returned to the police, and had to fight hard for compensation, finally receiving a cheque for £750,000 and a belated apology. But the murder of Marion Ross, the starting point for the strange case of Shirley McKie, remained unsolved.

A DAY IN THE LIFE OF SCOTLAND

I

AT ONE MINUTE PAST MIDNIGHT, JAMES (JIMMY) HALLIDAY, a former chairman of the Scottish National Party, opened his diary for 6 May 1999 with the reflection that it felt like New Year: a moment for remembrance and sentiment. Seven hours on, the polls would be open for the election to the first Scottish Parliament for almost 300 years; yet Halliday, who had worked all his life for the home rule cause, could feel no elation. 'What really matters,' he wrote, 'is Scotland in relation to the wider world. Without powers and functions in that area, our parliament must remain only "parliament". How can four years of sensible political debate be sustained on the topics within its permitted range? Topics which, once principles to guide action have been established, could safely be left to civil servants and professional functionaries.'

For Halliday, devolution would never be enough. For another of the early morning diarists that day, Tam Dalyell, it was a dangerous step too far. But when the Labour MP for Linlithgow woke at 2 am, it was not the potential break-up of the UK that was disturbing his sleep but NATO's military intervention in Yugoslavia and Britain's commitment to it: 'I ponder over the meeting at which I had been the opening speaker a few hours earlier. An eve-of-poll rally in Scotland? No such thing. The venue was the huge Methodist Hall opposite Westminster Abbey where 1,700 people, standing 10 deep in the aisles, listened to passionate speeches for the end of bombing.' Dalyell added a scathing reference to the

Defence Secretary, George Robertson ('It would have been better if he had never gone near defence and stuck to devolution') before switching on the radio, where he discovered, perhaps to his grim satisfaction, that the Scottish Parliament was the last item on the BBC's World Service news.

Another of the insomniacs, R.D. Kernohan, a former director of the Scottish Conservatives, was likewise thinking about Belgrade: 'Deliver us from the evil we have aggravated,' he prayed. 'Forgive us our miscalculations.' As he was drifting back to sleep, it occurred to him that he had better pray for Scotland too.

At the same tender hour – 4 am – the Lord Lieutenant of Shetland, John Scott, was already at work in remote Bressay: 'First light to the lambing ewes. Two needing help. 400 lambed, 500 to go. A cloudless dawn with a brisk east wind off the North Sea.' It was a day of personal significance for the Scott family: his son Tavish was hoping to become the Liberal Democrat MSP for Shetland. (And did.) But his first entry made no mention of politics: the fragility of new life took priority.

These diaries, and many others, were kept at the request of a journalist (the author of this book) as an informal record of 24 hours in the life of Scotland. There was no obligation to make them specifically political (the principal of Strathclyde University, Sir John Arbuthnott, managed to get through a day of meetings without ever mentioning the election), but for most of the diarists the renewal of parliamentary democracy in Scotland was the background theme, and for some it was the dominant one.

By 5.30 am, Scotland had dropped off the World Service agenda. 'Of a historic day in a little country on the north-west edge of Europe,' noted the journalist Fiona MacDonald, 'not a word'. On the domestic front pages, however, there was little else. The *Scotsman*'s 'Scotland makes history' and the *Sun*'s 'This is the day you make history' earned few marks for originality, while readers of the Labour-voting *Daily Record* might have been mystified rather than enlightened by the splash headline 'Make it a double Dewars' – which combined an incongruous reference to the prospective First Minister (not the most hospitable character in British public life) with a jaunty nod to the voting system for the new parliament, the first in the UK to be elected by proportional representation. The people had two votes: one for their constituency MSP, elected in the traditional first-past-the-post fashion, the other for a 'regional' member appointed by the parties themselves from a pecking order known as 'the list' – a system of PR which had the perverse effect of allowing some of the losers in the constituency contests to sit in the parliament with the same status and privileges as directly elected members. The only regional candidates named on the ballot paper were independents, if there were any; supporters of the big battalions were expected to vote for the party rather than for named individuals. Whatever the merits of proportional representation in theory, the practice in Scotland was undemocratic from the start.

The *Herald* invited its readers to vote 'with clarity in your head' – a tall order in the circumstances – but also 'with pride in your heart' – a tendentious message reinforced by the caption beneath a front-page photograph of a baby with a bottle in its mouth and a saltire in its pram: 'A toast to the future. A child enjoys his milk, and the sun, at a nationalist rally in Edinburgh. The grown-ups would have more serious thoughts in mind as Scotland's new era beckons.' At home in Brodick, the editor of the *Arran Banner*, John Millar, observed in his diary: 'The grown-ups are not so grown-up, I think. They are tribalist, they are smug, they are racist. This is playing to the gallery. And the gallery means the mob.'

At 6.30 am, the architect Sir James Dunbar-Nasmith, chairman of the Scottish Civic Trust, was listening on Radio Scotland to church bells playing 'Why am I so sad on this my wedding day?', apparently the tune of choice at St Giles Cathedral on the morning of the Act of Union. Another listener to *Good Morning Scotland*, Dr Charles Allison, a hospital consultant in Brechin, was thankful to the presenter, the phlegmatic John Milne, for 'resisting all that grandiose "date with destiny" stuff'.

The head of A&E at Ayr Hospital, Dr Leo Murray, who has made a previous appearance tending to the dead and dying from Hanger 13, began his working day at 7.50 am by reviewing the records of patients seen overnight: 'Man breathless with chronic lung disease; young woman with chest pain; male overdose; child with abdominal pain – nothing serious; young man with appendicitis; another young man in police custody having cut himself with a knife; well-known alcoholic with further episode of pancreatitis; elderly man with fractured femur; old lady with heart attack; young woman with bronchitis; man with gastro-enteritis. Routine night's work'.

Among the many who would not be voting with clarity in their head and pride in their heart was Hannah Downie, a third-year pupil at Marr College in Troon, who was not yet eligible to vote at all. 8.30 am: 'Hazel (the neighbour from across the road) meets me outside our front garden. She launches straight into: "Ugh! I hate this election!". This negative statement deflates my bad mood into a very bad mood as we set off for school . . . Fortunately, on the winding path (created in order to dodge the fallen trees of the Boxing Day storm), I suddenly have a little epiphany – everything slots into place. All around me nature is working its miracle of springtime. I now feel much more confident and happy.'

The broadcaster Ian Mackenzie had hoped to walk to the polling station on a carpet of glorious pink, but when he peeked out the window of his Helensburgh villa at first light he saw that an overnight gale had swept away the last of the cherry blossom. 'Tread softly,' he had intended to write in his diary, 'for you tread on the dream of a new Scotland.' It was such a good line that he included it anyway. At 8.45 am, Mackenzie marked the first of his crosses against the SNP candidate, a weather-man with Scottish Television. The party leader, Alex Salmond, had addressed a meeting in the town 11 days earlier:

'Jolly on occasion, he was straight on all key questions . . . I'm happy today to be voting for him.'

Meanwhile, Norman Gillies, the principal of Sabhal mor Ostaig, the new Gaelic college on Skye, was driving the two miles to work unimpeded by traffic lights or roundabouts: 'just a nice meander along the sea wall, admiring the views across the Sound of Sleat and into the mouths of two sea lochs, Loch Nevis and Loch Houra'; in Glasgow, Hamish Whyte of the Mariscat Press was opening the mail, a cheque for £6.44 from Kelvin Books ('any cheque brightens the day of a small publisher'); and in Langbank the radio presenter Iain Anderson was taking a flask of tea to the polling station, where he found his brother in earnest conversation with a clan chief, George MacMillan, the latter sporting the blue rosette of the Conservative Party.

At 9.30 am, the Reverend Roddy MacLeod, minister of Cumlodden, Lochfyneside and Lochgair – a parish name rich in evocative images – voted in Furnace Village Hall: 'Para Handy attended a ball in this very hall . . . Strongly tempted to give second vote to Robbie the Pict, who had the best election slogan: Pick the Pict for Parliament on the Peachy Paper Please.' The candidate with the talent for alliteration, an intrepid campaigner for the removal of tolls on the Skye bridge, would have added a welcome eccentricity to the new legislature. He suffered instead the almost inevitable fate of fringe candidates on the discreditable 'list': the Pict on the peachy paper was duly crushed by the combined weight of the party machines.

A second minister, the Reverend David Graham of Rosemount Parish Church in Aberdeen, found nothing in the newspapers 'worth tearing out for a Scottish future'. He was unimpressed by the *Herald*'s essayist of the day, Alasdair Gray, novelist and artist, who had implored readers to vote anything but Labour. 'Long ago,' wrote Graham, 'we employed him on a Glasgow community programme. Only for half a day; by lunchtime he had a better offer from the owners of the Ubiquitous Chip restaurant, who asked him to paint murals.'

At 10.15 am, the Bressay postman, George Birnie, arrived at John Scott's farmhouse with the mail. 'Says quite a few Bressay folk have voted already. Tavish off to Noss with David Manson and Robert Henderson and the dogs to gather the ewes. His way of relaxing after a hectic campaign.'

Fifteen minutes later, 400 miles to the south, Ian Mackenzie witnessed the start of a routine morning in Glasgow District Court: 'A broken-faced, broken-brained youth talks interminably at the magistrate in a monotone like Lucky in *Waiting for Godot*. A plump teenager with a pony tail grunts yes and no. As he is led away, I see his face. The eyes are dead, the expression stony. These are human? If to be human is to be free, these aren't. They're ghosts, devoid of the power to control their future.'

Across the city, Ronald Mavor entered in his diary the names of dead patriots. Mavor, son of the playwright James Bridie, a playwright himself, a physician, critic and arts administrator in his time, had returned from exile in Canada to retirement in a changed Glasgow, where he never seemed completely at ease. He listed, among those who had not lived to celebrate the great day, the novelist Compton Mackenzie, the writer George Scott Moncrieff, the poet and classicist Douglas Young, the editor Alastair Dunnett, the politician John P. Mackintosh and the lawyer John MacCormick, none of whom had been remembered by the *Herald* that morning in a piece claiming to honour the great home-rule campaigners.

The omission of MacCormick, founder of the Scottish Covenant movement after the Second World War, was particularly revealing of the media's short memory. Mavor recalled meeting him regularly 'late at night and not always entirely sober, in the Art Club on my fortnightly day off from the Victoria Infirmary'. Having paid £5 for a certificate from the Scottish Covenant redeemable in the event of a Scottish Parliament, Mavor hunted his flat for the proof, but without success. MacCormick was long dead, the certificate lost, the fiver unredeemed; but at last Scotland was about to have the desired outcome: a parliament.

Apart from Jimmy Halliday, three prominent nationalists of the pre-war or immediate post-war era did live to see the great day, and in the case of Ian Hamilton QC, MacCormick's friend and assistant in the Covenant movement, even take part in it as a candidate. The others were Nigel Tranter, who wrote his novels into a weatherproof notebook as he strode back and forth along the beach at Aberlady, and the ecclesiastical historian Elizabeth Whitley, alone in her farmhouse in Galloway since the death of her husband Harry, former minister of St Giles. At 10.45 am, Whitley recorded in her diary: 'Put on skirt, as for Sundays, to collect pension and vote. Decide I will wear the silver SNP badge given to me by those voters daft enough to ask me to stand against Sir Alec D Home – that hater of independence – in Perthshire.' She took the coast road from her cottage in the hamlet of Southwick, driving through bluebell woods and moorland, to the polling station and was back in time for 'the country dinner hour': noon.

James Gunn Henderson, a newspaperman from the far north, arrived in Inverness at lunchtime: 'Hailed by my old pal Charles Kennedy MP as I approach the cafe in the Eastgate shopping centre, in company with Lib Dem candidate John Farquhar Munro and his agent. Charles offers me a coffee and the other half of his "prime Ross-shire beef" sandwich, which I readily accept.' Kennedy had not been tempted to forsake Westminster, with its heady atmosphere, where important decisions were taken in one of the world's great capital cities – unlike Scotland's own capital, which came fully alive only for three weeks in August. Kennedy, clever and personable, was as seduced by London as the other Scottish stars in UK politics – though had he settled for a duller life in the Edinburgh parliament he might have lived longer. When he handed James Gunn Henderson the remains of his beef sandwich, he was within three months of being elected leader of his party, a bad career move for anyone with a drink problem.

At 1.20 pm, the new edition of the *Arran Banner* was ready for publication: 'The building is alive when the printing press is thumping away,' wrote its editor, John Millar. On another Scottish island, John Scott, up since 4 am, was having an early afternoon 'shepherd's sleep'. In a Glasgow studio, Iain Anderson was preparing for his daily programme on Radio Scotland, *Mr Anderson's Fine Tunes*; and soon, in Furnace, Argyll, the Reverend Roddy McLeod would be listening to it as he prepared his sermon for Sunday. Eileen Dunlop, a children's author, was at home in Dollar working out the plot of a novel for her Dublin-based publisher: 'I think how wonderful it would be if, in our "new" Scotland, a publisher appeared with flair and enthusiasm for children's literature . . . But I shall not hold my breath.' In Aberfoyle a retired businessman, John Blanche, was writing the latest instalment in his journal of family history and putting a note in his diary about the parliament in Edinburgh: 'It will be a worthwhile innovation if it can hold the government more accountable for its actions in Scotland. The old Scottish Office was never very willing to change its mind in the face of reasonable representations.' He speculated that it might be the first step towards a federal UK.

At Charing Cross in Glasgow, George Chalmers, who had served a total of 12 years in prison for a succession of bungled bank robberies, ran into some acquaintances. 'Were you at court thi day?' one of them asked him.

'No – a funeral – Rab Reed.'

'Whit wiz it – o.d.?'

'No, silent pneumonia.'

'First thing he kept quiet aboot, eh?'

Not far away in the west end, Ronald Mavor was arranging his flat for an election-night party, wheeling the television through from the bedroom into the drawing room. He looked out and watched workmen throw slates and bags of cement from a scaffolded building, badly damaged by winter storms, down great chutes of multi-coloured barrels, and wondered why there was not dancing in the streets in anticipation of the parliament, 'surely a more wonderful event than the mathematically doubtful millennium'. In Bressay, John Scott had stirred from his shepherd's sleep and gone out to vote – for his son. In Galloway, Elizabeth Whitley's hungry hens were grumbling at the gate, reminding her of a mutinous Woman's Guild. She brought them mash and collected their eggs.

Lucy Anderson, another of the third-year pupils at Marr College in Troon, wrote in her diary at the end of the school day that there had been no discussion of 'the greatness' of the occasion: 'We spent the day revising for the umpteen tests that are the lot of the Scottish child. I'd like to be able to report that we spent our free time discussing the election. However, we spent it practising our wolf whistles.'

In the late afternoon, the Roman Catholic bishop of Aberdeen, Mario Conti, called in at the offices of the church's millennium appeal and spoke to the co-ordinator, one of whose sons was voting for the first time. It prompted a comment in his diary about 'the extraordinary nature of the democratic system whereby the vote of one young person is of the same value, in effect, as that of a bishop, who has seen many administrations both locally and nationally and has had, by reason of his very office, to reflect on what are the foundations of a just society and to judge individuals and their parties thereby.'

'Have an egg to my tea,' wrote Elizabeth Whitley at 6 pm. 'They really are different from shop ones.' The polls were closing in four hours and she would not be staying up.

Early in the evening, as he ferried Labour supporters to the polling stations in Linlithgow, Tam Dalyell decided that he would not attend the count – 'because if I did go I could not restrain myself from entering a steaming row with Robin Cook [Foreign Secretary in the Blair government] who I blame in great measure, along with his odious friend Madeleine Albright, for the Balkans war.'

Around 8 pm, Martin T. Warren, a Cistercian monk at Nunraw Abbey, having been up since 3.15 am, was preparing for bed: 'Lock up. Apple blossom in profusion, thick fog and an easterly breeze. A portly crow on the garth getting a last bite before shut-eye, bunnies scatter at my coming, silence – the great silence – the sacrament of the night – no talking.' At the same time, Rose Galt, a retired teacher and Labour Party activist, was arriving at the flat of her brother and sister-in-law in Glasgow, bearing pizzas and wine: 'Waiting for results is essentially a communal activity.' The sacrament of the night did not apply in her case.

A little later, Fiona MacDonald spoke to a fisherman striding up the quay at Troon: Jim Brown, just off the *Southern Sun*. He hadn't voted. 'No polling stations out there and by the time I get home they'll be closed.'

By 9.15 pm, Iain Anderson was installed at the controller's party at BBC Scotland – 'The purvey here is seriously good' – and noting the presence of such luminaries as the novelist William McIlvanney. Sixteen minutes into the bulletin, there was the first mention of the Scottish election on the BBC's *Nine O'Clock News*. 'London does not like it,' noted John Scott in Bressay.

Some sensed that they had not been invited to the party: at the controller's, at Ronald Mavor's, at Rose Galt's brother's, or anywhere else. The editor of the *Arran Banner*, John Millar, stayed at home, disenchanted by the day's events: 'I have to confess that all this talk of a new Scottish pride makes me rather sad, makes me feel like an outsider in my own country. I love Scotland, but there are many things about my fellow Scots, especially the nationalists and all the thinly disguised anti-Englishness, which make me ashamed.'

A few seconds after 10 pm, Tam Dalyell heard the first exit polls on the BBC: his party would have no overall majority; it would be dependent on its coalition partner, the Liberal Democrats. 'Many in the Labour Party will ask: why did we sweat our guts out to hold the Labour Party together for 18 years simply to get a coalition? Will activists bother to do the hard work in future when they see Dewar and the Lib Dems carving up decisions in public?' He was disdainful of the minority party: 'deeply anti-socialist at home and hawks for military adventures abroad.'

Dr Leo Murray wondered what difference the day would make to the 153 people who had attended his A&E department: 'To the 46 admitted to hospital? To the lady with cancer spread to her bones? To the man with the brain tumour? To the boy with his first epileptic fit? To the six people with heart attacks? To the person suddenly blind in one eye? To the man in police custody? To me? To you?'

Lucy Anderson was sitting on her bed in Troon with two thoughts in her mind: 'Who is going to win the election? And, more importantly, what am I going to wear to tomorrow's "no uniform day" at school?'

But first there were the votes to count. Kirsty Wark, who had incurred the wrath of James Dunbar-Nasmith for her combative interviewing during the campaign, introduced the BBC's election night coverage with the puzzling statement: 'All the indications are that you have voted in your droves.' Puzzling, because even at that stage all the indications were that the Scots had not voted in their droves. 'The low turnout [58%] is disappointing,' wrote Rose Galt, 'and you can't put it all down to the weather – we're Scots for God's sake.' She hoped that 'by tomorrow we'll have a parliament in which no one party – even mine – has an overall majority'. She got her wish: after the arcane requirements of proportional representation had been satisfied, Labour had 56 seats, the SNP 35, the Conservatives 18, the Liberal Democrats 17, the Green Party 1 and the Scottish Socialists 1 (their leader, Tommy Sheridan, who wasted no time in introducing the first reforming measure of the parliament, a private member's bill abolishing warrant sales).

The supposed triumph of the new democracy was heavily qual-ified – by the failure of 42% of the electorate to vote, the absence of independent voices (apart from Dennis Canavan), the unwillingness of senior Labour politicians to commit to the fledgling parliament, the embarrassing mediocrity of many of the newly-elected members, some of whom had problems with basic articulation, and not least the absurdities thrown up by PR. In West Renfrewshire, for example, the runner-up (the nationalist) and the third-placed candidate (the Tory, Annabel Goldie, a long way back) were both beneficiaries of the list system, while the smartest in the field, Neal Ascherson, got nothing out of the experience apart from a few newspaper columns. He claimed to have 'loved all the hand shaking and baby kissing', of which, by his account, there was quite a lot, even in Port Glasgow. Ascherson had once been the resident brain in Jim Sillars's long-defunct break-away Scottish Labour Party, but by 1999 had drifted into the Liberal Democrats, to the general astonishment of his fellow journalists. Next door, in Greenock and Inverclyde, the pedigree of another good man – Ian Hamilton QC – likewise counted for little. The pioneer of the devolution scheme, Kenyon Wright, who stood as an independent on one of the regional lists, failed to be elected to his own parliament. Either the Scots mistakenly felt that they had an embarrassment of riches from which to choose, and could afford to discard such people, or they were ignorant of their own country and blind to its best interests.

Steve Bruce, professor of sociology at Aberdeen University, contributed the last of the diaries on 6 May 1999, offering a midnight prediction for the parliament: 'Much about it will be good: better gender balance, sensible working hours, little pomp, no huge majorities. Long-term, demarcation disputes will lead to greater ill-feeling between Scotland and London. In the lifetime of my children, the UK will break up and I cannot say I mind the thought.'

And that was how it felt, on the day Scotland elected a parliament.

II

The building itself – the inspiration of a Catalan architect, Enric Miralles, who died before its completion – was hailed by some as a masterpiece of modern design, by others as an eyesore. It came at spectacular expense and over-budget; and it was behind schedule. Its situation at the tatty extreme of the Royal Mile allowed it to adopt the generic name Holyrood, even when the legislators were obliged to meet elsewhere. The parliament found a temporary home in the Assembly Hall of the Church of Scotland on the Mound, and it was there, six days after the election, that it convened for the first time. Winifred Ewing, the oldest member, briefly occupied the chair until the appointment of Lord Steel of Aikwood as presiding officer. (Though the much-garlanded former Liberal leader preferred to be known as Sir David when in Scotland.)

Seven weeks then elapsed before the official opening by the Queen, time enough for the new administration led by Donald Dewar and his Liberal Democrat deputy, Jim Wallace, to settle in; and for the Scots to discover that their parliament was neither a house of varieties nor a chamber of horrors. The journalists who reported its affairs craved drama and sensation and were deriving neither from the dour First Minister and his administration's pedestrian agenda. There was also a question of style: the desire of the parliament's creators for a less confrontational politics seemed in reality to be more of an obstacle than a blessing. But what had the critics expected? A great deal of business – of any parliament – was necessarily methodical. As the seasoned Magnus Linklater wrote in *Scotland on Sunday*: 'There is not much point in pretending that banner headlines will greet clause-by-clause debate on the abolition of feudalism, or that the Finance Bill is going to electrify the nation.'

Nevertheless, the palpable sense of anticlimax and disillusion could not be ignored. Something had to be pulled out of the bag – an entertainment of some sort. It was left to Lord Steel – Sir David – The Boy David as he had been known in days almost beyond recall – to put together a programme for the royal event on 1 July.

The night before, there were two rival attractions in Edinburgh. In a recently opened science centre called Dynamic Earth, the latest

Secretary of State for Scotland, John Reid, hosted a gala dinner. It came as something of a surprise that a cabinet post of that title was required post-devolution and something of a mystery that Reid had anything useful to do in it. His gala dinner gave him a public profile if nothing else, but it was not much of a draw compared with the counter-attraction: the premiere of Sean Connery's new film, *Entrapment*, at the Odeon followed by a reception for 700 guests at Prestonfield House. The SNP leader, Alex Salmond, and his business manager Mike Russell, decided they would rather be at Prestonfield House, 'rubbing shoulders with the stars' as the *Scotsman* had it, rather than rubbing shoulders at Dynamic Earth with the likes of John Reid. The decision was made for them by the presence of Connery himself, the SNP's most celebrated supporter, accompanied by his glamorous young co-star, Catherine Zeta-Jones and her partner, the actor Michael Douglas. After weeks of dreary Holyrood, Edinburgh had Hollywood on its doorstep for a few hours – even if the film itself was the cinematic equivalent of a debate on the Finance Bill.

The Scottish media at its provincial worst fawned over Connery – 'the most famous living Scotsman' – and tactfully overlooked his decades of exile in a friendlier tax regime, where he was able to champion the cause of Scottish independence without the least risk of ever having to contribute to the bill. 'I've been waiting nearly 40 years for this,' he said. 'I think it's certainly the most important day of my life.' He admitted to mild disappointment with the parliament's performance to date: 'I don't think it's been at its best – it's been a dry rehearsal without the jokes, I suppose.' He hoped that 'the political gloves' would soon come off.

In the morning, the newspapers emphasised the momentous nature of the day ahead by publishing pull-out souvenir supplements. The *Scotsman* carried a thoughtful leader reminding its readers of a fact some might have forgotten: that when the Queen formally opened the parliament, Scotland would obtain what the *Scotsman* had asked for as long ago as 4 February 1887 ('An Assembly to relieve

Parliament by taking up at its request purely local-national affairs') and had continued to ask for periodically ever since. But there was no point in pretending – as romantic nationalists pretended – that the pre-1707 era in Scotland was somehow a golden age. The paper acknowledged that the last parliament had been elected by only two thousand people and that its final act was to enforce the serfdom of workers in salt pans: 'That was why, come the age of Enlightenment, the old parliament was scarcely missed. This time it must be different.' The leader finished with a challenging question: 'We may now have the power, but will we wield it wisely and dynamically?'

Despite James Halliday's lament for its limited focus, there was no lack of raw material for a domestic parliament with tax-raising powers. In the spring of 1999, a report on poverty in Glasgow revealed that nearly half the city's schoolchildren were deprived enough to qualify for free school meals and that more than half were entitled to clothing and footwear grants. In addressing the plight of the urban poor, a wise and dynamic parliament would find endless scope for new and more creative thinking. It would surely also be actively concerned about the scourge of racism – again in the headlines over the case of an 89-year-old partially sighted man, Shulam Rabbani, who, having been mugged in a Glasgow street after evening prayer at the Central Mosque, was casually treated by the police and sent home on a bus, injured and unaided. And a wise and dynamic parliament might further wish to do something about the depressed state of Scotland's towns after the Consumers Association's indictment of Ayr for the seediness of its seafront.

The disastrous national diet: that too demanded attention. While the political class headed for Edinburgh, a team of Japanese scientists were on their way to Skye to introduce the islanders to a new soya product, a jelly with the flavour of red wine and yoghurt. Professor Yukio Yamori of Kyoto University had been commissioned by the World Health Organisation to road-taste Japanese-style food in the hope of improving life expectancy in countries with an exceptional incidence of coronary heart disease. Yamori was dismayed by what he found in Scotland. He agreed that the French, like the Scots, had high cholesterol levels, but explained an essential difference between the partners in the Auld Alliance: the French diet contained more fruit and veg and the French drank red wine, which the professor considered beneficial in moderation. He then drew an unfavourable comparison with his own country. 'The Japanese like to eat fish a lot, raw fish,' he said, 'but in Scotland, when it comes to fish, it seems it is only fish and chips. To me, that is the worst way to eat fish.' Notwithstanding this sound advice, the islanders evinced little enthusiasm for the red wine and yoghurt alternative. Only a wise and dynamic parliament could change the national habits of a lifetime, and it would be doing well if it made the slightest difference.

But it was not a day for wisdom or dynamism. That would come later, if it came at all. It was a day for flummery.

The sun shone. We had the word of the columnist Ian Bell for that. 'Sunshine on Leith,' his sketch of the day began. 'Sunshine folding over New Town and Old. Sunshine bent over every northern vista in Edinburgh, poured in warm streams northwards to the expanse of the Forth and south to the green Borders. Sunshine, with a fleck of white cloud here and there, turning the morning grey into soft browns and yellows.' And later: 'Sunshine blessed the old stones of the capital.' There seemed no doubt about it: there had been sunshine. But the weather, like so much else about the project, was a matter of opinion. The *Guardian*'s Matthew Engel, a day visitor from the pampered south, was less impressed: to him it felt like 'one of those clear and fresh breezy mornings which in Edinburgh pass as high summer'.

There was, however, near-unanimity about the baroque presentation of the principal guest. Bell observed that 'Edinburgh saw its favourite son dressed as the laird of Fountainbridge' while Engel's more detailed fashion note had him 'clad in a ruff and kilt in green McNotice-me tartan'. If Connery really thought it was the most important day of his life, wrote Engel, it would confirm the view that film stars led lives of surprising emptiness; and if Lord Steel was accurate in his claim that it was the most historic event in Scotland for nearly 300 years, 'it does not say a huge amount for the past three centuries'. Among the commentariat in general, almost as much attention was lavished on the absentees. The second most famous living Scotsman, the comedian Billy Connolly, whose opinion of the scheme was never high (he dismissed it as 'a pretendy wee parliament'), and the third most famous, the football manager Alex Ferguson, a confirmed Unionist and Old Labour figure, both stayed away, but the media were then struggling to find no-shows worthy of comment. The best they could find – or, rather, not find – was the Z-list former Secretary of State for Scotland, Malcolm Rifkind, and two incorrigible rebels, Dennis Canavan and Tommy Sheridan.

Even the wittily cynical Matthew Engel had to admit that the ceremony itself went rather well, though it was not without hitches of protocol. For some reason the leader of Her Majesty's Opposition, William Hague, was not invited to join the formal procession along the High Street and had to sit in the Assembly Hall for an hour and three quarters, his expression ever more thunderous, until the official party arrived. The Duke of Hamilton then carried the crown of Scotland on a velvet cushion and the monarch was correctly introduced as the Queen of Scots.

The brass section of the Royal Scottish National Orchestra struck up a fanfare composed for the occasion – the Speaker of the House of Commons, Betty Boothroyd, looked not at all amused by this frolicsome touch – after which Sheena Wellington, a traditional singer, performed Robert Burns's anthem to democracy, *A Man's a Man for A' That*, MSPs spontaneously joining in the last verse. Victoria Joffe, a 17-year-old pupil of Craigholme School in Glasgow, read a poem by someone even younger: 11-year-old Amy Linekar of Miller Academy in Thurso, who had won a writing competition in celebration of the new parliament. The poem, *How to create a great country*, was cruelly dismissed as 'ludicrous' by a column-writing Tory, Gerald Warner. It was far from ludicrous; indeed it was funny and touching.

And there were speeches (of course). In the Assembly Hall, three: from the presiding officer, the First Minister and the Queen, who declared optimistically that she had trust in the good judgement of the Scottish people. A few hundred yards away in Parliament Hall, there were several more, including a mildly subversive address by Alex Salmond.

The next morning, the *Scotsman* splashed across most of its front page a photograph of the royal carriage in procession along the Royal Mile, under a heading borrowed from Donald Dewar's speech: 'A moment anchored in Scotland's history'. If this was laboured, the accompanying text was in danger of drowning in its own platitudes: 'A date with destiny . . . They came in their thousands to witness a scene, the like of which has not graced the capital for nearly 300 years. The months of eager anticipation reached a climax when the Queen, in an open coach, made her way to the Assembly Hall to open Scotland's parliament.'

Inside the paper, there was not much space for anything else. The Tory grandee Willie Whitelaw, who had once accused the Labour Party of going around the country stirring up apathy, thought so much of the new parliament that he died on its official birthday. A Scot, though not widely regarded as one, Whitelaw was brought up on the family estate near Nairn. He was a lonely child – his father and three uncles having been killed in the First World War – and, later, not the most confident public speaker. Despite his position on the left of the party, Whitelaw served for years as a lieutenant of Margaret Thatcher, who admitted frankly that every Prime Minister needed a Willie; and, of the faithful Whitelaw, it was true.

Among other news, the EIS ('Scotland's largest teachers' union') announced that it was challenging plans to make it a criminal offence for teachers to form relationships with pupils who were over the age of consent. The same organisation had resisted the abolition of corporal punishment until its members had their belts more or less prised from their hands. Another fallible institution, BBC Scotland, in a concession to the new spirit of self-determination, proposed a 20-minute opt-out from the London-based *Newsnight*, which its London-based presenter, Jeremy Paxman, denounced as 'a damn fool idea' and many in Scotland thought insulting; but on this matter, reserved by Westminster, the Scottish Parliament was powerless. The opt-out went ahead.

In 1999, the Scottish broadsheet papers were heavy with lucrative advertising for houses and jobs – it would be some time before these sources of revenue migrated to the internet – and, preceding the arrival of online chat rooms, with classified ads from the unattached or semi-detached. On the day the parliament opened, this appeared in the lonely hearts column of the *Scotsman*: 'Mad about town? Blonde F, 30s, likes music, theatre, travel, opera, books, sport, etc, seeks tall, kind, honest, slightly mad male, 35-45, for possible relationship. Glasgow'. After a day in which so much vanity had been indulged, so much grandiose pretension spent, it was a reminder of the unexamined life beyond politics.

III

By the weekend any honeymoon that the parliament might have enjoyed was abruptly terminated: it was back to business as usual. *Scotland on Sunday*, sister paper of the *Scotsman*, both of which were now owned by the reclusive Barclay brothers, turned up on doorsteps in a particularly sour mood. The proprietors' representative on earth, Andrew Neil, whose libertarian outlook inspired the visceral loathing of the Scottish thinking classes, set the tone with a piece dripping in sarcasm. He attacked the 'dire performance' of the parliament, poured scorn on MSPs ('poor dears') for requiring a long holiday immediately after the opening ceremony, and derided the timid legislative programme lined up by the coalition partners.

Elsewhere in the same edition, Katie Grant observed presciently that 'the gaunt and ramshackle Donald Dewar looks nowadays as if he has been alive since the last parliament was disbanded', while Iain Martin's assessment of the First Minister was peppered with disobliging anonymous quotes. In one of them he was insulted as 'an intellectual and social snob who does not listen to anyone he thinks is beneath him'. According to Martin, Dewar might have had his day and the real power in Scotland would shortly pass to John Reid: a discouraging prospect, though the author refrained from saying so.

For the other dominant personality in Scottish politics, the reception was little better. The political commentator Peter MacMahon wrote that Alex Salmond had seemed 'less than happy' on the big day and that he might be 'losing the acute political judgement he once had'. MacMahon pressed on: 'Could it be that the SNP leader, who before May had convinced himself that he would be in government, albeit probably in a coalition, has looked to the future, seen four years of the impotence of opposition facing him, and begun to wonder about his future?' The piece ended by asking whether Salmond 'still has the stomach for the fight'.

The denouement of this complicated plot did not materalise in any predictable way. Sixteen months later, Donald Dewar – 'father of the nation' – died suddenly at the age of 63. A green statue in his honour was erected in Buchanan Street, Glasgow, and because of repeated vandalism had to be raised to a level beyond the reach of the disrespectful public. The abrasive John Reid got a proper job as Secretary of State for Northern Ireland, maintaining his giddy progress through the departments of the UK government before his elevation to the chairmanship of Celtic Football Club and a seat in the House of Lords with the title Baron Reid of Cardowan. The Scottish Parliament slowly established itself as competent if uninspired, earning the guarded trust of most of those who had voted for it. Alex Salmond, far from having no stomach for the fight, showed a wily grasp of strategy, confirming his party as a credible left-of-centre alternative to

Labour, and within eight years was First Minister in a minority SNP government. Among the supporting cast, Sean Connery, denied high honour by Dewar on account of his nationalist sympathies, was finally knighted; Andrew Neil soon had no further business in Scotland; and Tommy Sheridan served a prison sentence for perjury. Victoria Joffe, who read the poem at the parliament's opening ceremony, went on to St Andrews University and into a career in television production.

It did become a criminal offence for teachers to form relationships with pupils who were over the age of consent, but other pressing questions in the month of the parliament's formal establishment were unresolved when this book came to be written long afterwards. The Scots, unimpressed by the Japanese diet of raw fish, persisted in eating unhealthily. The condition of the seaside town of Ayr further deteriorated. The parliament chose not to exercise its tax-raising powers for such purposes as the eradication of poverty in Glasgow, where life expectancy did not markedly improve. Schoolchildren went on being obsessively tested – more than ever when the Scottish National Party acquired a majority and Alex Salmond was succeeded as First Minister by his acolyte Nicola Sturgeon. Devolution, supposedly the settled will of the Scottish people, made the natives impatient for more. In 2014, given the chance of a divorce from the rest of the UK, they seriously flirted with independence before rejecting it, though perhaps only for the time being. By the following May, there was one Labour MP left in Scotland – representing affluent Morningside, where the funeral of John Smith of the settled will theory had taken place 21 years earlier. Considering itself materially disadvantaged in relation to its larger neighbour, the little country on the north-west edge of Europe could at least claim to be rich in irony.

INDEX

Barlinnie Prison, Glasgow, 26, 33, 66, 70
Barlinnie special unit, 33, 36, 172
Barmulloch Majorettes, 45
Barnsley, Maretta, 25
Barr, Brian, 237, 240–41
Barrow, Geoffrey, 351
Bateman, Derek, 144, 174
BBC, 31, 37–39, 68–69, 88–89, 101, 158, 160, 169, 178, 185, 206, 216, 236–41, 245, 249–50, 255, 296, 345, 354, 376, 435, 446, 455, 472, 489
Beath High School, Cowdenbeath, 1, 120
Beckett, Margaret, 441
Bedford, John, 306–07
Begg, Anne, 441
Beider, Harris, 454
Bell, Alexander, 226, 229
Bell, David, 351
Bell, Ian, 354, 424, 486
Bell, Maggie, 249
Bell, Walter, 210
Bell, William, 159
Bellahouston Park, Glasgow, 138–39, 145
Beltrami, Joseph, 8
Benn, Tony, 259
Besser, Mike, 441
Bilston Glen colliery, 173–78, 180, 182, 187
Bird, Bob, 350
Birnie, George, 476
Birt, Hugh, 204
Bissett-Johnston, Alastair, 338
Black, Douglas, 231
Black, Malcolm, 154
Black, Robert, 307
Black, Sue, 30
Blackburn, Granville, 166
Blair, Cherie, 444
Blair, Tony, 382, 438, 441, 444–46, 448–49, 479
Blake, Mary, 417–18

Blanche, John, 478
Blane, Colin, 185
Blue Oyster bar, Edinburgh, 279
Blumfield, Clifford, 225
Blyth, Larry, 21
Blyth, William, 128
Boesky, Ivan, 224
Bogside colliery, 178
Bolton, George, 182
Bo'ness Academy, 48
Bonnie Prince Charlie, 72
Bonomy, Iain, 431
Boothroyd, Betty, 487
Borthwick, Ken, 211–13, 216
Boscombe Down, 385
Boswell, James, 373
Bovey, Keith, 56
Boyd, Colin, 433
Boyd, Edward, 31, 66
Boyle, Jimmy, 34–36
Boyle, Penny, 228
BP, 41
Brading, John, 264
Brasher, Chris, 216
Brave Don't Cry, The, 358
Braveheart, 371
Bray, Jeremy, 348
Brazil, Alan, 203–04
Bremner, Alex, 38
Brennan, Tommy, 179, 260, 342, 355
Bridie, James, 476
Britain's Secret War, 191
British Aluminium plant, Fort William, 84
British Caledonian Airways, 45
British Medical Association, 231
British Medical Journal, 152, 236
British National Party, 450
British Nuclear Fuels, 229
British Rail, 71
British Steel Corporation, 179, 260, 340–49
British Tourist Authority, 110
Brittan, Leon, 108, 237

McManus, Mark, 249
McMenamin, Frances, 462–63
MacMillan, George, 475
McMillan, Joyce, 354
Macmillan, William, 251
McMurdo, Douglas, 426–32
McNeil, Anne, 136
McNeil, Hector, 60
Macpherson, Archie, 53–54, 202
Macpherson, William, 455–60
McQuarrie, Albert, 246
McQueenie, John, 135
MacRae, Andrew, 27–28
MacRae, Gordon, 28–30
MacRae, Renee, 27–29, 44
MacRae, William, 188–97
Macvicar, Neil, 137, 144–45
McWhinnie, Arnot, 97
Maan, Bashir, 453
Macari, Lou, 204–05
'magic circle', 270–82
Magnusson, Magnus, 38–39
Maguire, John, 401–02
Mail on Sunday, 329, 465
Mair, Dennis, 149–51
Major, John, 346, 354, 423, 438, 440,
    442–43
Malone, Gerry, 135, 245, 352, 355
Manchester United Football Club, 55,
    201
Manly, Raymond, 309–10
Man's a Man for A' That, A, 487
Manson, David, 476
manufacturing output, 344
Mariscat Press, 475
Marquis de Sade, 7
Marquise, Richard, 302
Marr College, Troon, 474, 479
marriage and divorce, 367
Marshall, David, 99
Marsland, David, 338
Martin, David, 38, 139
Martin, Iain, 490
Martin, Michael, 255
Martin, Robert, 220–21

Mary, Queen of Scots, 351
Mary's House, 307–09
Massie, Allan, 354
Massie Ferguson plant, Kilmarnock,
    84
Mas'ud, Abu Agila, 309
Mates, Michael, 254
Matheson, Alasdair, 263
Matheson, James, 159
Mavor, Ronald, 476, 478, 480
Maxwell, Jim, 356
Maxwell, Robert, 212–19, 218, 221,
    224
Maxwell, Stephen, 79, 125
Maxwelltown estate, Dundee, 454
May, Gordon Michael, 278
Mayor, Esther, 422
Mayor, Gwen, 417–20, 422
Medical Research Council, 235
Meehan, Patrick, 7–17, 94, 132, 387
Meek, Brian, 244, 248
Meek, James, 438
Meek, Jeffrey, 388
Mercer, Carol Anne, 393
Messer, Dorothy, 189, 193
Methodist Hall, London, 471
Metropolitan Police, 311
Michie, Ray, 245
Middleton, Francis, 163
Mihlon, Larry, 84–85
Miles, Lise, 62–63
Militant, 258–59
Millan, Bruce, 8–9, 10, 19, 35, 59, 99
Millar, John, 473, 478, 480
Millar, Robert, 39
Millar, Susan, 316, 318, 320–23,
    331–32, 334, 337–39
Miller Academy, Thurso, 487
Miller, Bill, 244–45
Miller, Leslie, 178
Miller, Michelle, 316, 331–2
Miller, Ron, 72–73
Miller, Willie, 53
Milligan, Eric, 290
Milligan, Lord, 278

Scholey, Robert, 260, 340–50, 355
school examinations, reform of, 116–17
Schulz, Carolyn, 26
Scientists against Nuclear Arms, 166
Scotland on Sunday, 354, 383, 452,
   463, 483, 489
Scotsman, The, 167, 242–43, 245, 259,
   282, 334, 344–45, 370, 390, 424,
   435, 460, 472, 484–85, 488–89
Scott, David, 418, 424
Scott, Hannah, 417
Scott, John, 472, 476, 478–80
Scott, Marion, 469
Scott, Tavish, 472, 476
Scottish Affairs, 455
Scottish Air Traffic Control (Military),
   375
Scottish Amicable, 223
Scottish Arts Council, 32
Scottish Catholic Observer, 128
Scottish Certificate of Education
   Examination Board, 118
Scottish Civic Trust, 473
Scottish Commission for Racial
   Equality, 460
Scottish Constitutional Convention,
   288–91
Scottish Council for Civil Liberties,
   6, 68
Scottish Court of Criminal Appeal, 9
Scottish covenant movement, 476
Scottish Crime Survey, 369
Scottish Criminal Cases Review
   Commission, 9, 150–51, 308
Scottish Criminal Record Office,
   466–69
Scottish Daily Express, 78
Scottish Dairy Council, 227
Scottish Development Agency, 66, 76,
   85, 247
Scottish Education Department, 2,
   6–7, 116
Scottish Enterprise, 349
Scottish Ethnic Minorities Research
   Unit, 453

Scottish Football Association, 49–53,
   202, 205
Scottish Grand Committee, 132–34
Scottish Homosexual Rights Group,
   390
Scottish Journey, 40
Scottish Labour Party (SLP), 56–60,
   482
Scottish Law Commission, 72
Scottish Movement, 126
Scottish National Liberation Army,
   194, 196
Scottish National Party, 56, 60–61,
   79, 81–84, 122–24, 140–45, 164,
   245–46, 289–91, 349–53, 446–47,
   481
Scottish Office, 5, 7–8, 18, 33, 63,
   77, 100, 199, 200, 214, 227, 230,
   347–48, 367, 381, 478
Scottish Parliament, opening of,
   482–91
Scottish Prison Officers Association,
   234
Scottish Prison Service, 403
Scottish Road Haulage Association,
   156
Scottish Sculpture Trust, 209
Scottish Socialist Party, 481
Scottish Standing Committee, 82
Scottish Television, 25, 51, 169, 244,
   249, 474
Scottish Theatre Ballet, 32
Scottish Trades Union Congress, 58,
   79, 82, 164, 247, 290
Scottish Universities Council on
   Entrance, 118
Scottish Women's Rural Institute, 62
Scotts shipyard, Greenock, 24
Scout Association, 413, 415
Seafield/Frances colliery, 178
Secker and Warburg, 370
Secret Society, 236–40, 250
Self, Will, 314
sermon on the Mound, 251
Sex Discrimination Act, 2